IT'S TIME

si unus es novem milium ad orbem terrarum tollendum
destinatorum, nunc est tempus

εἰ σὺ τῶν ἐννεακισχιλίων εἶ, οἷς πέπρωται τήν
γῆν ἆραι, ἐφῆκεν χρόνος

 डि यखु रे खने खड तहे ९००० थहख रे
देसतनिद तख लडितौ रतहति सि
तमि

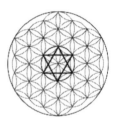

יתקמין בן ארעא
אן את זה יתה עשתיד אלכין

གལ་ཏེ་ཁྱེད་འཛམ་གླིང་འགེལ་གྱིས་མཡབ་ ༩༠༠༠ ཡོད་པའི་ནང་ནས་གཅིག་ཡིན་ན། ད
ནི་ལ་ཚོད་རན་འག

⠠⠊⠋ ⠽⠕⠥ ⠁⠗⠑ ⠕⠝⠑
⠕⠋ ⠞⠓⠑ ⠝⠊⠝⠑ ⠞⠓⠕⠥⠎⠁⠝⠙ ⠙⠑⠎⠞⠊⠝⠑⠙ ⠞⠕
⠗⠁⠊⠎⠑ ⠞⠓⠑ ⠑⠁⠗⠞⠓⠂ ⠝⠕⠺ ⠊⠎ ⠞⠓⠑ ⠞⠊⠍⠑

9000@andsobeit.com

IT'S TIME

CONVERSATION WITH ANGELS
VOLUME III

Dror B. Ashuah

EPIGRAPH BOOKS
RHINEBECK ~ NEW YORK

IT'S TIME: CONVERSATION WITH ANGELS VOLUME III © 2012 by
Dror B. Ashuah

ISBN 978-1-936940-42-4

Book and cover design by Barbara Patterson

Library of Congress Control Number: 2012946608

Bulk purchase discounts for educational or promotional purposes
are available.

To continue the conversation: www.andsobeit.com

Epigraph
22 East Market Street, Suite 304
Rhinebeck, New York 12572
www.epigraphps.com

Contents

Dedication

*I chose to dedicate this book to Luise Light,
a light warrior, who passed away in April 2010.
Your light is still with me. Your guidance and laughter
will stay with me forever. Thank you for your support,
encouragement, trust, and help as I was considering
making this material public. You are missed.
You will always be in my heart.*

Foreword

IT IS OVERCAST IN Tulum, Mexico, on this 21st day of June, 2012. Looking out my porch at the blue-green water, I am being absorbed by this sensual, emotional paradise. Waves crashing against the sand seem to penetrate my heart. The wind blowing, the intermittent downpours, the thick clouds, the lightning flaring on the horizon, all as if luring me to delve inside and contemplate the past three years since my last book, *And So Be It*, came out. It has been raining on and off for the past few days. I am renting Maria's Palapa, fifteen yards from the water, with nothing but white sand in between and nests of giant turtles scattered about. She named her home Casa Amor, or House of Love. How appropriate, I am thinking to myself with a bittersweet smile. For the past three years it has been my journey and struggle surfing waves of emotional storms, desperately trying to remain above water with love, not always sure what this word meant, rather than be drowned and buried by the anguish which appeared like flash floods twisting and turning me, leaving me shaken to my core.

Meditating over my personal journey, I can more clearly feel what the messages describe as upward spiral movement. The wind is sending high waves crashing against the large rock shaped like a jaguar's head. Calmness fills my heart; being here signifies for me coming full circle. I can now view the past three years as if from above, knowing with all my being that I am where I am meant to be. I can now more fully "see" the perfection of all that I experienced, feeling gratitude for the love and light that guided me on this journey.

My Personal Process

The first book, *Conversation with Angels*, was written in less than three months; the second book, *And So Be It*, was completed in about nine months; this book, *It's Time*, took about three years to complete. Since I had my first physical encounter with the angels on December 10, 2007, at Starbucks on the corner of Reade Street and Broadway, downtown Manhattan until today, summer solstice of 2012, my life has spiraled and every aspect of my reality has shifted. I feel I have become a different person despite my bedroom mirror, which insists otherwise.

One challenge in receiving these messages was creating an internal space of receptivity and peace while much of my physical life was upside-down and swirling. I had to gather all my strength and surrender in order to be in a vibration where I could sustain the link-up. Many of the messages would announce themselves to me only when I was ready, whereas before I would just sit and invite the angels to begin. I would be given advance notice: "We are ready; be ready to receive our message on Monday," for example. Often it was after I went through my own growing pains and deep realizations. I was working hard on myself, struggling to remain balanced and in the vibration of love. Many beautiful souls came at the right time to support me and guide me through. The messages came as if to offer support and at the same time as a confirmation that I am still walking my true path. At times I felt that I had to earn these messages by passing certain initiations and transformations so I would be aligned vibrationally. Mostly, I had to trust the process.

Not too long ago I was saying to myself, "This third volume is not really necessary to manifest. I have no energy to deal with it, and besides, very few will ever get to read it." I was told in a typical light tone sprinkled with angelic humor, simply, "It is not only about you."

Snapshot from September 2009

I was sitting in front of my computer in our apartment in downtown Manhattan, noticing that the words on the screen are blurring and twisting, as if I were reading under water. It was mid-September of 2009, and my daughter was in school, while my wife (then) was visiting her parents in Europe. I was composing the foreword to my second book, *And So Be It*. Words did not come easy then and they surely do not flow easily now. Despite working on my third book, I am still contemplating and struggling to find the illusive "right" words to describe this unlikely journey. Looking back on that day, I still had my family intact, although I was in denial of the fact that we were already coming apart at the seams.

Perturbed by the distorted vision, I decided to visit an optometrist who happened to reside on the first floor of our building. I quickly calculated that it was three in the afternoon and I had until four to pick up my daughter. Riding down in the elevator, I was thinking to myself, "What now? Is it not enough that I have to finish this book? I cannot even make out the words on the screen and on top of everything else seeming to go haywire around me—our finances, my relationship—all is crashing into pieces, and now my vision, too? What is going on? What is wrong with this picture?"

I saw myself pushing the "send" button of that thought to the "winged ones," wherever they are, hoping it would not be directed to their spam folder.

My mind kept turning until I heard the eye doctor telling me that I had to rush immediately to the emergency eye surgeon. His secretary, he said, already called the doctor's office and I should be there in one hour.

"What? Why?" I demanded, as my plans for the day were being flushed down the drain.

"This is a condition you do not want to delay checking," he said in a serious voice, "but it may very well be nothing. Just to be safe."

I proceeded to pick up my daughter from school while trying to calmly explain to her as best as I could that I needed to have my eyes checked right away. She was reluctant but agreed to stay by herself for a few hours while I explored this unexpected twist on my busy Friday afternoon.

The high-tech eye doctor's office was littered with incredible-looking machines. I could imagine actually enjoying this visit if I were not feeling so cold on this warm fall day. I sensed anxiety climbing up my spine. After several hours of torture which included dripping a variety of "cocktails" into my eyes, a verdict was announced. The sweet female doctor said in a stern voice, "We checked your condition and it is with absolute certainty that you have (three Latin words), a potentially quickly degenerative condition that can lead to blindness. I recommend beginning treatment right now to stop it. I will need to insert a syringe into your retina every day for one week starting today." And she continued to describe the process in clinical terms. Scenes continued to unfold like a horrible plot in a third-rate movie, and I could not help but wonder if I was the director of this "bad scene." I could hardly make sense of her next sentence: "This remedy will not heal your condition, but may stop the deterioration. You need to sign a waiver in case you become blind from the injections. Shall we proceed?"

Something deep inside of me felt so defeated, and yet another part of me felt that I had a choice here. I heard myself saying to her, "Hold off. I need to think about it and feel what is going on. I'll be back Monday and we can begin the treatment then." She looked at me, puzzled. "You are taking a risk, sir. It could be too late by Monday." I heard myself saying in a clearer voice, "I will take my chances." "Very well," she said. "Please make an appointment for Monday on your way out."

It was so bright once I exited the doctor's office. My retina was enlarged to allow more light in. Tasteless joke I thought, as I felt in such darkness. At the moment I stepped out of the clinic, all I could think of is that all humanity is divided in two—sick and healthy—

and everyone on the street seemed to be healthier than me. The prospect of losing my vision was utterly terrifying to me.

Later, back in the apartment, my daughter wanted to play. I was presented with my moment of truth. I knew I had a choice. I knew I did not have much time. I had to get to work, and my whole being was vibrating with this knowing. I heard myself telling her, "I need to meditate a lot this weekend, and I will not have time for much else." She looked at me, puzzled, and I could see her worried face asking why, but she agreed to let me. Deep inside her she seemed to know what was going on; I could see it in her eyes. From Friday afternoon until Monday morning I spent most of my time in the meditation room, diving deep into my inner workings. My eyes were swollen from tears and realizations. Silently I had a long overdue conversation with my deceased grandfather whom I'd never met. He died from eye cancer in Jerusalem all alone during a siege, away from his loved ones. My middle name, Baruch (which means "blessed one" in Hebrew), was his name. I never really liked that name, and now it was time to make peace with it. I visualized myself microscopic so that I could explore my left eye, seeing what was wrong, sealing, repairing, and healing what I could observe. I visualized taking an elevator down into my akashic library, questioning why I needed this learning at this time, realizing it was not set in stone. I followed by clearing that lesson. For the next seventy-two hours I used every tool I had in my possession to understand, correct, and find peace with what was happening to me.

On Monday morning something within me shifted. I felt more peaceful. Whatever was going to happen, I was ready. I felt detached from the unfolding drama. I had not shared it with anyone, yet within me I was resolved that I did all I could. I was prepared to accept this invasive treatment if that was what I needed to experience.

Back at the clinic later that day, the doctor seemed pleased that I came back and my vision had not gotten any worse. She ran additional tests to confirm the exact spot for the injection. I did not say a word. When she came back with the printout, there was a look of surprise on her face. "Hmmm, this is atypical," she said. "What do you mean?" I asked. "The signs are not there anymore. This is very strange," she said, visibly uncomfortable. "I have never seen this condition reverse itself, ever. What did you do?" she asked in a forced humorous tone with a bit of suspicion. "I meditated," I answered with a half smile. Inside of me, however, a huge bright smile was forming. "Whatever you did, keep doing it," she said, trying to cover her slight embarrassment.

"I do not think we should inject anything at the moment, but I am sure this condition will come back. Return in one week and we'll run additional tests," she said more confidently, regaining her composure. At her insistence I came back after a week, a month, three months, and then six months. The tests all showed that this condition was no longer present.

Many of the angels' messages speak of our power to change that which we wish for and to heal ourselves. Before my "eye experience" this was more of a nice idea. After healing took place I understood the profundity of this truth. I "saw" this truth using both my eyes.

The messages written in the third book were no longer just theory that I shared as a conduit. Often I had to experience firsthand, in the deepest sense of the word, the path described in the messages. And it was not always a walk in the park.

Snapshot from December 2010

It was the third anniversary since my encounter with the angels in New York City, a cold December night. By that time, my life had turned upside-down once more. My heart was torn. I often felt heavy shadows around me as I was trying to sort out what was happening to my life. Living by myself, marriage broken, the family I was so proud to be a part of was no longer. We used to be inseparable, like one unit, yet now each of us was hiding in the darkness of winter, in pain, curled in their corner.

My "nature walk" never failed to lift the heaviness I carried inside. I would walk near my Woodstock home, feeling and connecting with the trees, birds, and animals that crossed my path. Usually, by the time I returned, that heaviness had lifted. On this particular cold night I found myself inspired to walk despite the late hour, my tiredness, and the chill. It was almost ten at night and the dirt road was icy and slippery, pitch dark with no sign of moonlight. After treading carefully for forty minutes, I decided to shorten the walk and make my way back. I aimed my flashlight at this large tree beside the dirt road which leads back to the house. I had never connected with that one, yet I felt as if I was called to go to it. I placed my hands around the trunk of the tree, pressing my torso and forehead against the bark, breathing deeply, becoming one with its magnificent energy, connecting to its power and roots. Suddenly, a shockwave pierced my heart. My whole body jerked upward by some immense force. The entire tree lifted, as if it hiccupped, ascended a few inches and crashed with a thunderous thump back to the ground. My body, as if ejected, landed back on the road. I could not believe I was still standing. "What was that?" I stuttered, feeling my legs visibly shaking, struggling to keep my balance. My whole body was "screaming" at me, "Let's get out of here." Thoughts were charging me like a freight train: "What was this thing that just moved? Was the tree trying to hug me back? Did its kundalini get activated? But it is a tree! This is unbelievable. Will I make it back home? Did I completely lose it?" For a moment I contemplated getting closer to this tree once more, but my legs refused to move. They were on strike, as if holding a clear sign: "You can try to go, but we aren't moving." I was standing there trying to negotiate with my body, but it refused to negotiate. Reluctantly, after ten minutes of standing there frozen and shaken, I made my way back home.

To this day, I have yet to discover any logical explanation that could ease my mind. I wished to share it as one example of many experiences that I have no way of explaining or making sense of. What I do know is that our perceived reality is but a small aspect of our existence. Being in tune and receptive opens the door to the mystery of this path on Earth. On my personal journey I have been gifted with experiences which humbled me to the core, left in me awe, and transformed me forever.

At the time of my eye incident in the fall of 2009, my marriage of fourteen years was falling apart; our financial situation was in a downward spiral; and the powerful, sacred love and trust bond that I had with my daughter was threatened and felt disjointed. On top of it my health was being challenged at different junctures. At each juncture, I felt I was facing a choice: to see the situation as terrible, painful, and become a victim, or to change the story altogether. Each time I succeeded in telling myself a different story an immense shift took place. A story of sadness turned out to be one of sacredness, growth, and heart-based love. Each time I accepted a new, higher-vibration story line, I was growing stronger. My trust in the divinity of my path was expanding, and my heart was slowly reopening. My physical reality was changing as if through miracles, and I began to get glimpses of what it means to be in higher vibration, fully trusting in the perfection of this path.

Since 2010 I've been called to work with Earth's sacred energy portals, and I followed this guidance wherever it took me, collecting magical moments and meeting incredible people everywhere I went.

The angels often speak of us being guided to walk our path and fulfill our mission. I want to briefly share two such moments out of many to illustrate the beauty, love, and support I felt while walking my path.

Snapshot from January 2011

I arrived in Cancun, Mexico, on January 5, 2011, and I knew I had only one day to prepare before I hit the road. The map and the temples I was supposed to visit were already laid out; I saw them in visions. I knew I had to cover a large territory in three states, traveling almost a thousand kilometers, locating the temples, identifying and sensing the portals of energy within their large areas, activating and clearing the way I was guided to. I knew that once the portal activation process starts, it is pure magic. On the road, often, I would be working eighteen-hour days without stopping. I would eat very little and sleep even less. The level of energy is immense, and my body vibrates so intensely that it feels like continual climax.

The first temple was in the Tulum ruins. The work felt powerful and aligned. The next morning I left for the Coba Temple, less than two hours' drive, taking only the basic necessities—my crystals and "tools." I figured I would come back to my hotel and leave the next day for the larger, more distant temples: Chichen–Itza, Uxmal, Kabah, and Kohunlich. I drove on the main *caretera* (Spanish for "road") to Coba, a narrow road piercing the jungle's thick vegetation that seemed to stretch in a straight line forever. Not even ten minutes into the drive I heard a loud thump and realized that something crashed against my windshield. I knew already that in Mexico when I do the work, every sign is a post and is significant. I stopped the car and drove back, parking on the side to see what it was. Indeed, it was a large bird that hit my window and instantly died, sprawled on the hot asphalt.

I slowly walked around the bird and felt the energy, blessing it for its sacrifice. I asked to be shown what it was about. I had never hit a bird before, ever. The sensation in my body was strong so I knew I would find out sooner or later. For a moment a thought crossed my mind that it may be a warning, but it did not feel that way inside of me.

I was certain something was up, but the road was narrow and the drivers nearby were speeding as if on a European autobahn. I lifted the dead bird and put it on the side of the road. Strangely, its wing stretched in the most unlikely way. I found myself staring, contemplating its position. It felt like sign language, as if it was trying to communicate something. I know inside it wanted to reveal something, but what? I pulled out my camera and took a picture.

An inner voice told me that I needed to record this for the future; it was just too strange. A car buzzed by, beeping loudly. I snapped out of the moment and decided to keep going.

I entered the car and heard a clear inner voice saying: "You must keep going all the way today and not return to Tulum or you will not complete the activation by 1/11/11." Without even a toothbrush or a change of clothing, I spent the next four days on the road with a small bag packed. In the funny red dented Nissan that I rented at the airport I covered hundreds of miles in remote areas by myself, hoping that the car would not break down on me. I stayed in motels in no-name villages just so that I could get up and continue. By January 11, 2011, I made it back to Tulum with an hour to spare. The final step was completed at 11:11 at night. As the last activation was completed it began to downpour. I was told it had not rained for two months. I took it as a blessing and offered my gratitude for the experience, never really figuring out what the dead bird was trying to tell me.

Later that month, I landed in Egypt on January 24. The next day I joined a cruise sailing on the Nile, working at the temples of Philae and Edfu. I felt tension in the air, but I did not have access to TV or newspapers, so I was unaware that a revolution had started in Cairo that day. After three days on the Nile River, we reached Luxor and I hooked up with my tour guide, an Egyptian Christian Copt named Bob. We covered the temples of Karnak and Luxor. After much "persuasion" and some money, we obtained army permits to travel to Abydos and Dendera. That morning, January 28, the police were visibly absent from the streets, and my eyes were burning and tearing. I asked the hotel clerk what was going on. He tried to smile and said, "Oh nothing, just the pollution." I did not buy the answer and repeated the question to my guide who just entered the lobby. Bob said, "The police were shooting tear gas at demonstrators. Not good for business, but something has to change in this corrupt government." I was a bit taken by his openness but chose to keep it to myself, and we proceeded. As we left Luxor I saw many tanks and armored vehicles, but I restrained myself from asking. In the afternoon, we reached Dendera. As soon as I walked the steps towards the temple in the desert harsh light, I knew I had been there before. Everything felt familiar. Walking into the Birth House, dedicated to the Goddess Hathor, representing sexuality and fertility, I was taken by the sensual, powerful feminine energy that was present. Each carving and wall I looked at told me a story. Intense visions flooded me in every room. Finally, I reached the top of the famous Dendera zodiac in the Chapel dedicated to Osiris. I was taken by how dark the ceiling was. Emotions were flooding me and I felt such joy at being there. Bob was waiting patiently as I explored every detail of the chapel. I knew I was looking for something but I was not sure what. I examined each wall and each drawing in the smoke covered walls and ceiling. Finally, on the corner at eye level I found what I was looking for. This relief was unmistakably pulsating from the wall. It was the bird from Mexico. Almost in the exact position it was laying on the side of the road to Coba. I felt my spine vibrating so strongly like a tuning fork. My heart was beating loud and for a moment I wondered if people could hear it as well.

I called Bob over and asked excitedly, "What does this image mean? I have not seen it in any of the temples we visited." His reply was, "The bird signifies walking, guided by destiny, fulfilling your highest path." He further explained that this symbol was the seal of approval showing that where you are headed is guided from above and therefore you are fulfilling your destiny and your mission. The particular words he used I'd heard many times in my meditations and while receiving the messages. There it was, the answer to the bird puzzle. It was like finding an ancient key that fits perfectly to a door that you are trying to open. I stood there for a while offering gratitude and taking in the moment, until Bob, visibly uneasy about disturbing me, said that we had to make it back through the army post before it got dark.

My exit from Luxor is a story in itself, but let's just say that it was miraculous, and when I landed in Vienna (managing to get on Niki airlines, the only Viennese charter flight out), the first thing I did after landing was to indulge in this mouthwatering Viennese strudel, taking it in with dark tea. And food never tasted so good.

Snapshot from April 2012

I arrived late in the afternoon to Glastonbury, the enchanted land of Avalon, in the Western part of England. The landscape smelled and felt like home. Soon after settling into my hotel, I decided to explore in the few hours I had left before darkness descended. I let my legs carry me and just wandered around. Soon I found myself walking in the fields surrounding the Tor with St. Michael's Chapel protruding as a magnificent symbol of time past and time to come. A farmer in tweed overalls holding a beautiful golden retriever by one hand and a walking cane in the other, approached me with a smile. I said hello, and he told me in a friendly British accent that there was an ancient oak tree that I needed to visit, and it was not too far. He said, "If you continue on this path, it is just a short walk, maybe a mile or two," and he pointed to a narrow cow path that stretched between the lush green fields. The sun was already setting in the west, casting long shadows. I hesitated for a moment. I was thinking to myself that I had just arrived and surely did not wish to get lost, as I was not familiar with the area. My inner guidance interjected and encouraged me to follow his advice. It confirmed what I already knew, that absolutely everything was divinely guided on these journeys.

The path was beautiful—cows roaming around and a tapestry of green fields stretched as far as the eye can see around what used to be called the Island of Avalon. Walking the narrow paths I began to wonder if I'd ever find the tree and my way back. The Tor, with its impressive chapel commanding over the hills, gave me some comfort that I would find my way back, especially as the moon was almost full.

Then I noticed the ancient oak tree. There were actually two of them, but one died. They seemed to be thousands of years old, used by the Druids for sacred ceremonies and rituals. There was barbed wire enclosing the tree. I climbed over and noticed a man sitting at the foot of the tree, drinking from a bottle of Scotch. I always liked to be by myself when I did energy work, and I hesitated if I should approach or come back another time. My instincts were on high alert, as I surely did not expect that someone would be there this late.

With the friendliest voice this chap introduced himself by the name Soul. I eased a little and asked him his whereabouts. He explained that he had come here every four years since he was twelve years old, and he always left a bottle of whiskey hidden just so he could have one more sip four years later. Smiling, he said, "Each time it tasted better and better." I relaxed as something in his friendly demeanor and tone felt familiar to me. I sat across from him and as we began to speak, I realized that this was not just an ordinary traveler. He spoke the magical language of the angelic messages as if he'd read everything that I had learned and written for the past few years and was nonchalantly spewing these profound truths. My mouth remained open and then was slowly replaced with a huge smile. For a moment there, I had to pinch myself to make sure I was not daydreaming. It was my turn to share and I told him that what he just spoke about was astonishingly similar to messages I have received and made into a book. He responded, saying that he could not read nor write, nor does he have a home, but he never felt homeless as Earth was his home, and he was so grateful being alive and having such a beautiful large space to call home. He then looked at me with a broad smile, his eyes looking through me and said, "We do not really need to learn anything, but mainly unlearn, as all the knowledge is already in our hearts. We just need to remember."

I felt a little dizzy and had this otherworldly sensation as if I were in between dimensions. We sat together for a few hours, and I just listened to him speak. Just as I was thinking how lucky I was not to have turned around he said, "I never met anyone when I came here. I know I was supposed to meet you here. This was meant to be." "Yes, indeed it was," I said.

Our meeting resonated deeply within me. I walk my walk, often not knowing anything and just trusting my inner feelings. Yet, deep inside, I hope for some validation. This beautiful soul, I felt, was assigned to hand me an angelic validation and a hug, in Glastonbury, beside an ancient oak tree, with a bottle of whiskey and a funny hat. Angels come in many different shapes, accents, and outfits.

Coming Back Full Circle to Snapshot June 21, 2012

Summer solstice today—a major celestial event, the longest day of the year, and a time marked by intense shifts. The ancient Mayans celebrated the summer solstice as a time for spiritual initiation and change. They held rituals on the solstice to balance Earth's energy.

A Mexican shaman is performing a solstice ceremony at Xel-Ha archeological site on the edge of the Mexican jungle. A fresh breeze blows gently on my face as this early morning's gathering takes shape. A group of thirty of us are standing in a circle, acknowledging the intense shift that humanity and each of us is experiencing. The Mayan priestess with long black hair dressed all in white speaks about the need to align with Earth's heart and connect the heart of heaven with the heart of Earth through our own heart. Her beautiful voice dances with the leaves and mixes with the singing of the birds. She describes the seemingly insurmountable obstacles that each of us is facing in our personal lives. It seems that just about everyone present in the circle nods in agreement. She looks around and says with a half smile, "We now are being presented with an opportunity to clean our 'house,' find peace with the process, and align with our truth. If we choose not to, well . . ." Her dark eyes seem to question the heart of each one of the participants. "It may get very challenging." Looking around, I feel that we are all in agreement that indeed there is work to do, and yes, I confirm within myself, I am no different.

During the solstice meditation I open my eyes and I see the beautiful light emanating from those standing around me: young and old, long hair, bald, in different outfits, from different countries, speaking different languages. I cannot help but smile, sensing a flutter in my heart as it whispers to me, "I am home." I am with my spiritual family, and despite the apparent differences, I feel that we are all deeply connected.

Another Mayan shaman dressed up in traditional colorful garb speaks of our relationships with flowers and all living things, our connection to the unseen world of elementals and angels, the world of energy and consciousness. He looks at us, slowly scanning us. He then shuts his eyes and says, "Look around you. We are all one with all that you see; we must protect all this because it is ourselves we are protecting." Carried by the love and beauty of the moment, I linger as the hugs and smiles dissipate. I find myself walking over to an ancient Mayan structure nearby. A plaque placed in front of it explains that it was named in ancient times the "House of Jaguar." Suddenly, I sense a movement near the thick vegetation and trees a few yards away. Raising my gaze, right in front of me a yellow jaguar jumps off the limb of the tree. The branch bows violently just to snap back up, and the jaguar disappears into the jungle like a phantom. Gina, a ballerina from Mexico City, lets out a shocking cry. Her voice hangs for a moment, then follows the jaguar and vanishes into the thick jungle. The rest of us fall into silence, feeling the sacredness of this moment. Walking to my car, I contemplate that this magnificent large cat was probably drawn by our vision of unity and may have been eavesdropping on this whole ceremony, making a dramatic exit just at the right moment, leaving me in awe.

These journeys always offer glimpses into the mysteries of life's interconnectedness and wholesomeness. Wherever I go, the hearts of all whom I encounter seek love, as if we are all one pulse yearning to merge with itself. Often we seem to be experiencing life through our individual stories yet more and more acknowledge how deeply connected we all are to the larger story.

From Guatemala, Mexico, Peru, Egypt, Hawaii, Sedona, Israel, Germany, England, wherever I journeyed, the buzzword was "change." A profound shift is taking place right now. If I had seen my life as it is now, three years ago, I would probably not have been able to accept it or even believe it. I could not have imagined living in my truth so completely and having so many beautiful human angels around me who embody a similar commitment to living their truth and to shining their light. My personal journey for the past three years, as arduous as it often seemed, was and is perfect and complete in every way possible. I feel gratitude from the depth of my soul for each moment I have on this Earth and for the privilege to be a conduit for these messages of love and light, sharing them with you. For the past few years I have seen people transform, lives

changed in miraculous ways. Each life that has transformed has made this planet brighter.

With infinite gratitude to you for shining your light.

The story of *It's Time* and how to read it.

The Title of the Book

This book's main message is, "It's time to wake up and align with your truth; it's time to live your mission; it's time to turn on your light and shine as you intended; it's time to claim your power, and it's time to let go of the idea that you have anything to lose. Now is the time and there is no other time. This is the reason you are here. It's time to remember who you are, why you are here, and to wake up."

How to Choose a Message

The messages come from the circle and are not in a linear order. You are asked to feel the book; ask to receive what you need to read at that moment to move forward and open the book seemingly arbitrarily. Trust that the page you are on is what you need to read and remain with that message. You can also choose based on the message directory in the back of the book. Remain with whatever grabs your attention. To receive the full benefit it is recommended not to read more than one message in any twenty-four-hour period. Staying with a message for one week invites you to go deeper, aligning with its vibration and through alchemy expanding your awareness. This compilation of messages can then take you through a one year cycle of awakening. You may read the same message a few times, but remain with that one message. Take time to meditate before reading a message. Ask for the message to guide you and shed light on your path, then let go. These messages connect vibrationally to your energetic field and not necessarily through your intellect, so you may just read them as if you read a mantra and then give yourself space to meditate, be receptive and in peace.

The Codes and How to Understand Them

Some of the messages are layered with codes. In order to fully understand these codes or hints, one must pass through vibrational gates or portals. We are asked to move through these portals and discover the mysteries of our power and divinity. The codes are there to guard the ascension process so one can only move as high as one's heart will allow. Once you move through a portal, some of the coded messages become clearer, and the "blanks" are being filled in for you directly with precision and accuracy. The messages offer us technology that is very potent to bring about a planetary transformation, and this technology must be used with love, trust, and pure intent. These messages help us remember our original vision and guide us to manifest this vision using powerful energetic tools. As you connect to the vibration emitted by these messages you are being activated and prepared to receive direct guidance and to further explore the depth and power of living your authentic light with an open heart and aligned with your true, highest path.

This is an illustration of the coded way these messages are delivered. I will use the first sentence as an example (see paragraph below).

In one of the messages the Angels tell us to:

Give intent to celebrate your body. Use your sexual energy often in a sacred form. Teach your body to be loved, allowing the knowledge embedded in your DNA to resurface and teach you all the unexplored pleasure zones and mysteries of your body. Never judge and always allow that which you experience to be used as building blocks for new awareness to guide you on your journey. There has never been a more potent time to make a shift in your life. You came this time around to experience a shift. We ask you with all love to move into the center of your truth and begin today. Use love, and your heart, in all that you do. Your whole reality is about to shift and as you enter into alignment with the center of your galaxy; simultaneously, you must align with your own center. This is your time. Do not fear love. Do not fear pleasure. Do not fear to experience life as a game and as an adventure. Play the game as if each day is the only day. Focus on the now and stay connected to your breath. Allow Mother Gaia to take your breath away with joy as you ascend to new heights. Stay connected to Gaia and ask to be guided. We are with you, celebrating, guiding, and hugging you, when you call us. We are your angels. For us you are the only one who matters, and so be it.

Let's look at the first few lines:

Talking about "celebrating the body," one may ask, "How?"

"Use your sexual energy often and in a sacred form," one may ask, "What is often?" and "How?"

"Teach your body to be loved," one may ask, "How?"

"Allow the knowledge embedded in your DNA to resurface," and yet again, "How?"

The answer is simple: Each of these instructions is an invitation to open a gateway inside of you. When you express intention to explore deeper and move higher, you will be guided expediently and accurately in a manner that is aligned with your individual path, where to go and what to do. The perfect guidance will appear in your life to shine on your path and move you forward. You will then have a choice to walk through that gateway or to keep it shut. You always have a choice.

Heaven and Earth Astrological Charts

In the beginning of each message I was guided to add an astrological chart of the exact reading of the planetary position from the place and time the message was received. You may use it like a mandala or an image to meditate over. There is no need to know anything about it other than to feel the image and gaze at it after you finish reading. It may take you to a greater knowing, linking you to the heavens. On the back of the celestial chart page I was guided to add a symbolic representation of life on Earth. This part was more challenging as I was guided to pick an email I received or sent around the date each particular message was given to me representing an Earth physical dimension to balance the celestial chart. In some instances parts of emails are omitted to avoid making it too personal. They are meant to be a symbolic snapshot in time structured like the sacred geometry form called Vesica Piscis, heaven, Earth, and the human angel balancing both dimensions. It turned out to be an interesting dance, a poignant reminder of the challenge of balancing life, finding peace within. The astrologic chart and the earthly chatter are a play in geometry and vibration, recording a moment in time and space.

You do not need to contemplate it too much but just glance at it if you are called to do so. It may hold a message for you or it may be just there to remind us that we are grounded in physical life but are multidimensional, expansive galactic beings with immense power, beauty, and capacity to love.

Vesica Piscis

Each page separating the chapters carries a symbol of the Vesica Piscis. This sacred geometry symbol embodies the concept of merging masculine and feminine to ignite creation, which is a mix of both divine essences. The Vesica Piscis motif is yonic-shaped, symbolizing the feminine Goddess role as the creator. This shape demonstrates the initial division of cells in the creation of all life. It is the foundation for the Flower of Life and Solomon's Seal geometrical gateways. In some traditions it represents the perfect balance between masculine and feminine energy, heaven and Earth, yin and yang, a bridge from duality to oneness. In Egyptian cosmology it represents "As Above, So Below." This symbol is embedded on the Chalice Well in Glastonbury, Western England, and represents for me the current shift in paradigm. It emanates the code of the new path being charted, embracing the sacred Goddess and holding the vision of human angels in balance and alignment with Earth. These are all energetic geometric activators to support the written messages. You may meditate over them, have fun with them, or ignore them altogether. I was guided to add them as support scaffolding to the written messages.

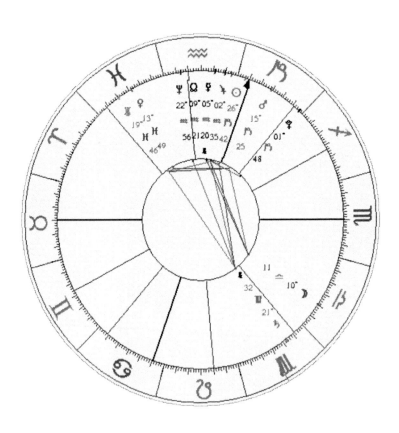

1/16/2009

Dear Nancy,

Thank you for spreading light. It is wonderful that you are doing this work and allowing people to know about it. (N's distribution center) At the moment I feel that I can not go out and promote the book. I do not feel strong enough to both deal with my personal life and keep writing. I am so grateful for your being and your energy.

I am sending you two messages. One deal with the transition of death and the other with constricted body mentally or otherwise. It is not specifically about dementia but it is the same idea. There is much that speaks of death and old age and she may want to go back and read "the tapestry". "the Runway". There is some more but I need to look a bit deeper

I cannot tell you enough how grateful I am for your work. You are giving me energy and the push to continue my work.

Much love

dror

The Golden Cage

*Y*OU ARE DEARLY LOVED.

You are back and we are back. You are on a journey and it is treacherous at times. You get scratched, you bleed a little, and you injure your knees, but you keep going. It is the journey which we hold sacred. Your journey is the reason for our celebration. We love you so and we see you in your struggles. We tell you that you are on the verge of the most astonishing leap, and we ask you to keep walking. Do not look at the peak of the mountain and say, "Oh, this is too difficult. It is too far and I do not have enough strength or equipment." We ask you to look at the vista and focus on the next step, on your breath, on your heartbeat, and celebrate moment by moment. You are not measured by how high you climb. Your treasure is in the thoughts and feelings that you radiate as you walk. In your culture, goals are being promoted as the end-all, and if you arrived second, you lost. Only the one who arrived first is the declared winner. In our game, at times, the one who arrived last is the declared winner. It is so, because she experienced joy as she defeated all odds just to be in the race and run with the pack. You are magnificent, and you win by being in the moment and being connected to yourself. When you are connected to yourself, you are connected to all and you are with joy, regardless of your outer circumstances. When you are one with yourself there is no outside authority that can declare you a winner. You already won. We ask you not to look for medals and recognition from your fellow angels as at times the price you pay is high, and you may win an approval, but you move away from yourself and become one more victim of a feeding frenzy of a society and culture that is searching for the next face to fill its empty stomachs. When the stomach of your culture becomes full of one face, that face, recognized as a treasure, becomes waste as a new face is crowned. We see a trail of "waste" and "lost" angels from those whom you considered "winners." Many become "victims" by buying into the role they play, thereby moving away from themselves. Your journey is about the integration of you with you. When you are one with yourself no outside power can ever sway you because you know who you are and what you are about.

What am I about, you may still ask?

You are about divinity and you are about love. Your story is so much grander than any trophy or title you may receive from your society. Your truth is your truth regardless of what everyone around tells you. Here is the mechanism of which we wish to speak. It is a cultural mechanism. We are naming it "the golden cage" and it has to do with neutralizing your idea of who you are and the power you possess. You are powerful to manifest that which you want, and you are one with the energy you named God. You are the creator of your reality. When you are on your path, be aware that there are those who specialize in channeling the energy of angels who are walking in blindness away from you and into hidden vaults where this energy can be used to feed "others." Those "others" are not known to you because they eat in the dark and do not declare their intention.

Should we fear them, you may ask?

As we hug you we say it to you again and again, that fear is exactly where "they" want you to be. Do not use fear. Fear feeds others. When you are in joy you feed yourself and thereby create light which in turn helps all to see. Your culture often creates fire to catch Moth and trap it in the golden cage. Moth symbolizes those angels who are being crowned by your establishments and are promoted to be the face of all of you. Many of them become victims because they believe that they are winners when in fact they know better. They know that they are no better than anyone else. When they sit

4

at home in the dark before going to bed and they take stock of their lives, many of them weep because they feel that something is very wrong. What is wrong is that they have replaced their own divinity with the image and adoration of the many. By doing so they gave up on realizing their own inner power. They moved away from themselves and became dependent on the way others see them. When they are perceived as winners they feel "good," and when they are seen as "losers" they feel bad. From where we sit, we see them wearing the geometry of isolation and they become lonely. Loneliness is not being by yourself on Thanksgiving. Loneliness, from where we sit, is removing yourself from your *self*. You can have a hundred people at your birthday party and still feel lonely.

We wish to tell you that even we, who are part of you, cannot get too close to you when you are not with yourself. Moth carries its own flame and when it replaces its inner flame with an outer flame it burns itself and disintegrates. With all love, we wish you to integrate rather than disintegrate. There is never a judgment and the way you learn is by walking. It is, however, your mission now to be one with *you*, to light your inner flame and let it soar.

Why do you tell us about Moth and fire, some of you may wonder?

We wish you to listen to your inner voice and to not become part of a mechanism that separates you from you. When your feelings are being channeled away from you they feed others. When you feed others rather than yourself, you add to the balance of darkness on your planet. We are light and you are light. When you are one with yourself you are magnificent in every way and there is no power in the universe that can harm you. You are *it* and we ask you to be it. It is never too late to claim your inner flame. Your flame is just waiting for you to claim it.

How do we find it, some may wonder? *We moved too far and now we are lost.*

You are never too far, is our answer.

All it takes is you telling your inner flame that it is time for a reunion. You ask yourself to join you and you become that which you are—magnificent.

How can we believe it, some may still doubt? *We tried healers; we tried yoga; we tried everything, and we still feel lonely.*

All you do on your path to become whole is sacred and honored. We see many of you who seek those whom you consider "whole" to help you move closer to yourself, when in fact all you need to do is to choose with pure heart to integrate. When you ask others to help you, many of you still maintain the same attitudes about self. You seek others, systems, beliefs, gurus, and healers to do the work for you. To some you pay good money, and you think that by doing so you earned your integration and it will be handed to you on a silver platter. We love you so and we wish to impart to you that the most powerful angels who play roles as healers cannot help you if you choose not to do the work. It is honored to seek help and to hire the support of others. For many, life has changed forever as a result and sacred healing took place. With all love, we wish to tell you that the power lies within you; it always has and it always will. No healer can heal you if you do not wish to be healed.

I do certainly wish to heal, some may say in dismay. *I have been going to the best people. I have spent all this money and all I wish is to be better.*

We know who you are. There is never a judgment as to the twists and turns that you take on your journey. We, however, see your geometry; we see your colors and we hear your melody. We do not see the value of the money you spend on this or that method, but we see your intention and we can tell you that when you choose to heal, you will. When you choose to go back to your inner sanctuary and become one with your self, you will do just that. Many of you give your power to others saying, "You do the work for me, while I wait for my body to get stronger and my soul to turn happy." With all love, we wish to impart to you that this is not how it works. You may be wasting precious time and money. You try and try only to find that you have moved nowhere.

What do we do, you may ask? *How do we know that we are in the right place with the right intention?*

We thought you'd never ask, we answer with a smile!

The answer is simple: you must allow change in your life to come and take you to where you need to be. You must let go of all the things that hold you separated from your self and surrender to the higher part of you so it can lead you. You must allow yourself, at times, when appropriate, to be turned upside down and go through twists and turns while remaining peaceful, knowing that healing takes place through change. Without change, healing cannot take place. Your disease or loneliness came to you to remind you that the place you are standing on may not be the right place for you and you must seek that place inside of you which feels right. We ask you not to fear change. Change will come whether you accept it or not. By trying to hold on to the old, you do not allow your circumstances to rearrange themselves for that healing which you claim you want to take place. We ask you to embrace change because when you come with pure heart and ask for healing, you must change. If you were integrated with you, you would not have to seek healing in the first place as you would be happy and vibrant where you are. With a hug, we wish to tell you that some of the circumstances that you perceive as painful, horrible, and tragic are your greatest gifts. They force you to accept change. We ask you to intend for the high road with less drama before you are forced. Moreover, when the circumstances in your life force change upon you, we ask you not to fight it, but embrace it, intend for it, and healing will come as it must. You are on a road to a place where the view has never been so beautiful. You are climbing and the path may be treacherous, but the reward is you being with you, experiencing light all the time. This is your paradise. Paradise is not a physical place but it is a state of being. You may experience paradise wherever you are. You are in paradise when you are on our side of things, as you are in harmony with all that is.

You are coming into a pattern where the energies of your planet will begin to create constant change and all that was will be changing. It is you who asked for it and it is upon you. It is the change that you seek to heal yourself and by doing so you are healing the planet. Our message to you is to not *brace* for change, but *embrace* the change. Surrender to the new and allow the old to be purged. You cannot hold on to heaviness when you create healing. Change can be forceful, and at times even violent, but it rearranges your reality so the old, that was unbalanced, is purged and burnt, with the buds of the new making their way through the ashes.

Are we to be fearful of some fire and storms, some ask?

You are to celebrate that which you are now experiencing at every moment without judgment. You see only that which is in front of you, but the road which you are now on is leading to a place which you have yet to see. It is around the corner and you cannot see around the corner. We wish to whisper in your ears that we can see the potential around the corner and it is magnificent. With all love, we wish you to allow change and surrender to that which comes to you with joy. Stay balanced and peaceful. Allow the healing of you and the planet to take place. You asked for healing. It must start with each angel individually. The more that healing takes place within, the energy of healing is transferred to Gaia and transforms the soil that you are walking on. You and Gaia are one. You are going though change together. We wish you to be healthy, vibrant, joyful and balanced, as it is your natural state of being. If you are not there, we ask you to intend for *you* to reunite with *you* and allow change, and so be it.

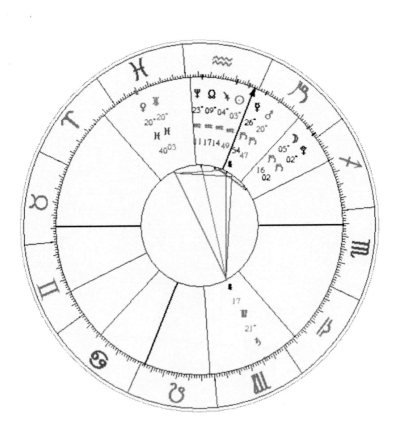

1/23/2009

Hola Dror,

I just read the message. It is powerful and something I think we both need to hear now. The ideas are complex and important. For example...

"Your journey is about integration of you with you. When you are one with yourself no outside power can ever sway you because you know what you are about."

"You are about divinity and you are about love. Your truth is your truth regardless of what everyone around you tells you." (This, I thought was for you - to not let arrows thrown at you stick)

"You are powerful to manifest that which you want and you are one with the energy you name God. You are the creator of your reality."

"The moth carries its own flame and when it replaces the inner flame with the outer flame it burns itself and disintegrates. With all love we wish you to integrate rather then disintegrate. There is never a judgment and the way you learn is by walking. It is however your mission now to be one with you, to light your inner flame and let it soar. Why do you tell us about moth and fire? Some of you may wonder. We ask you to begin to listen to your inner voice and do not become part of the mechanisms that separate you from you. When your feelings are being channeled away from you they feed others. When you feed others rather then yourself you add to the balance of darkness on your planet. We are light and you are light. When you are with you, you are magnificent in every way and there is no power in the universe that can harm you."

The part about seeking healers outside yourself...I received this advice recently. I was told not to give authority to voices outside yourself. Also to not allow outside voices to be misinterpreted as inner voices.

But it is ok, as the angels indicated, to seek help outside yourself but don't expect to not have to do the work of change.

Being at peace with change seems important here and knowing that healing comes with change.

I at first thought perhaps they were referring to personal relationships (I thinking of my relationship with J. – and you with d.) Then they mentioned just trusting that change will come and it will be forceful or not but it will be healing. Just be at peace with it.

Well, there could be more to say as the messages are dense. But that is all for now.

Thanks for sending this one.
un abrazo
love,
Nancy

Monsters Under Your Bed

YOU ARE DEARLY LOVED.

What you have been doing is taking one step at a time. You are honored for your walk, and again we wish to embrace you and congratulate you on your path. What you do affects us all, and we are with you all the time. We wish to take you by the hand and allow the road to open up so you can see the vista. There is so much beauty that many of you miss as you move along your journey to become whole with yourself. We come to you in many ways and ask you to open up and learn the subtle signs that are pointing to the highway so you will not get lost.

What are those signs, some may wonder?

As we hold your hands, we ask you to close your eyes so you can *feel* rather than *see* where you are going. No matter what lighting conditions surround you, when you do not rely on vision to navigate, you do not get lost. Your vision is limited to what the brain can interpret. When you see things which don't add up your brain freezes, so to speak. It may choose to ignore what it sees, or it sends you into fear, which freezes your organs and prevents you from vibrating in harmony with all that is.

What are we expected to see that will freeze us, some may ask in dismay?

Your landscape is changing, and your resistance to flowing with that change can create visions that are new to you. We ask you at this time to allow all that you experience to flow through you without trying to hold on to the poles of safety. These poles will be shifting, and the only place where you will find balance, peace, and safety is within. Close your eyes and look into that place which is eternal and full of love—your home.

Am I expected to just ignore whatever is around me and go inside, some may still inquire?

It requires practice, and like anything else that you wish to learn, you must find a way, a space, and the time to become proficient. It will serve you well. You are renegades and you are at the forefront of the energy of change that is sweeping across the planet, and it will touch upon all of you. This energy is powerful because you are powerful. You created it within you and manifested it in your world. You first created it inside, and then you have shifted the atoms around you to reflect your intent. Now when your outer experience begins to reflect your intent, we ask you to celebrate it and not say, "Stop, I did not really mean it," or "Wait, I wanted just a little bit, but not that way." Moving upward requires fearlessness, and fearlessness requires you to practice conquering fear. Fear is part of your humanness and it is built in you. It is biological; it protects you and it helps you to survive. What we ask you, with all love, is to conquer fear by learning to redirect the energy of fear from you to Gaia so it can be transformed rather than freeze you.

How do we do that? Is it even possible, some may ask in disbelief?

You have done it before, is our answer. Many of you have been shamans in past cycles, and your knowledge is never lost. It is inside of you. Ask your cells to wake up so you can recall the memory of how to transfer heavy energy from you to the planet. You are connected all the time to Gaia. Gaia is conscious. She knows where you are and what you are doing. She responds to you even when you think you are forsaken and forgotten.

That is all theoretical. How do we actually do it, some may still insist?

As you stand in the midst of a reality that is swirling and howling, close your eyes and breathe into the earth. Ask Gaia to take whatever it is that you fear and transform it. Look down with your eyes still closed and "see" through the dirt. When you do this with pure heart, she will open her heart to you and embrace you. It will feel like a mother's embrace and it will be full of love. This is how you transform fear. You send your fear to your mother Gaia, and she hugs you in return.

Is it that simple, some may ask in disbelief?

It is even simpler. Everything that we tell you, you already know. You did it when you were a child. When you cried at night and asked your mother to stay by your bed until you fell asleep, you did just that. You transferred the energy of fear and in exchange received love. All of you have done it in one form or another. It requires you to surrender and stay open so that fear can be taken away from you, making space for love. When you were a child and you saw imaginary monsters under your bed, your remedy was to call out, asking your mother to take them away. Gaia is your mother and you are her child. She is connected to you like a mother and supports you like a mother. When you fear and you call out, she will come to you.

There are many of you who say "I wish it were that easy," and you dismiss it as nonsense. With all love, we wish to impart to you that you are loved just the same. However, when you are in fear and you do not transfer the energy because you do not believe that it actually works, it will stay with you and you may freeze. When you freeze you do not vibrate in harmony and you feed darkness rather than create light. There is never a judgment and you are loved the same if you take our hands or ignore our hands, dismissing our messages altogether.

We are available for all of you, but only those who open their eyes and give intent to walk hand in hand with their higher part will experience the high road. This is a free-will universe and you are powerful in both directions. You are powerful to create light and you are powerful to block your light, thereby giving a stage for darkness to take hold. When you move in your world, you sound a melody that is sent to all directions, and it tells us of your feelings. Feelings form the strings that connect you with us and with yourself. We see many of you who are playing the melody of mistrust. When you mistrust, you are walking on a path that is dim as you cannot clearly see where you are going. The energy of mistrust is associated with the color blue and it carries its own geometric shape. From where we sit, it looks like a circle that is broken into pieces where each piece is floating and disconnected from the other piece. Each piece begins from the center outward. The simplest way to visualize it is by comparing it to a slice of pizza. These slices of pizza want to come together, but the energy of mistrust is keeping them floating and disconnected as if on a mobile in a child's room. You are a circle and you desire to become whole. When you are in that energy you feel insecure, as the pieces that make you whole are wobbly and discombobulated.

Why are you telling us of these shapes and why should we care, some of you may wonder?

We connect with you through feelings and we wish to paint a picture that stirs your feeling center so you can link with us to a higher ground where your perception can shift. To us you look like geometric shapes moving around. As you move around, you emit light and you create music. Your thoughts and feelings conduct your melody. When you are in the energy of mistrust it is as if you conduct with a broken wand. We love you and we wish to impart to you that trust is needed for you to move to a higher ground.

We hear you say, "I trust myself but I do not trust my partner." Others say, "Whenever I trusted someone they betrayed me, so I have no more trust for anyone. This way I do not get disappointed and hurt." We know your pain; we can see where you have been and why these people who have hurt you in past cycles are back again to teach you about trust. They are here to teach you about you, to help you move away from hurt and to find peace. Many of them played the part of the untrustworthy angel so you could begin your healing from the point where you had left off last time and begin to integrate. Trust is one of your biggest challenges at this time as fearlessness and trust go together like the ingredients of ginger carrot soup. You cannot separate the ginger from the carrot—the soup will become something else. You cannot separate them because they make the flavor that you require to ascend in vibration. Many of you are being tested, as each time the slice of pizza moves away from the center you become unstable and unbalanced. The geometry yearns to be united, and it must unite first in you so your outer reality will create trust. Trust is love. When you carry the energy of love within you, do not move away from trust, as trust is the glue that holds the pieces together. When you face a situation where your pieces come apart because of a test, when someone you love has betrayed your trust, moving away from your bond, leaving you in pain to repair and glue the pieces back, you must use the remedy of self-love. You must hug yourself first. Then know that even the most painful betrayal comes to teach you about finding your own power and igniting your inner light. You are one consciousness exploring yourself. The one who moves away from you and "betrays you" is also the one who paves the way for you to find the part in you that can never be betrayed.

I am in pain and you are telling me about self-love, some of you may ask? *How can I love myself when the one I love the most hurt me,* others may wonder?

It is you who is walking the walk of a master and you must not forget it, not even for a moment. The one who betrayed you and the one who cannot be trusted is your teacher, so always know that he or she is only playing a role in the drama you call human journey... and your journey. You must know that you are exploring your own energy from all angles and the way you learn about yourself is through relationships.

Why am I always attracted to relationships where I have trust issues with my partner, some of you may inquire?

You are so dearly loved. It is you who is searching for trust, and you bond into relationships where you are challenged. Your challenge is not to find someone you can trust. You are here to find joy and you are here to move higher, finding the divinity inside. When you feel that your partner moves away from you, when your pieces begin to wobble, know that the test is about you staying balanced and integrated, moving back into your center by using the adhesive of self-love. We are not here to find a solution for the partner that cannot be trusted. They use "betrayal" as a substitute for their own lack of self-trust. They are on their own journey, and when they use an unbalanced energy to try to complete the lack they feel in themselves, they create an imbalance within that will need to be balanced at a different time through karma. They are facilitating your lesson and you are facilitating theirs.

It is you who seeks to grow in that aspect and to learn about trust. Trust is love. The feeling of being betrayed causes you to move away from love, experiencing a form of disconnect, as if someone severed a cord between you and you. This cord is the connection that you feel between you and your own eternal self that is all about love. When you do not trust, you experience fear. Fear is translated into resentment, and often, into anger. You feel as if your heart has been pulled away from your body and you fear that you will "die" without it. It is a devastating feeling to many of you, and you become very vulnerable. When you are in mistrust you emit powerful vibrations of mistrust which are not easily balanced. We wish to impart to you that trust and love are one and the same. When you feel unloved you do not trust, and when you feel untrusting you do not love.

How can I feel love toward the one who is hurting me, some may ask?

It is about you and you are all about love. We ask you to see yourself as a master and understand that even the one who hurts you is your teacher.

What do they teach me besides making me angry and in pain, some may wonder?

They are your messengers and they are showing you that you have a choice to go with the dark or to go with the light. When you go with the light, staying centered, with love, you will teach all, including them, the treasure of trust. If you move away from your center, allowing their energy to sideswipe you into anger and resentment, it is as if you told them, "I am not there yet, please show me more betrayal so I can learn to stay balanced with myself."

Do you want to tell me that I must stay in relationships when my partner betrays me, some may ask?

This journey is about you with you. There is never a judgment if you wish to stay or move away from your relationships. We see that, at times, moving away from a relationship is the most appropriate step for your growth, and at times, staying in a relationship is the most appropriate step for your growth. Whatever you choose to do, know that you are always loved. If you choose to allow the relationships to sway you and allow your pieces to dangle, you have work to do.

What should I do with my relationship? It is my main concern, some may still insist. *Should I stay or should I leave?*

As we hug you we wish to tell you that it is all about you and your inner journey. Your relationships are part of you. At times it is appropriate to shed parts of you so other parts can grow and blossom. Do not fear moving away from part of yourself as it may allow you to learn other aspects of yourself. Your relationships feel at times as if they are part of your body and, as you move away from a relationship, it is as if you have severed part of your body. We know your pain and we know who you are. We are with you in the trenches every day that you are on this planet walking blindfolded.

We still do not know what to do, you may insist.

You are beautiful and you are divine. We ask you to wake up to your power and know that you are all about love. Nothing should ever move you from the link between you and you. When you move into the energy of mistrust you are disconnecting from your link to your love center. Those who are searching to unload thoughts of heaviness or darkness have access to your magnetic field, and often they move in to insert heaviness into you, thereby filling up the gap. Often when you are in the energy of mistrust you experience your heart as heavy. This heaviness is inserted, magnetizing your heart center, creating weight and pain. This is one gift we ask you not to accept. Your own heaviness acts as a magnet for heaviness that is floating in your universe. It is in the geometry of your thoughts and it happens automatically. It is no wonder that so much violence and pain is created in the name of "betrayal and mistrust." When your partner, friend, or spouse whom you have trusted went against you, it is as if you have been torn apart. They represent an aspect of you and by moving away they have shattered your sense of wholeness. When you "allow" your core to wobble and float away, know that you may also allow heavy energies to fill the gap between these slices of pizza. The taste— we can assure you—is not fresh.

What do we do then, you may ask?

Send love to the one who you feel betrayed you, is our answer. By doing so you counter the drifting and shattering forces. As if by magic, then, you deflect all that heaviness away from you. It is not as hard as you may think. By sending love to your partner or friend, you are composing a melody that resounds in the heavens.

How can I send love to the one who has broken my trust, you may still ask?

With all love, we wish to tell you that from where we sit it is the surest way to graduate this lesson and move away to a higher ground. When you send love to the one who you believe "betrayed" you, you become whole, as you experience the integration of you by accepting all aspects of yourself. You become whole through loving the parts that you perceive as positive as well as the parts that you perceive as negative. When you do, you neutralize the heavy energy and send a beam of light not only to your partner but to the planet. This journey is about your own transformation. We wish to tell you that when you truly send love to the one who "betrayed" you, you will also have the power to move away from them, graduating this lesson with honors, without experiencing the feeling of loss of self. With all love, we wish to impart to you that, from our perspective, there is no one that can ever betray you. When you ask someone to be only yours and to show you that you are one, a lesson may ensue to teach you that you do not need anyone to show you that you are one. You are one as it is inscribed in your divinity. We see many of you give your power to others so they can mirror for you your own value. When the mirror reflects you to yourself, you break the mirror because you do not like what you see. With all love, we wish to impart to you that what you see is your own lack of trust reflected. Trust or broken trust, from our perch, is not about husband cheating on wife or girlfriend dating someone other than her boyfriend. This is just part of your drama of learning about your journey of being a human.

What is betrayal then, some may wonder?

From our vantage point, betrayal is when you asked someone to complete you and help you become whole just to realize that this power is not with them but it is inside of you. You then feel disappointed and broken because your expectations were not met. You feel that you have built your inner power on relationships that cannot sustain your expectations. You are taking your relationships seriously because you think that you are not whole by yourself. You contain within you the entire reflection of your wholeness. In each lifetime you allow part of that reflection to be expressed and manifested. Then, you can learn and grow within the eternal journey of moving upward to become one. It is your limited vision which shows you only as far as the edge of your nose. Love is trust and trust is love. Your journey is about finding love in all aspects of your human experience. When you feel that you have experienced the pain of mistrust, use your inner power to send love to the one who broke your trust. By doing so you have integrated all our teachings and bonded all your parts into an unshakable divine circle of one. You are beautiful and you are divine. Whatever experience you attract is the one that, within you, must be transformed. You are a master and you are walking the walk of an angel in duality pretending to be a human. As we hug you, we whisper in your ear that you are love, you are one, and you are perfect. Know that you do not need anyone to be whole. It is your birthright. We wish you to shine the most luminous light, playing the most divine melody—one that will resound across the universe, transforming all that comes in contact with you and the planet, and so be it.

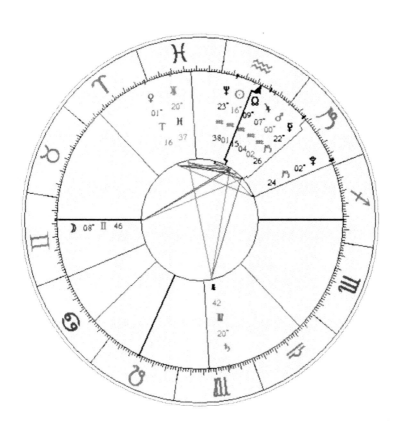

2-4-2009
Hello Dror,

Read the beautiful email I received from a friend in S.C. about you and your work. My Israeli name is Amnon, been living in Jacksonville, FL for 31 years, learning to let go of the separation/alienation from God and stay aware of the divine source, the true nature of beingness. I would love to connect with you if you are up to call or receive a call from another soul. It feels like it will be a celebration of Love and Light.

From the Essence that Connects,
Amnon Shomlo

Subject: Wanted to share

Akexander,
Wanted to share this with you.
This past Sunday I attended a gathering to hear a gentleman by the name of Dror Ashuah, born in Israel and a graduate of Mass. College of Art and Harvard University. He has published 2 books entitled "Conversations With Angels". He is a very well educated, humble man who has had encounters with angels who impart information to him. Yeah, I know, I was skeptical but curious...until I met him. Everything he talked about resonated with pure truth... you know that deep recognition, intuitive insight ahh-ha kind of knowing that just has to be true by the impact it has on your heart? I think he's worth reading.
He is so intent on sharing this information with everyone that you can read both volumes free on line in their entirety!
Log on to his website at www.andsobeit.com
If you are not familiar with him, I think you will find it informative and interesting.   I think, like me, you'll find the perspective,
insight, unadorned explanations, and deep wisdom quite simply perceptive, beautifully stated, and resolutely true.
There's something here and I wanted to share it with you.
Joyous blessings and love,
~ Michele

The Fountain of Youth

YOU ARE DEARLY LOVED.

It is not the end of the story. It is a beginning.

Beginning of what, you may ask?

It is a beginning of you moving away from the idea of who you were and dressing up in a new outfit.

What outfit might that be, some may wonder?

It is you who asked to move away from your current groove so you could avert the potential you had of ending human life on Earth. You said that you wanted to do the work and complete the journey. You had a certain amount of time to graduate and this time is upon you. You are graduating from one lesson and moving on to the next. As you know from your school systems, before graduation you must go through a series of tests.

Why do we need those tests, some may inquire?

As we hug you we wish to tell you that the tests are there so you will integrate the knowledge that you have accumulated over a period of many cycles. You are now in the energy of the tests. After the tests come the evaluation and the graduation. You are very close to completing a course of study that has lasted from the beginning of your recorded history.

We do not want any tests; we just want to have a secure life without too much drama, many will argue. *We want to relax a little*, you say.

There is much to do in a short time, is our answer. In your linear reality time is accelerating, and resting will not be an easy option for most of you. This is why we ask you to slow down so you will not get lost in the acceleration of the illusion of time. You are eternal, and time is manufactured for you by you. It is accelerating now so you will graduate on time. In the season of tests in your school and university system there is a period where you have to prepare. Then, you have a period where you have to face the exams. The time of preparation is over and you are facing the time of exams. These exams are there to bring you to a higher place where you will be awarded a diploma. In your culture, those who obtain advanced degrees are rewarded. In this energy the advanced degree is earned by you staying with love and in peace in the midst of turmoil and chaos.

What are we to do and how should we prepare, some may ask?

You have all the tools inside of you and you are ready, is our answer.

We ask you now to trust yourself and know that when you are at a place when things do not make sense anymore, close your eyes and go inside. Sit down and allow the light to emanate from your core. Hold your light high and breathe. Allow your breath to be filled with joy, knowing that you are fulfilling your mission and passing the exam by doing exactly that. We ask you to trust. Trust that the movement taking place around you is a divine expression of your intention to graduate. Trust that you can never be harmed, that you are made of light and love. Know that darkness can never get too close to the light. Know that when light gets near darkness, darkness transforms. Know that we are with you, hugging you, all the time, and you are never, ever alone. Know that you are the most powerful force in the universe and you contain within you, collectively, the energy you named God. This knowing and trusting is your divine expression of harmony. When you are in harmony you vibrate with all that is and you act as a vessel of the energy of love. When your vibration is aligned with the universal vibration of love energy you are creating the bridge of light which catapults you to a new consciousness. This is the glory that is upon you. We ask you to be in gratitude and in joy while all this is taking place around you.

This is impossible and inhuman, some of you may claim.

As we hug you, we ask you to expand your idea of your "humanness" and become the multidimensional expanded angel that you are. Many of you will choose to experience fear, desperation, pain, and suffering. Some will choose to step off the planet for a while. Surely they will be coming back later on to experience the tail end of this transformation. We ask you to honor the lesson of your fellow angels, knowing that there is never a judgment on how far you go or the choices you make on your path. Know that the most you can do to elevate your planet's state of being, bringing peace and abundance closer, will be transforming yourself to vibrate with the energy we call love. Your power is immense and yet we see so many of you give away your power to others in the hope that it will create a better world.

How do we give away our power, some may wonder?

It is the human who vibrates love from within who is changing the Earth and allowing others to see through her light. In your culture many find that they are not enough and they need to find others to admire for their power. We ask you to love yourself. Refrain from admiring others, knowing that, like you, all are playing their unique role. Your mission is to play your role but not anyone else's. You are beautiful and you are powerful. We see many who are looking at themselves in the mirror and saying, "I am not powerful and I am not beautiful; let the powerful and beautiful one carry my light for me because they have what it takes but I do not." We ask you to hold on to your light and carry it within because you are here at a time when each light that shines from within makes a difference, bringing peace on Earth closer. When you allow others to use your light, you are no t fully occupying the space that was given to you as your birthright.

When I look in the mirror I see an old face with tired eyes. How can I see myself as beautiful or powerful, you may ask?

Close your eyes and consult your feeling center. It will tell you your story better than any mirror. Your biology is just one small aspect of who you are. It is a vehicle, and like you do not think that you are the car that you drive, we ask you to not think that you are your body. Give yourself a hug and smile. It may be hard in the beginning, but it will become easy through practice. Walk your walk with a smile. By smiling you allow the energy of gratitude a space and you are deflecting the energy of victimhood.

What am I to do, you wish to know?

You are to shine your light from a place of gratitude and joy while walking on your path doing what you are doing. We wish you to congratulate yourself, honoring yourself and your body for carrying you through. Do not look at magazines and say to yourself, "She is beautiful and I am not." We wish you to say, "I celebrate the diversity of this planet and the role that each of us chooses to play. I especially honor my role, as it is sacred and the most appropriate for me at this time, as I am beautiful, as I am divine."

You are honored and this is a free-choice place where all angels walking in duality are hugged the same. We ask you to keep your power inside and allow it to transform all that come in contact with you from within you. When you give away your power to others, often it is being misused to create darkness. Your power comes from you occupying your biology and creating joy within. When you are fully connected to yourself, you are a magician and an alchemist. If you could join us and fly above for a moment, you would know that things are not gloomy. You would carry the perspective of Spirit and you would celebrate every day you progress toward a new reality which some are calling the "New Sun."

For human life to be sprouted on your planet, many cosmic events had to take place. As they did, you waited patiently on the sidelines observing and anticipating your humanness to gel as it formed. You have been floating in a reality that is joyful and full of light, waiting for the opportunity to be challenged in a reality that is heavy, where light is a choice, not a natural state. You wanted to explore all aspects of the energy we named "free choice." You wanted to know that when given a choice you will choose light over dark and light over heavy. This experiment was celebrated, being observed by many in your universe and other universes, since your walking on this planet began. Can you imagine the anticipation now as you near graduation? We ask you to fly with us, if not physically, then in your dreams, and allow the vision you had to manifest the bridge of light bringing you closer to peace on Earth.

We wish to speak with you about an aspect of your humanness which you named aging. From our perspective you never age. You are eternal and, while you move through bodies, your energy stays ageless. It is an aspect of your walking in the dimension of time which brings about changes in your biology that many of you dread. The changes that seemingly are imposed on your biology are your choice. It is written in your contract and you signed it. You asked for your reality to continually change so you will be led to growth and to explore the energy of your journey from multiple perspectives.

Why did we choose to experience the pain and degradation of our physical bodies, some of you may wonder? *It is horrible to lose our abilities and become limited*, others may say.

You are so dearly loved, and your walk is about you bridging your reality to the reality of your eternal self, thereby awakening to your divinity, your essence, which is love. What better way to accomplish it than through time? As your biology changes and your cells age, you slow down. It is then that you begin the journey inside. You have been searching for eternity for the fountain of youth, not realizing that even as you age, you are always youthful and always young. Youth is a state of being and not a physical age. From our side of the veil, you are all ageless. Your body is part of your divine expression which takes you through the journey you call human life. Your body is programmed to show you who you are and to express the energy of your eternal self through this vehicle. You create your body before you come to this planet from a thought and an intention. You continue to create and recreate your body as an expression of your thought, with intention, while walking blindfolded on the planet. Your body responds to you as you are the driver.

We know someone who is no longer in the driver's seat, and they no longer know where they are or what they are doing. How do they benefit from this ride, some may question? Others will say how terrible it is to see someone who was strong and vital become incapacitated by this or that ailment.

With all love, we wish to impart to you that you are so dearly loved and those of you who are going through the experience of forgetfulness or incapacitation are those who are learning to feel rather than control their environment through reason. Many of you who are in the company of angels who are forgetting or are incapacitated by limitation of their mental abilities believe that they are not aware of their environment. On some level it is true and on some level those who experience the deterioration of their mental capacity are going through unlearning one lesson while learning another.

What might that be, some may ask?

They may seem to lose their ability to communicate rationally and operate effectively in your world but they do not lose their ability to feel. Feeling is the language of Spirit and they are preparing to cross that bridge through connecting their feeling centers. There are those who experience in the later part of their cycle the most profound lesson of all—the lesson of feeling and allowing the logical mind to disintegrate. It is a choice. As painful as it seems to you, son or daughter, know that it is a sacred time and an honored aspect of their journey.

It is so painful to see my dad who was so proud become so helpless and frail, some will say. *It is so painful to see my mother who raised me not being able to care for herself.*

Yes, is our answer. Now it is their opportunity to learn to receive, and we ask you not to take this lesson away from them. Yes, it is painful, we say, if you choose to see it as such, but with all love, we ask you to honor their choice, their lesson, allowing them to be the one receiving the care. Allow them to feel love because, through their forgetfulness, the feeling part is enhanced. They know how you feel, knowing if you get angry or resentful, or if you feel love and compassion towards them. They know it because it is their opportunity to go inside, experiencing emotions and being in the now. Some may lose their ability to communicate how they feel in a rational, linear manner, crying when they are sad or stamping their feet when they are angry. We ask you to love them. We ask you to teach them how to receive by giving them what they are asking for: love. You have found that as you walk on your journey, you form an idea of what is positive and what is negative. We hear many of you saying to yourself at night, "I would rather be dead than suffer like that, being taken care of, not knowing where I am or what goes on around me. I would kill myself if I ever get to where my father or mother is at this time. It is terrible; it is awful; it is hell." Dear son and daughter, know that this part of your parent's journey is where they have asked to learn about surrendering. They may wish to experience the path you call dementia so they can "see" a new reflection of reality. They may wish to teach you about giving, about compassion, while experiencing the helplessness and the humbleness of no longer being in control. It is an intense learning and it is sacred. Some of you may feel, as you walk on your path, that you were meant to learn by feeling wonderful and being healthy. When you become disabled and sad, though, somehow that was not meant to be. With all love, we wish to impart to you that your natural state is of health and joy, but at times your higher part seeks to expand your idea of who you are through limitation. When an angel's capacity is becoming restricted they may initially go through fear and hopelessness; it is in the geometry of this lesson. With all love, we wish to whisper in your ears that once they have moved through and under that bridge, something miraculous begins to happen. They let go. They open the palms of their hands and surrender. They give up the fight and they let go of what once was unthinkable. They give up on thinking that they need to be and act in a certain way. They allow others to handle their physical bodies and they allow Spirit to come in, teaching them about love. Some lessons may be brief but intense, and some will last for a long time; it is a choice of the one going through this lesson. The energy of the soul is not afraid to be humiliated because it knows of its own divinity. The energy of one's eternal self is not afraid to go through the deterioration of the body and of the mind because it knows that it is eternal. When you see your loved one unable to dress herself without help and in need of having her body washed, requiring assistance in attending to her most basic needs, you feel sorry for her. You judge her lesson as being terrible. We ask you to move away from your limited vision and climb to the top of the mountain. This lesson is as valuable as a lesson of winning a race or being victorious. Do not put plus and minus signs in front of your dear one's choices of learning. We ask you to love them without conditions and honor their learning. Know that they chose to learn by experiencing limitations, as it was appropriate for them on the eternal journey of becoming one. Know that when they volunteer to go through limitation they extend their hands to you to join them in the learning. They wish to teach you as well. So do not judge, just love and support them, as well as yourself, throughout this journey. If you are angry, if you are in pain, know that you are loved and accept those emotions, allowing them through. Forgive yourself and love yourself, knowing that it is all sacred. In the end of it all there is only love. We wish you not to wait for the end to realize it.

How do I go about the day today, some may wonder? *I can hardly make it through a day without crying.*

We know who you are and we cry with you when you cry. We laugh with you when you laugh, and we are around you throughout it all. This lesson has to do with being in the now. It is so, also, for your loved one who is becoming incapacitated. They lose their fear of the future because they are busy with the present. They know when they are hungry and they know when they are tired. We ask you to be in the present as well, as it is the only time you have. Focus on transforming one minute at a time and do not think about the next. When you are with your loved ones and they cry because they wanted an orange but when they asked for it you brought them an apple, they did not realize that they asked for an apple when in fact they meant orange. When you are in front of a dear one who is crying and you do not know why, allow them to express, and be with them. Understand the sacredness of their feelings and stay with them. Give them a hug or hold their hand and know that it is the most you can do. They must experience their own journey as you must experience yours. You help each other grow, and it is not always pretty, but the potential for the most brilliant luminosity is there at any given moment.

You are coming to a physical reality where all your lessons seem to be piling on top of your head until you can no longer sort them. It is an overwhelming feeling and you may stop walking. We ask you to keep breathing slowly and feel your heartbeat. Know that this is exam time and to pass with distinction you must be in the now, holding your light, knowing that all that crosses your path is divine. Smile, knowing that every breath is an opportunity to transform heavy to light and sadness to joy. Allow those you love to experience what they must and love them through it all. They have indeed lost their ability to communicate, but they feel everything. In fact, they are like a newborn baby who has the knowledge of the whole universe trapped in a helpless, limited body. Physical ability alone cannot translate the knowing, so the infant must surrender and wait.

It is the same at the end portion of the journey. The feeling and knowing is all there. The physical body, though, is unable to translate it into words and actions. There is so much that is hidden from you. Much like an iceberg, most of the action takes place under water and you can only see the surface. With all love, we ask you not to judge the learning of your loved ones as positive or negative. Honor their journey and take care of yourself. Allow them to undergo their own transformation by accepting it and supporting them. Know that they feel everything and are aware of everything without the ability to communicate back. We wish you to talk to them. Explain to them how you feel and tell them often that you love them. We know who you are and we know what you are going through; we wish to hug you all the time. You are so honored for coming down to the energy we call the human body and taking on a lesson that is not easy. The universe and the billions of us are in awe of you. We ask you to open yourself so you can receive the love and light from beyond the veil. We ask you to walk the walk of a master knowing that you are divine. Your journey is about finding love in all aspects of your experience, and so be it.

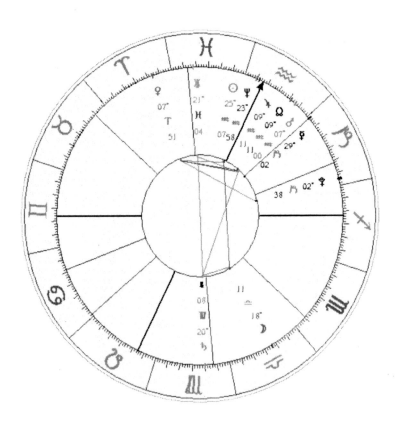

2-13-2009

Dear Brother

I know of a book you wrote, what is it? It's an enviable ability to write a book.

The ability to create art in general gives me great jealousy, no envy of the desire to take Anyone what he had, but a good one. I wants me to have this ability to describe, see and feel.

Happy to hear more.
What other book?

Happy to hear about Z, I have a regret that she grew up without that beautiful relationship between all other cousins. I know I asked her circumstances but I can not help thinking that with degree of sorrow, for what might have been, and probably will not happen. *

Perhaps through creativity, it will be possible to think and come up with that track.
Mama told me (of course too late) that you had a frightening and difficult experience in India. What was that?

Love

Your Brother

Gil

The Dot

YOU ARE DEARLY LOVED.

We are with you all the time; fear not, as the path ahead of you is wide open. You are paving the road as you go. Your moment-by-moment thoughts, and feelings, continuously rearrange the atoms and molecules around you, supporting you on your journey. Fear not, as there is no time on our side and miracles are the name of the game. "Magic" is the manner by which your reality conjures itself when there is no time. One potential can be replaced by another in a matter of a nanosecond. You will not even notice that your reality has switched. It may happen faster than a blink of an eye. This is how powerful you are. There are some who may tell you that you have no power and you are a victim. Exercise discernment accepting help from those who seemingly try to "save" you because their stated intention may not be what they declare it to be. You are the only one who knows your path. It is your choice to progress and follow your highest trajectory. At times those around you may "market to you" that you are weak and they offer their hands. What they are actually saying is that you are not sovereign and you cannot change that which is in front of you. Know that you can un-create what you create, that you can recreate the new and move away from old at any moment. You are the master of your universe and we ask you to hold on to the crown of your own kingdom. Hold on to your light. Your light is your power. When enough angels turn on their light, the immense luminosity created will light your planet like a light bulb and create a protective layer of love frequency that will reach all. The halo of the planet can become the guiding force rendering actions which go against the energy of love to be unsupported.

Do you still doubt the importance of your mission? Do not flinch; do not hesitate. Use love in all your interactions. Always come back to balance and joy. The change is upon you. You are paving the road for a new energy to become your new air, your new soil, your new gravity, and your new language. This new energy is of higher vibration and it is becoming your new reality, permeating every facet of your layered life. Actions which go counter to the new frequency may no longer hold the same traction. A room that is well lit has no place for shadows to hide. All darkness must transform. This is your potential. You asked to graduate and we ask you to keep walking.

We have so much to fear, some will claim, *the economy, our future, our safety, the climate, our children, everything. What should we do?*

You are to walk the walk of a master, is our answer. It is always the same answer. For you to walk that walk, you must first awaken and become aware of your divinity. When you are awakened and you radiate the energy of love there are fewer fears, fewer questions.

How should we do that, some may still inquire?

You are already doing it, is our answer.

We ask you to be in the now. When you are in the now, you are walking hand in hand with your breath and your heartbeat, connected to all that is. When you walk with the joy of occupying your biology and radiating the moment by moment joy of breathing, you are a master. It is so much simpler than some of you may envision. There are those who believe that they have to become masters by practicing breathing for twenty years before becoming it, while others may go through self-deprecation and deprivation to experience enlightenment. With all love, from our perch, it is not necessary. Your choices are honored and sacred. Whatever discipline you choose to learn from and undertake to reach higher awareness is always sacred. Becoming a "blind" devotee of any discipline may hold you back because it was charted by someone other than you.

You may follow someone else's steps hoping to reach the same place as they. You may, however, discover that you can only walk so far. The masters discovered their own journey and it applied to their story perfectly. Now it is your turn to be the master and find your own story. Their "stories," although helpful, do not offer you all the answers. You are the Master, the Priest, the Imam, the Rabbi, and the Guru, as well as your own disciple. It is on you to connect with you, so all of the yous who make up the energy of divinity can unite and coil together to reach the light, creating light. From where we sit watching you, the path to higher awareness is very simple. You may use complicated language; you may embed the path in difficult practices, but at the end of the sentence there is always a dot, and the dot is where the whole story is hiding.

Tell us about the "dot," you request.

We ask you to be in the now; that is all. When you are in the now we ask you to be in the awareness of love; that is all. When you are in that awareness of love we ask you to be in the awareness of gratitude to all that is coming to you or crossing your path; that is all. When you have achieved those three simple stages, you are a master. Your reality will bow at your feet and will lift you to the top of the mountain where you can see a wide- open vista, experiencing the joy of light.

How can that be, many may ask in dismay? *We are told that we need to learn the scriptures and know how to walk on fire. We are taught that we must perfect our bodies and exercise discipline.*

Yes, is our answer. Whatever you choose to do is where your intention lies and if you choose with a pure heart to move higher, indeed you will. It is not the type of discipline you choose that matters the most, but it is your intention to move higher which propels you forward. Your chosen discipline may only take you so far. Like a child who learns to ride a bicycle, she begins with a small bicycle which has an extra set of training wheels to keep her from falling. These extra wheels help her keep her body upright while learning to ride her bike. At some point, however, the two extra wheels become an obstacle as they block learning balance. You can always use the extra set of training wheels, but know that at some point, you will need to let them go.

We are in love with you. We look at you and we shed tears of joy. You are beautiful and your choices are honored. We ask those of you who intend to discover their own divinity to let go of the fear. Do not fear riding your bicycle without training wheels. You were meant to be able to ride without even using a bicycle.

How can we ride without a bicycle, some may wonder?

You are an alchemist and you can transform your vehicle at any point to become that which you desire. You are energy, and as energy, you can be that which you wish. When we speak of peace on Earth, it is not limited only to people not having wars. We are speaking of harmony that vibrates with love and creates a new reality on every level of existence on your planet. When we speak of abundance, we speak of you not being worried about having your next meal.

This is not possible; the world is becoming worse by the day, many will claim. *We only see poverty, dis-ease, wars, and threats from seemingly everywhere.*

It is your choice to see what you wish and your choice is sacred. With a hug, we whisper in your ears that we can see your potential and it looks very different. You are learning to ride your bicycle without having training wheels. Perhaps you will get scratched and bruised in the process. You, however, are determined to ride and you are well on your way. We ask you to keep your vision aimed at your breath and your heartbeat. Do not allow the illusion of the movie that is currently playing in your theater to distract you away from balance.

Why do we feel the way we do, some may ask? *Why are we facing so many challenges at the moment?*

When you watch a movie on your TV screen you see things happening and events following events. The events in your movie seem to take their own linear progression. Now we ask you to turn off the sound and advance the film on fast-forward. Watch the silent movie for a moment and understand that, metaphorically, it is what you are going through at this time. Your movie is being fast-forwarded and events that were stretched over an hour are taking place instead within a few minutes. It is why we ask you to slow down your system, focusing on your breath and heartbeat. Put your left hand on your heart and your right hand on your third eye and close your eyes. This may act as a reset button to bring you back to a rhythm that is in harmony with your system. No one knows better than you what it is that you need to do. Your biology is changing and your reality is moving as if on whitewater rapids. You try to steer your canoes left, then right, to avoid the rocks and danger. You are coming to a stretch in the river that will present you with relentless challenges. These challenges may present themselves on the internal personal playing field as well as your physical external playing field.

We have told you that you all had to make a choice of either moving with the new or staying with the old, as staying in the energy of neutrality and not joining the game will not be an option. As your planet is moving to higher planes, all of you will have to shift your positions and adjust. Sleeping will not be an option. We ask you to wake up to the beauty of your journey and enjoy the vista. Allow your attention to be in the moment and you will be in the most glorious of energies—the energy of ascension. You are beautiful and you are powerful. You do not need to do anything or prove anything. It is not in the contour of your face that your beauty lies, and it is it not in your muscles that your power hides. Transforming within is why you came to this planet. This inner transformation is then applied to your outer reality, transforming your planet. Keep walking. Do not stop. We ask you to learn to enjoy the vista rather than fear what is coming. You are eternal and you are beautiful. When you are with us you do not fear anything. There is never a judgment and you are loved for walking the walk of an angel disguised as a human. Intend to find your own divinity and understand that your path is sacred. We wish you to be all you can. The age of miracles is upon you. We ask you to create miracles as you walk. You are always connected to all that is and what you do is felt everywhere in the universe. We congratulate you on your journey, asking you to create the miracle of joy, balance, and love at every turn of your journey, and so be it.

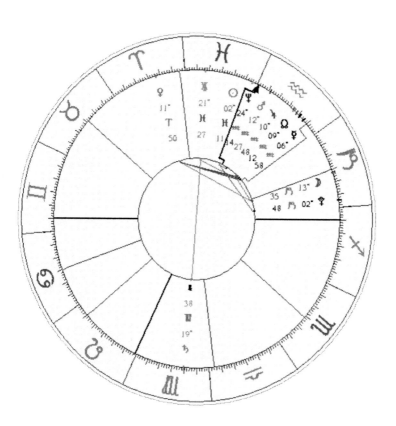

2-20-2009

Greetings and Blessings.

Rev. S. B.

Ancient Egyptians believed that upon death they would be asked two questions and their answers would determine whether they could continue their journey in the afterlife. The first question was, `Did  you bring joy?' The second was, `Did you find joy?'"

--Leo Buscaglia, 1924-1998

Gadgets Stop Ringing

YOU ARE DEARLY LOVED.

You are never alone. You are always connected with invisible strings to all that is. We see many of you who bathe in the geometry of isolation. When you are in the energy of isolation, many of you feel like a cooking appliance that is disconnected from its power source—be it gas or electric—rendering it useless. Isolation is the energy of disconnection and it has to do with your feeling of rootlessness from the energy of Gaia. When you are connected to the energy of your mother it allows your geometry to be in harmony with all that is. Isolation, from our perch, is not about being alone without a partner or family. Isolation is, to us, geometry: a melody and a color of disconnect from your own life source—the life source that connects you to your planet. We see it in terms of cords. These cords vary in color. They come from your first and second energy centers (chakras) and allow you to walk as one with your biology.

Why do you tell us about isolation, some may wonder?

Many of you moved away from the embrace of your Mother Earth and thereby experience the feeling of isolation. When you feel isolated you do not honor Gaia because you are not connected to her. As you moved further and further away from the way of life that was in line with nature—the animals, your food—you have become increasingly disconnected. As a result of your moving away from your connectedness to the source of life that is under your feet, you have created artificial ways to try to link yourself with the source of life. We see many of you trying to connect and communicate all the time. This is because of the fear that, when the gadgets you have stop ringing, you may have to face yourself and be in the energy of isolation. For some of you, being away from instruments that link you to others is a terrifying experience. That is why we see so many of you communicating incessantly with so many, all over. From where we sit, we see you communicating indiscriminately in search of meaning, when in fact the geometry of fear of not existing is all over that communication. We wish to ask you then, how would you feel if all your communication devices stopped functioning? What if your TV, radio, phones, and internet devices no longer transmitted to you the artificial connectedness so many of you crave?

We see many of you who rely on this communication to define yourself, rather than looking inside, proving to yourself that you actually exist. We see many of you who like your devices better than you like to be around live humans. These devices are your link. You become reliant on them to know who you are and what you are about. With all love, we ask you to find a way to reconnect with your environment and Gaia. It will serve you well. Your isolation is one of the reasons many of you seek relationships that are not in balance with the heart center. Many of you are not connecting through your physical energy centers because you are so used to having them inactive. Your physical body responds to your intent, and when you close up your heart, your ability to stay connected becomes limited. Your heart center honors your intent and closes down. It is then that you cannot tell the difference between heart connection and the artificial connection that comes from your devices. We see many of you develop virtual relationships with your instruments and walk hand in hand with them, thereby moving into the geometry of disconnection from your heart, from Gaia. We see many who feel more comfortable having a digital companion that speaks to them, moving them further away from themselves. There is never a judgment and you are loved regardless of your choices.

You are now in the energy of reconnecting with yourself, becoming one. Gaia knows who you are and all the energies around you know who you are, the trillions of us know you. We wish you, too, to know yourself. With all love, we wish to tell you that the energy of isolation is the energy of darkness. It makes you reliant on a virtual persona that can be manipulated at the push of a button. When your heart center is not active you may not notice that you are drifting further away from yourself. Into that drifting space, darkness moves. When light moves out, darkness replaces it. It is the way it works in your reality. We ask you to be connected with yourself and limit your reliance on instruments. We wish you to relearn the language of Gaia, as it will open your heart and allow you to see truth from falsehood. There are those who operate in the dark who control some of your devices. When many of you rely on these devices to feed you information that you take in as truth, you are vulnerable; you are susceptible to being taken over, getting manipulated by those who want you to stay at a place of isolation. When you are removed from your self, it is easier to sell you things and to "convince" you to consume. The consumption is about "re-educating" you about who you are and what you need to be in order to be part of life. The more isolated you are, the more susceptible you are to consume what you are sold on, so you will "feel better" about yourself.

With a hug, we wish to impart to you that the pendulum is swinging away from the direction of isolation and your current financial condition is one way that allows you to move closer to yourself, taking stock of yourself. During hardship many must look inside. You may not like what you see. When you cannot distract yourself through spending, many find that they need to rediscover new meaning. There are no coincidences. We ask you to look at your current financial reality, seeing it as an opportunity to chart a new path back to balance and integrity.

When you are isolated you are not in a place of love. Love is connectedness and love is being in harmony with the universe. When you are in that energy you are vibrating with the energy of Gaia and of all that is. It is then that you are fulfilling your mission. When we are with you and you are in the vibration of love, you are celebrated by the multitudes. With all love, we wish to impart to you that the pull of dark and light is in a tug of war. Like a pendulum the energy moves from one side to the other. We ask you to find the fulcrum point where you will not be susceptible to the movement of others around you. When you are in the energy of balance, you allow others to find balance. Balance is connectedness to your divinity.

Why are you telling us about devices and isolation, some may inquire? *We need those devices to communicate and be in the world; we need them to make a living.*

With all love, we do not ask you to give up your devices but to not give up your connectedness to your self. We see those who use these devices as an excuse to develop virtual relationships with the world around them. Their relationships carry the geometry of 2-D. It shows in the heart center and in the throat center. Both centers are not aligned with truth and love. They are channeled to be in the energy of isolation and separation. When we speak of isolation and separation, it is not from society, it is from self. With a hug, we wish to tell you that when you are not with yourself, you cannot be in truth with others, as it will not move you forward. When you are in virtual mode with self you apply the same energy to your relationships with others and you do not move in the trajectory of the new energy. You are on a journey. Your journey is about climbing up and seeing the larger picture. It is your mission to be connected with self and know that you are part of all that is. The planet is moving faster and faster upward. In order to stay in balance you must stay with the energy of love and balance. As the planet is ascending, you must shift as well. With a hug, we wish to tell you that separation from self may feel uncomfortable, as it is unsupported by the magnetics of your planet. You are in the energy that is moving toward the center, truth, and light. Those who are walking in the direction of this center may experience life very differently than those who move in the opposite direction. We wish you to be in a place of love and joy on this journey.

We ask you to keep your power and hold your light high. You signed up for this mission, and it is testing you to your limits. You are powerful when you are connected with your self and you are vulnerable when you are in the geometry of isolation. When you develop a virtual world and relationships, you are moving away from Gaia. It is then that you are likely to not move in the direction of an ascending planet. With all love, we ask you to slow down, take the time to walk in the woods, touch the leaves of the trees, lean against their trunks, and feel the earth under you. Take time to observe the birds and the animals; talk to your plants. With a smile, we offer to you that, at times, a conversation with your plants will be more rewarding than your virtual conversation on your computer. It is a conversation that will align you back into the energy of harmony with all that is.

You are alive in the most magnificent of times. It is a time of changes, and what we speak about will become clear to you sooner or later. We wish you to enjoy the ride, knowing that it is what you asked for and that change is upon you. We wish you to stay with balance, love and joy, and so be it.

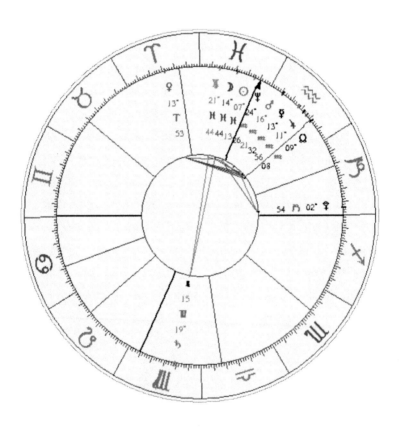

2/25/09

Hi,

I have two friends in dire need of all the prayers they can get.

The first is my friend June John's father, Bob's. He had successful open heart surgery last Friday. However, he became agitated yesterday and the hospital over-medicated him to calm him down and messed up his liver and kidney. He is on dialysis now and in a confused state. Please join me in praying for his complete recovery.

The second is my friend Corry Fisch. I mentioned her once before. She is a mother of two pre-teens, who's had a brain tumor since before she was married (over 15 years ago)with. She's been in and out of hospitals and coping fairly well (with chemo, etc.) until recently. Her condition has definitely been diagnosed as inoperable, and the cancer is spreading into more of her brain. The worst latest symptom is her short term memory is going very quickly, so family members have to continually answer the same questions and remind her of things. She can still move about at home, but she now can't be left alone with her children and the prognosis is that she'll continue to get worse until she eventually dies.

Please join me in praying for the best quality of life she and her family can get while she is still here with us and her family; and for a peaceful transition for her and her family when her time to move to the next level approaches.

Many thanks to all,

Jan

Shades of Grey

*Y*OU ARE DEARLY LOVED.

It is no coincidence: when you walk the walk and you find a treasure on the side of the road, know that it has come to meet you. You and we are like partners. We are collaborating together on creating light. When you walk, you are using a stick to feel your way around, as your vision is limited. It is then that we offer you guidance.

How do you offer your guidance, some may inquire?

We work with your frequency and we communicate directly to your geometry. We do not insert thoughts per se, but we ride on your frequency wave, allowing your thoughts to fork so you can "see" an alternative. We do so, so you may be able to choose. When you are about to act and a thought is moving into you showing you, in a split second, a vision of the possible results of your action, know that it is your angels working with you, shining light around you so you can see, acting then, from awareness.

At times you will not have the necessary energy to move away from your planned action, even though you know that it does not serve your highest potential. You are loved and hugged just the same. There is never a judgment on how you act. We respect your free-will universe and you are never forced to choose one road over the other. The power is within you. Know that you always have a choice between dark and light. Often your choice will not present itself solely as dark or light but rather in shades of grey. Even in the spectrum of shades of grey, there is always a lighter shade of grey and a darker shade. Your mission is to become aware, to awaken, so you will always move towards the lighter shade, spiraling, ascending, toward purer and purer light. Our responsibility is to "show" you the possible results of your actions when you are using love and the results of actions that are devoid of love. For you it may appear as a split-second thought or vision of what's to come, a dreamlike flash which melts away as soon as you try to grab on to it, but leaving you with an impression and a feeling. This is the mechanism of the love of Spirit interacting with your biology.

For you it may feel as if a choice or an alternative just presented itself seemingly from nowhere. When you are in a place of darkness, you can all of a sudden "see" your choices of dark or light. It is still your choice, but it is an alternative you may have not considered a moment earlier. This alternative miraculously appears within you just when you thought you had no other choice, but now this new one is available to you. When you choose light you are celebrated by all of us; when you choose darkness you are loved just the same. With a sweet, loving hug, we wish to impart to you that you may not take part in the celebration because you may be crying under your blanket. Choosing light does not mean taking the easy road. It means a choice that is, at times, the more difficult one, but it moves you away from your groove of karma, catapulting you towards mastery.

Why do you speak to us about our choices, some may wonder?

You had a choice to move away from your test, and from our perspective, it was the easier choice. It was just a short shift of energy, and you could have been back home but yet you have chosen to stay. From our perspective this was the harder choice, but one that has the potential to create magnificent luminosity, transforming the universe—yours and ours. We wish to shine light around you, allowing you to see how connected you are to the mechanism of spirit. In your day-to-day, many of you feel that you are separated from Spirit and you are on your own, moving alone. Many of you hold the belief that unless you go to church, synagogue, mosque, or a temple, you are not connected to your divinity; you are forsaken and forgotten. With all love, we wish to tell you that it is never the case. You do not need to go anywhere to be connected.

How do I know that it is the truth, some may ask?

Give us a hand, ask for us to reveal ourselves, and let go. The answer to your question will come to you in many different forms. You must ask for that which you wish to experience. If you ask for a fancy car to materialize in front of your eyes, you do not yet fully understand the mechanism of spirit. If you ask for your angels to make their presence known through a feeling, you will not sleep at night because of an all-night celebration that will take place around your bed.

We wish to speak to you about a choice that an angel on their journey may face at times. This choice is considered in your culture a taboo, and we wish to shed light on this taboo. Taboos are your society's or culture's agreed-upon walls of darkness, as they block you from seeing the mechanism of divinity in all processes that you are experiencing as an angel in disguise. When an angel decides to shorten their journey and go back home, many of you who were close to this angel feel ashamed.

Why ashamed, some may wonder?

Your guilty feelings come from a place that is very deep. You wonder whether there was something you could have done to prevent this angel from moving into desperation and hopelessness, resulting in their choice to end their own life. Your society condemns such action, and you create rituals which do not allow you to fully process the path you named suicide. In some cultures you do not bury the ones who committed suicide with those who died from natural causes. At times your religions ostracize and condemn such humans. Taking one's own life carries an immense power. It shows you the power that you possess in your hands—the power of life and the power to end your own life. With a hug, we wish to remind you that you can never end your life, but you can cut a lesson short. You are eternal, and what you call "life" never ends. You move into a body because of a wish to express and grow through a lesson that is accelerated. Earth journey is always an accelerated path. It takes immense courage and will to come into this dimension to walk the walk. This is why we ask you to keep walking. You are here to express through your biology. Your biology is sacred. Intuitively, all of you know and feel the sacredness of your temple. Many of you fight for your life and, when an angel chooses of their own free will to cut their journey short, they create a vibration, a geometry, that reaches out, shifting all who are involved with such an angel. When you walk the walk, you have a built-in biological mechanism which keeps you connected to life, finding creative ways to continue and strive under even the most difficult circumstances. We wish to use a metaphor to describe the feeling that suicide may create in some of you. It is as if you were standing in line for a long time waiting to receive a gift that is cherished, held sacred by all. When, then, you finally get to the front of the line, receiving your beautiful gift, you do not fully open it. As you struggle with unwinding the packaging, you get frustrated and choose to throw away the whole gift box still unopened. When you discard your gift, all the others waiting in line are shocked as they cannot fathom how one can dare do such a thing.

We wish to speak with you at this time about this process, as the energy for it is ripe. The process is complex and layered. There are many angled mirrors on your disco ball that reflect back to you who you are and how you appear to yourself. You are light and your geometry spans all dimensions. As you become multidimensional we wish to shine light through reflection on some, more challenging, aspects of your divinity. It is not an easy subject for most of you to ingest, especially those of you who had loved ones who ended their journey early. We ask you at this time to hug yourself and know that you are loved and the one who you have lost is loved just the same. Their choice was a sacred choice and it was honored. We wish to begin by reminding you that you never die. The process of moving away from your biology is a simple shift of dimension that you have done hundreds and thousands of times before. You know what to do and it is natural to all of you. We see many of you who believe that this is your first time and you are so excited to have this opportunity to express. With a wink, we wish to tell you that it is the beauty of being in duality. Every time is like the first time. It is as if you take on a short-term memory disorder so you can experience the joy and thrill of tasting, all over again, your favorite flavor of ice cream just as it was the first time. When you taste the ice cream we hear you say to yourself, "Wow, this is good; I will never let it go." What if, to some, the flavor was not completely forgotten? The flavor was buried in their cellular memory and they know of their flavors. They hold the memory of how it feels after you eat too much or when the initial sugar rush has subsided, giving way to a low. They remember, on a cellular level, the journey you call Earth life, and they are fearful of what is to come. Many try to drown their memory by ingesting substances or moving out of their day to day reality, separating from their biology through depression, psychosis, and other forms. They chose this journey, but on some level, once the memory kicked back in, they changed their tune. At times the memory is expressed as uncontrollable anger from what was done to them. They wish to hurt others to balance what was done to them, destroying themselves in the process. Others may express their fear and pain by creating such an imbalanced life that inevitably it leads them to cut their journey short, either intentionally or not, but always by choice. With all love, we wish to impart to you that some angels work very hard to distance themselves from themselves, sometimes through power and fame. Sometimes, though, it may be through poverty and depression. One is not better than the other. They manufacture a persona that is based mainly on illusions, so much so that they lose the relationship to their divinity. It is hidden inside but they can no longer find it. Those angels, no matter how powerful they may appear in the physical limited dimension, hold very little light, and when their illusion pops like a balloon, they choose to end their cycle rather than face themselves.

Some also remember the difficulties of the journey and the challenges that lie ahead. They know and remember their tests. If you ask them, they would not be able to articulate it, but they can feel it. Some may even believe that they do not hold the power to transform what they came here to transform. They also know that they can start over at any point and there will be no judgment if they cut their journey short. With a hug, we wish to impart to you that when they do choose to move away from their lesson, at times they will choose a subsequent life that begins in a circumstance that is challenging, picking up where they left off, therefore learning to cherish the gift of life by having to struggle for survival, and learning to hold sacred such a gift. Often they will choose to experience a subsequent life where life is hanging by a thread and they must keep on fighting just to learn about the beauty of such expression. When an angel contemplates ending her own life, she often came with this challenge. It may have been a memory from a previous expression or a lesson of learning to honor life by being in the energy of despair and hopelessness. Here the opportunity for self-transformation is abundant and glorious.

You have chosen to come to this planet of free choice, and ending your life is one of your choices. You have asked to come back, promising to honor life, transform the darkness to light discovering your own divinity, awakening to the sacred journey of expressing life though your biology, of expressing all your energy of thoughts and feelings. When an angel chooses to end their journey early, in most cases it is through darkness that this choice is made. There are circumstances, however, that the choice to end one's life, moving to the next lesson, holds the energy of neutrality, not creating the imbalance which asks to be balanced though karma. You are energy. You make a contract with your biology that you will meld, working together as one, for the sake of learning about energy and about self. For self to learn about self it must have an aspect of reality that reflects self. Your entire reality is manufactured for the purpose of reflecting self. When you are in your body connected to your biology, all that you encounter is manufactured for you by you. There are no arbitrary aspects of your reality that are not by choice— your choice. Your self in duality is not always aware of your power to manufacture your own reality, and many of you who pray at night for an "easier life" create challenges during the rest of the day. These challenges are created through thoughts, feelings, and lessons that are chosen through the energy of balancing past actions. When an angel occupies her biology and fills up the space that was allotted to her, she carries within her the power to transform all aspects of her reality, becoming the alchemist, turning the lead into gold.

What space do I need to fill, some may inquire?

When you are size 8 but you wear an outfit that is size 13, you leave space for another to move in and help you fill up your outfit. Your biology is a vehicle that your energy of light must meld into and work with in order to create harmony. Through harmony, you move closer to your oneness, thereby moving upward in vibration, getting closer to self.

How do we create harmony and oneness, some may ask?

When you realize the immense power you possess to create your own reality. When you move in your day-to-day connected to your biology and in the now, you are well on your way to realizing your power. There are angels who slowly move away from their biological vehicle, allowing holes to be formed in their energetic bodies. It may be in the mental, emotional, or astral bodies. These holes are created by moving away from oneness, not occupying your space, and not being in mastery of your own reality. It is then that other energies may enter and wreak havoc in your energetic bodies by occupying these holes, thereby creating disconnected, discombobulated geometry.

What "other energies" are out there, you may ask?

The unseen universe is abundant with conscious life and many are on a path that is different than yours. They, too, wish to express but do not occupy a vehicle with which they can express. Some are on a path that is of a different learning and they do not hold the sacredness of life as you do. Some are marching on a path that does not have love in it like you do, and they wish to learn about it by attaching themselves to vacant seats. When you vacate your seat we can assure you that there will be plenty of volunteers to fill this space.

These energies do not have a biology, but they look for gaps and holes. These energies can wreak havoc in your energetic structure.

Are they evil, some may wonder?

With a smile, we ask you: Is a bee evil for stinging you when you sit on it by mistake? No, there is no evil; there are various levels of conscious energies and all are on a path of learning. They are playing their parts as you play yours.

How do these energies work on us, some may inquire?

It is as if you had a body that was meant to weigh 150 pounds and instead you carry a body of 300 pounds. The extra 150 pounds are not part of your original intention or your original blueprint. It is added on through imbalance within the energetic structure which then manifests in your biology. Your biology follows your instruction and, when you choose to move away from self, your biology expresses it.

How is it being expressed, some may wonder?

There is never a judgment in our hearts, and you are on a glorious path that is held sacred by all of us. It is, however, our intention to light your surroundings so you can learn about yourself through reflection. Your society and culture developed many ways to lure you aside so that you will be removed from yourself, becoming vulnerable and susceptible.

Susceptible to what, some may ask?

You are powerful. When you are in your power, you can tell truth from falsehood and you are in balance. When you are in balance you do not consume more than you need, you do not hurt other life forms, you do not create imbalance in your environment or in nature. You walk in harmony with Gaia and what you do is supported by the elements around you. Being in balance does not make a very good business model because it does not create outer growth. Growth within is what is created. Great effort was made to find ways to move you away from yourself in order to create imbalance. This imbalance is a geometry that is out of balance with your biological vehicle and the planet. You and Gaia are connected, so any imbalance within you inevitably creates imbalance for your planet.

How are these imbalances expressed, some may still inquire?

They are expressed through dis-ease like the AIDS epidemic, obesity, diabetes, cancer, mental disorders—

mainly depression, pollution of your natural resources, drug and alcohol abuse, abuse of sexual energy. It is expressed through addictions to food, sex, drugs, TV, and even work, as well as being medicated by numbing psycho-pharmaceutical drugs which keep you away from yourself. The imbalance is also expressed through violence, wars, and overconsumption, fueled by greed, then imploding to return to balance. As you move from yourself you damage your vehicle, and when many choose the path of moving away from their own vehicle, they are walking the path of destruction. Just like the angel who chooses to end her own life, it is the same with humanity; through lack of awareness we walk the path of self-destruction. This, however, was your potential but you moved away from it at the last minute, choosing to reclaim your vehicle and create light which exposes some of the methods that were utilized to move you away from self.

But I was helped by some drugs that helped me cope and healed others, too, some may claim.

There is never a judgment, and the path of moving away from self began a long time ago. Now it is time to come back to yourself, reclaiming your power and revealing your divinity. When you are powerful, you are in balance as you do not need to rely on things outside yourself to keep you content. We wish you to awaken. We wish you to open up and embrace this time, as it is glorious. You are on a path to create a leap that will transform all of you. We wish to shine light on aspects of your journey so you will find balance and peace within to keep walking, shining your light.

At times the energy of an angel is so far removed from their original intention when descending to the Earth plane that they believe they do not possess the power to transform their own reality and move closer to self. The only path they see is the one of destroying their biological vehicle to reunite with themselves. You come here to explore energy and to become one with self. Through exploring different aspects of you, exploring energy, you move closer and closer to self. You create more light, discovering your own divinity and power. The journey of walking the walk offers many routes; some that your society often promotes are the ones which move you away from yourself. The path of destroying oneself has many layers. One layer may be expressed through misuse of one's biology and the abuse of one's environment. A different layer may be expressed by an angel actively choosing to destroy their own vehicle. Many who are consuming self-destructive substances are on the same path as the one who jumps off of high places, but it is not as literal and graphic. Ironically, some of the self-destructive substances are actually being promoted by your culture.

Your journey is about honoring life and about discovering the link of love in all that is, moving closer to your true interdimensional self, walking the walk of a master. We ask you at this time to honor those who choose to cut their journey short because, by doing so, they allow all the people around them to realize and become aware of the gift of life. The geometry of suicide is one that rearranges all the shapes around them. The melody of such an act throws into question many of the things many of you take for granted. From our perspective, those who move away from you "too soon" give you a gift of becoming aware of the fragility and the sacredness of life. They ask you to learn from them and choose life, thereby rearranging your priorities so they will reflect light. They ask you to be yourself so you can avoid their path. They ask you to have joy in your life and be in the now. They are your messengers. Through their action, they ask you to re-evaluate, re-arranging your priorities, choosing light over dark and being one with self. It is a painful event to all who witness and are connected to a person who has chosen to commit suicide, but many more in your culture are on the same path that is not as literal; they are on a path of self-destruction by moving away from self through lack of awareness. You have chosen to come here to learn and grow. You always come with the potential to cut your lesson short. The lesson has to do with moving away from self-destruction and hate into self-love.

You, who knew the one who chose to end their life, know that they are loved just like you and their choice was honored. Within their darkness they could not find the light. In the midst of hopelessness and depression they have chosen to start over.

It is your responsibility now to shine your own light. We ask you not to use guilt or shame. The angels who have chosen to move away are back with you and they are again learning the precious lesson of honoring life. Those who cut their journey short know, as soon as they are back home, that there were other ways to deal with their reality. They know and are shown all the potentials, and they realize that there were other ways to move along their path. When they go back, many require rest and restoration. Their energy must be healed and repaired so they can come back for another challenging lesson. Honoring the gift of life is a major lesson and one that is held sacred by all of us. You are eternal and you are loved. We ask you to know that whatever you encounter on your path is there by design—your design. Know that for every challenge that you have orchestrated for yourself you also designed a solution to move away from the challenge. Know that no challenge in your life was meant to end with self-destruction. You do come with karma. The path to becoming liberated from karma is always through awakening and experiencing, not through destruction of self.

We ask those of you who see and live with the one who you believe is contemplating suicide to know that you must take care of yourself, shining your inner light. That is the greatest contribution and service you can give to your loved ones. If you join them in darkness, you add to the balance of darkness. When you shine your light, you allow them the option to see. Know that you cannot change others. You can only change self. By changing self you affect all. We ask you to find love in all that you encounter, knowing that for those who choose to be in darkness, it is their choice, and you must come to peace with their journey. Each of you has your own journey and you intersect with others so that you can learn about self. Those who choose to end their life teach you about honoring the gift of life. Honor their choice and honor yours. Life is your biggest gift and it comes with much responsibility. You came here to discover your true nature and shine your light, allowing all to see. You came here at this time to be the lighthouse and show others the path to safety. You came here to awaken to your divinity and walk the walk of a master knowing that all that you encounter at the end of the day comes from love. We ask you to be in the now, connect to your biology, honor yourself, honor life, and honor Gaia. Love yourself first and through self-love, spread it to all who come in contact with you. We wish you to wear the outfit of a master under your plain everyday clothes. We ask you to awaken to your purpose, becoming it, and so be it.

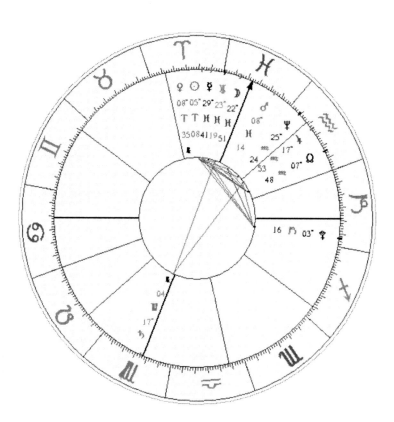

3-25-2009

Maintenance Bill

Hi Dror,

Here is the info for the door repair. The hinges
were $14.00.

I have to go out of town this week so will tackle the
list when I get back. I will check my email or you can
call me anytime.

Steve

Thank you Steve

Next priority is the ceiling in the bathroom of
Foster street #4

it is in pretty bad shape

let me know

Grateful
Dror

Planetary Healers

YOU ARE DEARLY LOVED.

The pain you feel is you asking to be whole.

Why does it have to be painful, some may ask?

It doesn't, is our answer. Your pain and your agony are choices. Your joy and happiness are also choices. At times you have to go through one to reach the other.

Why is it so, some may still insist?

You are so loved and your path is one of wonders. When you begin to walk you can only see what is in front of you. The views may be painful to your senses, but they may be taking you through mayhem and through thorns to a place that is elevated, offering an open, beautiful vista. Things are often different than what they seem. We ask you to move with trust and fear not. You are eternal and you are loved. We wish to remind you that you are part of creation. You always were and always will be. You come by choice to experience and explore energy from all perspectives. There is no perspective that is more valued than another. It is your awareness and awakening which add the flavor of light or the flavor of darkness to your chosen dish. We are here to walk with you and hold your hand when you let us. We are here to hug you when you need a hug and cry with you when you need to shed a tear. Your emotions and feelings are your most powerful tools at this time. They carry the energy that is the energy of spirit. This is how we communicate and connect with you. This is how you are linked to us and to spirit. We ask you to stay in touch with your feelings. We ask you not to numb your emotions and to not try to be the one who behaves according to your acceptable rules because "people will talk." You are renegades and you are here to create a new reality. Do you think that you create anything new by conforming to the old? You signed up to build something that was never there before. You must be fully with your emotions and your biology so you can act as a vessel for the new energy, not for the energy of conformity. You are coming to a time where you will need all your resources to stay balanced. The wind will be blowing and the earth under your feet may feel unstable. The old must be destroyed so the new can be built.

We do not like hearing that. Are we to expect destruction, some may wonder?

Indeed, you must destroy your ideas of who you are so a new you can emerge. Some may experience it internally and some externally, but all must shift. The process of destruction can be fearful or joyful. It is your choice.

Should we be worried, some may wonder?

With a hug, we ask you to not worry. You signed up for this mission. When you know that you are at the right place and the right time, fulfilling your mission with love in your heart, you are invincible. When fear comes we ask you to greet it like an old friend and tell it that this time you are unavailable. Your "old friend" will persist and so must you. There is no space for fear when you are the lighthouse whose task is to shine light and guide others to safety. Your mission is to remain balanced and peaceful. You must build inside of you the new and then let go of the old. Your inner process then manifests in your outer reality. When you fear, the vibration that you emit is weak and you cannot transform the old nor can you create a new reality. We ask you to be aware of your eternity and awaken to your awesome powers. When you walk in your power, activated and aware, connected to your true knowing and feeling, your thoughts manifest instantly.

We do not believe it, some may state. *How is that possible*, others may wonder?

With a hug, we wish to remind you that everything that was ever created in your 4-D reality was created from your thoughts and emotions. Do you think that your reality is created by your hands and your physical power? With all love, we wish to tell you that nothing was ever created in your physical reality that was not created within first. When you are in your power, the dimension of time disappears and you create what you need instantly. Your power is within you. When you project it toward inner harmony, balance, peace, and love, you literally give birth to that which you project by transforming vibration into physical matter which manifests in your experiential reality. We wish to impart to you that you are walking into a new reality which can be compared to an aquarium of sorts, where your surroundings are transparent and the energy that you are walking into is like your modern day X-ray. You can no longer claim that you want peace and at the same time act in the opposite direction from your stated intention. You are at a place where the magnetic fields around you will no longer support actions that are hiding in the shade. The dark will be as powerful as it always was but it can no longer put on the costume of light and pretend. Dark will be exposed as dark and light will be as light.

It is time to speak about your path and where it is leading you.

Will you tell us the future, some ask in excitement?

No, is our answer; we wish to talk to you about your past. You are now creating your future by being in the now, one thought at a time and one feeling at a time.

What does the past have to do with the future, you may wonder in confusion?

The past is your future, is our answer.

Why is it so, some may ask?

You now must use all your past experiences to create the future, is our answer. All you need to know is stored within you. All of you who are on this mission have done it before. We ask you to activate your past knowledge so you can transform your "now." By transforming your now you are transforming your future. It is that easy. You are eternal. You are here at this time to reunite with self, shining your light, becoming the beacon of strength and hope to all those who come in contact with you. You are enabled and all of our teachings are known to you. You carry inside of you all of your tools, and they are not in your backpack but embedded in your biology. You've had many lives—all of you—where you used different types of energy. You have learned how to create magic, how to heal your friends, create peace with your enemies, and balance Gaia. A time will come when you will need to bring back much of the knowledge that you once had— knowledge of which you are no longer aware. We wish to tell you how to access this information. Healing is a power that you have in you. You can heal yourself and you can facilitate healing of others. It is a time of healing, and with each and every healing that you facilitate you lead Gaia closer into balance. Healing is always energetic first. When you try to heal symptoms without addressing the underlying cause, it is as if you put a bandage over an amputated limb, rendering the healing ineffective.

We are with you all the time, and when you come with pure intent to a fellow angel who asks to be healed, you are a healer. There are many who believe that they need to have knowledge of what is wrong, that they need to know how to manipulate energy and how to ask for specific results. With a hug, we wish to tell you that many healers at this time approach healing from a limited linear reality. We exist in the circle and part of you exists in the circle. When you and we hold hands above the one who needs healing, it is your linearity that you need to move aside so your circular portion can be activated. When the energy from the circle interacts with your biology, the melody that is being transmitted is one of harmony, and it creates a pitch or a tone that is harmonious with your cells, bringing them back into balance. Some of you really enjoy music. We know who you are. When you go to a concert, hearing a divine piece of music, you feel as if your whole body is vibrating and your spine is all bubbly. The music that you hear is not only aimed at your ears nor does it create joy exclusively for your eardrums. The music that you hear is vibrating throughout your whole being. It is the same with healing energy. The energy that you transmit is working on your own vibration, aligning it with the harmonious resonance of love. Love is balance. When you become one with the energy that you transmit, you create healing within your own biology as well as the one you attempt to heal.

Is it hard to learn how to do it, some may wonder? *I wish to heal my loved one who is sick; can I do it?*

Yes, you can, is our short answer. You must have the one who heals set pure intent to allow healing energy to come through without agendas and preconceived ideas. The one who wishes to be healed must also come to the healing with pure intent, asking to be balanced. When both parties join with pure intent to create harmony, healing takes place. It is then that you must trust, allowing that which comes to unfold, knowing that you are a vessel, and that your task is to *allow* healing, not to *create* healing. Healing is created within the person who is healed. You are a lightning rod for energy. The one who heals must have all the "credit" and the one who facilitates healing must be in awareness that she must not take "credit" for herself, whether healing took place or not. The healer is a vessel and the one who is healed is the actual creator of the healing. When you heal someone you must stay loving and balanced, detached from the end results of your work. If you take "credit" for healing, you then must take credit when healing does not occur. It is then that you lose the purity of the vessel as you become attached through an agenda to the results. Any agenda limits your ability to act as a pure vessel.

At times the most profound healing takes place by going through a dis-ease. Healing of the body is not always the path that leads to the most profound growth. At times a dis-ease of the body brings about deeper healing which is of the eternal self. That is why we keep singing you the melody that you are powerful. You are powerful to manifest dis-ease. You are also powerful to heal yourself and facilitate healing for others.

Your society created a mechanism whose stated purpose is to heal you and it is called modern medicine. Most of your modern medicine works on repairing damage that was created through imbalanced energy. Not all of you can repair damage that was already done. In fact, you spend most of your healing resources on repairing damages rather than on healing. If we had to estimate, we would say that 0.01 percent of your resources is spent on healing and 99.99 percent is spent on repairing. The reason your priorities are such is that it makes a good business model. The more imbalanced your society becomes, the more resources you spend on repairing others. The sicker your society becomes, the larger the business of "repairing" grows. This is your current business model and it is about to change.

Healing can be facilitated by anyone. Repair has to be done by specialists who spent many years studying and practicing, connecting what is disconnected, repairing what is damaged. We congratulate you for developing ingenious methods to repair damaged tissues and save lives. You are honored for your creation. It is valuable and sacred. With all love, we wish to impart to you that you can heal most of your imbalances, worldwide, without needing to spend even one day in medical school. Each and every one of you has the power to heal yourself and others. If only two out of a thousand angels use their healing powers worldwide, you will have a dis-ease-free society.

How can we heal if we do not know what to do, you question?

You do know what to do, is our answer. When we tell you that you have all the tools inside of you we mean it.

Can we heal AIDS, other epidemics and dis-eases, some may ask in disbelief?

You can create a reality where you no longer need to experience epidemics and dis-eases to bring you back to balance because you will be balanced, is our answer. All you need is to remember.

How do I remember, some may inquire?

It is not through your mind that you need to re-member, but through your feelings. You heal by feeling love towards the one on whom you are working. We ask you to learn to love.

How can I love someone that I do not know, some may wonder?

You begin by learning to love yourself. In the circle you are in love all the time. Love is not limited to your idea of one person who has love for another person. Love is a state of being. It is about becoming an embodiment of love. Close your eyes. Allow the love that is always around you a passage so it can go through you and be channeled to the one you wish to heal.

That is impossible, many may grin in disbelief.

There is nothing impossible when you deal with love. You can heal yourself and others by simply being in that energy, allowing it to pass through you. You do not need to know where the liver is and how the heart functions. You do not need to know if the person is diabetic or has cancer. You do not need to study even one day or to take any courses. You need to be that which you are: a vessel which carries the energy of love.

If it were that simple, everyone would do it, some may reason.

You are right; it is not simple only because many of you have developed blocks as obstacles that interfere with the free flow of the energy of love. You do not need to learn how to heal because all you need to do is allow healing to pass through you. It is, however, your task to become pure and block free so you can allow that energy to flow. For that, however, many of you need to go to schools and ask for guidance. It is not the type of guidance that speaks of the human body and its dis-eases. It is the guidance which focuses on transforming from within yourself. You are all natural healers. For you to exercise your powers you must unlearn much of what you know, becoming one with yourself, clear and clean.

Are we not clean, some may frown?

You are a vibration, and when you ingest energies that do not support your own biology you limit your healing power. If a healer comes to her session with a pack of cigarettes, we can assure you that her healing power is limited, blocked, and therefore ineffective. In the energy of transparency, a healer who abuses her body can no longer facilitate healing of others effectively. The energy will not flow freely through her and therefore will not transmit to another. We ask you to become a healer. Start with self. We ask you to learn how to balance your biology and how to become clear. When you are there, then you are ready to heal others. We ask you to become clear and to become clean, so your energy field will allow the love vibration to pass through you. When you become a vessel to love energy you no longer harm or hurt others, you are in harmony with your own cells, and you resonate with Gaia. This is why we ask you awaken now and become a healer.

Can we start asking for money as healers, some may ask?

It is humorous to us that as soon as you realize your power you wish to be paid for it. When healing is your chosen path it is appropriate to ask for energetic return in a form of money. In your current state of awareness there is no appropriate alternative which allows you to function effectively. Money is an energy that is pure. Your effort and time must be balanced through receiving as well as giving.

We wish to speak to those who can heal without choosing the path and journey of a healer. Healing power is given to all of you equally and in abundance. Do you pay for air, is our question? Do you get paid for kissing your child at night or giving a hug to your partner? If you do, you can also ask money for healing. In the circle, the money that you would have asked for was already given to you because when you facilitate another, the love healing energy must first pass through you bringing balance to your own biology. You are therefore being paid precisely the amount that you are owed with energy. As you heal another you are healed. With a smile we can assure you that you can never overcharge for your session.

Can we contract dis-ease if we work on another, some may inquire?

When you become clear and clean you do not attract that which you balance. If you yourself are not balanced, you may manifest your own imbalance through healing work. This is why we ask you to heal yourself first. Through healing yourself you receive your certificate and become a healer. Once you are clear you no longer attract that which is around you. Your safety net is your own healing process. If you attempt to heal others before you have worked on yourself, you may attract imbalance instead of sending balance to others. To us you appear as beautiful swirling multidimensional geometric shapes made of sound, color, and light. The larger your shapes, the brighter your colors, the more harmonious your melody, the more ready you are to work on others. When your own colors are not bright and your melody is out of tune, instead of healing others you may attract what others have. If we could tell you of the potential healings that are all around you all day long, you would not believe it. As your medical establishment is trying to figure out how to keep the population healthy by developing drugs and vaccines, we are telling you that you are the medicine and your energy is the vaccine. This is what is needed to heal you, your brothers, sisters, and the planet at this time. We love you so. We wish you to awaken to your healing powers, beginning to use them first on yourself and then on others.

How do I begin, some may still wonder?

You begin by expressing intention to become clear and clean so you can act as a pure vessel for healing energy.

What then, some may ask?

Ask to be shown the way to bring healing to yourself and others. Sit in front of a candle and ask your cells to awaken, and to remember that which will lead you on your path.

Then what, some may still persist?

Ask for all the knowledge embedded in your cellular memory and DNA to awaken. Ask it to bubble to the forefront so it can meld with your awareness and be accessed at will.

What if we ask and nothing happens, some skeptics may inquire?

This is why we love you so. You want proof, dear human. You want to see it written in black and white in a medical journal before you believe it. This is not the way of spirit. You must walk the walk and trust, as the miracles manifest only as far as your trust. If you ask with pure intent you will receive. This is the way of it. Whether you accept the results or are happy with the results is your choice. Healing must take place when you ask for it. Ask for it and it will be handed to you. Do not ask for proof because the proof will never come the way you envision it. Ask and embrace that which comes your way, as it is sacred. The story is much grander than you can ever imagine. We ask you to trust and walk, activating your powers, becoming the master that you are.

How do we know that this is the truth, some may wonder?

Why won't you try, is our answer.

To heal another is an effortless process. To become clean and free of blocks is hard work at times. We ask you to give intent so you can become one of the energy holders of the place you call home, Planet Earth.

The more healers awaken to their powers, the more balanced a planet you will have and the less dis-ease will manifest. You came here to work and to awaken. It's time. We ask you to open your eyes. Begin today, for today is the best day to become that which you are, a planetary healer, and so be it.

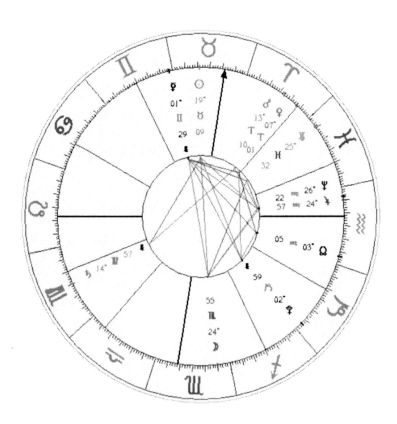

5/9/2009
Hola Dror,

Crazy day with J.

As I suspected he doesn't have the money for the mortgage this month. Asked to borrow money from me to make up what was missing from the account. Now he owes me even more money.

I said I wanted to put the house up for sale in July. He said I was looking on the dark side and I was bringing darkness. He made a statement that darkness was around him and it was the people around him that doubted him. He "didn't blame me".

In the past he said that everything he did worked, he had a golden touch now nothing is working. He thinks it is all because he is not doing God's work. He said he used to go to church more and help out more in the church. But I am not sure that was true. I said that it sounded like the things he did in business lacked integrity, he was a womanizer and then everything came crashing down.

Tough to listen to when I know we manifest everything in our lives.

Interesting contrast how you experience me as light and he as darkness.

un beso,

N.

The Dye of Love

YOU ARE DEARLY LOVED.

You are at a crossroads and all that you experience seems to pull you away from your path. It is a test and a test it is. Now you must decipher what your aim is and stay focused.

What is my aim, you may ask?

Your aim is to be one with yourself and as you move forward, know that you are loved every moment. You have been riding on a roller coaster. The twists and turns are getting sharper. The ride is accelerating. Staying balanced and connected to your center is your goal. We are here to hold your hand when you need us but we cannot do the work for you. It is on you to create the bridge between you and us. We are here waiting and you are to open your cellular memory so you can receive that which is all around you.

What are my cells to remember and I to receive, you may inquire?

With a smile we hug you and say, "Love." What else!

Why then am I having so much difficulty with my relationships, some may wonder?

You are now reliving all the residues of past expressions in one lifetime—this one. It is intense and it is necessary for you in order to progress.

Why is it so, some may inquire?

It is the season of tests. You must pass final exams where you can utilize all you have learned in order to graduate. You must use your mastery to navigate between all the unfinished lessons of past expressions, clearing them one by one as you move higher and higher to a place where your vibration reaches the intersection where *your* dimension meets the *other* dimension—the dimension of spirit. This is your goal.

Why must it be so painful, some may wonder?

With all love, it is not, is our answer.

Know that as you move from one test to another you must hug yourself all the time and love yourself all the time. Take care of your biology. Become one with your vessel. To move upward you must have energy, and your "fuel" must be flowing with no blocks so you can be one with the energy of acceleration. It is more important than ever to sleep enough and rest enough. Much of your work is done while sleeping, and we ask you to listen to your body. When you are tired, do not fuel your body with artificial accelerators, but allow it to rest.

When is it going to end, some may want to know?

This is just the beginning, is our answer.

From our vantage point you are at the edge of the joy ride. You are still at the "flat" section moving and edging closer to the "drop." Once the "joy ride" begins you must go along with it, and all you can do, all you must do, is surrender to it, becoming one with the ride. With all love, we wish to impart to you that you must be in a love state all the time. This is your goal and your challenge. You will face continuous challenges and obstacles. Your goal is to allow that which comes to pass through you, and as it moves through you, to sprinkle it with love vibration, adding light to it. You are energy and vibration. You are connected to *all that is* all the time. We wish to use a metaphor to allow you to feel the process. When you pour a drop of food-coloring dye into clear water the whole glass of water becomes colored by the drop of dye. You are the dye and the drop is the drop of "love." When you mix your environment with just one drop of a concentrated dye, all who are around you will be colored by your energy. It is the way of it.

How do we practically do it, some may wonder?

We ask you to be in the awareness of Hollywood.

We thought Hollywood was all fake and manufactured, some may ask in dismay?

This is precisely your story. We wish to use metaphors again so you can *feel* rather than *intellectualize* your reality. You are in a movie theater. All that you now experience are reruns of segments and programs that have played in your past expressions but were not resolved. You are in a loop of sorts. Your goal is to allow these reruns to take place without believing them or becoming entangled in the scenes. These reruns offer great temptation for you because they carry an emotional residue of unfinished business, so they are very alluring. You may feel enticed to become part of that scene and to play your role all over again. With a hug we wish to tell you that the reruns will return as they must. The surest way to not be anchored by endless reruns is to be in the awareness that you are seeing old movies from past expressions that no longer offer you the same learning as they did in the past. These movies are there to show you bits and pieces of uncompleted learning so you can become peaceful, releasing them.

Why are there so many, some may complain?

You are all old souls and you have traveled on Earth many times, therefore you have accumulated many unfinished stories. Now it is a time of graduation and you must finish all the unfinished homework in a relatively short period of time.

How, some may ask again?

Become peaceful, go inside and become the observer. Do not try to understand what is going on because at times it may be inaccessible to you. View it like you are watching a movie and understand that you are not the movie, but a spectator. Form a feeling about the scene that is unfolding in front of you. Breathe this scene into you, exhaling it once and for all. With each breath, exhale that unfinished scene. As you let it go, add your dye of love potion to it. You must observe and remain peaceful. If you choose to become involved in the movie that is playing, claiming once again that you are "right" or you are the "victor," you again keep the energy of the movie alive to be played over again as a rerun. We know how much some of you love your reruns on TV. We know that it is comforting to some knowing what will happen and how it will end. We ask you to become the director of a new movie and to let the rerun aspects of your unfinished lessons clear away. It may be entertaining to watch all over again your favorite "episode" on TV, but contrary to your reruns on TV, these offer mainly unfinished aspects that you may perceive as negative or heavy. It may be expressed in your relationships or your biological vehicle. You are watching many reruns at the moment. Since you have experienced these episodes before and you know the endings, we ask you to stay balanced this time. The reason the rerun comes back yet again is because last time you were not balanced and did not use love when it was appropriate. Know that this is how you move from the old to the new. You must stay balanced. Even if the episode playing out is one that carries intense emotional energy, breathe it in all the way and exhale it using love. Each breath you take, remaining balanced and using love, you are releasing old scripts, making space for the new movie to be created—a movie where you are the director.

How do we know that we are doing the right thing, some may inquire?

It is simple to tell, is our answer.

When you watch the episode taking place and you become involved in the episode you must then go through it again. There is never a judgment. You are loved and honored the same. Why would you want to do it again, is our question to you? When the familiar "episode" is coming again, always on time, you watch it unfold, staying calm. You observe the pattern and geometry of the interaction or the action of the movie. You say to yourself, "Wow, this is so familiar. It is a rerun and I am going to observe this one from the side." Then when the whole thing plays out, you breathe it in as if it was air, then you exhale it. As you let it go, spray it with love, and we can assure you that this same rerun will not return. It may try again at times but you must remember what you did and do the same.

Does it mean that we need not talk or act, some may ask for clarification?

The rerun involved you, so at times you must talk and act. It is in the awareness that the key to this release is hidden. When you feel the old familiar opening act of this "episode" that you have watched so many times before, we ask you to become the observer of the movie. Tell yourself that now you are aware that it is a movie playing in front of you and allow it to play as it must. At this time you are facing many reruns which hold you back from moving into your mission—becoming the director of your movie. You are dearly loved and you are the ones who chose to be the warriors coming to a dimension where there is much more hidden from you than revealed. You are an angel and you are powerful to create within this dimension that which you choose. You may create joy or pain, light or darkness. Ascension is alchemical transformation. Any powerful transformation must begin with awareness. Any powerful transformation must begin with love and must also begin with intention. When you create the triangle of *awareness*, *love*, and *intent*, you will remain balanced like a pyramid—your wide base anchored in the Earth, your awareness in the heavens, the dimension of spirit. The spiraling of energy must begin from the wide base coiling higher and higher to the dimension where you meet your self with wings. This is the melding of body and spirit. There are so many who wish to become one with God through neglecting and abusing their bodies. It is through the body that you must ascend. Without a body you do not need to ascend because you have already ascended. The marriage of body and Spirit must encompass loving your vehicle and accepting all parts of it. Some of your religions and spiritual establishments teach about moving higher by separating body from spirit. They actually are asking you to remove your engine before you begin the journey of ascension. Your engine is your sexual energy; it has been so corrupted intentionally by those who wish you to be weak and malleable that it is your greatest challenge at this time…to transform your idea about sexuality, using it to move higher.

You have been given a body and it is sacred. All of it. The parts of the body that are meant to give you pleasure are the opening vortexes to your higher dimensions. You link through pleasure. Some of your institutions knew of the power of pleasure. They knew that a society that is guided by pleasure and freedom to explore will not seek war, dominance, or instability. Instability is how your society and institutions believe that you create growth. When your body is out of balance it creates growth which manifests as cancer. The same "cancerous growth" also applies to your society and your planet. Progress in your current awareness is created through instability, through wars, through famine, through pain. Your society first creates imbalance and then develops ingenious ways to balance that which is out of balance. If you look back at your science, so much of your current understanding of the physics and mechanics of your resources was developed through wars, through painful imbalances. Much of your progress in medicine is fueled by your need to address modern imbalances from polluted natural resources and lifestyle. With all love, we wish to impart to you that, when a negative stamp was placed on your sexual energy, it began the path of moving away from the sacred feminine Goddess to a place of imbalance. The feminine Goddess energy holds the key to a balanced planet, and it must come back to its central role. It is pivotal that you go through the memory and pain of repressed sexual cellular memory, releasing it.

How do we do that, some may wonder? *Do you wish us to become promiscuous and have more sex with others,* some may inquire?

With a hug, we wish to tell you that you are linear and you see only that which is in front of you. We ask you to use great discretion when you use this energy. Create sacredness around your sexual energy; never use it with negative intent. Honor your own sexuality and honor yourself when you use sexuality. We see many who use this energy in a way that diminishes, not honors, the self. We ask you to be in the awareness that it is your most powerful tool at this time to move forward, so learn about yourself, ask to be guided and to be shown ways to connect with your sacred vortexes. Do not use it without mixing it with love and without mixing it with awareness. Do not fear it and do not avoid it, but always be in the awareness that you hold the key to your own ascension. You cannot, though, move very high without releasing the pain stored within your cellular memory. Many of your reruns involved sexual energy. Many of your "dramas" and "episodes" come back to you because of unresolved issues. We ask you to purify and create a sacred space before you mix. Hold a ceremony. Ask to be shown the way to release and celebrate your power. Do not mix when your body is numbed or enticed by substances because that is how you invite lower vibrational frequencies to your energy fields. Your intoxication allows space in your field for energies that do not have your best interest in mind. They find it much easier to "take over" when your senses are influenced by drugs, alcohol, and other substances or medications. These energies are attracted to sexual energy because it gives them a boost as well. They ride on it for their own pleasure and learning. We impart to you that you must be fully present with your biology and awareness when you mix with another or use sexual energy. Create a space that is protected, always asking for the highest outcome, using only love and light as purifiers for any intruders. This journey is about you moving closer to yourself. You know all that we know. You came here to awaken, to shine your light during the most challenging and glorious time in human history. It is time to get out of your beds and walk the walk of a master using your tools. You have sent for us to join you. We ask you, with all love, to wake up, to become the master that you are, and so be it.

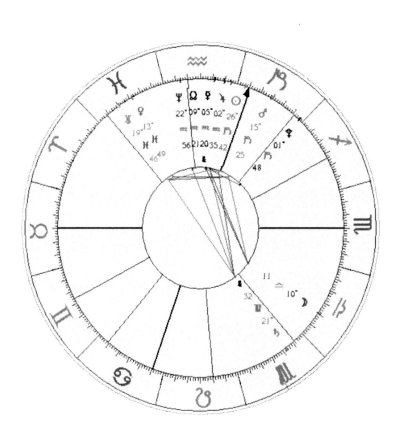

6-7-2009

Dear Dror,

many many thanks for sending the books so quickly.
Unfortunately...there is a slight complication,
because the customs officials here in Germany are
sitting on the books....they didn't realize that they
were intended as a gift. Would it be possible for
you that you send me a couple of lines in a word-
document with your letterhead stating that I am
acting as your literary agent and that the books
represent complimentary copies / desk copies for
potential publishers and that you are making the
books available to me free of charge? And then send
it over by email? they're very strict with imports
from the U.S. Red tape bureaucratic procedures...

Thanks very much for your efforts.

Hope all is well with you.

Best wishes from Munich,

Caroline.

What Am I Doing Here?

*Y*OU ARE DEARLY LOVED.

"Why?" is a question many of you are asking at this time. You want to know "why." You feel that you have the right. You wish to know "why" this had happened and that had happened, "why" it happened to you and not to your friend. You ask your angels "why" as if the answer will take the weight off your shoulders and miraculously make everything better. Your main question is "why?" followed by "why me?" Our answer to you is: do not ask "why" but "how."

How what, you may wonder? *How do I move from the place I am, into a higher place where the vista will open up and allow me an entryway to the whys?*

When you ask for the "why," you wish to receive a simple explanation that will allow your linear mind to find peace. You wish to receive a story like in your holy texts where you have done so and so, and that is why you are receiving such and such. With a smile, we wish to impart to you that the story is much larger than you can ever imagine. The story of the "whys" is always in the circle, whereas the mechanism of the "whys" is in the 4-D physical reality. You can only imagine what you see, and when you do not see or sense something, you are not able to imagine it. You are told from an early age to stop imagining things and get back to reality. Your reality is limited by what you can and cannot imagine. Those things that you are able to conceive can also be manifested in your physical reality.

Why are you telling us about these confusing ideas, some may wonder?

It's time, is our answer.

You have asked to know and we are here to tell you what you need to know so you can advance on your journey. We wish to take you with us one more time on our imaginary spaceship and show you what your Earth looks like from above. It is beautiful. It looks like a blue pearl shining and glowing in the vast empty space that surrounds it. From our spaceship you can see the ocean currents and you can see clouds. You can see the light parts, and the dark comes in as the Earth is rotating on its axis, moving along its trajectory around the sun. When we bring the spaceship a little closer, you begin to see shapes and colors, light radiating from everywhere. You can hear overlapping melodies, and when observed all together it is as if you are watching the ultimate Broadway show or Hollywood special effects movie. Then you get closer and you see the individual human as she walks on her way to somewhere. All around her there are geometric shapes and colors continuously changing. She is also emitting a melodic sound that is unheard by the human ear but it is heard loud and clear by all of us. Then we take you even closer inside that human. There you become aware of trillions of actions taking place simultaneously, keeping that human alive and functioning. As we get closer and closer, taking our spaceship into one of the blood vessels of that individual, you begin to understand the mechanics of spirit.

From the far reaches of the universe to the individual cell that is inside an angel, God is at work. When a person sits down to meditate there are trillions and trillions of energetic conversations, exchanges of energy happening within that individual. At the same time that this individual is sitting to meditate, we ask you to zoom in your imagination to a place one thousand light-years away into the center of a beautiful, magical galaxy. There you will find trillions and trillions of energetic exchanges in conversation taking place as well. You are a piece of biology with a twist, and the twist is that you carry the seed of God in each one of your cells. The mechanics of your biology hold the key to the universe. It is why we tell you that you contain all you need, and you create what you need *when you are in the now.*

What does it mean, you may still wonder?

It means that you are the creator. As a creator you hold within you the key to unraveling the full scope of the magnificent creation that expresses itself all around you. We ask you in so many ways to wake up to your power because you hold the key. It is inside of you. Our spaceship is able to move from one thousand light-years away into the blood vessel of a human walking on your street in a matter of a thought which is not even in the realm of a nanosecond. In your current level of technology it would be considered instantaneous. Size is never an issue and space is never an issue. Traveling in the vast space of your visible universe does not require time.

How does one travel, some of you may want to know?

Traveling happens through thoughts. As you imagine where you are, you are already there. That is why we speak to you about your limited imagination. The key to your ascension in vibration is hidden in your awareness and ability to imagine who you are. When you let your imagination free, you are free, and when you control it, directing it to where you think you should be, it is as if you are writing yourself the script to your dream world. Your dream time is when you travel in an instant because you are not limited by your logical mind which asks you for "whys" and "hows."

Why are you telling us about all this, some may ask in frustration?

The "whys" of your life are not as important as the awareness of the "hows."

How do I move forward when my reality does not add up in my logical mind? What do I hold on to at such a time?

With love, we wish you that you hold on to your divinity, hold on to love, hold on to trust, and hug yourself all the time. There is a magnificent story that is being told and it is unfolding as we speak. Our spaceship can pick you up and shuttle you from a place full of light one thousand light-years away into the blood vessel of a human walking or shopping at a store in an instant. Your ability to move within this vast space/time dimension is part of the story that is now unfolding. You must learn to shut down your senses and ignite your imagination. This is why we ask you to be childlike. Children are your guides at this time. They show you that there are no limits to what magic reality holds. Reality is a story that they create as they walk through their enchanted forest encountering fairies and imaginary friends. They also can see leprechauns, elves, trolls, and other magical creatures. Some of your children can also see the geometric shapes around you, hear your melody, and see your aura. They are coming here more enabled than you are because they represent your evolutionary path.

Did we tell you yet that we love you?

You tell us all the time but we do not sense it, some may say.

Love is not the love you are exchanging between people. Love is the energetic substance that makes the reality of God, and that is the most ample in our realm. When we tell you that you are loved, we are inviting you to our realm and link you to your expanded dimension. Words carry a vibration that rides on your frequency and creates a link. Through that link, the energy from the different dimensions is being transferred.

Where am I going, you want to know?

You are changing, is our answer. You are moving higher. You are becoming lighter.

Good, some of you may say, *I have been trying to lose those pounds for years.*

Yes, indeed, we say with a smile. The gravity that holds you anchored to this planet is easing up and your energetic body is now allowed to expand. There will be some who will begin to experience the type of traveling we described by will and not as a one-time occurrence. This is enabled at this time. The only thing that holds you from exploring dimensions and realities beyond your wildest dreams is your imagination. You must let it loose and become free of the way things "ought" to be.

We still do not get what it is about, some may claim.

It is about expansion of your awareness of who you are and what your mission on Earth is at this time. Your mission is to awaken to who you really are. When you do, you see divinity everywhere you look. It is then that you shine your light and emit love to yourself, knowing that all you encounter is there to lead you to your highest potential. When you are in that place of love you radiate that energy to all those who come in contact with you and to the elements of nature. You also change the electromagnetic structure of the soil you walk on so it will be in support of an ascending planet. When you walk immersed in the vibration of love you move into alignment, harmonizing with the resonance of the natural world and the dimensions of spirit. When you are in this elevated resonance you are celebrated because you are home—linked with your higher part walking the elevated path. You contain within you all the universes in all dimensions, and there are more than a few. You, the one reading these lines, are the key to the unfolding of the biggest shift in consciousness your planet has seen since its birth.

Are you still feeling powerless?

The way you are built and the cellular structure of your biology is a hologram. Like your DNA that holds the blueprint to your whole being, you are holding the key to the blueprint of the entire universe. What you do affects all of us. When you change one DNA coding, you are changing the entire blueprint. We ask you to awaken because when you are in your power shining your light, you are changing the entire planetary blueprint. It is as if an architect took a pencil and began to draw on the existing plans. The ones who are reading these messages, and who resonate with our words, are the architects of the shift in the planetary blueprint—no small task. It is why we ask you to come to your power beginning now, as now is the only time that is aligned between you and spirit. Our dimension has no tomorrow and no yesterday; it is all in the "now."

What should we do then, some may still wonder?

Sit down, close your eyes, sense your breath, and connect with your heartbeat. Touch your heart with your hand and say out loud, "I am divinity; I am love; I am honored; I am in my power; I am open now to be shown the high road to where I can be fully in my mission. I have no fear; I have only trust and love." Open the palm of your hands and allow our vibration to tingle through your fingers. Give yourself a hug and allow yourself to feel our hugs. Know that we shed tears of joy with you. The power of your intent is the step necessary to join your melody with others, creating a symphony that is changing the planetary blueprint towards peace on Earth, and so be it.

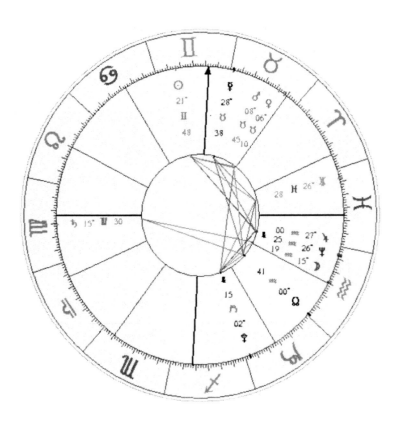

6-12-2009

Dear Dror,

I sure did. I had fun sending them off to a couple of awakening friends and we have enjoyed e-mailing to each other about them. I forgot to acknowledge and share my gratitude with you . . . many thanks! They were great! We so appreciate them . . . anytime.

It feels to me and many others that energies have been intense this week . . . perhaps building up to something. A big shift has been intuited by several wise intuitives. Have you picked up anything from the angels?

I hope your week settles down for you. Hecticness is so draining for those of us that are shifting so much internally!

Much love, radiant light and deep gratitude to you, Jenny.

Rise of the Goddess

YOU ARE DEARLY LOVED.

So it has been a winding road for you. You feel at times as if you get nauseated by the constant turns and bumps. Your nausea may be caused by your balance being challenged. Your body is built with sensors which keep it balanced in relation to Earth's rotational and gravitational forces. When these forces begin to shift ever so slightly, you may feel dizzy, as if you are not standing on solid ground.

Can you tell us what is going on? We wish to know where we stand, some may ask.

It is a time like no other, is our answer. You are loved, and you are the master of your own reality. There is nothing else you can hold on to at this time. Shields that you built inside of you and in your physical reality to keep you away from yourself will be disintegrating—some gradually, others overnight. Some institutions that you once thought were invincible will vanish into thin air. Some ideas that you have held about the "truth" of your existence will be shifting dramatically. The movie that you are now watching offers many surprises as the actors must take off their costumes and move closer to their real essence. You are experiencing a shift that is expressed through the peeling of external barriers and hidden truths. Many of the walls and protections you created in your past are now being weakened by your desire to discover your truth, your divinity. Corporations, establishments, structures, and governments are being challenged daily by what seems to be a change in paradigm. What was once considered predictable is so no longer. The only predictable thing is that there will be constant change in all aspects of your life. The rules of the game are changing and very few seem to have a handle on the new set of rules. With all love, we wish to impart to you that you must feel the new rules and not have them handed down to you by authorities, the media, or your peers. You are now experiencing the magnificent rise of the feminine Goddess energy in all her glory. The feminine energy is based on feelings, and many of your structures are based on masculine patriarchal foundations, immersed in logic, control, and fear.

Wow, we hear some of you say to yourselves, and *what now?*

It is time to surrender; let go of your walls. Allow all the emotions that you held at bay to be expressed within you and through you so they can be released. Learn to feel again. Learn to trust that you are loved and protected. You are moving into harmony, aligning with the powerful energy of the Goddess, dependent on your willingness to let go of the poles that hold you anchored in shame, guilt, and separation.

Do you wish us to start telling everyone how we really feel about them, some may ask, puzzled?

My dear angel, you think you are linear; however, within you there are so many dimensions that are operating together to take you higher. We ask you to do the work internally. Allow yourself to feel. Take time to feel; allow sadness, when it comes, to cover you and go through you. Allow pain to come in, and move through you; do not numb it and do not suppress it. Do not take substances to cover that which you are experiencing. Fear not, as the feminine principle is the essence of the warrioress, and she is fearless. When you give pure intent to progress on your journey, aligning with the new energy, everything will rearrange itself to support you on that path. When you are not awakened to your mission, all the magnificent sights that are coming your way may cause you to freeze in fear, looking for a place to hide. We wish you to stand tall and shine your light when it is time. Lighthouses do not hide. They stand tall and raise their light high for all to see.

How will we know when it's time, you may wonder?

The time is now and you know it because you designed it to be that way. There is so much that is dependent on your awakening. When you awaken, you see your reality from a higher perspective. You walk with the knowing that all that faces you in the physical dimension is of your choosing. You also become aware that when you find yourself on one path, you can always un-choose it and create a new path. You were on target to end human life and you chose in the last moment to shift directions. You can choose to change anything in your life even if everyone tells you that it is too late and nothing more can be done.

How do we change things when everything seems to be changing around us without our control, some may wonder?

One way is to connect to the essence of the Goddess within you. That is our short answer. The feminine energy is powerful and it is now aligned with aspects of your planet to pick you up and move you higher. One attribute of the feminine energy is represented by the substance of water. It is a nurturing, life-giving substance that you all need in order to exist. It can give life, but can become destructive as well. Are you wondering why water is on the front pages of your media and minds? Your water cycles are all changing. The rising of water levels and the warming of the planet is closely related to the rising of the Goddess. Water in all forms is one consciousness. All water molecules are connected in quantum space and, as the shift in water cycles happens outside of you, it is also happening inside you. The water inside of you and the water outside of you know each other, metaphorically.

We wish to speak to you about water because it is time. Water's molecular structure is simply two parts hydrogen and one part oxygen. The hydrogen represents the feminine aspect and the oxygen represents the masculine. Two parts out of the three represent the feminine aspect of the most ample substance on your planet which holds your ecosystem in equilibrium. When you disturb this balance, this substance may no longer support your biology. As the micro is structured, so is the macro. When you disturb the feminine/masculine ratio which is part of the original blueprint of this creation, you move into manifesting a planet that may not support life. When you ask your fish to live in polluted lakes, rivers, or oceans, many of them say no and die. The natural world is part of you and you are part of it. When you damage the natural environment around you, you damage your own self. You see a "fish," for example, as separated from yourself, but we see the "fish" element within you. We see many of you who receive messages about the dying of the natural world and you say to yourselves, "How does it pertain to me? I have water to drink, why should I bother about 'fish' dying in some lake?" The fish have so much compassion for angels walking in blindness that they are willing to die so that you will wake up. When you hurt the natural world you hurt an energetic part of yourself. The geometry of the planet is intimately tied to yours. You cannot exist without the planet holding your physical vibration intact.

Why do you speak to us about fish, you may inquire?

"Fish," with other aquatic life, hold your energy linked to the feminine aspect of yourself and the planet. There is a story that is unfolding at the moment which involves the rise of the Goddess energy, water and the life it supports. The three aspects co-create a geometric shape of a triangle.

Why a triangle, some may wonder?

Water is rising now both energetically and figuratively to reclaim its central role in the return of the feminine/masculine balance on your blue planet. Water can purify, nurture, and be life-giving. It can also be destructive and furious. You entered a period when the water element will play a central role in the lives of many of the inhabitants on your planet. Water has a cleansing property and it is a substance that is closely related to your biology. As water is being polluted on the planet it also affects your body's balance and equilibrium. We wish to hug you one more time and impart to you that *you are the planet*. Your energetic core is linked to the core of your planet. You cannot separate the two.

The water of the planet has consciousness. On some level, each water molecule knows its central role in the creation and sustenance of life on Earth. When you create an environment that does not honor your life-sustaining substance, you do not honor yourself. There are those amongst you who took it upon yourselves to change course, bringing this planet back into equilibrium and balance. It is a sacred mission changing the course of humanity, allowing your journey to continue. Those of you who are reading our messages will know that you are the ones who are assigned to bring back the balance. In order to align yourself with your mission, you must align with the feminine part in you. It does not matter if you happened to choose a male body or a female body, as feminine energy exists in all aspects of life.

With a smile, we acknowledge that angels dressed up in female bodies may have some advantage because of a natural inclination and wiring of your biology. You are intuitively wired to be connected to your emotions and intuition, as it allows you to create life. Many angels in female bodies moved away from their natural inclination so they could cope better in a patriarchally structured world. We know who you are and some of you must work as hard as your male counterparts to align with the Goddess energy. When we speak of the "Goddess energy" we speak of an energetic aspect that exists in all of you, that is linked to creation and to your planet. Metaphorically, the Goddess aspect is the creator of life as the male aspect is the sustainer of life. Together, creation is being carried out and expressed through biological forms. With a hug, we must tell you that feminine energy is not exclusively expressed through females and masculine energy is not exclusively expressed by males. Again, it is a choice and inclination that determines the ratio of feminine/masculine balance in your life.

What are we to do with this information, you ask?

We thought you'd never ask, we answer with a smile. You are a divine being walking into a reality of the Goddess where the feminine aspect of all of you will act as a catalyst for change in every human life on Earth.

What does it really mean in my life, you may wonder?

In order for you to move with ease in this shifting and ascending planet you must be linked to that aspect of yourself.

How do I link, you may inquire?

You take time to feel. You consult your feelings for every decision that you make. You take the time to intuit and sense your path. You make all important decisions based on feelings first, not logic. You ask yourself, "Does it feel right?" and not, "Does it add up?" Many of those who host the body of a female must clear out the residue of the fear of expression and layers of repression. You must activate your Shakti, or your female sexual power, suppressed and repressed for thousands of years. The pendulum is swinging back to balance and with it, all of you must shift. The mission of many of you in female bodies is to awaken and express your power through inner transformation. Your first and second chakras, or energy vortexes, are connected to the belly of Gaia, to the force of creation. It is your sexual centers which propel all aspects of creation. When this center is hidden or covered with layers of guilt, shame, anger, and resentment, your power is limited. It may even be used destructively, rather than for the purpose of creation, nurturing, balance, and love. We do not ask you to preach or have followers, but we ask you to walk activated and empowered. You must work to clear yourself from any anchors that hold you in a place of repression.

We see many of you who "empower" yourselves by wearing supporting mechanisms to make you more attractive to men and, seemingly, more attractive to yourselves. This is not what we mean.

Walking empowered and activated means loving yourself, loving your body. Honor yourself and know the role that you play in the game of creation. Playing the female role is very different than being the Goddess walking activated and empowered. You must feel your body and be connected to your womb, to your sexual centers. You must be connected to the soil that you walk on grounded in your power. In each decision that faces you, no matter how challenging it may appear, take the time to link to your womb, as it is the core of creation which holds the power of your femininity. We ask you to look at the mirror often just so you can move away from the anchors of what your society tells you are beautiful, attractive, and desirable. Learn to see your authentic beauty, strength, and power, discarding the filters "gifted" to you. Many of you hold an image of what a female should look like, how she should behave and act. This image is embedded in your cellular memory from past cycles. This image is further reinforced through your culture and media. It is camouflaged as the advertising and marketing of different products or ideals. This image we speak of was created mainly by males for the service of male/masculine energy in a patriarchal structure. This is now changing as it must. You must develop a new identity which is linked to your true power and not to the one sold to you through the pages of your magazines, media outlets, or fear-based politics, ideology, or religion. Your outer image has very little to do with what we view as authentic beauty; your body shape has very little to do with authentic sexuality and creation. Your creative power and beauty are your birthright, having little to do with the role you play as an angel. Those whom your society considers attractive and desirable are, from our perspective, an effective campaign of manipulating the Goddess to hand out her power. This is now changing and you must play a role in this shift to allow the Goddess to return to her authentic, rightful place in the game of creation.

Shakti is the Goddess's power. When you walk linked to your Shakti you are beautiful and powerful. We observe from our perch many female angels moving away from their Shakti by trying to live up to an impossible image of eternal youth and outer beauty. With so much love, we must impart to you that the stretching, stapling, and covering of your true essence takes away from your feminine power. There is never a judgment in our hearts, and you are so honored for just walking the walk, being on this planet at this time. It is, however, our mission to awaken you by illuminating your path so you can see. When your multidimensional eyes are open in the center of your forehead you may make decisions that are based on light, love, and true inner knowing.

What should we do, some may still wonder? *How do we connect to this Shakti?*

We ask you to take off all your masks and clothing, standing in front of the mirror as naked as the moment you were born. Begin from your feet and move upward. Begin to send love to every part of your body. As you move upward you may encounter a body part, let's say the knee, for example. You may not like the shape of your knee. We know who you are. We are aware of the parts that you like and the parts that you do not. Your body is also aware of your liking and not liking. We ask you to stay with this part of your body examining it and observing it until such time that you start loving it. You must love every part of your body as it is. After you have given a hug to yourself we ask you to sit on the floor, connecting to Earth through your sexual center and womb. You do that by breathing up from the core of the Earth and hold the air in your womb. As you exhale, imagine that the energy moves to all directions from that center. There are many different schools which can teach you how to link and get in touch to your feminine/Shakti power. Seek what feels right for you. There is no school that is more honored than another. Each of you must find what is appropriate for you. It is you who is honored; your intent and search that is sacred. You are the teachers; the leaders of this shift. You must be in your power so you can show others the path to a higher ground. You are the lighthouses and your Shakti power is the light. We ask you to turn it on, and so be it.

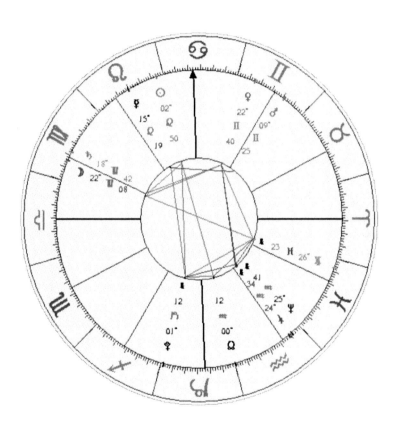

7-25-2009

Hi Dror

I already knew about your radio interview. I found out by chance online last night, and told another friend of mine, Jane, who is also very connected to your work.

I miss you and your messages. I've been thinking about you a lot. I would like to meet you and talk more about angels, spirit, love and light.

I would like to ask you something, if that is OK? I have a friend who is very sensitive and is literally feeling like she lost connection with herself and wants to re-create that. But she doesn't know what to do exactly. She feels like she doesn't know what she wants for her life, although she is very aware. She feels like she keeps searching for something but doesn't know what it is. I bet that is spirit nagging her.

Love.

Arella

The Wave

YOU ARE DEARLY LOVED.

The aches and pains that you feel are your body changing.

Why is that so, some may ask?

There is a story and this story is unfolding as you read these words. The story is about your evolution from one level of awareness to the next. Evolution never ends, but when there is a leap in evolution it carries cosmic and universal ramifications.

Why is it changing, some may ask?

Your body is being prepared to align itself with the new energy that is now permeating your planet. The magnetic coordinates of your planet have shifted as well as your planet's gravitational pull and magnetic polarity. The new radiation that is being directed to your planet from outer space is altering ever so slightly the atomic structure and molecular bonds of every living and nonliving aspect of your Earth.

No one ever told you that you will be the same after all this is over. With a smile, we wish to tell you that it is never really over. Your next step is biological as well as spiritual. You must work on being grounded, removing much of the toxins in your body, as well as in your life, so you can transform with ease and less pain. The pains and aches are most likely from the resistance of your cells to mutate due to the rigidity formed from lifestyle choice, as well as ingesting a certain diet. Some substances may anchor your body, not allowing the flexibility required to mutate with ease.

If you have been out of shape for a long time, then all of a sudden, you need to do heavy lifting, you may feel sore and in pain the next day. From where we sit it is imperative that you take care of your body, keeping it clean and cleansed of toxins. Keep it balanced and nourished. Rest often, drink a lot of pure water. Eat pure foods that are alive and made with love. Keeping your body in shape has never been more important than it is right now. The physical demands on your vehicles are straining them to capacity. Your body must feel light and balanced to move upward with ease.

What is happening to us, some may still ask?

You are ascending, is the short answer. You are becoming multidimensional. Your body is being prepared to link you to other dimensions and realities. You are opening up hidden vortexes that were dormant for eons. You are activating parts of your DNA that were waiting for that special "wake up" call. Much has been written about your DNA but much is yet to be discovered. Some of those parts that your geneticists believed were useless will light up all of a sudden and will correlate to certain functions that were not before observed. It will be so dramatic that even your scientific community will begin to acknowledge that indeed a magnificent change is on its way in the human body.

You are preparing to open up to the galactic activity that is all around you. Your cells are being activated and your senses enhanced. This is just the first step and it is a big one.

We ask you in so many ways to slow down and re-discover your inner balance as it is the only thing that you can hold on to at this time of change. There are many who walk oblivious to this change, and they are honored just like you. There are many who feel something but they do not know what to call it so they just dismiss it by saying they feel weird, or they numb the unsettling feelings with substances; they are honored as well. And then there are those of you who are in the forefront of this change. You came to this planet at this time to see it through, and you know the meaning of all the commotion around you.

There are nights you cannot sleep because your body twitches. You feel the strong vibrations. Your cells are all excited and tingly. You know deeply that "this is it" and you wish to prepare. This message is for you.

Metaphorically, this change is like a large wave approaching, and like water does, it lifts everything lighter on its path. You know that you must be lifted or you will drown. You know that, to move with the strong upward motion of the wave, you must know how to swim and how to breathe air without taking in water. You also want to feel light and in shape. Every choice you make in your daily life is part of the path of moving with this wave. When choosing, you may want to ask yourself, "Will I be lighter or heavier as a result of this choice?" You are always loved and never judged. Your choices are sacred no matter what. We, however, illuminate your path so you can see all your choices.

We wish to speak with you about your human relationships. If each one of you is being lifted by the wave, what then happens to your families or your partners? Yes, indeed they all must shift as well. It is part of the strains and stresses on your system that you are now experiencing. Your relationships bonded when you were in a specific composition. Your composition is now changing, as well as those of your partner, spouse, family members, and friends. Even your children's composition is changing. When we speak of composition we speak of your melody, geometry, and the colors that you emit as you walk as an angel in a human costume. All your relationships are now in transition. When an individual is changing and growing it may feel threatening to his/her environment because the relationship dynamic of the past no longer holds the same power. Many of you resist change even though the current state is not one of great satisfaction. You wish to maintain what you know rather than explore new realms. Safety is an important glue that holds together many of your human ties. There is a powerful upward pressure to grow which can no longer be ignored by you. As it pushes and pulls on your system, you have an option to resist or to flow with the movement. Resisting may be perceived as more painful, as all of you must adjust at some point. Resisting the pressure may only delay your progress and make the perception of the experience seem more challenging. There is no sitting this one out. All of you are changing. This change is intense and faster than you have ever experienced in your history as humans.

When all of you are shifting, everyone is exposed to feeling the insecurities and fragility of their human relationships more intensely. The rules of the game are also changing, and the only stable pole that you can hold on to through this period of formation of the new paradigm is the pole that runs through your central nervous system or column, anchored by your heart. The stability will exist in one place, inside of you. Do not look for it outside as it will not be there.

What do we do, some may wonder?

We wish you to remember why you are here. Your main mission is to shine your light so all those who are around you can see. It is therefore your responsibility to take care of yourself, finding a balanced space inside of you so you can be in the energy of change and growth, while maintaining your inner peace and calm.

You are so dearly loved for choosing to walk this walk. We wish to remind you that it was your choice to be here and it is you who signed up for this mission. We are here just to hold your hand when you ask for it and to illuminate your journey. There is much pressure in the relationship department. Toxicity and imbalances that were contained in the past are now enhanced by the new light that is shining everywhere. There is no hiding. Many of you face newly discovered realizations which are uncomfortable and which you feel "were better left covered." With the planet becoming brighter nothing can stay in the dark. All that is hidden must and will be illuminated. It is therefore time to let go of buried feelings of shame and guilt. These feelings only lead to anger, resentment, and fear. The movement upward has to do with shedding the heaviness of the past and severing cords which hold all humanity anchored into lower levels of awareness. To truly become one with oneself, you must let all that does not belong to you be discarded. You hold the belief that the heavy, buried feelings are your baggage. Many still hold on to their heaviness and we must impart to you that you cannot easily float with the coming of the high water surge if you hold on to wet suitcases. You may go under with your "precious" belongings. With all love, we ask you to hold on to the only precious thing that you are responsible for on this journey, you and your biological vehicle. As all of you yearn to remain buoyant,, each and everyone is responsible for oneself. When you take care of yourself first, automatically you benefit all those who are around you.

You attempt to hold your relationships in a "comfort zone" that used to serve you but no longer does. The movement upward is sacred and powerful, so there is no staying put. Your resistance to the change may only cause you to delay your movement forward. Do not try to hold on to the old. You are in the energy of the *new* and you must flow with it. You are all connected. You are all a part of one consciousness exploring its own magnificence. You are never too far from your family, friends, children, partners, or spouses. Even if you do not communicate you are still part of one. When you leave this place you will have a reunion of sorts with all those who you felt were separated from you. You will laugh about the times you felt alienated and alone. You are never, ever alone and you are always part of all those who have crossed your path. After the dust settles there is always an appropriateness and love connection which links all of your relationships. If you try to hold on to your relationships so you can feel more secure, you will discover it is no longer possible. The sense of security must be generated *within you* as you are walking on a whitewater raft and everything is in a constant state of flux.

It is all magnificent. There is a cacophony of colors, shapes, and melodies which cover your precious planet. All your galactic neighbors are in awe of the sights they perceive. It is truly a grand party and you are the guest of honor.

What do we do with all that information, some may rightly ask?

We never said that it would be easy, but we can assure you that it is the time and the place you have asked to be to play your part. You have asked, "What do I do?" and we ask you first to hug yourself, then let us join in with the hug. Place your left hand on your heart and your right on you solar plexus. Tell yourself that you are loved and that you love yourself.

What then, some ask?

Slow down, is our answer. Take time to reflect and feel. Take time to sense your path. Do not rush and do not react. Process everything you perceive through your feeling center and ask for feedback in the form of a feeling. Follow your feelings.

What should we do with our relationships, you may wonder?

Ask for clarity for yourself and your relationships. Allow that which comes to come, and remain the observer. Do not fall into the traps of drama, as it will only move you away from your inner knowing. Real knowing comes from peace and calm. We ask you to love yourself all the time. When you stop loving, fear comes in: fear of separation, fear of abandonment, fear of rejection, fear of loneliness, fear of survival. All fears must be vanquished in the face of love. Fill yourself with love and the rest will come to you.

How do we do that, some may still wonder?

Look in the mirror and tell yourself that you are loved. Tell yourself that you love whom you see in the mirror. Love is your weapon and your armor. Love shields you, keeping you protected and balanced through this shift.

What if we do not like what we see in the mirror, some may still wonder?

This is your mission. Learn to love what you see in the mirror as the whole universe is reflected in the one you see in the mirror. You hold the key to your own reality. It all starts and ends with loving the one you see in the mirror. We would not tell you that if it were not so. You are the key. We ask you to open up to your own magnificence, and everything else will follow, and so be it.

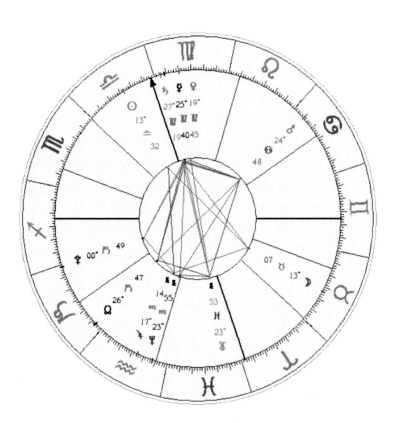

10-6-2009

Dear Dror

The pleasure is mine in meeting you. I know that we
were all brought together at the beginning of this
year for a reason...the reason is slowly manifesting
itself, like a beautiful flower unfolding, each petal,
one at a time, in its own time.

I know we were put on the same train together—
embarking on an incredible journey, where the vistas
are majestic mountains, hidden rainbows, four leaf
clovers, and where eagles fly, so high, the song of the
Creator gives music to the flight of their wings.

Dror, you are a special friend to me...

M.

I Want

YOU ARE DEARLY LOVED.

Hello, hello, and again hello. It has been a rocky ride and you have remained seated in the saddle. We have been watching you, following your actions and reactions; you have chosen light at each intersection. With a hug we welcome you back and are delighted to speak with you again.

What happens next, you may want to know? *Where is it all leading to?*

No one really knows, as the next destination is of your choosing. We are here to guide you through light and love to your highest path. Like a road sign, we can point the direction, but it is up to you to choose it, walking the walk. Before you is a mountain. It seems high and the climb is steep. There are many obstacles and thorny bushes on the way. You are at base camp now and you are about to embark on the journey to conquer the peak. You know that it is not easy and you know that all the obstacles that will appear before you come from within you, but you are determined to walk the path.

Why should I get all the way up there? What is awaiting me at the peak, some may wonder?

Your crown is waiting for you—the crown of your divinity. When you reach the top you can see the view clearly. The open vista, free of obstacles, is your reward. The communication from Spirit will be clear as there will be no obstructions between you and the transmitter.

Is it worth the effort, you may want to know?

This is your path; you may try to go around and around, but at some point you will need to find a way to conquer this mountain. All the elements support you at this time, but if you choose to wait, there is no judgment, and you are loved just the same. The peak is inside of you waiting for you to climb it. Like this metaphoric peak, light exists regardless of whether there is someone who witnesses it or not. Light will continue to fulfill its mission regardless of whether you choose to open your eyes or not. We ask you to choose to go with light as this is your mission at this time. Darkness offers comfort, at times, that light cannot.

What are you speaking of, some of you may inquire?

Light shows everything without judgment. From your perspective you assign it a positive or negative mark. Darkness hides everything regardless of whether you consider it "good" or "bad."

Are you seeking to experience your truth or do you wish to hide it for a little longer, is our question to you?

You are coming to a time where all that was hidden must be exposed. You chose light, and we ask you not to hide what you may consider to be negative. Your walk is sacred. The negative, like the positive, adds to your learning and to your masterpiece. When you paint a painting and, deep inside of you, you know that it is a masterpiece, you do not judge one brushstroke as positive while another you consider negative. It is all part of the painting. You must see yourself as a whole, not from the limited vantage point where you happen to be, at the moment. We ask you to look at yourself from the peak of the mountain, as if you are already there. When you see yourself on top, to reach it is just a matter of allowing yourself to be guided. You will not get lost. Many of you know where you are and you know where you are going. Your destination is clear inside of you. For many, however, fear comes in and distracts you from your path. It is the season of tests, and fear is what we call the last resort of darkness to absorb light.

You are therefore about to experience many "scary sights" in the illusion you call your reality. Your movement upward is on many dimensions and not only on the dimension of your Earth plane. There are many players in the game of manufactured reality. All have agendas of their own and none have your best interest in mind. You are the only one who knows what is best for you, so we ask you to never judge what is best for your brother and sister. Honor their path and walk your path. Be in gratitude and use love in all your energy exchanges, and you will walk the high road of a master.

What scary sights may I expect, you want to know?

You exist in a world of pure energy manifesting as physical reality through "song and dance." The energy creates sights, smells, and sensual experiences that you perceive as your "true reality." You all agreed to experience this "reality" and accept it for the duration of your visit as angels on planet Earth. As the battle rages over control of your resources of energy, the main venues by which you are controlled and manipulated will offer you challenge. As light exposes the way by which your energy is harvested, you must reclaim your power, redirecting the energy to self first. This is part of the mission for which you have trained. Some of the main energy rivers which flow in your 3-D reality are money, sexual energy, energy resources, natural resources, air, water, and fire. All will be shifting, changing at a growing pace as they react to the pull and push coming from all directions. Your mission is to stay balanced and not join this battle. You win by staying balanced, with love. This is your power. In the game of resource control the individual has the ultimate say as to her own light. It is your birthright.

Many have been robbed of their light over many years through marketing campaigns selling you on the fact that you have no power; you must do this and that in order to survive. You have been programmed on how to give away your light to others, spreading your power to an extent that you were left with just enough to survive and keep giving. The lies and deceits you have been fed for millennia are now being exposed, more so now than ever before.

It is the age of truth. It is on you to wake up now and stand tall, shining your light. No one ever said that this time will be a walk in the park. You will need all your tools, all your resourcefulness, to stay balanced and peaceful. You will need to go deep inside so you can emanate love to all.

We wish to speak to you about your "wanting" as this is one way that has been cultivated, in your collective consciousness, to make you move away from your power and deeper into illusion. Your archeologists, when digging in the earth, find many objects that they describe as tools of primitive cultures. As they approach the more recent cultures they speculate on the advancement of these cultures technologically and scientifically. What they lack in their observation is how many of the ancient cultures were far more advanced in the realm of Spirit knowledge, that is, in their relationships and interactions with the galactic universe around them. You are pure energy manifesting your desire through matter. In the physical world the atoms and molecules adhere to your wishes. They create what you wish for within the rules of time and physics. You can choose at any given moment how to use your power to manifest and create. As the creator, your power is limitless. You can create that which you imagine, and the *only limitation is your imagination*. You have learned over time to focus your desires and wanting on creating matter. This is because you believed matter would give you more of what you need in order to thrive, ultimately be more fulfilled, becoming happy.

There were those who exploited your ability to create. They began a campaign a long time ago of moving you away from your innate inner power towards external power. The further you moved away from self and internal desires, the weaker you became. As you redirected your creative energy from inner desires towards external desires, you moved away from your equilibrium, your inner abundance, your link to self and Spirit. This is what your archeologists fail to observe. Your connection to Spirit and your internal abilities in your distant past were much greater than today. You did not need all the technology to know who you are and what your mission was about. You created that which you needed internally, and the external reality was secondary. That is why there was not much to be found externally in your distant past. As you have moved away from your inner wealth and power, you have felt a strong yearning and desire to rediscover the same sensations of bliss, connectedness to spirit, your own divinity, and power that you once held.

The more you created and advanced in your external physical reality, the further you moved away from self. You have shifted your creative energy externally, searching for power in *things*, love in *things*, and connectedness in *things*. The physical and technological advancement that you made gave you a short-lived feeling of satisfaction, power, control, love, yes, even connectedness. Like an addict, you felt that you needed more, always more, in order to feed your inner void of security, power, love, balance, and peace.

This dynamic was fully exploited by the dark that saw an opportunity to separate you from your core power by promoting short-lived highs and illusions of power through wanting and through desire. The powerful desire that is currently dominating your modern society was born and cultivated to move you away from your core mission, redirecting your creative energy away from self. There is no inherent "bad" in creating in the external reality. You have, however, replaced the internal with the external. This same dynamic happened in Atlantis, and that society had to be rebooted, as your expression goes. They had to start over. Your creations, your advancements, although magnificent in scope, are dwarfed in comparison to your power as an angel who knows your role and mission. The more you have relied on your environment and created things to support you, the further you moved from the tools you had to control your inner reality. Your golden age of technology is now the dark age of your spirit. Your power to create was directed by the masculine energy, out of balance with the direction of the planet's trajectory of ascension, as was appropriate to your level of awareness, by your own choice. Your path was leading you to termination as it moved too far away from your core path and mission. Then a shift happened where many intuitively felt the need to reclaim their light, rediscovering equilibrium within, bringing back the feminine energy, reconnecting to their own core power, their light. Through those angels your termination was averted and you have started to write the new chapter that you are now experiencing.

Do you see the power that you possess? It is awesome. Your power to manifest your external reality is limitless, yet many of you direct it to money, security, and things. You feel that if you only have so much money you will feel better, or if you only have this person in your life you will feel loved. Your wanting is insatiable as you are all looking to feel a certain way and to connect with self. What you are looking for, no object or person can ever give you. Many of you believe that if you could only get more of what you already have, you will experience that feeling of being loved, secure, connected, happy, and joyful. The more you learned to create things that seemingly helped you experience bliss, the less you have been able to create those feelings inside of you. Your wanting, desires, and yearnings brought you to astonishing technological advancements, also leading you to the lowest ebb in your evolution as Spirit commanding a human body. Your cultures, societies, your power players, your architects of your manufactured reality further reinforced your belief that through external creation, you will get to experience joy, bliss, love, security, and balance.

You have been put on a treadmill and sold on a one-way ticket that the faster you move the further you will reach, when in actuality you have not moved anywhere. Your external physical reality is a manifestation of misdirected core energy that moved away from its purpose, supplanting higher levels of awareness with creation of technological advancement to facilitate your life.

What is wrong with wanting and desires, you may ask?

It is a fine question. Wanting is always based in lack, which is rooted in feeling. If you wish for a better car, it is not for the purpose of arriving faster to work, but it is rooted in the belief that you will be happier as a result. Feelings of lack fuel your current state of wanting and desires.

We love you and we ask you: do you really believe that by having this diamond ring you will feel more loved? And the answer is *yes*…momentarily. The moment-to-moment yearning is what fuels your economy, desires, and misdirected creative energy. Some of you have truly bought the idea that your life will improve as a result of *things*. Our question to you: do you think that your Western technologically advanced societies are internally, psychologically, and spiritually better off than indigenous, or what you call third-world, cultures? We'll let you ponder this question.

The reason that your global economy seems to be crumbling is the same reason that many of you begin to reevaluate your priorities. Many of you have discovered that what you believed would bring you happiness and joy did not. More so, it made you dependent on so many outer circumstances that you have forgotten who you are and what the purpose of your journey is. We are here today to remind you. We spoke about wanting and how to link to what is truly missing in your life. No material wealth—no matter how extensive—will ever be enough. It is from within that your feeling of lack has to be fulfilled. Next time you sit to meditate and speak to spirit, ask not for more money but feel the feeling that you yearn to experience. Imagine feeling love; imagine feeling peace; imagine experiencing balance; imagine experiencing abundance; then let go and trust that you are the creator manifesting all that which you wish for. Allow your reality to rearrange itself according to your imagined feelings and let go. You add flavor to whatever you manifest in your reality. We ask you to become the flavor of peace, balance, love, and joy. You will have a choice of whether to rely on your external reality or to go inside, finding that which you look for, catapulting your vibration to a new dimension.

We hear you say, however, *Yes, all that is true, but please give me the extra money so I can focus on other things, not worrying about rent.*

We know who you are and we can see your tests. It is up to you to create your reality within because only then true abundance will manifest in your life. Until you have mastered and fulfilled your inner yearnings, your desires, you will never have enough. When you have mastered and fulfilled your inner desires you will always have plenty. That is your choice. We ask you to celebrate it at every moment, remembering who you are, and so be it.

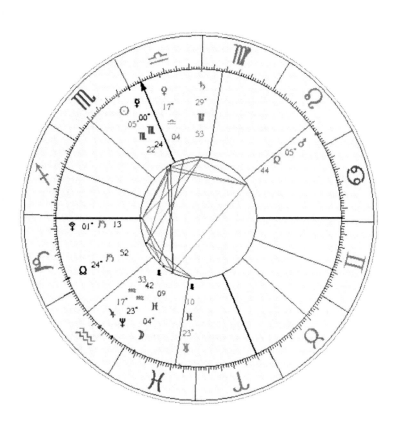

10-28-2009

Dror - thanks. In reference to inner turmoil, I must say honestly that I am more centered internally now than I have ever
been. I have had much more "turmoil" in the distant past, but
have
also done a lot of therapy work in the past too. The emotions
that come up in reference to the Holocaust I regard as "positive" in the sense that some of the suppression is coming up for
resolution.

best, Daniel
_____

(from Dror)

Dear Daniel

This is a tough subject which puts every peaceful soul to the
test.

I received a message today but it has to do with the inner
turmoil that each and every one of us in now experiencing and
what it means.

I will ask if there is particular information that can be of
help. You have asked now about the cruelty to animals and the
Holocaust. I hope to respond soon.

Love

Dror

The Blender

*Y*OU ARE DEARLY LOVED.

Smile, all is well. No one, anywhere, can take away your smile! When you smile, you are lifting the vibration of yourself and the ones who are near you.

We have no reason to smile, some of you may claim.

Are you breathing, we ask?

Of course, you answer. Here is your reason, we reply.

What is going on, some may want to know?

Imagine a giant column of sorts that swivels rapidly and it collects everything on its path. You can compare it to a huge vacuum cleaner. The column is the link between your Earth and the heavens. As it turns, like a tornado, it pulls you upward.

Why is it so, some may wonder?

You have collectively asked to move higher. As you do, your outer reality is shifting to accommodate and create space for the new energy to replace the old. The immense forces that pull on your light bodies can create a sense of imbalance in your physical body. There is so much going on within you that you cannot sleep at night. The dynamic forces acting within your visible sensual reality create a sense of instability. These forces are part of your collective yearning to ascend, but individually you perceive them as disconcerting or threatening. What you feel is the small wave that precedes the large wave. The effects of this immense wave that we see approaching will continue for a long time after 2012 is no longer in the news. You are now experiencing small, rapidly moving waves of galactic energy turning you upside down, twisting you, making you feel disoriented and confused. We have asked you in so many ways to be prepared because stability in your outer reality will not be there for your support. You must link to the place inside of you that offers you the peace you need to stay standing, shining your light.

When we tell you that there will be no place to hide we mean that what you experience outside is only a small part of the story. It is your inside which will be going through some very exciting rides, and you will feel at times like a blender. Your inner structure will be twisting and turning where your outer reality will appear as if all is as usual. You are Spirit and what happens outside of you happens also inside. The space/time delay between your true essence and your hidden essence is shrinking. As you move higher, the outer reality and inner reality will begin to mirror each other more closely, more expediently. In your past there was a delay of time inserted between your intention, your inner state and its manifestation in your outer reality. Your physical body is experiencing what we call an adjustment period where it is being furnished interdimensionally with tools to maneuver and function in this new world that is being created. It is part of your evolution as angels disguised as humans. You have earned an upgrade—being dressed up with new and exciting tools.

What are these tools, some may wonder?

Your glands will become more sensitive to pressure.

Why pressure, you may inquire?

The gravitational pull of your planet is changing slightly. Your glands that control the release of hormones, which hold conversations with your cells, are being recalibrated; your nervous system is being upgraded.

Why is it so, some may ask?

Your nerves are like antennas. They are sensitive to subtle changes in your electromagnetic circuitry as well as the planet's magnetic polarity. Without these upgrades you may feel disoriented, as if you and your body are not connected. You will feel like you are outside of your body. This can create immense pressure on your adrenal glands and your kidneys because your fight/flight survival mechanism may be called into action, rendering your system malleable and therefore vulnerable. You may experience an inner sense of anxiety, fear, and panic that relates to your biology not harmonizing with the new resonance of your changing planet.

How can we confirm that indeed these upgrades are taking place, you wonder?

You cannot confirm it because most of the changes will happen in the realm of interdimensional quantum space. You will, though, experience exponential growth in anxiety- or panic-related disorders, as well as neuroses that have to do with disorientation and inner confusion.

It all sounds terrible, some may say.

With a hug, we must impart to you that it is magnificent, glorious, and sacred. Like a preteen who is moving into adolescence, many bodily changes are taking place in her to facilitate this transformation. So it is with you. Those of you who take the time to learn to link with your inner light, invoking your full power, creating the protective layer of a master, will experience this time as nothing but glorious, yet others may experience it as "terrible."

Again, it is your choice. We are your flashlights. We are shining our beam of light on the signs so you can focus your attention on the up-and-coming curves in the road, but we cannot do the driving for you.

How do we make sure that we pay attention to the signs, some may rightly ask?

Slow down, is our short answer. When you begin to realize that nothing ever escapes from you, you are in fact eternal, and whatever it is that you are chasing is already inside of you, you have little justification not to slow down. You see the futility of trying to hurry up and move to a place that you are already occupying.

Slowing down is a prerequisite to getting in touch with the up-and-coming changes. You must allow your biology and perception time to adjust. Your next step to align with the changes is connecting to Gaia. We cannot say it enough as it is in the core of your moving upward. Like an airplane, your planet is taking off, and to take off with it you must be seated in the plane. We wish you to smell flowers, talk to squirrels, hug trees, and walk amongst nature, as it is part of you. You have been weakened by moving away from your natural space into virtual spaces. It is essential for you to reconnect with your birds, animals, plants, and trees. They have so much love for you. As you link with the natural world, all the elements embrace your energy, hugging you and taking you in, so you become part of the change, not feeling left out.

So you say, *I have no time to slow down; there is so much to do and so little time to do it.*

And we ask you, who is controlling your schedule? Is it you?

My boss is pressuring me, as are my kids, spouse, relatives, and friends. All want my attention and I have no time to breathe.

Are you making all of them happy, is our question?

No, is your likely answer, I am not because there's just not enough time for everything.

Precisely. We ask you to slow down because you manifest your reality and your reality dances based on the tune you play. When you slow down, all those around you will reflect the same to you and will slow down. When you take care of yourself, creating joy within, your outer reality will dance that same tune, reflecting back to you the joy that you have created within. You are the master of your own reality, and when you say "there is not enough time" it is as if you at that moment wrote your own script which reflects your belief: "no time and no joy."

Imagine a world where everyone knew that they were eternal and masters of their reality. Everybody knew that all they needed to "do" is be in the now and in a place of joy. They knew that their reality must rearrange itself according to their belief and intent. Do you know what happens when enough of you understand these simple mechanics of your dimension? You have brought heaven upon you. Wouldn't you like to be the bringer of heaven on Earth? We have done just that, so we speak from experience. We are light like you. We have been with you from before the beginning and will continue to be with you after the end. You are eternal. We ask you to slow down because, wherever you think you must get to, you have plenty of time. With a smile, we hug you once more, asking you to be an instrument for creating heaven for your own self and those around you. You have the power at any given moment to shift your reality. We ask you to start now, and so be it.

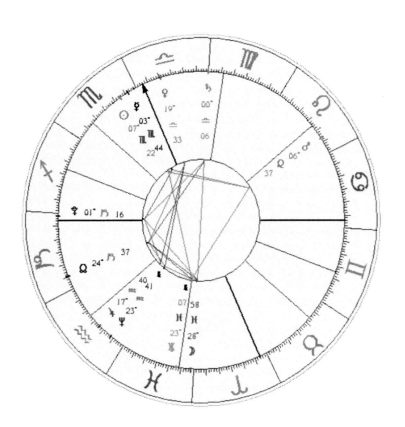

10-30-2009

Dear Dror
I wanted to share with you this song—don't the
angels say they act as DJ's sometimes.

Thanks for today.
. . . .
Don't ask me
What you know is true
Don't have to tell you
I love your precious heart

I..........I was standing
You were there
Two worlds collided
And they could never tear us apart

We could live for a thousand years
But if I hurt you
I'd make wine from your tears

I told you
That we could fly
Cause we all have wings
But some of us don't know why
Li-or

Show Me the Money

*Y*OU ARE DEARLY LOVED.

Can we do it, some of you ask?

Yes, you can, we answer. There is a beautiful, colorful rainbow inside each of you which shows you the way. For the rainbow to appear, your sun must be shining. Your inner sun will bring about the rainbow. We observe many of you who are struggling at this time in your current reality, as though there is a shadow hiding behind each day. You are just waiting for it to jump out and frighten you. You have a twenty-four hour period which you define as a day. If you divide it into slices like a pie, on average, one-third of the day you work, another third you live your private life, and the last third is for sleeping, collecting yourself to face the next pie. What if you change the order of these slices and imagine a pie where the time that you work is actually the time that you sleep? The time that you would normally work during the day would be the time of rest. Can you imagine being at work as restful and relaxed as when you are sleeping, getting everything needed easily done?

183

That is impossible, most will say!

It is on you to be in the reality of your choosing. Most of you define work as something that you must do in order to get something else. Most of you say, "Without work I cannot support myself and pay my bills. Without paying my bills I will not have a place to live. I therefore need and must work no matter what." Most of you see work as something you are forced to do for your survival. You define it as work and it is where you are mostly doing what you are told to do.

Where are you going with this, some may inquire?

We see you walking the walk of an angel disguised as human. You allocate your energy and intention mostly in a pattern that does not leave you with light when you need it. Light is something you carry within, and when you interact with your surroundings, you shine your light. When you sleep, the light is still with you but you keep it to yourself and your angelic group. It is not being exchanged with other humans. We can see your tendencies and we can see your challenges. Many of your challenges are presented to you as a result of the way you perceive your situation. When you feel restful and joyful in an environment, it will allow you to rest, recharge, enjoy. If you come to a place where you are already in the mind frame that it is going to be challenging, difficult, and that you will have to face many obstacles, indeed you will. No one tells you how to feel inside of you. You are being told who you are, how you need to dress up, how you need to act in the world almost from birth, but feelings are something that you carry inside of you, and it is the "dress" and the "actions" of these feelings that we see. We do not care if you wear a designer suit or rags; we see your "inner outfit." When you begin to move closer into the circle you discover that, like a magician, you can shift your reality in an instant. You are moving into a period of pure magic. The more linear your thoughts are, the less your reality will make sense to you. The more "circular" you become, the greater the satisfaction and joy you will experience.

Most of you desire money; you believe that it will really facilitate your life. You uphold money as your "God." It has such impact on your life that many of you believe that it holds the key to your happiness. We hear many of you say to yourselves, "Just give me more of 'that stuff' and I will be all set." We hear you pray for it at night as if it were the real God. You say all these sweet prayers and at the end you ask for the payback: "I will do good and I want to have money." What many of you are saying is that it is not you who holds the power to your own reality, but it is the energy of money which holds the power. Money is a curious thing from our perspective. It is a concept that was created seemingly from nowhere to make your life simpler. Instead of exchanging goods, your ancestors felt that it would be easier to equate the goods with a substance which would symbolically mean the same thing, but be easier to carry and trade. Well, that was some time ago. Where are you now? You are at a place where that energy was, again, redirected from its original purpose; instead of facilitating trade, it made it so abstract that the relationship between the energy and you has very little correlation. Your society therefore determined that an hour of one person's time is worth a fortune, where another person's time—who happens to do menial labor—is worth much less. Why is it so? You have, as a society, made the energy serve some and exclude others. Those who control much of your resources created a value system where certain talents or attributes are praised and others not. As money is energy, it must move in order to fulfill its purpose. It must circulate. Like life force in your body, when it is stagnant, you may develop a dis-ease. In your physical reality, when the energy of money—which is the life force of your economies—stops circulating, you experience energetic blockages, manifesting shifts that you perceive as negative and damaging.

Why are you speaking to us about money? It is all known and obvious, some frown in frustration.

Yes, indeed it is, but why is it, then, that so many of you are having difficulty with it? When we see you from above, we do not see your bank accounts. We see the geometry of the energy of money in disharmony with your light body. We wish to ask you, if all is so clear, with you knowing all you need to know about the energy of money, why is it that angels from all walks of life—economic backgrounds, education, creeds, races, and religions—find the biggest challenge with this energy. The only place you will not find the energy of money as the most prevailing challenge is when the geometry of religion is dominating, overshadowing the geometry of money.

Will you tell us how to make more? What is the secret to being rich, some excitedly ask?

The secret is that having more is not the answer; therefore, the path to abundance is, once again, in the realm of the circle and not in the realm of adding up your pennies. Money is energy like food is energy, and like wind or your sun. This energy propels you to act and do things in your world. You believe that without it you are weak and helpless. You also believe that money can come to you only in certain ways and not others. You have, by way of your awareness and your acceptance of what reality is, made money different than any other energy source on your planet. You made it scarce.

It may be a surprise for you, but your planet produces enough food for all humans, and then some. The sun energy gifts you with enough energy to propel all your energy needs forever, and then some. Your natural energy sources outside of money are limitless. Some of you may argue the scientific validation of such a statement, but you were born into a reality where, in potential, all your needs are given to you as your birthright. From such an entry point you are charting your own path, and, based on your choices, creating your individual reality as well as your shared reality.

Can you tell us something we do not know, some of you will ask in frustration?

Money was produced on the premise of scarcity. It is therefore a self-fulfilling prophecy that you choose to tie yourself to a treadmill where the chase after sufficient energy is bound to be your path, unless of course, you step off the treadmill.

What then, some may wonder? *We will be broke and homeless.*

That is also a choice, but we had a different idea in mind.

Can you please tell us, some may ask?

You are powerful; your reality changes based on your intention, trust, and fearlessness.

Money, as energy, was created such that when you have a lot of it, inevitably it must come from someplace, thereby creating scarcity. You have created it so it will be in perpetual scarcity, so no matter how many of you will get some, others will never have enough. It is, therefore, those who you consider powerful who must guard this resource so they can horde enough of it. Do you see armed guards protecting the sun so only some will enjoy its radiation and not others? Do you see armies protecting the wind or gravity? Do you see air being rationed so some of you can breathe and others cannot? Air is your most precious energy source because it keeps your biological vehicle alive. It gives you your life force so your cells metabolize and move energy in your body. Without air you cannot survive for more than a few minutes; do you see any armed patrol protection around this precious resource?

Many of you will tell us that again, this is obvious, and nothing new was said. With all love, we wish to tell you that all we speak of is known to you. We are just here to remind you of what you already know. It is, therefore, our contention that your desire to accumulate energy that is scarce will accelerate your scarcity, creating further imbalance on your planet.

What is the remedy then, some may wonder? *Is there a solution?*

We speak to you individually. We are not attempting to solve your world's problems, nor do we try to save its economies. The current system is based on lack and not abundance; therefore, as long as you are part of the system, it is part of the limitation of this game. We ask you at this time to move out of the game, imagining that which you wish to feel. Imagine abundance, that you have stepped off the treadmill and away from the game of scarcity. Imagine how the abundance feels: you are loved, taken care of, there is nothing you need more than what you already have. By using your power and light, you create your reality. The feeling of abundance will then present itself in your life as it must. Do not ask for money, as money is energy based on lack. Money has no meaning on its own. It is neutral until it is in your hand. You, therefore, will attract this energy by not seeking it. When you create that which you need in your awareness, it must come to you. *Your ability to create is rooted in feelings and not in your linear mind.* The power of your feelings moves the molecules, not the idea itself. If you wish to create something that was not there before, you must attach it to a powerful feeling. Without feeling, the idea may stay on the drawing board unrealized. The same is true with money; if you wish to have this energy, ask not for this energy, but create a visual picture for the *feeling* of what you wish.

We spoke to you about your "wanting." When you ask for things, it is not the "thing" that you really desire, but it is the *feeling that you believe will be created* from having this "thing." We ask you to step into the circle and visualize that feeling rather than experience the arduous task of using lack to create abundance. Money is energy when it is flowing between various pockets. When it is being horded it loses its energetic property and becomes stagnant. Once money is being accumulated, it is not being used as energy, but as a misdirected tool to control others and to create scarcity. It is as if one of your corporations covered the face of the Earth and allowed only those with resources the privilege of sunlight. Inevitably the value of sunlight would increase because scarcity was created.

What do we do about it, some may wonder? *We still do not understand. How are we supposed to have more money?*

You are moving into a new reality where you will face the limitation of your systems. Their flaws, then, will be exposed and challenged. The first thing we ask you to know is that, in order to experience abundance, you must step off your treadmills. Your self-perpetuated yearning for more only creates more scarcity, not only in your individual reality, but as a whole. In addition, we wish you to understand that money is an energy that needs to be circulated and flowing in order to express its energetic quality. To attract money to your reality, it is not money that you need to ask for, but the *feeling of abundance* that you are asked to visualize. Abundance is a feeling of wholeness where all your needs are met and you lack nothing. Money can never give you that feeling because it was created on the opposite premise of scarcity. Your abundance comes from awareness. When you move consciously into a place of abundance, it will manifest in your life, as it is true, with peace, with love, and with joy. When you develop the awareness that abundance does not come from money, but from an awareness of who you are and what your mission is about, you become the symbol of everlasting wealth, never lacking ... ever. It is so, as it must be. You are the master and you control your own awareness. Your consciousness controls your reality, and when you brought abundance to your awareness, you created that reality in an instant. Your physical reality will move somewhat slower to meet with your intention, as it must. Be patient and trust. You came here at this time to allow light through you, bringing yourself to your highest potential and manifesting change that can only be described as glorious. You have the potential to create peace and abundance, first in you, then from you to everyone else. We ask you to know your powers and to begin using them now. Now it's time, as there is no other time, and so be it.

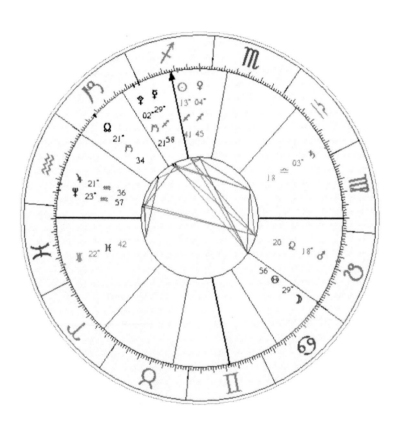

12/5/09

Dear Dror,
What can I say. My heart has opened so much over the last month
as I have read the beautiful words that you have received from
the Angels. Sunday was magnificent and I cannot thank you
enough for spending your time with this beautiful group of healers.
Your words touched so many and created such a shift.

Ok so this is going to sound a little "nuts", but you are used to this
I'm sure. From the first time that I read your email, there was
something familiar with your energy that was part of this world
and part out of it. I know that the Angels say that we are all
this way, so I will clarify that you have an enhanced awareness of
this paradigm and how to use it. Having spent quite a bit of time
working within the energy of Jesus, I feel very strongly that this
is the energy that I was feeling with you. As you spoke Sunday,
that became apparent to me. It is a very powerful, but loving and
calm energy. I guess what I am saying is that I feel that you have
taken on many of the attributes of the energy of Jesus. It is such
a gift to be able to communicate in such a way.

I have enclosed all of the emails of individuals that wanted the up-
dates on your healing messages. I know that you are leaving soon,
so if you would prefer that I send the email out just let me know.

I am wishing you and your family all the best this holiday season
and a safe trip to Israel !

With much love,

M.

It's Time

YOU ARE DEARLY LOVED.

Where should we begin? In the beginning, some may answer. There is, however, no beginning and no end. You are in the circle and so are we. All the answers you are looking for are within you, and all you need to do is link to the circle within you. You are it. You are the source of all that you need and you create that which you desire as spirit, walking, commanding a biological vehicle. You are a driver of the divine energy you call God. You choose your vehicle, you choose your route, and you choose your end destination. There is no one out there more powerful than you regarding your own life. You are a master; it is time for you to acknowledge it, moving forward, knowing that there are no victims, no coincidences, and no accidents in the journey you call human life. There is you and your awareness. When you are awake, acting from awareness of your own divinity, you are powerful, as you are linked to the energy of God and love. When you are asleep, acting without awareness, you are disconnected from the energy of love and the actions you bring forth may need to be balanced through karma. Actions done from love release and clear karmic debt; actions done from energy other than love often increase your karmic balance sheet. The days are getting shorter as you are moving from one phase of your journey to the next. This journey never ends, but it changes. You are in the midst of that change and many of you are aware of the instability of the fulcrum point inside of you. It feels wobbly like seesaw riding. Even those of you who used to be in a place of balance find it challenging to stay still. Your nights are less restful and your days offer you many opportunities to test your place of awareness. It is the time of initiation and tests; many of you feel that you want to get off this train, but it does not stop. With all love, we embrace you with our wings and whisper in your ears that it's time.

What should we do with this information, many ask?

Sit down and smile to yourself knowing that you are the one in control of your journey. Smile because as long as you breathe, you know that you can shine light and bring transformation to where it is needed. Your thoughts, feelings, and actions are the fuel of the change you are now experiencing. We ask you to wake up to the immense responsibility you are carrying.

What's next, you may want to know?

Next is you coming to a meeting. In that meeting, the "other you" will be present; you introduce yourself to yourself and walk hand in hand. This is the coveted reunion about which everyone is talking. Imagine two brothers who never met, only communicating through an interpreter. Finally they get to meet face to face, embracing, and telling each other all that they have been through.

Where will the meeting take place, you may want to know?

In the circle, is our answer.

In the past the linking of you with you was facilitated by others, whether it be a holy person or through religions. You have relied on a middle person because you felt that it was the only way to meet your lost or hidden part. This attribute is now changing. The space separating you from you is becoming thinner and thinner. The information that you are now receiving regarding your life journey comes quickly and with less distortion. Some of you are becoming so clear in your relationships with your higher part that you appear to us as a walking Spirit glowing in its full magnificence and splendor.

It is time to speak to those of you who facilitate healing, helping to balance those angels who are unbalanced. We embrace you with our wings, and hug you, as your mission is sacred beyond your wildest dreams. As we watch you from above, or view you from below, we are in awe of the work that is being done in some of your backrooms and self-made facilities. We see magic and miracles wherever we look. Many of you are breaking the rules because you know why these rules were written in the first place. You know that healing is pure magic which is facilitated through love and pure intent. You know that the manuals, or the protocols, are there to assist you to break free from manuals and protocols. You have to start somewhere. Many of you who are hard at work following the set of instructions taught to them by their masters, gurus or healing teachers find that the results are less predictable than in the past, and in some cases do not work at all.

What happens? Why is that so, you wish to know?

There is a grid that holds all your vibrations intact and it is facilitated by the other side. There is a shift in the oscillation of the planetary vibratory rate which changes the way energy is being transmitted from one to another. It is part of the attribute of easier communication between you and the other you. Your vibratory rate and Earth's vibratory rate have increased, so that you find yourself following the same protocol that used to work but the results seem to be less than before. In some cases nothing happens and you find yourself wondering if you lost your touch. We hear you speaking to yourself questioning if maybe it is time to go back to that bookkeeping position you left ten years ago when you chose to pursue your life's purpose of becoming a healer. We know who you are. It is a grand time indeed. Healing energy is not only helping the person that is being healed, but also the healer and the planet. When you balance a biological vehicle driven by spirit, you are healing spirit. The consciousness of Gaia, or the planet, is carried through angels walking in duality, so when you are healing a person, you are also balancing and healing the planet. It is a profound, sacred mission that many of you are aware of, pursuing it with a purity of intent and love.

What happens during healing from our perspective? Energy is being transmitted from a place we can only describe as the space of love. This energy is directed through the healer to the one being healed. The source of that energy is infinite and it resonates with the frequency of healthy cells, the building blocks of your biology. Once the love melody is being played, it stimulates the unbalanced cell to move back to balance where it is aligned with the universal resonance of love. When the person being healed is being electrified with healing energy, he or she may move closer to balance. When the underlying energy patterns of imbalance are not being addressed, it is most likely that the imbalance will resurface. It may appear in the same form or take a new form. This is not new and all of you are aware of it.

So tell us what is new, you may ask?

What is new is that you now have the ability to address the underlying issue causing the imbalance in the first place, creating real, long-lasting life change, eliminating the need for your client to come back over and over again. Now, that may not sound like a great business plan as you may fear that you will run out of clients. With all love, we do not see that happening anytime soon. We see more and more people coming to you as the word spreads that a real shift, a real healing, is taking place among your clients.

What is required, some may wish to know?

As you may have guessed, be childlike while being fearless at the same time. From where you are standing, looking at the person who seeks to be healed (no matter how familiar you are with the mechanics of the body and its various functions), you will not be able to match the knowing of your higher part with that of the body being healed. You may know the shapes and functions of the nadis, chakras, all the meridians; you may know where each organ is placed and its function; you may even know the language of color, flower essences and crystals. You may, indeed, know all the different pressure points and may have memorized all the healing mantras, yet you will still fall short.

Why is it so, you may ask?

Healing comes from love. Blocked systems develop due to lack of love caused by challenges from this life or previous cycles. From our perspective, your mission is not to know and not to analyze what had gone wrong or who had done what to whom. In the circle all is perfect and has a purpose. You must begin by envisioning the perfection of the system and bow to it. Hold that perfection in your vision as sacred. Understand that all that happens and will happen comes from one source: LOVE. When you hold that vision, you now have the most difficult challenge of all: letting go of all that you have learned. Press the delete button and then press enter. Allow all that you know to vanish as you make space for divinity to stream through you to the person asking to be balanced. When you begin your process from a place of not knowing, true knowing will come to you. When it does, you must again be fearless and act on what is being offered to you. We wish you to be childlike in a toy room, using whatever is available even if you do not hold a certificate in that specific domain. Healing comes from the circle and the body system is linked to the circle. When you hold the perfect image of the body in the circle, it will give you instructions on how to apply it to the physical body to bring forth healing. Many of you train in a specific system, having received a certification stating that, indeed you are authorized, are ready to heal people and that you may charge for your service. This is appropriate and necessary in your society's current state of awareness. Hang your certificate *outside* the healing room as your certification must change once you enter the room and give intention for healing to take place. Your certificate is given to you through your intent and it is signed with the word "love." If you follow a manual of any tradition to the letter getting a perfect score every time, we assure you that it will still shy of the power of healing you exercise through not knowing.

You do not have to take the angelic word for it; try it and compare. Keep notes and check for yourself. It is appropriate to educate yourself in the language of the different healing schools and methods. We ask you to expose yourself to as many modalities as you can. Again, be childlike, seeking healings for yourself from your healer friends and colleagues. Allow your body to absorb the innate knowledge buried in you from the different schools. Many of you have been involved in healings in some of your past expressions, and all you need to do is allow the memory to surface when it is appropriate. It may not come with clear explanation and it may sound weird, but we must impart to you that the potential for deep transformation is magnificent. You are a vessel, and as such, your mission is to allow that energy of love to flow through you. That energy, then, can take over for the time of the healing and may facilitate balancing the one lying on the healing table.

Many of you believe that you must use the one method you were taught and that your method can heal all ailments. With all love, we wish to impart to you that healing can be facilitated through the many different modalities not because of the modality, but because of you. It is you who activates the energy. The crystal by itself or the flower essence by itself will not be as potent or as transformative when it is bought from a store by the patient and applied. You must charge it with your intent. It is your energy mixed with that essence which imbues love and intent into the formula making it powerfully transformative.

I am only trained in massage and Reiki, some will claim. *I know nothing about flower essences and crystals.*

Well, it is time that you enter the toy room and begin to play. Everything is available to you and all the knowledge you need is imbued in the delete button. Learn and play with as many methods and modalities as your heart desires. You do not need to become a master of all but expose yourself and awaken your inner knowing. Once you enter the healing space, placing your hand above your client, we ask you to now move aside, delete all you know, and wait. Visualize your patient in his/her perfect form as if there were no ailment. See them as healed and do not ask for specifics as if healing has already happened. Trust that once you clear yourself from expectation, stop looking for this or that sign of imbalance, trying to remember what to do, that the love frequency from the circle will operate through you. It is our promise, then, that you will experience miracles.

What kind of miracles, you may inquire?

Deep, transformative healing must always come from the realm of multiple dimensions working on all levels, subtle and physical. At times changes in the akash must take place for blocks to be cleared. Can you do all of it in a matter of 60 minutes? When you see a block in the liver and you send your energy to that area or massage it, can you tell from where the underlying imbalance comes? Miracles are possible when you no longer try to control the outcome of your actions. You are no longer the driver of the healing; *you are a spectator*. You move aside and allow your body to be used from the highest place of love to facilitate healing in another. When you are experiencing that place, not only will your client be transformed, but you will be, as well. More so, you will be capable of addressing more people without being drained of energy. In actuality, your energy will only increase as you allow love through you to another without holding on to anything. Your primary role is to set a pure intention and to be in a place of balance and clarity yourself, seeing your patient in his/her perfect form as if all ailments miraculously have already healed, which requires nothing. It is then that the universe will align with your coherent vision acting as an instrument for healing.

So how come not everyone is doing it? It sounds so easy, some may claim.

This is the best part which, of course, comes last. The greatest effort is not in facilitating healing but in being in a place of balance yourself. The attribute of the new healing energetic exchange brings about miracles when you, yourself, master the art of balance, peace, and self-love. Your own blocks may limit the transformative power of your healings. We started the message by telling you about your power. The first mission of

any healer is to heal yourself. Through your own process you facilitate others. If you choose to be a martyr
and neglect the self, giving everything to others, with
a smile we say, all the neglect of self will show up in
your healings by blocking your healing energy, limiting your power. Being a healer *always must start with
self.* When we see those of you who carry heavy energy into your healing sessions, we must tell you that you
may be inflicting more damage than good. The magic
key to transformative healings is becoming balanced. If
you ingest drugs or smoke, treating your own body in
an unbalanced or unloving way, how can you act as a
pure vessel for another? When the healing energy passes through you it collects all of your unresolved issues.
All that we speak of is already in you, as you are a master, powerfully creating miracles in your life. Miracles
are transformations that are not linear, but which come
from the circle. When you see miracles, they may come
in a form of a sick person who everyone said was ter-
minal. You may see the incurable person being healed
quickly. You may see ailments that have no known rem-
edies walk off to never come back. The most potent
healer is the spectator who trusts and follows her higher guidance. Your mission, as always, is to work on self.
Your reality is your own construct rippling outward, so
when you are healed, you are healing the planet, and
so be it.

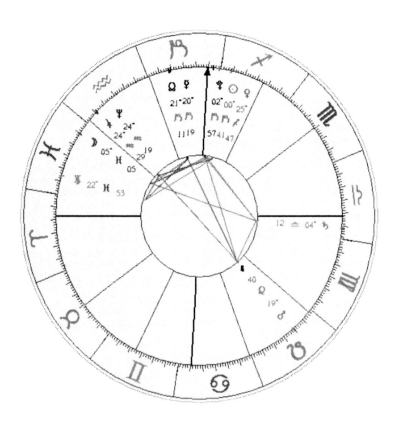

12-22-2009

Hi Dror,

It sounds like you had an amazing walk last night. How magical.

I just wanted to let you know that I felt a shift and that I am feeling ready again to take on the work actively. I feel more balanced and like I am melting again and letting go.

I actually was still doing the work but in a more passive way, just letting the energy of all the lessons settle in.

I feel that you have sent some positive energy in my direction and I want to thank you for that.

I feel a lot of gratitude for you.

I did yoga this morning and my practice is really rewarding. My body is learning to let go and go deeper into the asanas. I can do a head stand away from the wall now which is very exciting for me. It is gratifying to see the improvements and the physical manifestation of letting go.

I am now at Garden Cafe and will be writing my intentions on this winter solstice. My main intention is to let my light shine through and to trust and let go rather than hold on.

Lots of love

Yasmin

Alchemy

*Y*OU ARE DEARLY LOVED.

Again, we thank you for your work and congratulate you for being an instrument. You have taken a path that is not easy and you keep walking the high road, skipping over potholes, moving around obstacles. There are many of you who are moving on this road determined to reach a higher ground and a wide open vista. Many of you give intent to move up but find yourselves looking down to avoid the many pits that are being introduced to you. You are so concerned with avoiding the pits that you forget to look up, reorienting yourselves with the direction of the mountain top. We know who you are and we ask you to know who we are. We are you, expanded. We are with you all the time. We are around you when you laugh and when you cry.

What is it that you are telling us, you may wonder?

You have chosen to come here for the sole purpose of living your truth awakened. You have come here to discover your purpose, and you have come here to show what this life is all about, through example. You have come here to create an energy vortex around you that will recalibrate the way people view their own reality—no small task.

How is that being done, some may want to know?

It is done through magnetics and it is done through alchemy. The process of alchemy happens when you walk in the knowledge of who you are. You create a vortex of energy around you which activates others. As you move around in life activating others, you create ripples of higher frequency which we also named "light." Others can use the higher frequency to ride on and bring about inner transformation from one state of awareness to another. This is alchemy. From heavy, you become light; from lead, become gold. From human you uncover your angelic essence. From a linear human you bridge up to the multidimensional circular reality of spirit. This is what we speak of when we say you are all alchemists. This is your purpose.

So why do we feel so dark at times? Why do we feel that we have it more challenging than others, some wonder?

Because you do, is our short answer. As all of you are on a path of learning, of growing, some of you are at a point on your journey where the learning appears easier, more rudimentary, while some others are here to pull humanity to a place it had never visited before.

Can you give us examples, some may ask?

Many on your planet are now experiencing a basic lesson that has to do with material reality. In one sentence we can sum it up: "It is not all about money." In order to learn this lesson many of you must first experience a reality where it is all about money, and then the constellation of your playing cards is being reshuffled so you can experience the other side of this reality. Often the mechanics of your lessons are you learning through opposites. The experience of lack allows you to learn abundance, fear guides you to fearlessness, and the material world takes you beyond the material world. For you to experience, and truly imbibe on a feeling level the hidden elements behind your biology and the observable reality that is around you, you must first experience swimming in that reality fully. Many of you learn the basic lesson of respecting life by experiencing a reality where human life is not being honored. Many of you who signed up to learn about Spirit are now completely absorbed in the world of matter. When that world collapses, the next lesson will be moving beyond matter.

All lessons are precious and all are valued. On a level of mass consciousness, you, as a group, are about to move from one state of awareness to another. You are moving into a state of higher consciousness which is very different from the state where many on your planet currently reside. Some of you have signed up to pave the roads so many will have a track to follow. You are groove creators. Energetically you move into a higher frequency of awareness, paving a pathway for others to follow. When people begin to feel that their current paradigm no longer holds water, nor makes sense, they will seek an alternative. You are therefore renegades, and you came here to break aspects of the old world so the new world can be established. Nature is your guide and in winter plants often die just so they can re-emerge in the spring. You break old-world energetic molds by not allowing your awareness to be diverted away from you or your power to be channeled away. When you are in your power and in awakened awareness no one can touch you. No one will even try because your magnetic resonance will repel those who try to de-power you from getting too close. When the time comes, there will be a mass awakening on a global scale and those who were operating without awareness will suddenly face a reality that clearly does not support their old ways. Then, they will look for renegades like you to show them a new way. We would not ask you to awaken if it was not your purpose. We would not tell you that time is short if it was not so. We would not tell you that you have the power and the tools if it was not so. We would not be keeping you awake at night if it did not serve a purpose. It's time, as there is no other.

Who are these groups who try to de-power the masses, some of you want to know?

We have said many times before that in your free-will universe, dark and light are allowed to be expressed equally. Both are part of your reality and you have the potential to be the darkest angel or the most illuminated angel. Lucifer, the fallen angel, can be any of you who through free will, choose to express through darkness. Darkness is lack of light, so it is void of truth and love. When one is feeding you with lies, in order to advance their agenda, they operate in the dark. When one knowingly manufactures or distributes products which are harmful to you and your planet, they are operating in the dark. Dark is not necessarily evil. Evil is darkness coupled with an intent to cause harm.

When you create something that unknowingly causes harm, it is not darkness. When you learn the consequences of your creation and you continue to distribute your creation, you move into the dark grey of the spectrum. When you intentionally use that same creation in order to cause harm, that can be tagged as evil. Dark and light are on one continuum; their placement on that continuum is determined by awareness and intent.

You exist in a layered, multifaceted, complicated reality, and all of you carry a unique version of your own reality. There are points where your different realities intersect to create a movement within mass consciousness on your planet. Those events which create powerful shifts are known to you. They are clearly depicted in your history books and your sacred texts. With a gentle hug, we ask you to prepare yourself for accelerated shifts larger than any written in any of the books you currently have.

Why is it so, you may wonder? *How should we be prepared*, others may ask? *Should we worry*, others may inquire?

The upcoming shifts are coming because of you. You have created them from a quantum space. You can explain them as geological or geographical shifts, but the movements are created from the larger consciousness of which you are a part. Collectively, everyone alive on your planet knew of these shifts, and all of you agreed to be here before you descended into the birth canal to emerge as a baby.

What should we do, some of you may wonder?

You are to awaken and give intent for your path to open up to you. Allow your reality to shift and stay open. In this accelerated reality, when you give pure intent to move into your purpose today, you may find yourself shifting tomorrow. Some of you may feel that it is too soon, but, with love, we ask you not to hold back. Allow yourself to be guided to where you are needed because the other option is not any easier.

What is that, some may wonder?

The other option is that you find yourself in a reality where you have no more options and you are forced, even in your physical reality, to shift. Reality that is forced upon you usually is delivered with powerful fear components. Fear holds you back from ascending. We ask you to glide into alignment with your life purpose so you can ride the shift, rather than be buried by it.

Are we to fear, you wonder?

We have spoken often of fear. Fear is your neutralizer. It carries a reverse alchemy where gold is being turned back to lead. Fear is your greatest challenge at this time. As renegades you must form your own ideas of your reality and not buy the one sold to you through your media. With a smile, we would pull the plug if we could to assist you in disconnecting from the source of information that feeds you fear, but we cannot. It is not our purpose. We are here to show you your options by using light. You know everything that we know and when you feel inside of you that something is wrong, follow your feelings; do not follow your mind. Some of your technology is used ingeniously to numb you and disconnect you from your source of power. Some of you are so plugged in to your instruments that, unless you get a splash of water, you will not believe you are being flooded, because that is not what your instruments say.

What am I to do with this information, you may ask?

You are angels of light and your mission is to shine. Your collective light is the shift for which everyone is waiting. The change is within you as you are a code-activating consciousness, and, through you, a ripple is created, moving in concentric circles, to engulf the rest of humanity. Your codes are linked to Gaia and when you are ready she will begin to shift. Like DNA, each code has its purpose and mission.

Why should we be in a hurry to bring about this shift, you rightfully ask?

Because you have a deadline. Your deadline is NOW.

Why is it so, you may wonder?

When you began your mission, a deadline was given to reach a certain vibration or frequency within this great journey of consciousness, moving and expanding to finally meet itself.

Who gave the deadline, you may ask?

The collective you did, and you are now moving into the final phase of a change that is internal, as well as external, which will carry you forward to your next chapter as humans on this planet. The year 2012 marks a beginning, and an ending to a journey that started eons ago. The aim and mission is to reach a point where you can finally become aware of the greater story of your existence. Become part of your galactic family and your expanded universe. This shift is within your reach but you must reach it internally before it is absorbed and expressed through Gaia. We ask you to celebrate the moment-by-moment that makes up your now and give intent to awaken to your purpose. It's time. And so be it.

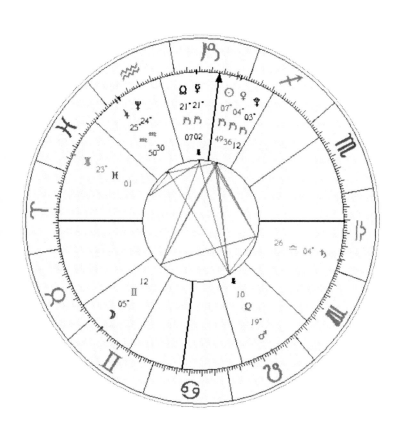

12-29-2009

Hi Dror,

Would you want to be in one of my radio shows in January. I am looking in scheduling them now and have the first and second Monday (4th or 11th) at 4 pm EST available to do this during my Dutch hour and rerun it on Wednesday at 8 pm EST.

No problem if you can't, so don't feel obligated.

Much Love,

Wilhelmina.

Learning to Fly

YOU ARE DEARLY LOVED.

If you were a bird you would not think twice before spreading your wings and flying. The process would have come to you as naturally as being alive. Birds do not fear flying, they just do it. There is much to learn from birds, as you carry wings as well. They are indeed hidden, but nevertheless they are on you and available to you all the time. You are an angel and you are so dearly loved. Like a chick in the nest, you grow; we, your brothers and sisters, are around you from before birth. We follow your every footstep; we love you without pauses and conditions. There is nothing you need to do or give in return. You are loved because you are family and you are part of us. As we look at you from above and below, hugging you, we ask you to open up your heart to the love from the other side. This love heals, as it nurtures. This love we direct to you is the substance we are made of, so we never lack. When you give us your hand we are already with you. Angels are everywhere. There are many of us assigned to each of you, so when you are in a body walking in duality, confused, in fear or pain, there are many of us who are walking with you holding your hands. Your journey is one of wonders. Many of you perceive your life as difficult, challenging, and indeed it can be. You came here to this heavy reality in order to learn that you really are not a human at all. You are an angel with wings and you came here to learn to fly.

Why do I have to come here, some may wish to know?

You come to this planet because this is where angels come to learn about their divinity. When you are with us you already know who you are so there is a different kind of learning. The journey through life takes you to experiences where you must face your limitations, your mortality, your fears. From such a place, you may emerge invincible, fearless and ready to do work—work that you came here to do—being a lighthouse. Angels are made of light and love. Angels can be in many places at the same time. Angels are vessels for energies which can reverse dis-ease and heal the sick. They heal by connecting, through love, with the one who has lost sight of who they are. When an angel shines light on the one in darkness, light takes over and illuminates that which was without light. When you come to this sacred place you call Earth, you are very much connected to the angelic realm because your memory is still intact. Babies come without the ability to talk because if they could they would tell all the secrets you came here to discover. They know it all and slowly they forget, as it is appropriate. When a baby looks at you and smiles she opens a space for you to join the angelic energy. At times she will follow you with her eyes, asking you to connect to the vortex of divinity that is hidden within her sweet gaze. Your journey starts from a place of knowing and ends when you have completed what you came here to learn. To some of you, friends, loved ones, and relatives left too soon, but it is not the life expectancy that determines the length of time you spend in a cycle, but your purpose for coming. Time is meaningless, as you are eternal. The dimension of time is only inserted for your growth and to create a richer environment for experiences. It gives you a context which you can use to understand the larger purpose of the system you named God.

Why do we need to learn about a system that we are a part of, some may question?

Because the larger consciousness you named God wishes to understand itself so it can become one with itself. It is the same with you. You carry within you the same micro purpose as the whole system. As you wish to be one with you, so the system God wishes to become one with itself.

What purpose will that serve, you may ask again?

All universes are birthed by what we call LOVE, which is source creative power that expresses itself through matter in many dimensions and realities. Through you the creative power of the system is being expressed. You carry the same frequency and purpose as the entire universe or system. You are all God messengers carrying, expressing, and delivering its creative power through fragments of energy. When those fragments of energy unite in the awareness of oneness, your mission is then completed, as you create light where light did not exist. It is your purpose and mission to create. When you mix light with light it creates more light, as you cannot distinguish one light photon from the next. They all merge to become one light source. Your purpose is similar. You are made out of light, and by merging your light with lights that are around you, you become one.

Why are you telling us all this, some may wonder?

It's time, is our short answer. With a smile we wish you to fly and experience your reality from a place that is elevated. You have a choice at any given moment in how to look at yourself and at your reality. When you wake up in the morning in gratitude for being alive, asking for the day to take you by the hand and lead you to where you are most luminescent, fulfilling your highest potential, you are in the realm of light emissary"-- a full fledge—a full-fledged angel with wings. When you wake up in the morning, wondering why you are here, anxiously awaiting the day to reveal itself in its burdens and drama, you are an angel in training, and we ask you to jump and take flight. There is never a judgment, and most of humanity are angels in training looking for their purpose. Those of you who are on this sacred mission of awakening, creating an energy vortex for peace on Earth to manifest, this is your time.

What is peace on Earth, some of you want to know?

Peace on Earth is the potential for this time. You have moved away from Armageddon, knowing that another choice was peace on Earth. Peace is not a practical political solution to your social and cultural conflicts, but a state of consciousness. You are getting closer to a vibration where the gap separating you from yourself is quickly closing like your hole in the ozone layer. You are approaching a state of awareness that embraces your oneness on a mass scale, holding a united vibration which can open up your dimension to the celebration that is all around you. We have told you many times that we like to party. There is a grand celebration scheduled and you are invited. The party is scheduled soon and your light is needed for this party to happen on time. Our question to you is, why would you want to miss this party?

How can we achieve peace on Earth, some may still ask?

Peace is your natural state, and when enough of you become peaceful, the vibratory rate of Gaia will come to meet this vibration, carrying you to a whole new reality—a reality that we can only describe as blissful or heavenly. It is as if you graduated one grade and moved on to the next. The first grade was one filled with drama, pain, fear, and hurt, as well as love and light. Your learning has the potential to move into a more subtle reality where your learning will evolve around melodic nuances and not ear-deafening explosions. This is what you came here for.

Will this reality be a part of everyone's reality, some may wonder?

Your planet is continuously renewing, and there are many of you who are in one body today and tomorrow they are in another. Like water streaming down a river, it looks as if the water is the same water, when in fact, the water is renewing continuously from the source. When a vibration of peace is powerful enough, a process will begin where those who do not match that vibration will choose to go home so they can refresh and come back more equipped while those who are aligned with this vibration will begin experiencing biological, spiritual, and physiological changes—even on the DNA level. This will affect not only their lifespan but also the physical perception and ability to intuit processes that are taking place around them. These qualities were not enabled since the time of Lemuria—over one hundred thousand years ago.

It is therefore that the two strands of the DNA in the double helix will grow and expand as more strands are activated in the twelve-strand system. From a human you are becoming an angel, or should we call it a galactic human with wings. There are many aspects of your journey that must align with the activation of your twelve strands of DNA, but the most essential component which activates and harmonizes your system rebuilding is—you guessed it—Love.

What kind of Earth will we have once we reach that vibration, some may wonder?

You are in a state of awareness where material wealth is a major concern to many. To others, food and water is their greatest need, and yet to others, feeling safe and secure is their current state of need. When enough reach the frequency of DNA activation through love, a change—slow at first but growing faster and faster—will begin to take place where your physical reality will begin to match your state of awareness.

What does it mean, some may wonder?

It means that the resource distribution, the safety, the abundance will be created from a place of equilibrium and integrity. It is then that the physical feminine vibration will align with Gaia to support life on Earth in a balanced way both within and in the outer physical reality. Your current state of awareness blocks Gaia from finding balance. When enough of you create within this balance, it will activate your dormant cellular memory, directing you towards a reality of the New Earth.

Is it grand enough for you, we ask with a smile?

So many of you knew of this potential and you also knew of the other potential where you looked for a new home in which to settle. You chose to stay on this beautiful blue pearl creating a change for the entire galactic system.

These changes are within your reach. We have promised you that we are always with you. You have promised us that you will wake up when we ring the bell. The bell is now ringing and it is your time to rise, and so be it.

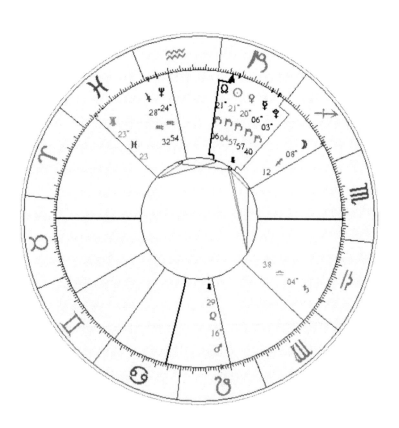

1/11/10

Dear Dror,
My apologies for how long it took me to edit the attached. It is brilliant and
and beautiful and I found it personally very helpful at this time.

Thank you for the privilege of healing with your words.

I will tackle the second piece later today. Please let me know that this arrived
in good form.

Blessings and love, dear one.

Light everlasting this year and forever!

With humble gratitude,
Luise

Dear Luise;
I have been thinking of you.

Thank you so very much. I just returned from traveling in the Negev Desert
and it was very cleansing and powerful experience

I miss talking to you. I will call next week

Love
Dror
Dear Dror
I look forward to that! I just now returned from another 4 days in the hospital
where they drained 5 liters of fluid from my legs and body. Feel much better
now. Making plans to hook up with specialists at Sloan Kettering who seem to
have experience with my type of tumor. More when we talk.

I want to hear about your journey in the desert...an Essence experience?

With love, honor and gratitude,
Luise

Sexual Energy Dance

YOU ARE DEARLY LOVED.

Many of you are lost at this time. You think the road leads you one way when in fact it is leading you to a destination very different than the one you imagined. This is part of the magic of being in a fog: you cannot see very far. You can shine your high beams all you want, but the reflection will blind you rather than show you your true destination. The next part of your journey must be *felt*.

There are many lightworkers now in a female body who carry a heavier burden.

It's not fair, some may claim. *Why is it so?*

It is so because not only must those females do their own work linking, staying balanced, and holding their own vibrations, they must also do the work for their male partners. The masculine energy is hovering above the crust of the planet and is not biologically linked to the crystalline grid hidden within the inner sanctuary of your Earth. The feminine energy is grounded and in alignment with Earth's vibratory frequency because it is biologically linked. The masculine therefore must go through stages to link with the planet's guiding forces. It must first find equilibrium within balancing male and female energies. Then it must link through a feminine vibration so it can be able to read and interpret the messages coming from Gaia. All of you carry both vibrations inside of you. The ratio of male to female vibration within you depends on your awareness as well as your ability to access memories from the time you were in both genders. For your memory to be accessible, your biology must be activated and you must be in touch with your feeling centers.

How do we know if we are in touch, some may ask?

The first indication is being in the now. If you are spending much of your time contemplating the past or the future, you are surely not in the now. Being in the now is being in touch with your breath and your heartbeat. All of you must breathe a few times each minute and your heart must beat many times a minute. The air you breathe delivers your life force which is absorbed by your lungs. Your heart then circulates the oxygen through the blood to all of your organs. Being in the awareness of your heartbeat and breath is you existing in the awareness of being alive in a body. It is also your best indication that you are in the now.

Feminine vibration is holding the key role in the planet's current energy shift. It is no surprise that we hug many more females than males at this time. It is not because we love you more in a female body, but because many more of you in female bodies give us your hand, asking us to lead you by shining light on your path. Do you think it is an accident that the women's liberation movement accelerated in the '60s? Intuitively you all knew that it was time for a big energetic shift. You also knew who was to lead that shift. The mass awakening of the '60s was the first indication that the prophesied trajectory of humanity was being challenged. All of you have danced in both genders many times, and as you have played your various roles, you learned about your uniqueness as well as your oneness in each role.

When you are with us you are energy without gender. You choose your gender based on your journey and lesson. When your lesson requires you to develop understanding of feminine qualities, for example, you may choose to be born in a body of the opposite gender in order to develop parts of you that are yet to mature.

Why is it so, some may wonder?

Accelerated learning is never easy, and when an angel wishes to learn about the feminine aspect of self, those aspects come as a challenge. Often, this angel will choose to be born as a male so it will be tested to learn through feeling rather than knowing. When you are born as a female it is not necessary that you learn about the feminine aspect, as it is your natural state. To learn about it you must at times experience it through the eyes of the other gender. Again, it is the circle that you come from, and within the circle logic does not always play by the rules.

You are a huge energy and as such you try to fit into a small biological vehicle. Not only is the vessel small, but it comes with further restrictions on how you must behave and operate. Most of the instructions have been written by those who wished you to be confined, obedient, and subservient.

Why was the feminine energy targeted particularly, some may wish to know?

The Goddess was not always under attack. There was a time when the Goddess ruled and there was a time she overstepped her powers. The pendulum then swung back with the masculine rising to correct and balance what was done. The masculine Gods then methodically, and over most of your recorded history, rewrote history, obliterating ancient records to be lost forever. The masculine created a reality where the feminine had to hand over most of her power through coercion, oppression, and subjugation.

This now is moving back yet again, and the rise of the Goddess power must come from a place of love and nurturing and not from a place of control and power. It is an interesting dance that you are now performing within your polarities. The roles of genders are in such a state of flux that many of you find your relationships disintegrating as a result. As you interchange roles, with females acting in male roles, as well as males acting in female roles, there is much insecurity within the familial and social framework. To add to that, the male now must concede to his feminine counterpart, so that she can move to center stage. This adds pressure to an already fragile union. Your relationships appear to us as if you were floating on a raft down a whitewater stretch and the river is raging. Your role is to stay balanced within yourself as you move down the river. Every time you choose a male or female body, you must take under consideration your place within the male/female lesson of balance. It is one of the most important obstacles you must jump over on your spiritual journey.

How do we balance our polarities, some may ask?

Your journey of understanding who you are and how to manage energies is in the forefront of the shift many of you are now experiencing. There are many levels of learning. The basic one is honoring the life of each other. The highest level is working within the realm of sexual energy. Within this spectrum you come together to create energy through merging your polarities. This energy may be directed to creating new life, but it may also be directed for the purpose of shifting and expanding your consciousness, directing you to new heights where the fabric of your reality opens to the multidimensional being that you are. Procreation is the basic premise of merging creative life force and sexual energy. However, most of humanity practices using these sacred energies without awareness, which keeps them earthbound and unable to fly.

When you begin to use sexual energy, connect with an open heart, and become a vessel for pure love energy, you create a divine dance which gives birth not to another human, but to a new Earth. The sheer power of this dance is enormous, as it uses your most potent source of power with the highest frequency available to you. Procreation is the physical manifestation of this dance, but when you climb beyond the physical, you give birth not to babies but to light. You impregnate Gaia with sacred energy which further increases her vibration and yours. You are a source creative power. You can manifest in the realm of the physical or in the realm of pure energy. When you direct your creative power and sexual energy to bring new life it is a sacred act, but not the highest in the realm of learning about energy. Most of humanity was directed to view procreation as the be-all and end-all for the use of sexual energy. From our perspective it is not so. The dance of sexual energy and love produces the most powerful luminosity in the realm of light. This love dance represents the greatest potential for a shift of human consciousness when done with awareness and pure intent.

How do we know if we use it with the right awareness, some may ask?

When you are exchanging being in the now without fear, guilt, or shame you are well on your way. Clearing yourself from these anchors is an essential step to becoming a pure vessel for love energy. This energy has been tainted for eons and has been tattooed into your cellular memory. To free yourself from these anchors you must be fearless and connected to your feeling centers. These old patterns are anchors that do not serve you and are there to limit your experience, holding you earthbound. Your aim is to fly. You may learn by going it alone, but relationships accelerate your learning and make your experience richer. Your current chapter reads that you are moving into an accelerated learning where the Goddess energy is taking center stage and the male partner must be in a supporting role. The Goddess role is not only to lead but to guide, nurture, and love so that those struggling with a sense of imbalance, or a lack of guidance, will be able to use this feminine energy to form a link.

We love you so, and we wish to use simple metaphors to describe your journey to you. For you to connect to the internet, many of you use a Wi-Fi signal. Without a signal you are unable to link to your source of information. The Goddess is the transmitter of that signal. We hear some of your masculine partners say, "How can that be? You surely are not speaking of my partner. My partner is not spiritual. When she speaks to me she makes no sense and she is often misleading me rather than guiding me." We do not see what you are telling us. With a smile, we hug you as we know who you are.

You have been both males and females. Some of you are also creating unions within the same gender. There is never a judgment as all is sacred and leads you forward. Within unions that are of same genders the masculine/feminine polarity still exists. When the electromagnetic attraction is weak, the union will be weak as well.

The guidance coming from the Goddess is sacred and revered at this time. This guidance we speak of is hidden in your biology and in the electromagnetic field that surrounds you. It is not in the words that gems are hidden, but within the subtle fields around the body. Although all fields are part of one electromagnetic continuous movement, the emotional field is the one linking you to your partner and to the source of information available to you. This field is accessed through the heart. It is therefore the type of connection that you hold with your partner that is important, and not the level of spiritual knowledge or verbal guidance that matters.

What do we do with that information, you inquire?

Keep your heart open to your partner. Work on allowing the flow of energy to exchange as it is in the core of the creation of new feminine/masculine balance on your precious planet. When your heart is open and you are exchanging, the work of linking the masculine energy to Gaia is done automatically. When her heart closes up, it is as if you have unplugged the source of the wireless signal and you can no longer link.

How do we keep our hearts open, some may wonder?

You are to stay in the now, feeling your breath and heartbeat. When you are in the past or in the future your heart may close up, but when you are in the now it stays open as it must. We love you so and we connect to you through your heart. When you place your left palm on your heart and your right index finger on your third eye, you allow your knowing to keep circulating. Place your attention on your heartbeat and breathe deeply. This simple act can keep you open and linked. Love is your magic carpet to higher vibration. We, therefore, wish you to be in the awareness that maintaining an open heart is part of your mission, and so be it.

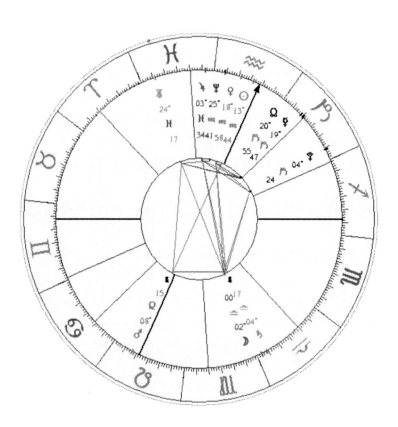

2-2-2012
Attention: QUESTIONS

Dear G.:
Thank you for your email. I am back. We can continue our conversation. I am also planning to come back sometime soon to the Yoga room.
Love

Thank you Dror.
I am at a difficult place in my life and I just don't know what to do quite honestly.

Hello Dror.
When we last emailed you told me that things are not always what they seem and you told me I would find out soon enough—I am still trying to understand what you meant by that—Since our last email I have been experiencing some spiritual awakenings. I listened to a message that told me to do something (go to the carwash, which I never do. My car is quite dirty and I did not have my car washed) but when I got to the car wash I saw my ex-boyfriend's co-worker driving the same truck that my ex-boyfriend drives. I am struggling with the break up, as it went unfinished and without closure. I was blown away and now realize that I am able to communicate with my angels and so happy about it— But now what? What did it mean at the carwash if anything???? I am so lost and confused. Any input would be greatly appreciated.
Thank you,
G.

Dear G.
This is your path and direction to open up and begin to communicate with your guides. Do not ask "now what?" Be grateful for every moment even if you do not feel great. Learn to work with your higher part. The break through is pre-sented to you on a silver platter but you have to choose to grab it. Say thank you to yourself for every moment that you awake and keep listening to the messages that come to you. That is the way which leads you to the treasure. If I will tell you the road and where it is treasure is hidden, you will not benefit from it. The treasure is within you and you are on your own treasure hunt. You can move away from your pain. You choose to be in pain and you can also choose to be in joy. Keep walking with gratitude. Find a healer nearby. You can call me if you wish.

Love, Dror

Move, Shake, Flood, Fire

YOU ARE DEARLY LOVED.

"Thank you," we hear you say. We hug you with tears in our angelic eyes and we say, "Thank *you*." You are moving upward in leaps and bounds while we are right here along with you leaping with joy. This is your time. We feel the fear that keeps crawling up your spine; we can see your geometry of insecurity and confusion. We can even see your dreams that are filled with unsettling sights. We sit by your bed holding your hands as you go through one of those seemingly endless, sleepless nights. We direct you to keep breathing, remaining calm, as you are facilitating work in your sleepless nights for others working on the other side, so the progress will continue according to plan. You are a facilitator of a shift that is now in the midst of its path, and your energy is needed to see humanity reach its destination.

What destination is that, you may ask?

You have come to create a shift so you can graduate from one lesson and move to the next higher vibration.

In the higher vibration many more mysteries will open up to you. Your sixth sense, as some of you like to call it, will become one of your main sensory tools through which you conduct and manage your life. You are well on your way to becoming a multidimensional galactic member of the universe around you. We speak often of "multidimensional" beings and we would like to pause for a moment, explaining to you what we mean by that. Your reality is being fed to you through your five senses. Your brain is programmed to analyze the signals being fed to it, organizing them into a picture, telling a story upon which you can then act. Many in your day-to-day do not look any further beyond what they see, feel, taste, hear, and smell. They walk on Earth acting and reacting from a place that interprets their life picture according to what they can sense: if it is not there, it does not exist. If you would ask a person to wear, for a moment, the sensory environment of a bee, a snake, or a bat, they would experience a reality that is very different than the one you experience, although you both would be looking at the same thing. You would be looking at a flower while the bee would miss the flower altogether and only see the pollen.

When you exist in a reality that is being fed by your senses, you are bound by the limits of your vehicle and cannot go beyond the frequency that your brain can interpret. This is a reality that you are now leaving behind, moving from a limited dimensional view to a multidimensional vista.

So what does it mean for us to be multidimensional, some may inquire?

It means that you begin to get glimpses of your oneness with everything that is around you. You are the bee, the flower, the snake, and the bat. You are expansive beyond your wildest imagination. When you begin to sense and experience your vastness, you begin to experience harmony with all that is, starting from your brothers and sisters, nature, the sky, the stars, and even visitors from other systems. You become an intergalactic member of your universe. When your awareness reaches the stage of oneness, a greatly richer picture of your reality presents itself to you through your newly heightened awareness, and you develop capabilities to process these new visions through your feeling centers. What it means is that many of you will begin to experience an expanded reality in your daily life.

It sounds pathological to us, some may say with a smile. *We hear of schizophrenics who see things that no one else can.*

Yes, we say as we hug you. Some of them indeed, can see what most cannot, but that is due to a faulty wiring of the brain. You, however, are moving into a vibratory rate where the ones with pathology will be those who cannot experience an expanded reality. This is the next phase of humanity's consciousness-evolution process, and the one who cannot keep up with the next step will be at a disadvantage.

Multidimensionality becomes your reality when you open up. You exist on many levels, realities, and dimensions, all of them overlapping, intersecting, in a web that is dizzying in its complex magnificence.

How do we open up to this expanded reality, some may wish to know?

You already exist in this reality, but the veil which hides you from your expanded you is thinning. That is why many of you experience sleepless nights, day-dreaming, and telepathic communication with relatives or friends. Many feel unexplainable anxiety and insecurities as if the ground is unstable. It is part of the shifting and expansion of your sensory system. It is being upgraded. You now are beginning to sense more and more thoughts which are floating in the ether. You begin to develop prophetic ability, almost anticipating what will happen both in your life and in the lives of those who are close to you. Some begin to get insights and visions of world or global events. All are potentials floating about, now being accessed by more and more angels walking in duality. If you think for a moment that this expanded reality will simplify your life, you are in for a bit of a surprise. Your action-packed movies are slow-motion merry-go-rounds in comparison to what you are about to sense. It is why we urge you to slow down, learn the art of inner balance, deciphering what is yours and what isn't. If you think your life is complicated now and your sensory systems are overstimulated, wait until you shift gears. Like a caterpillar, you exist in a reality where you are mostly aware of the leaf in front of you. You are about to enter into a short cocoon phase where many of you will begin to grow wings, and wham, you soon emerge on the other side as a butterfly. Reality looks very different to a caterpillar than to a butterfly.

Why are you telling us all of this, some ask for the hundredth time?

Because we love you, is our short answer. We have been through this journey before and we know the road. We know the pains, the joys, and we know your destination. We see you walking on the highway north as if you know where you are going. You are in a state of transition from one level to the next. This has never happened before in your recorded history as a human on this planet. The dial is turning and you are moving upward. Many of you experience this turning internally as a stomach-twisting sensation of unexplainable anxiety. The body translates the different sensory stimulations unfamiliar to it with overburden on the kidneys, specifically the adrenal glands. We wish to hold your hands, leading you to a place where you can find answers to what is happening around you, as well as inside of you. Nothing outside of you can give you the appropriate answer. We ask you to learn to breathe, slow down, and keep your biology well nurtured and balanced. Eat healthy, drink lots of pure water. Do not ingest substances which numb you. Filter the sources of information that feed you your news. We ask you to understand that everything you sense, you also digest. Learn to pick your diet carefully. Do not allow junk to be fed to you too often. Your energy and balance are at the core of moving through this phase with joy and health.

Your attitude is your guide through this phase. Find the time to offer gratitude to yourself, your partner, and those who are around you, to the trees, the birds, the soil, the sun, your food, your mother-in-law. Yes, her too. We know who you are and your attitude reorganizes your reality so you can ride on the highest frequency. Walk in an awareness that all around you is an external manifestation of the creative power of love, no matter how difficult it may seem to believe. Your source of creative power and that of the universe is love. When you melt your own borders, reaching out to the elements that surround you, you become the bird, the tree, the food, and yes, your mother-in-law. There is no more separation between you and the world around you. You have entered the dimension of oneness, the multidimensional reality of which we speak. Many of you only experience this sensation as a baby and as an adult for a brief moment through orgasm. Some advanced angels can enter oneness through meditation and spiritual rituals. From our perch, the vibration of humanity is heading to a greater sense of oneness than ever before. It may appear at times that the opposite is true, and for some, reality will appear as though it is going the other way. However, the vibration of the planet is moving away from duality to the direction of unity consciousness. As soon as you begin to separate one thing from another you find yourself moving away from oneness. With all love, we wish to impart to you that when large movements take place in your physical dimension like floods, hurricanes, or earthquakes, your planet becomes, for a short moment, united in the energy of sympathy and compassion. Every moment of such magnitude creates a step for humanity to climb upward. After each event that has shaken your physical landscape, the wave of united emotions flooding your Earth is like a tsunami which pushes the larger consciousness, of which you are a part, towards the realization that you are all connected, all part of the One. Humanity can be compared to one body. However, some may still say, "My finger is inflamed but my toe feels great." The body part of the one entity that is out of balance would certainly affect the balance of the whole entity.

You are the sum of all of your parts. When one part is sick, you are sick. You do not say, "My liver is sick but I am healthy." Whatever part is imbalanced within you must be healed for you to be healthy. Again, like the human body, each part of that body is essential to maintain the health of the whole. When you say "I" you do not refer to only your toe, but you include all that is you: the fingers, legs, hands, head, and all the rest. Earth seeks to find equilibrium of her different systems. As Earth aligns, she must shift, move, shake, flood, and spew fire. The effects of her physical alignment ripple to your hearts, guiding humanity to a higher consciousness. Earth, through her powerful dance, creates portals for global moments of oneness. Some "devastating" events serve the process of ascension, and the planetary consciousness is climbing as a result. With all love, we know of your fears; we know of the process of pain and suffering on your precious planet. We know of each baby, each child, that is buried under the rubble and drowned under the waves. We hug each of them individually, welcoming them back into the celebration, congratulating them on fulfilling their mission of assisting the greatest shift humanity has ever experienced. All those affected knew of this potential before they came down through the birth canal and they volunteered to steer humanity higher. We know the pain of losing a loved one and it is sacred. You are an angel going through a human experience, and your journey is the most revered journey anyone can take. You are so dearly loved just for being here, doing what you are doing. You are never alone; we are always there waiting for you to look up, or down, and greet us. As we hug you one last time today, as well as every day from now on until eternity, we ask you to wake up to your mission and understand the power that each of you holds in this great game of creation. Each of you holds the key within to the whole. You are an angel and so are we. As we merge our light and love together, we illuminate the sky and the Earth so all can see. And so be it.

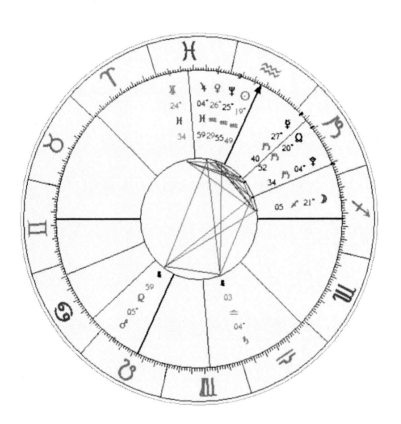

2/8/2010

Dear Dror

Ok, I digested. It is being absorbed right now. I am
at work. I can hear from my left and from my right
children receiving dental care, crying in pain and
fear. This is the way we (mis)treat our children in
the XXI century, with all resources we have in this
rich, well-educated place. This is how we are forming the new generation of health-professionals. I just
can't conform and subscribe to this.

Your welcoming open heart and love remind me and
help me to maintain my light up, sending love and
healing energy, instead of feeling sorrow for them.

You must also know that I hold you dearly in my
heart all day and all night long. I had so many
dreams I can't count them anymore.

I would like to tell you about writing the angels messages for children and adolescents when we talk.

Love

Oriee

Sleepless Nights

*Y*OU ARE DEARLY LOVED.

Thank you, we say. And again, we hug you.

Didn't we already do that, you ask?

Yes, dear brother and sister. Every time we meet family, we greet with hugs. It is how you know we are around you. It is a sacred act for an angel to be called and summoned by a human. When you create the sacred space in your heart aligning with that space inside of you where the angelic frequency is residing, we come to you, celebrating through song and dance. We are in love with you and there is no greater honor for us than to be holding your hand, sending you a frequency that we can only describe as love. You and we are connected through strings of love. We hear you all the time. We listen to your thoughts. We know how to interpret your dreams. We can read the language of multidimensions. It is our vocabulary that you use when you are asleep. It is easier for us to communicate with you when you are asleep. To many of you, our frequency keeps your nights less restful. When we contact you in your sleep, you are hovering in the deep sleep state. Once we begin to communicate with you, you remain in this deep sleep state, but you may feel as if you are completely awake. It is not a dream per se that you are experiencing, but an activation of the larger you, expanding, as your mind is off guard. To many, our meetings feel like a hangover after an all-night party. Once the intoxication ends, you lie exhausted in bed but unable to sleep. To some, you feel like the bed is vibrating and your cells are tingly. Sound familiar, we ask with a smile? We know who you are.

We need our sleep, many of you will claim. *How can we reclaim our nights*, you may wish to know?

You simply must ask, is our short answer.

Many of you are being upgraded while you are asleep. Your biology is being furnished with new abilities and your "software" is being enhanced. This takes time as your biology must integrate your new tools. The tools are being sent to you and delivered through the rays of sun, as well as unseen high-energy particles that are coming from outer space. You have asked to move upward, ascending in vibration, and your sleepless nights are part of this path. As we hug you, we ask you to sit for a few minutes before going to bed and speak to your winged friends. Ask your angels for a good night's sleep once in a while so you can recharge. Make a ceremony around your night. Hug yourself and ask them to stand around the bed but not *on* the bed so you can get the energy needed to continue your path. You are the master of your journey and your intent is honored always. You are so dearly loved just for being here, walking the walk. Ask for what you need and you will receive. We cannot promise all nights will be restful but at least some of them will give you the nourishment you need. After all, you have asked to move forward and we need to help you fulfill that wish as well.

You can be in that space of expanded awareness when you are awake in your daily lives; however, to many of you the mind hinders the attempt of the greater knowing to come to the surface. As you begin to expand in daydreams, or are flooded with intense feelings, the mind steps in, asking the brain to interpret these signals, thereby channelling the feelings and emotions through the intellect. Usually it is stopped by fear, the survival mechanism kicks in, and halts the process of the expanded consciousness moving into your awareness. To many of you it is so threatening to expand because there are no words which can describe these sensations; there is no imagery that you can use to frame what you feel. Expansion means one thing: being in the moment, one with all that is around you, allowing the movement of your feelings to guide you through your mystery to where there is no more why, how, what, and if.

What next, some may wish to know?

You are nearing the next phase of your journey where some may feel as if the acceleration was carried out by a rocket booster into outer space orbit.

Why so, some may wonder?

The accumulative energy now stored on the surface of your planet held by Gaia and angels like you is reaching a critical point where the new trajectory of your journey into the new era will become more apparent. You are renegades. As such, you lead the pack, as your biology is integrated with the new tools, giving a sense of urgency and importance to your awakening. Most of humanity is still in a sleeping state. The next planetary shift will involve jolts and tremors that aim to awaken energetically many more of you who are still in bed. All of you must awaken each from within your own individual path and journey. Some of you will experience the jolts within, some on the physical plane; all is appropriate and by design. Each jolt will be catered to the one experiencing it. There are no co-incidences or accidents, and there are no victims on this journey. Whatever you experience comes from the same divine source, which is the source of love. It may come in forms which you may not be able to comprehend, but this game has divinity in each atom of each molecule of each cell. There are no atoms which are out of line with divinity. Your journey into and out of a physical body is but a small fraction of your essence. You are God dressed in human clothes going through a human experience which aims to awaken you to your divinity from a place of choice. Many have experienced lifetime after lifetime where you had no access to this link between your human costume and your divinity. In this lifetime everyone will get a chance to awaken to the part in them that is expanded and will receive an introduction to membership in the expanded galactic club of which we all are members. Each will get their own custom- designed script, and to some it may come at the last moment before going back home.

Are we to fear, some may wonder?

There is neither time nor space to be in fear. It is time for celebration; it is time for joy. It is time to free yourself from the limited idea of who you are and learn to fly. You learn to fly by flying and not by reading about flying. Sure, you first must prepare, but then comes a time when you must jump. The moment in time when you must let go of reading about flying to jump, to spread your wings, is getting closer and closer. All of you can fly. Fear is the only energy which can freeze your wings and give gravity the upper hand. Fearlessness is the hot air under your wings which carries you to the top of the mountain.

What do you mean by flying, some may still wonder?

Flying means opening your expanded awareness, using it to navigate your now at every moment, even in your sleep. Flying means being in the moment-by-moment of your life, seeing all through the eye of a master shining light and love to your environment, allowing the miracles that are part of your angelic birthright to manifest without you trying to control or explain their origin. Flying means being in the knowing of who you really are, as well as the power that you possess to manifest and experience that which you choose. Flying means allowing your expanded self to lead your day-to-day, as if life is being handed to you with a magic manual giving you the set of instructions exactly when you need them and not a moment too soon. Flying means trusting that whatever crosses your path comes from divinity and tells you your own story. Flying means experiencing your life on a heartbeat-by-heartbeat, breath-by-breath level, knowing that all is the eternal gift, all coming from the one source. It means that the fragmented realities experienced through your senses all are aspects of that one source. Those fragments are all connect through love. Your journey is about soaring above your physical reality while being part of that reality, keeping a balanced connection both to the divine and to Gaia, knowing that you are all of it. It is time, and no long preparation is needed to awaken. All the preparation was done before you came here. You are ready and we are ready to guide you towards the next chapter of your story as an angel on a journey through the magnificent mystery of existence, and so be it.

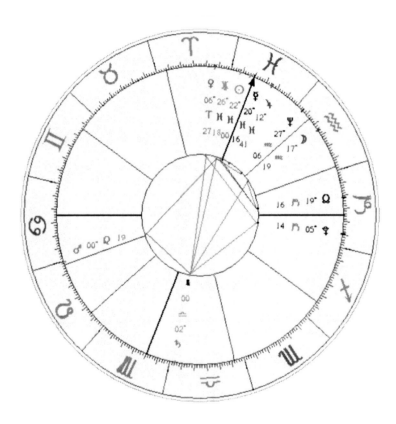

3-12-2010

M. I have had such trouble writing this. Maybe because I am so excited and am over-thinking this whole process. I hope this is what
you needed. I asked the angels...

Reflex Sympathetic Dystrophy-a neuropathic pain disease that
effects all sympathetic nervous symptoms at different times. It
has affected my arms, legs, stomach, and is bothering my neck/back
of my head (r side) presently.

I have noticed that it has a lot to do with emotions, stressors,
seasons, weather, and I am thinking diet plays a significant role as
well. It may be going to the organs or it may not. I am currently
having problems with my bladder and my kidneys. I have yet to find
a doctor who knows enough about the spread of this disease to
know what it can or can't do or how to decipher if it is the disease
or something else until the limb is balloon-like or frozen.

At one time I could tell what was the disease and what was just
an ailment but these days things are meshing together. I have been
fighting sinus? headache symptoms w/ double earaches pretty
much all winter and 4 doctors cannot decide between it being a
sinus infection or the RSD. I have given it to GOD and his angels
because it is too big for me.

For everything I have gained from this I have to keep reminding
myself I am the lucky one.

Thank you

N.

And So Be It

YOU ARE DEARLY LOVED.

We are still waiting for you, hugging you, and holding you in our arms. Through this ordeal, not once are you left alone. Not once are you forsaken, and you are always loved. Our commitment is for eternity. We are always by your side no matter how challenging and difficult your path may seem.

Why are you telling us this again, some may wonder?

For a moment you have forgotten that you have an entourage at your service. At times we see you walking your path as if you are alone. As we wrap our wings around your fragile frame, we ask you to close your eyes, activate your inner vision, and feel us hovering all around you. Some of you may even smell our fragrance. We wish you to open up your inner vision, allow our love to be felt, and allow us to guide you on your journey. Your journey is second to none in this universe of free choice, and you are the one who directs, at any given moment, the movie of your choosing. You select the players, the scenery, the timing, and you create the storyboard—all for one purpose.

What is that purpose, some may wonder?

The purpose is to find yourself, your own divinity, and truly discover who you are. You come here to this remote planet in a hidden, scarcely populated area of your galaxy, believing that you are separated from everything, and through your inner process you must discover your oneness with all that is. Your oneness must be found within you. Once you discover who you are and begin to live your mission, the road opens up and you create ripples of oneness which circulate. Like a magnet, you attract all the pieces of your life together into one unified field. That unified field is made out of the substance of love. Once you radiate love, you are shining and sparkling like a star in the night sky. Many of you believe that the process of becoming one is through serving God. Belief in God is equivalent to belief in self. Belief in self must come from love of self. Many of you begin by loving God, wanting to serve, yet you soon find out that the road reaches a dead end so you can no longer advance.

Why is that so, some may wish to know?

It is because you started from the end. Who do you think God is? When you begin searching outside yourself you give your love to God, and we see some of you wondering when you will receive love in return. This puzzle has been waiting for you to discover from the day you began your journey. Collectively, you are God. You are *it*, and when we say to you "And So Be It," we ask you to awaken to your *divinity*.

We are here to awaken you to your true identity so you can act as the lighthouse you were meant to be. When we take you by the hand, we ask you to trust your path, knowing that you are being shown the highway to a new reality. Nothing that you know will stay the same; all of you are undergoing a shift that is spiritual, biological, and physical. You are moving from one level to the next higher level. It is not a choice anymore whether to ascend or not, as your planet is ascending so that all of you must either join this ride or step off the planet, recharge, and come back more equipped. We know who you are, and you are so dearly loved. There is a powerful yearning for some of you who are of high vibration to help us from our side. We ask you to stay where you are because your light is needed here on your planet. On our side there is only light, and you will join us soon enough. You are never judged; your choices are sacred, and you are honored above all. You are part of the energy of Gaia, and where she goes, you go. You may resist, but that may only make your journey more challenging.

What are you telling us, some may ask?

We are asking you to open up to the mechanics of your journey, trusting that you are loved and cared for. We are asking you to follow your feelings as they represent the guidance from spirit. We ask you to use love in your interactions with your brothers and sisters, your Earth, the natural world—most importantly, with yourself. We ask you to walk as if there is an entourage of angels all around you caring for you, because in all truth, we are around you and we never leave.

We wish to speak to you about your next step. Your biology is now changing and your cells are being furnished with new capabilities. Many of you are losing sleep because the body must reintegrate the new coding that is being sent to you from the galactic transmitters and facilitators, delivered mostly through your sun. You think you are alone in the universe. If you could see the preparation that is taking place all around your precious planet in anticipation of its graduation, you would be in awe.

The next chapter in the story, now unfolding, is that many of you must clear up your past anchors, strings, and the heavy residues accumulated through the cycles, so you may become lighter, vibrating at your highest potential. To many of you it feels as if the opposite is happening, and that you are being held back by seemingly endless problems and obstacles, which show up as health, financial, relationship, and emotional issues. Understand the sacredness of these signposts. You are here to clear all that needed to be cleared and to do it now. The meaning of accelerated time is that you are now living, reliving, and clearing all your clutter buried deep in your drawers, stored in the akashic library, so you can make room for a new blueprint to manifest itself. This new blueprint will manifest into a New Earth. Many of you lightworkers who signed up to shine your light feel that you are carrying the load for everyone else, and there are many roadblocks on your path to shining. We hear you say at night, "If you wish me to shine, why do you place so many blocks in my way?" We know who you are. Trust that all these blocks and issues are just an illusion waiting to be blown away, swept to the side. It feels insurmountable but it is not. Your linear time is just an illusion. If you try to resolve everything on your plate through your linear thinking and calculating, we promise you that you will have plenty of clutter left. The accelerated path has to be walked one leg on Earth and the other in heaven. You must be connected to your higher guidance, following it with trust.

It is the age of miracles, and you cannot expect magic when you are in your logical frame of mind. You must be open and trusting to allow the energy of magic to flow so it will interact with your biology, with your environment. The history of your stored heavy residue archived in your akash is being cleared worldwide. The akashic records are stored in crystals buried deep in the belly of Gaia. They are now being reprogrammed, through the crystalline grid, to prepare for a new vision of Earth. It is a magnificent sight. There are many bumps in this road, and as you move faster it feels like the ground is shaking under your feet. In fact, since it is you who are moving faster, you must then jump over many more of these hurdles to become clear and free. We wish to tell you that when you move away from heaviness, you are like us—an angel. Once gravity loosens up its grip, you can fly.

Your mission now is to become aware and to awaken, so you can transform what you experience, elevating your vibration as high as you can. Being in higher vibration does not mean that drama disappears and you have no more challenges. Higher vibration means that everything that presents itself to you is seen as sacred. Receive it as a gift and welcome it with gratitude. You then clear this gift by purifying it using the spray of self-love and sending it back to Gaia. Gaia will transform it. The residues that you clear will never come back. Your mission is to rewrite your storyboard, implanting it back into your akashic library so it can manifest the new vision for you and the planet. Your single candle can create such luminosity that you gift your family/friends circle with a sacred choice to awaken and begin to see, as well.

Yes, that is nice, but I am sick and I feel old, tired. I am also not doing well financially, we hear some of you whisper to yourselves. *How can we carry our burden as well as shine our light?*

With a hug, we wish to tell you that this is your mission. What you carry is a choice that you made, and you have a choice to clear this burden, moving higher at any moment. You wanted to clear your heavy part and this is your chance. "I am tired," we hear you say to yourself so no one could hear. We hear you and we know who you are. We know that you are tired and we ask you to give us a hand so we can help pull you. Some of you give us a hand and then also use a cane. When you ask for help, trust that you will be shown the way. Clearing is a sacred process and at times may feel unpleasant. If you hold on to your current pole, then set intent to clear, understand that you are resisting your own movement forward. To clear in this accelerated time you must let go of the "must do" and "must have." Then, let go of the "what if" and "how will I?" When you wake up in the morning, give yourself a hug and ask to be shown the way to clear the heaviness from your life, moving forward. Ask to be shown the way to balance and health, then let go. Ask to create love within you; trust and let go. Your entourage will spring into action, as your request is sacred, and you will be given not one hand but a dozen to pull you forward. Quiet yourself enough to hear the directions, and slow your pace enough to see the road signs. All you need is catered to you. Many of you are conditioned to follow a path that was already paved by others. It is a new era, and you are the one who must pave your own path using your own compass. You are built for it; you have the power, and you came for this purpose. We ask you to release your resistance so you can allow the heaviness to stay on the ground and become part of the soil where it belongs.

We are afraid that we will lose everything, we hear you say.

Indeed you will, we say with a smile. You will lose some weight, you may lose your fears, and you may lose your health issues. You may even lose your drama. You could also lose a friend or two, but you will gain mastery over gravity. An angel is one who can fly. It is your mission at this time to spread your wings and ascend. This is your purpose, and your wings are built into your vessel. We love you. With a hug, we ask you to awaken to the grandest time of human history, play your part, and so be it.

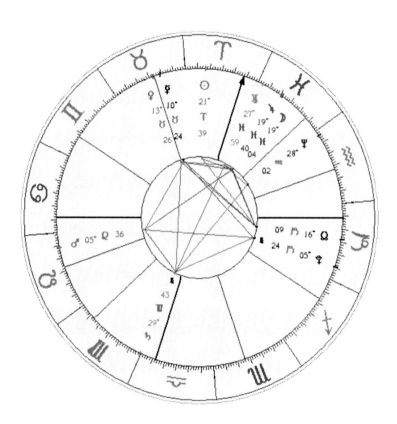

4-11-2010

Dearest Dror,

Thank you so much for sharing that about M. and the girls; it is what I feel most of the time but then the ego fear steps in. Thank you for everything else that we share.
I felt such a powerful force just before you hung up the other day. I keep remembering that you were the last one I saw before I came into this life. I don't know what it means or where we are going but I am so so grateful for every moment of connection with you. As you said the not knowing is sacred too.

I have been calling upon all that I have learned in my past lives to be with me recently (Maria shared the concept with me) and I have felt my role in the Mystery Schools paralleling what I am doing now... holding this space, healing, and loving....it brings me strength.

Love

Nicki

Slowing Down

YOU ARE DEARLY LOVED.

Where have you been, we ask with a smile?

I am not sure, you answer.

There is so much confusion permeating every facet of your day-to-day. We see many of you walking fast, juggling so many balls at the same time, but at night when you take stock of the day, you are not sure of the purpose of all the running and juggling. Many of you are walking on your treadmills as if possessed by an inner force that moves you faster and faster, when in fact you have stayed at the exact same place. Moving forward has to do with slowing down, which is again counterintuitive, as are many aspects of your ascension.

What does it mean to slow down, some may wonder?

Slowing down means that you must begin to feel the inner workings of yourself rather than figure out the outer workings of your external reality. To move into your power, you must realize that *you create inter-*

nally everything that shows up in your physical reality. We ask you to connect to the place where everything that you experience emanates from—*inside* you. We see those of you who are trying to figure out the politics of your environment so you can be more effective and influence those around you, believing that this facilitates your progress, helping you to move forward. With all love, we ask you to know where you are heading before you press on. Moving forward has very little to do with your external environment and everything to do with your internal politics. You are a powerful angel, and as such, you create your world every moment. Even during your sleep you are working on creating. The purpose of your life is creation. Creation is a magnificent aspect of coming down to this planet and wearing a human costume. At home, creation happens instantly following a thought. In your linear, limited reality as a human, the same happens but with the delay of time. Knowingly or unknowingly, thoughts and feelings are the power behind all creations. It is why we ask you to slow down—so you can become aware of the chatter that takes place within. As you move from point to point, thinking and feeling without awareness, you continually create, but the creation is like a car driving on the highway without a driver—as if you were a passenger in a driverless taxi. Not a recommended safe path for you to reach your destination.

Many of your obstacles and blocks are created within you while you are busy running on your treadmill, making things happen. Often, as you think you are moving forward, you encounter insurmountable blocks that you yourself created while being busy, and then you blame karma or whoever volunteered to play the blocking role for you as the culprit. With all love, we wish you to understand that there is no one out there who is more powerful than you regarding your own journey. You are the God that you pray for at night. You are the angels, and you are divinity. We are part of you, and when you slow down enough to feel all the forces that are part of your entourage, there is nothing that can ever block your path, your potential, or your destiny. When we say "destiny" we refer to your highest potential as an angel. Destiny is not a set, predetermined aspect of your life, but your highest manifested potential—the one you aspired to while planning your life on the Earth plane. Your destiny means the completion of your contracts, the clearing of your karma and becoming the highest vibrational light being. You become a full-fledged angel walking in a human body spreading love and light wherever you are.

That is your mission and there is no greater mission at this time of Earth ascension. All of you came here to play a role in the most profound change this planet has ever seen in human consciousness. You are the instigators and renegades who must break free from the idea of being a human, moving closer and closer to becoming an angel in human costume. When enough of you shine your light you will illuminate the whole planet and all those areas dominated by darkness will be transformed. This is the power of which we speak. It all begins with you becoming aware of your thoughts and feelings. For that you must slow down and quiet your inner noise. Become aware of your breath, your heartbeats, your "now" . . . and from that place creation will begin to reflect your highest potential.

What now, you may wonder?

Now it is time for the wind to blow, for the Earth to shake, both within you and externally. You are moving into the energy of sharp and abrupt changes that has to do with global adjustments to the entire planetary consciousness. We see phenomena that will be perceived as irregular all around you, in nature, and within you. Thoughts and feelings that are new to many of you will begin to move into your wakened mind, lighting up a part of your brain that was mostly dormant up until now. We see many begin to sense events before they occur and receive clearer communication from the circle. There is a greater communication between our dimension and yours now than there has ever been on your planet since the time of Lemuria. We see vortexes of communication opening worldwide like your World Wide Web. The communication that was reserved for only shamans, high priests, and holy persons is now becoming an everyday occurrence for many of you. We see many of you who fear these new tools and use them with caution as if you might break or lose something if you overuse it. With a smile, we wish to use an analogy so that you may *feel* rather than *analyze* your paradigm. You are like a toddler who is learning to speak. As she begins to get used to her vocal cords, much of what you call gibberish is taking place, and many of you enjoy it as parents. It is, however, an essential component of learning to control and use the vocal cords. The same goes for using your intuition, power of extrasensory perception, premonition, and higher guidance: the more you use it, the more proficient you will become. You are evolving at a tremendous speed, and we see many of you who are fearful of using your newly found power in your day-to-day. We see that some of you reserve it to use only in spiritual forums or when you are alone in the room with your candle. This power we speak of was always there for you, but now more and more of you are remembering how to use it. In the past, only a few renegades had access to it. The multitudes are now becoming activated humans through intent. Our mission is to activate more of you so you will remember who you are, awakening to your power and divinity. It is up to you, however, to choose if you wish to use your new tools or hide them in a drawer. There is never a judgment. You are loved just for being here on this dense reality learning about energy and creation.

Why are you telling us about all that, many of you may wonder?

It's time, we answer with a smile. These tools we speak of are the ones you need to maneuver your new reality. The more you become adept in utilizing them, the more joy, peace, love, abundance, and overall well-being you will experience. There is a split. The split is between light and dark, new energy and old energy. The ones using their new tools are the ones who will be able to navigate in the new energy with greater ease. If you try to find your way using an old energy compass you may get lost—and many of you are lost at this time.

To us it all sounds too abstract, some may claim. *There is really nothing concrete to hold on to*, others may complain.

If you are using the new tools, you know of what we are speaking, and we can see it in your geometry. We know who you are, as we are with you every single day that you are alive on this planet and then afterwards as well.

If you are one of those who has no idea about what we are saying, we ask you to slow down. Take time to walk in nature, observe trees, roll in the grass. Take time to speak to animals and birds, touch crystals and stare at the night sky. Sit down in front of a candle and just hug yourself. These acts, which may seem like a waste of time, are the most valuable gifts you can give yourself in order to learn the language of the new energy. You must return to your center and introduce yourself to your environment. Move away from all modern communication gadgets at times and just be quiet in silence. Listen to the chatter that takes place inside of you, and when the chatter quiets down, you will hear us. It is then that you will feel our hugs, and the feeling of love will bubble up inside of you, creating ripples in your cells. Inside you is where the meeting takes place, and when you get "there" you will feel it. This is our promise to you.

Nothing that we tell you is new to you. We are your brothers and sisters of light, and we come from your future to awaken you. You have asked to be awakened and we came to fulfill your request. We cannot awaken you if you do not wish for it. Your planet is governed by free will. If you are one of the angels who can read our messages so that they are resonating within you, know that it is your time to awaken to love, health, and joy, riding on the highest frequency now available. Your example will illuminate others and will pave the way for a new dawn for humanity. We love you and we are part of your essence. We have come to meet family. There is nothing more sacred than the hug between an angel and a human. We hug you now, wishing you to become all that you can be in this cycle as this is your mission, and so be it.

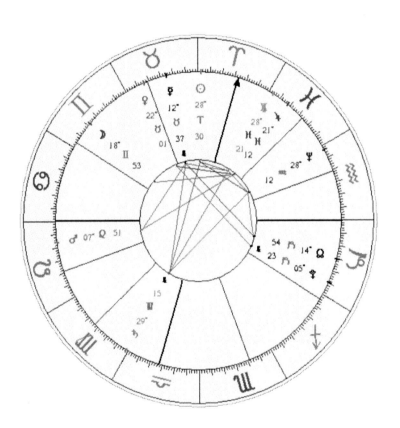

4-18-2010

Dear Dror,

I didn't know why i told you about the child i lost. But i do
know now.
The moment she died, she came into my heart. Her name
is F, what means little woman. For 30 years she was with
me, always, night and day. She was so beautiful. She was
my guide, my angel. She left me this morning, to be born
again. I think i knew on a deeper level this would happen
when the time was right.
I never felt so alone.
My classes were amazing this morning, i didn't know who
gave them, not me, and nobody moved after the last three
Om's, i didn't dare to move myself. I think it was her but
she was not present.
When i came home today i started to cry for hours and
i think i just stopped, don't no for shore. I feel totally
empty, there's nothing to hold on to.
I trust it is my journey but oh God, i wish that i knew
what to do.

I just wanted to share, but maybe you saw it already.

Love,

N.

Notes from 4/18/10 – Woodstock, New York
(Luise Light was buried today in Rodef Shalom
cemetery, New York. She came through in the
beginning of the message.)

Self-Love

Hello, I am okay. It has been an amazing journey and I am now on the other side of the fence looking in. Before, I was on the duality side, and now I am whole. It is sunny and warm. I am surrounded by loved ones and friends. I feel love and I emanate love to all of you who journeyed with me when I was in a body. I feel only joy. There is much to do and I will be working tirelessly to bring about the vibrational shift that we all seek. There is a great excitement here and all are talking about the trajectory of humanity at this time towards higher ground. I am with the angels and they all say, "Hi." They send their love and they do have wings. I have been on this journey before and now I am flying again. How I've longed to fly. I wanted my wings back. I wanted to see the light shining all the time and I wanted to be home. It feels so much like the home I was always looking for.

What a joy bubbling in me as I connect to you and allow my thoughts to stream through you. There is a large group of angels who are assigned to facilitate this change on Earth, and they know each and every one of you by name. This journey I was on felt so familiar, and once I left my old body it was as if I knew the way. All the signs were clear, and the love and light I feel all around is a sensation I could never have imagined possible until I felt it. I am one of the angels, and I will be walking hand in hand with those of you who seek my guidance. I have been longing to guide and I asked for it. I am grateful for having had a fulfilling cycle and I will be back for sure. For now, I am here where I belong . . . at home.

Now the angels are coming through:

YOU ARE DEARLY LOVED.

Communication with the other side is always sacred. We celebrate the golden bridge created between your dimension and ours. The process of transition is one of great joy both to those who come home and to those who receive them at the gate. The gate is full of flowers and it is always open. When one enters this gate they have made the transition from a human in duality back to an angel, and there is no going back in the same body. One must return to the selection room and choose a new one. We are all here celebrating the return of one of our dear ones and there is only joy. We ask you to understand that there is no death—only changes from one state of awareness to another. We are part of humanity. As we celebrate the return of family, we also allow you to feel the love and joy that we feel if you quiet your senses, joining us for just a moment. When you walk across the threshold, arriving back home, you are part of the family of angels that guides and directs humanity from this side. There is no time delay, as there is no time on the other side. We hold you dear and always make your return a reason to celebrate, honoring your path. Many of you believe that your journey is about one thing. However, from the other side of the veil, it is another. You celebrate one's life based on what they achieve, and we celebrate one's life just for walking the walk, viewing this life based on how they felt while doing whatever they were doing. From here everything that you do is similar in importance and honored by all. A janitor and the chairman of the corporation that heads the physical space in which this janitor works are looked upon as equal. It is their individual thoughts, feelings, and vibrations that we celebrate after one's cycle ends since none of the trophies, certificates, or the fortunes one collected throughout a physical life can be taken back with them. Your thoughts, feelings, and vibrations, however, stay with you for eternity. None of what you have achieved on your spiritual journey is ever lost as you accumulate power, wisdom, and spiritual fortune from one lifetime to another. Karmic debts—cleared and paid off—will never come back. The wisdom you gained and the light you created to illuminate your surroundings do accumulate, and are deposited in your akashic bank account for eternity.

Your journey looks very different to us, from our perch, than it does to some of you who are walking the walk of a human in duality. There is a great story that is now unfolding in front of your eyes and it is the merging of our dimension with yours. In fact, both of the dimensions are merged; they always were and always will be.

So what is the difference, some of you may wish to know?

The difference is that we always had access to yours, but now more and more of you have access to our dimension. Once you gain that access, you instantly expand the idea of who you are, beginning to realize, then, the mission and role that you came down here to play. You call this process enlightenment or ascension, and we call it coming home. You have been walking in the thick forest looking for answers, trying to find clues as to who you are, what the purpose is of all this pain, this suffering, this hate on the one side, while on the other side there is only joy, happiness, and love. As we hug you tightly we say: this is the most sacred journey an angel can make when she wants to learn about energy. You are a vibrating manifestation of spirit. You contain within you aspects of God, and as such, you wish to explore your own magnificence through creation. In this unique place you are shielded from your true identity and you have free choice at any given moment. Your free will is expressed through the choices you make and the energy that you emanate while making those choices. The walk of an angel on this planet is known to all as this journey is one which offers you the widest spectrum of energy from which to choose. You can be the brightest star or a black hole. Both options are available to you and whatever you choose is honored. When you come home you do not pay for the choices you have made. You only "pay" for the energy you created when you return to the same playing field through the law of karma.

Your idea about heaven and hell was attributed to the life you lead after your life in this physical dimension ends. However, it was meant to refer to your life in the physical dimension. None of the rules of your duality apply when you come back home.

What do you wish us to do, some may wonder?

Celebrate, we say with a smile. Celebrate, *celebrate because you are eternal*, and what most of you are fearful of is death. When you know that no such thing exists, you are free to fly and soar above the reality of survival, becoming the angel. Your awareness is the fortune that you accumulate throughout your cycles in this physical third dimension. Everything around you is created for you to have context so you can grow and learn. You live, breathe, give birth, and go through physical death in a holographic movie created for the purpose of your exploration of energy. What we ask you, then, is to explore, fear not, live and breathe every moment knowing that you have asked to be here so you can grow, adding to the system you call God.

Some of you may ask, *So what is the purpose of all this lightwork that we are asked to do?*

You are so dearly loved, and as we hug you we remind you that you have asked to be on this planet so you can fulfill a mission, a desire, that you have held for eons throughout your many cycles. You were waiting for this time when the biggest shift happens so you can play your part using all the knowledge you have gained throughout your many lives. You have asked us to remind you and you have promised yourself that this time you will remember. The time is now and we are your alarm clock. You set up the timer to ring at the eleventh hour and it's time. You are ready and you have all the know-how within you. When you awaken, all your cells begin to sing a different tune which is heard in heaven, supporting the alignment of Earth's vibration with higher dimensions. You are the piece that this puzzle is missing in order to be complete. For this puzzle to be whole, you must wake up and begin to vibrate at your highest potential. When you do, you, your brothers and your sisters worldwide create a web that links all of you like a grid. You may then elevate the rest of humanity through your own resonance. You do not need to know the others, nor do you need to be aware of the type of energy that you emit. The work is to become one with self.

How do we become one with self, some may ask?

Through self-love, we answer with a smile. It is always the same answer. Love is the highest frequency, bridging all dimensions and realities. For you to ascend to the next level you must vibrate with love. First to self and, as you walk with self-love, your resonance begins to spread to others. We never said that vibrating with love is like a walk in the park. You have walked, you have learned all the skills needed to vibrate with love, but accessing them, clearing away those parts which block love from flowing freely through you, is your mission. It is, indeed, the most sacred mission at this time. You are asked to elevate your whole existence and begin to levitate rather than walk. The process of becoming lighter is through allowing more light into your system. We ask you to allow more light to flood your physical vessel from within. It will support your cellular structure and help you cleanse. The more light you allow inside, the lighter you become and the easier it will be for you to levitate, defying the forces of gravity. Love is light; the sun emits light; light is stored in chlorophyll, and light is part of each cell in your body. You are light and we are light. When you give us your hand you allow even more light into your system. It is a joyful time for us to be bridging our dimension and touching your heart. If you wish to link with us just hold your left hand on your heart with your right hand on top of the left. You will feel us, then, all around joining in with our invisible hands. You have asked us to be here with you. Now you must trust that we heard you, that we are here ready to guide you and to love you throughout this journey. You are so dearly loved, and so be it.

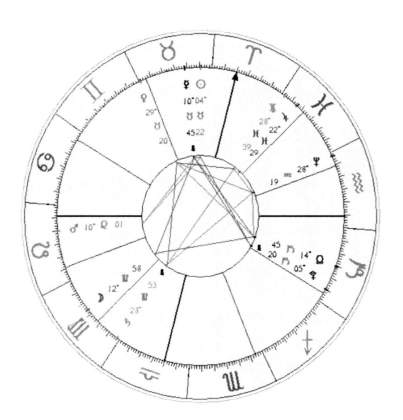

4-24-10

Dearest Dror,

The concert went 'very well'. I picked up M. and we needed
half an hour to find a parking spot, only half an hour to dance
salsa left, with sooooooo many people around and than the band
from Haiti came, it was horrible, very dark energy, i got scared
and wanted to go home. It was good, i was home early and
enjoyed reading and thinking of you.

I still have something to share about Thursday with you. But
maybe i will not be able to reach you before you leave. So here
it is: The moment you felt and communicated we were too
vulnerable, i saw you as a light, connecting, all most merging
with my soul or my light and i saw you at that moment, and i
understood. You are amazingly beautiful and dear. There was
a presence of a Goddess behind you she had sort of horns on
her head, but it was not scary, little bit like my funny hair but
bigger and she was soft and sweet. There are not really words
to tell you how amazing it is to share all of this in grace with
you.

I went to a numerologist today, his wife was in my yoga class
and invited me over, she liked my number? So funny, it was very
interesting what he told about me and about the changes on
earth. He could see very clearly what is happening with me
these day's. Some life we have to live on this earth. WOW!

Have a safe trip and i would love to join Saturday Night.

take good care,

N.

Leaking Roof

YOU ARE DEARLY LOVED.

It's beautiful. The vista is always magnificent. Whether you walk up the mountain or down the valley, what you see is just a small portion of the story. Your "true" story unfolds under your feet, though you cannot see it, and above your head which you can see. But when you look up during the day all you can see is blue sky or clouds which holds you in separation from the vast space that is all around you. When night falls some of you get scared because there are no defined boundaries to that space above you. It seems to stretch forever. You always look for the borders and lines which can define who you are. Your mind always looks to hang on to limits. What happens when you choose to expand beyond the limitation of your mind? You guessed it—you have to trust and move through fear.

You are all beautiful angels who came from the vastness of being one with all that is. Without mass you are very expansive. When you squeeze your vastness into a form, you must begin to examine where you begin and where you do not begin. You spend much of your time trying to discover your own boundaries when in fact you have none. These boundaries are only a construct of your mind holding you in an illusion of separation from all that is. Your *body* does have defined boundaries, but it is not *you*. It is just your borrowed vessel for the duration of your trip across the mountains and valleys. When you complete the trip, you allow the vessel to return to its origin, becoming part of the mountains and valleys. You then expand and return to your vastness again.

As always, we try to wrap you up with love and describe to you your journey the way it appears from our perch. Many of you believe that truth matters. How would you explain to an angel child, who sees you as geometric patterns and a beautiful display of lights swiveling in all directions, that this is not the truth? The angel child will say, "But I can see it." A human child who looks in the same direction will say, "I can see this woman. She has curly hair and she is wearing a striped dress." If the two children stand next to each other and each describes her version of reality, who would be telling the truth?

We ask you to go out on a limb, trusting that you are vast without really seeing it. Trust that you are powerful without really sensing it. Trust that you are beautiful despite the mirror which may insists otherwise. We know that we ask plenty. We know that it is not easy.

We know you and we love you. We wish you to know yourself and love yourself. When you do, you enter into the circle, connecting to family and connecting to God. When you love self, you have moved onto the dance floor of spirit. There is nothing more sacred than an angel in human costume loving herself, celebrating her own form. The fallen angel was the one who could not find, within, the love. He therefore fell from the heavens and became earthbound. Love is the fuel which propels you higher and higher. Self-love is the foundation of love. It is always within, where all your experiences begin. You are the source of your reality and whatever you accomplish in your external reality must first, within, be created. We have said that before, and with a smile, we may say that again in your future.

How do I start to love myself, some may wonder? *I do not like the one staring at me from the other side of the mirror*, others may claim.

Love is the air you breathe when you are not in a body. Love is your essence, and to begin loving yourself, you have to link to your essence. We would carry you on our wings to that place where love hides but it is against the rules of the game. It is on you to find us and it is on you to give intent to find the love inside of you that is so elusive. The seed of self-love is planted into your consciousness as part of your original blueprint. Seeds carry the original blueprint regardless of whether they have the conditions to sprout. So do you. All of you carry the seed of self-love, as it was given to you as your birthright walking in duality in this challenging school called Earth.

What now, some may wonder?

It is on you to discover those places where the conditions will support the sprouting of your seed.

What are those, some may wonder?

Water and sun, is our short answer. If you live in an environment which does not allow these conditions to manifest, you must either consider moving to a new environment or change the conditions. If you are under a roof where there is neither rain nor sun, you may wait for a long, long time for the right conditions to manifest. When these conditions finally arrive, do not be surprised that they arrive in the form of a powerful tornado which blows the roof off your structure. Some of you may wish to wait for the storm and we promise you that storms will come both internally and externally, but your learning has to do with manifesting the change within, not waiting for help from Gaia. Gaia will help and many roofs will be blown off in the wind, as collectively you have asked to grow, becoming the potential stored within the seed form.

The purpose of a seed is to sprout and become a plant or a tree. Your purpose is the same. You must become who you are by creating and negotiating the conditions which allow you to sprout, growing to your full potential. Some may say, "But I cannot move or change because this is what I was given. I am stuck." With a smile and a soft hug we say to you: you have been there before, remember? You have been, before, the victim. This time you said to us and yourself before coming down that you will try harder to change what seems to be unchangeable. We keep repeating that you are the master because, unlike the seed of a tree, you are a miracle seed which can bring rain onto you when you choose to and find also sunlight when you so choose. It is your purpose to grow, but when you do not, there is never a judgment, and you remain a potential, like the seed. Seeds can remain in a seed form for a long time until such time that the conditions change and you sprout. You are here at this time to sprout. We represent, for some of you, the first rain and the first rays of sun here for your awakening. You must remember your original form, as many of you find it comforting to remain a seed. Some of you feel that it is nice to know that you have a potential, but why bother making an effort? Seed form will do just fine. You are loved regardless of your choices, and your free will is honored above all, but we must whisper in your ears that this time is different. Your sprouting has the potential to create a magnificent tree and that tree will create a new type of seed. These new seeds can grow to create a new version of humanity, one that is closer and more in touch with the original intention—the one many of you have forgotten. You are here at a special time and it is not a coincidence. You have asked to be here and have stood in a very long line, waiting for the right condition to manifest, so you can experience this time in a mature body which can create, manifesting miracles. Our question to you is: what are you waiting for? The sun shines regardless of whether you see it or not. Rain falls regardless of whether you are experiencing it. All of the elements are there, and it is on you to bring them into your reality so you can rise from the ground toward the heavens.

Yes, some may claim, *but we have a spouse who blocks our sun and a financial condition which blocks the rain.*

As we hug you from all directions, we wish to remind you that last time it was for different reasons, and you remained in a seed form as well.

How do we change what seems to be unchangeable, you may ask?

Nothing in your reality is unchangeable. What seems unchangeable is your own fear and belief that things cannot be different. When you give intent, with a pure heart, to find the love inside of you, your reality will begin to shift and change to reflect your new direction. If you are under a sealed roof, holes will form so as to allow moisture and sunlight to penetrate. When holes are formed we see many of you who rush very quickly to cover the leaking roof overhead, again blocking the rain and the sun. Your outer circumstances must change for you to move from a place of dry darkness to a place of moisture and luminosity. For those conditions to manifest, at times you must allow the roof to leak and not rush to repair it. We see many of you who fear change, and we must impart to you that change is coming. It is on you to embrace it or try to block it. The new flow of energy is all about moving you to higher ground through change. We ask you to celebrate that which you have asked for, beginning by intending for the change to start with your seed. Your sprouting is the beginning of the New Earth and it is magnificent. We wish you to celebrate walking the mountains and valleys, knowing that, as you walk awakened, you plant new seeds, the foundation for the New Earth. This is

a sacred journey that begins with you loving yourself,
and so be it.

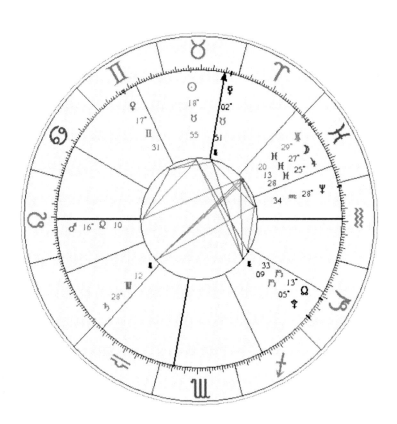

5-9-2010

Good morning Dror,

It is a gloriously beautiful day here. I hope it is also in Woodstock.

When we spoke on the phone yesterday you asked if I wanted to tell you what had happened the day before and I just didn't want to dredge it up again. So, I hope you don't mind, but feel that I can open up to you about yesterday.

I felt really off-kilter yesterday (and Friday as well) and after work I went to visit the woman in whose shop I am thinking of opening my own business. We took some measurements of areas I can work out of and talked more. I went home and just basically made a deal with myself that I was going to be "bad" since I had been so "good" whilst going through all kinds of stress this last couple of weeks. So I did. I drank several glasses of wine, ate some things I normally wouldn't have (some snacky stuff which wasn't really too bad, but it was processed and I haven't been eating processed stuff, and about 12 pieces of chocolate), didn't do my spiritual evening practice, just basically let myself go out of control.

Well, I woke up just as out of control. My thoughts and feelings were swirling - felt like a thousand things were going through my head and my body was feeling all kinds of feelings and I kept trying to center myself, but as soon as I did, I was swirling again. I felt like I have so many things to do and so many decisions to make but unable to do them. I feel like I need some kind of energy work to get me through this.

I know there are a number of things going on besides the stuff I am facing, such as processing the therapy I had two weeks ago, I am also in a weekly class which is designed to bring up our "stuff" so we can recognize and deal with it in a better way, and shift our consciousness. Mercury is in retrograde. And then, I opened my email today and check out the Weekly Kabbalah Tuneup from Yehuda Berg:

L. K.

Being Still

YOU ARE DEARLY LOVED.

There is much movement all around you. It is the age of movement, and in order to be one with the movement you must learn to be still.

Why still, some may wonder? *Aren't we supposed to be moving?*

The movement that is taking place all around you directs you towards your highest path. When you are still you can feel the guidance coming from the wind and follow it. Many of you feel that you are moving in circles and in some ways you are correct. The movement is indeed in circles with the direction upward, which creates a spiral. Another word for an upward spiral is ascension. Both you and Gaia are spiraling together. When a leaf falls from a tree, often it spirals its way upward or downward. The leaf has no agenda and it allows the movement of the wind to carry it. Many of you are trying to control your path to such an extent that you are resisting the guidance that is gifted to you from Gaia and your angelic entourage. We ask you, when appropriate, to ease up and be like the leaf. Allow the wind to carry you to where you need to be and to twirl you up, down or sideways, letting go of fear about the landing. Trust that you will land where it is appropriate for you to fulfill your mission. Your next chapter is about learning to let go of so much and to remain light.

We see many who try to gain so much knowledge about their path that, when the time comes to use their knowledge, they still try to control the outcome. The outcome is always guided by your intention. There is a wonderful simplicity in the way energy is translated into matter. Your thoughts and feelings are like a set of instructions that come from the master commander to its troops. Once the order is given, the master must allow the troops to fulfill their mission by following the instructions. We ask you to be still so you can focus on the set of instructions you are sending, rather than micromanaging the troops who are following the higher order of instructions. There are many layers to your reality, and we ask you at this time to follow the path which directs you to reunite you with your real power. As an awakened master you must realize your power, using it not only when you are walking in your day-to-day but when you are asleep as well. We never ask you to let go of what serves you. You are only asked to let go of what does not serve you. By doing so you are moving into your power and aligning with your true path. You are so dearly loved. The angels are always with you, ready and always waiting for your instructions. It is on you to make the step forward, asking for what you wish by becoming still, giving intention to move up to your highest path. Once you do, you must trust that your intent was recorded and celebrated.

Your angels do not wait too long, as time is short on this path. Soon you will begin to receive directions about where to go and what to do. These directions came from you through your intent. You then must follow the intention with action while staying still and balanced inside. As you do, you begin to see the love connection that weaves all the different circumstances creating your life. You will then begin to see yourself as a masterpiece in which every part of that masterpiece serves a purpose. You no longer judge good or bad, but you become peaceful with what was and become grateful for what is. Experiencing your life from a place filled with peace and gratitude aligns you with your highest path. These directions are the simplest, most profound set of instructions to move you into the spiral of ascension. You are living in times of great upheaval. Much of the turmoil is presented to you from within your close circle. As your inner cellular structure is aligning with the new electromagnetic frequency of Gaia, your inner structures must follow and align with your higher purpose as well. The set of instructions coming from the powerful feminine Goddess who is now rising is affecting all of you. Many paradigms around you are now shifting. It is on you to weave them all together by being still and flexible so the new you can emerge rather than break apart. Many of the shifts are coming from your close circle because they act as your mirror to you while you act as a mirror to them. Your close circle is the first ripple in the change that you must experience; however, we see many of you who try to bypass this ripple and become lighthouses before taking care of the core ripple. Your close circle is your mirror and you must deal with it first.

How do we deal with it, some may ask?

You must become peaceful with your mirror so when you look at it the one reflected in it feels balanced. Your mission must grow in concentric circles and it must begin at home. Your truth, power, balance, and peace must be exercised at home before it can be translated to transformative light which facilitates others. Often your close circle is the most challenging because it reflects you back to you. When you conquer your mirror and you emanate love to the one who is reflected to you from your mirror, you are then ready to shine your light fully, beaming it from the top of the lighthouse to those lost at sea.

Do I have to love those who are hurting me, some may wonder?

With a hug, we ask you to see the magnificence of your masterpiece and by realizing that you create everything in your life, you can then infer that you can, as well, un-create everything that you have unconsciously created, changing all that feels heavy. You do not need to stay with those who hurt you, but you must realize your part in attracting someone who hurts you, becoming more peaceful with your painting. You can then move into gratitude, allowing yourself to actually thank the one who hurt you for showing you those parts of you that need work. Once you understand your own dynamic, you may move from the one who hurt you to the one who loves you. When you love self you can no longer attract people who hurt you. There will be no magnetic polarity to attract them. You will become invisible to the energy of the abuser and will become visible to the energy of the lover. You have a choice at any given moment to change your life from the darker spectrum to the lightest spectrum by claiming your power and light. Your light is always there, but at times, like a pilot light, it is very low, remaining just enough to sustain your flame. Your mission is to shine fully, allowing your light to be visible. Your spouse, children, relatives, friends, coworkers, and those who you interact with in your day-to-day are your mirrors. When you look at the mirror in the morning, feeling love for the one reflected, your close circle will begin to rearrange the constellation and positions of its members. You, therefore, may lose those who do not match the way you feel about yourself.

You are the center of the ripple, and you create your reality around you based on the energy you emit. Your own energy is at the core of all movement. We wish you to never allow your thoughts and feelings to be those of victimhood. Victims have no power as they believe that everything that is happening to them is a result of circumstances and greater powers. There is no greater power than you to manifest your own journey and it is time to awaken to this knowing. Over millennia many of you have given your power to anyone who asked for it. It is time to ask for it to be returned to you with interest.

How do we get interest on our power, some may ask with a smile?

What you have given is yours. When you ask for your power to return to you, some of you will experience it as coming back tenfold to that which you have lost. The reason is that you are now ready to host a higher vibration as your body is upgraded and able to carry a greater capacity of energy in comparison to the power you once gave away.

How do we start, some may wonder?

You begin with your body. First and foremost you must become peaceful with your vessel. You must activate your chakras, allowing the cords of shame, guilt, and fear to be cleared from your sexual centers. You must work on self-love until such time that your body vibrates with love. Your greatest challenge is to clear your sexual centers and begin to sound the divine music that your body was meant to play. Your sexuality is at the core of the campaign to limit your power. You must free yourself from all the "downloads" that were "gifted" to you by your institutions and religions. Your vessel is divine and sacred, not just your head. We ask you to begin there. Loving yourself will begin to ripple to your close circle, and they will react to your new frequency. Many will resist you if this frequency is new to you because of their fear of losing you or their own fear of change. You must then continue with the path of self-love becoming like a pendulum learning the art of returning to peace and balance. Everything around you will begin to shift as you walk the walk of mastery. Your cells will vibrate differently, your body will begin to sing a new tune, and your close circle will begin to change, to mirror this new you.

How do we learn to love our bodies, some may ask?

You begin by caressing it, is our answer. What a mother does to her child is caressing; what a couple in love do is caressing. We ask you to do the same. Learn to love yourself. Get reacquainted with parts of your body that you have not looked at closely for a very long time. We know who you are and we are in love with you. There is never a judgment to how you walk, as your walk by itself is celebrated by all of us. It is you who asked us to remind you, awakening you to your path, and we are here through your invitation. Always create a ceremony around your body; honor your sacredness before you eat. Honor it before you exercise or mix sexually with yourself or another. Honor your body, creating a ceremony around all activities relating to your vessel, and your body will "hear" it so that your cells will begin singing a harmonious tune resounding in heaven.

You are a master and we ask you to give intent for your path to be revealed to you. When your path opens up in front of you we wish you to take the first step, then the next and the next, trusting that you are fulfilling the greatest mission you have been waiting for— being an activated, awakened angel walking on Earth, vibrating with love, and so be it.

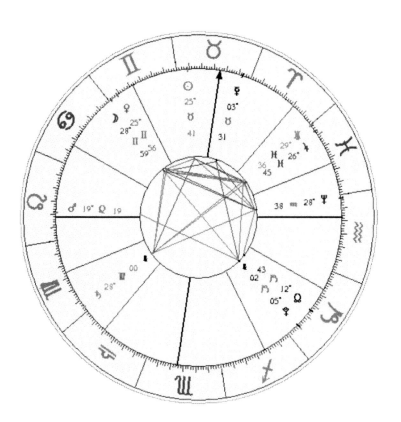

5/16/2010

Dearest Yasmin:
I was happy to connect with you at Tara.
I have been going inside today. Needed some rest
I am doing fasting and silence just meditating.   I felt like I
needed to get back my energy and ground. I worked in the
garden planting seeds. It was a beautiful day

  Let connect tomorrow

Much love and hugs

Dror

Follow the Beat

*Y*OU ARE DEARLY LOVED.

Yes, we can see that you are ready, and we are ready as well. Some of you feel anticipation for something, but you are not sure from where it is coming or what it is you are anticipating. Your cells know of the shift that is taking place in the electromagnetic fields around you but your body cannot interpret the signs because they are not being delivered in a linear fashion.

I feel confused, I feel lonely, I am tired. These are the comments we hear often. *I want to go to sleep and wake up when all this is over. What should I do?*

We answer with so much love: sit down and hug yourself; take time to love yourself.

What is happening to us, you want to know?

You are changing, but the change is not only in your perception of reality, it is also in the way your cells sing. The tone and frequency of your living tissue is changing, and as your physical body shifts, so must you. Everything around you seems the same but it is not. In time your scientific community will look back and say, "How could we have missed the signs?" There are so many of them, but fear is your biggest challenge. When science walks halfway across the bridge and meets Spirit, new doors will open to link the brain's left hemisphere with the right hemisphere so that the next leap will be more supported. At the moment, all that is happening must be processed from within. It is a new type of skill and many do not like it. You feel strange that you need to rely on feelings rather than facts. There are many who subscribe to the reality of facts, and indeed your reality is delivered to you through your senses in a linear fashion. This reality was created within you and that is why it adheres to your instructions. If you choose not to see something, it will not be there. Those who wish to have proof of all that is a happening around them may need to wait for a long time. When finally the "proof" will be "corroborated" you may look back and say to yourself, "How could I have missed what was in front of my eyes?"

We ask you over and over to focus on *unlearning* rather than learning. At times it is more difficult to allow the new to enter consciousness without the benefit of the intellect explaining what it means. To many of you the concept of the unknown is terrifying. You want to know as much as possible so you can be prepared. What if the next step has not been written yet and it is on you to pave it? How can you create something completely new if you hang on to the old? The new is so new that the only dance you can follow is to allow your legs and hands to be carried by the beat without controlling or even knowing the name of the dance. You must trust that the movement of your hands or legs will respond to the beat when it is playing, and move flowingly. There is no right or wrong. There is only you learning to fly when before you thought you could only walk. This journey requires you to learn a whole new language that is yet to be part of your day-to-day vocabulary. Learning and being prepared from a 3-D perspective is like a toddler who wishes to get ready for her pilot license. The learning has to come slowly and your set of skills must build up one on top of the other. You first must learn to walk, and then to talk, and then to read before you try to fly a plane. Try to be childlike and open to whatever comes to you and learn through experience. Most toddlers do not need a teacher to learn to walk or talk. They are open and by being in a stimulating environment they absorb the information. Advance that toddler forty years, place her in a foreign country, and the task of learning a new language appears more challenging.

We see so many who take the Spirit dimension seriously, digesting so much of the information available to instruct you on how to advance and move forward. With all love, we must tell you even there to slow down. You are the master. You chose your path. Your choices, then, are always sacred and honored above all. However, we—your brothers and sisters who have been where you are now—must impart to you that the next step is more about letting go of what you know. All you need to know is within you as it always has been. Your link to Spirit is your birthright and if you wish to study it in a book, that book may direct you to some method, but it may not be your method. We ask you to open your own manual and get the access card to your own library. The knowing is part of your biology and can be accessed at any time. You access it by intending to open your own book. Many of you search and search; that search then is sacred. It is, however, the opening of your own library and accessing your own resources which moves you from one plane of reality to another.

Ascension rarely comes from studying mantras or sacred texts. Your vibration is linked to your biological vehicle and cannot be experienced only in your mind. The next step in your evolution must be *felt within and experienced*. You can talk all day long about a beautiful piece of music or the divine taste of dark chocolate, but the reading and hearing about it can never take you to the actual experience of listening to the music or tasting the chocolate. You come here to this planet to experience a version of reality that bridges matter and spirit. On your journey, some of you may move to mainly Spirit or mainly matter, but only the balance of the two achieves the purpose of spiraling upward in this divine school. Many of you speak of love. When you actually experience love through your inner and outer senses, realizing that it is everywhere, it is then that your reality shifts.

This is all too abstract, we hear you thinking to yourself. *We wish to have concrete steps of what we need to do.*

Give us a hand and let's move to the beat. Allow your body to be absorbed in the music and let go of definitions or methods of dance. Allow your deepest knowing to be expressed through you.

How can we go through our busy schedules and day-to-day busy lives with such an attitude, some may complain?

You must slow down a little, is our short answer. If you are so busy planning and scheduling everything in your life, when will you make space for magic? Can you schedule ascension or connecting through love? Can you schedule flying lessons or dancing with your angels? Of course you can, but it may not appear right on schedule. In your 3-D reality angels are notoriously too late or too early depending on with whom you speak. Angels do not keep watches because, from the dimension of Spirit, they are always on time.

How should we walk in both worlds, some may ask in frustration?

You already are walking in both worlds and the question we wish to ask you is: have you noticed? Your choices in every moment that you walk the walk of an angel in human clothes determine your experiences. Many of you experience miracles and magic but never slow down enough to even realize it and be grateful. You are on the most magnificent journey. We are in awe of the leaps and bounds that some of you make on your path. You are beautiful and loved beyond your wildest dreams. We are here with you every day and every hour, reminding you what your journey is about, perhaps nagging you a little so you may remember your divinity and move into your power. We are always available to dance with you. Just give us your hand; we will be there, and so be it.

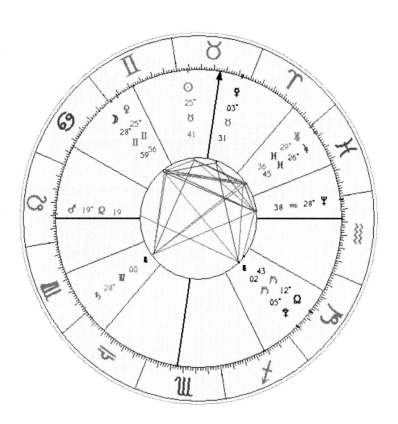

6-19-2010

hi dror,

I am in Tel Aviv... feeling much better but still have a bit of
nausea and the burping sometimes... but we're have a place here
and are traveling less for the time being so much better. i'm
eating a lot more and have a much bigger appetite though no
meat at all... I'm getting pretty tired here not sure if it's bc of
the heat or lack of iron but am taking a multi vitamin and will
start to eat a tiny bit of red meat to see if it helps.

hope you are well... i'm still puzzled by these symptoms and hope
that they don't continue for India and Turkey???

love,

Sara

Dearest I:
I am happy to hear you are doing better. I was wandering if
the Dr. diagnosed you?

I am traveling at the moment and will be back in Woodstock
next week. Enjoy Italy.

Much love

Dror
Sent via BlackBerry from T-Mobile.

Left Ankle

YOU ARE DEARLY LOVED.

From where do you think your wishes come? They come from lack of trust. When you wish for something, it is only because you believe that you will not receive that which you believe you need.

You have been walking the accelerated path, moving around and over obstacles. At times you even bleed a little. You injure yourself, but you keep moving. We see the parts of you that are hurting and we can feel the doubts moving up your spine.

We hear many of you asking yourselves, "Is it worth it?" We hear you whisper to yourself, "I have no idea where am I going and what will happen next." So you ask yourself, "Did I lose it completely? I am not sure what to do or how to continue from here. It all seems to be too much to carry."

We did not promise that this portion of your journey would be easy, did we? We have told you in many of the messages that this is where it gets exciting. This portion of the journey is all about faith. You must let go of the "know-how" method and move into the "I will be shown when I am ready" method. So much of what you believed would unfold did not, yet you met many miracles and many are still to come. There is a larger story that is unfolding, and we speak about this story. It is your story, as you are moving from one chapter to the next in your evolutionary journey toward integration of all the "yous." We have been following you. You have stumbled and fallen many times, but we celebrate each time you get up, bruised and in pain. Yet you keep walking. We are in awe of all of you who do your lightwork every day despite the seemingly insurmountable blocks you are facing.

I am tired, we hear you say.

We know, as we are with you every day and every night.

What is it that we are asked to do at this time, some may still wonder?

Your bodies are now in the midst of transition, and as your biology is being upgraded, some of you are experiencing various new ailments that were not there before. These are ailments that are connected to energy vortexes in your bodies that are yet to be cleared. You exist in a symbolic universe where the parts of your body that are not in balance correspond to your path of learning and your ailments correspond to the blocks that you now must clear. If your sciatic nerve is pinching, you may need to reexamine the direction of your journey. It may tell you that you need to adjust as you are not moving in alignment with your current purpose. If your left ankle or knee is in pain and you are having a difficult time stepping fully on your left foot, you may need to examine whether you are fully in your feminine power. You must clear those blocks so you can step fully into your role. When your digestion is not in alignment you may need to examine the energies that you ingest and the energies that you express. The digestive tract is one of great symbolism. It directs you toward fully digesting your role and mission: whenever you are out of line with this role, the food or energies will not be processed and create imbalance within you. Every single imbalance carries, as you know, a corresponding soul imbalance. Now, more than ever before, every tone you play that is off key may be shown to you clearly and almost instantaneously within your physical system. There is less and less of a delay between your choices along the path, resulting in the manifestation of those choices on your physical vehicle. With much love, we must impart that the opposite is also true. When you move into your role, understanding the mission and aligning yourself, your body will begin to sing a harmonious tune as if it happened overnight. Your bodies are becoming more and more multidimensional, reflecting the sum of your choices more clearly, faster than ever before.

Why is it so, some may wonder?

Your cells are now being furnished with a more direct link to the universal conversation that is happening all around you. This upgrade is part of you being prepared to meet the other players on this vast playing field and also realizing your role in this game of creation. Your cells are communicating more closely with you and they let you know when you are in line or out of line with the direction of your path. So much is still hidden from you. There are great portions of the mystery of your existence still to unfold as you move through 2012 and beyond. The great majority of your brothers and sisters will be so much in survival mode that many of the new realizations will be missed by them. Many of you, though, will be watching, observing that the rules of the game are indeed being changed and there is no going back, only forward.

What rules are you speaking of, some may still want to know?

There is a profound change that is now taking place within the rules by which power is being used in your politics, your governments, your businesses and commerce.

We do not see any profound change, some may claim!

There is less and less tolerance for lack of integrity; there is less tolerance for playing by the old rules of manipulation and lies. The game is moving to a new field where integrity and collaboration from a place of unity will begin to take precedence over local or tribal barriers. Much of what was hidden and disguised as old politics will now be exposed, as the light emanating from above allows all to see that which is hidden. It will be increasingly more difficult to hide truths and to manipulate people. A great cry and yearning for truth, for integrity, will sound from many places that are seemingly not connected around the globe. The trajectory of your journey now is no longer linear, but circular. What this means is that events from very different geographical locales will appear to be coordinated, pushing your consciousness to a higher elevation.

The integrity and well-being of the planet is, more than before, linked to your own physical body. Many, then, will begin to sense within them the state of the planetary body. Events that are harmful to the planet will be felt within your body and can no longer be ignored. You are moving closer into the realm of unity consciousness where all that is not in line with the trajectory of the New Earth must be transformed. Great movements are then to be anticipated, and you are prepared. The movement within Earth and within you will be felt by all. For a while, it will be constant and unrelenting. Much of the old must be cleared so the new can find clear space to sprout. It is a time like no other. Those of you who are here now know of your responsibility to hold the space of balance in an external reality of chaos, holding the vibration of love in an external expression of anger and hate directed at systems that no longer fulfill the need of evolving consciousness.

There are so many angles to each of you. All we are doing is waiting for you to look up, saying to us, "Give me your hands and let's go." This journey is about walking fearlessly, one step at a time, knowing that whatever faces you, you are ready. The sights and visions that will appear as if from all around you are just a holographic movie designed to halt your progress, scrambling your clarity. Your power lies in awareness that all is appropriate and all is by design to move you to the next phase of the human evolutionary stage. You have asked for it. Now this time is upon you. Many events that are seemingly unrelated are created to move you into a position that is more in line with unity consciousness.

You and the planet are one and the same. With all love, we must tell you that when you feel united, within you and with the natural world, your body will sing joyfully as all the elements around you join in, in support. Those elements may include wild animals, birds, fish, frogs, spiders, bees, your pets, and even the weather. When you are not within the awareness of unity, you may face many small or large lessons aimed at redirecting you toward unity awareness. Maintaining the link that you are one with all that is, which includes those within your inner circle as well as those who cross your path, is essential to navigating the next phase. With love, we ask you to be aware that all the obstacles and incidents that greet you on your path are there to slow you enough that you can become the witness of your own journey, within the framework of unity.

We are not sure what you are speaking of, some may wonder.

We see many of you who are facing great obstacles and we see others who seemingly glide on a magic carpet. Know that what you see is reflected back to you in direct relation to unity consciousness. When you believe that all is there to support your path and you are one with all that is, your reality will shift as if through miracles. If your awareness is still in the old energy of separation, what is yours and mine, you may face more of that energy. The light shining on you mercilessly now is the light of information and truth. This light will show you exactly what you are about as well as who you are. It is a light permeating all layers and there is no place to hide. It is time to own all that is now around you and to begin by being grateful. Once you understand the magnificence of all the support that you have around you, ask to be shown the way and do not set a timetable on your request. Trust that you were heard. When you get up in the morning, observe all that is around you and start slowly. Allow yourself to be immersed in the holographic scene of unity and begin the day from that awareness. Know that all the scenes that are now playing in your private movie theater were directed by you and for you. Tread slowly and peacefully, learning to be still. Listen within to the conversation. You are a magician and your role is to move all aspects of your awareness from the role of the actor to the one of the director. You are a director of a movie. The movie is all about clearing the past, moving into a new understanding of what reality is about and how it is being created.

As the director you choose how to interpret each event that crosses your path. There are events that seem so dark because they offer you the opportunity to see the pain that is within you and within Earth. You may choose to be in pain or you may choose to see the magnificence of such events in the game of reality creation. Events that reach all of you create a ripple which allows unity consciousness to permeate all who are affected. The vibratory rate of Gaia is intimately linked to that of humanity. When global events occur and a large amount of energy is exerted towards a specific event, it creates a step for humanity to climb up to the next level. Many of the scenes in the movie now playing in your private theaters are there to steer you to where you need to be. Know that you are the director and do not freeze when the scenes look too real. Understand that your reality is just a choice at any given moment. Answer with gratitude that you can play your part in a mission that has the universe around you holding its breath in anticipation of every move. There is a great joy felt on the other side and even greater support for your path. We love you so and we ask you to keep walking with the awareness that you asked to be here at this time, promising to shine your light, helping to facilitate the greatest shift humanity has ever experienced. With one last hug, we remind you that it's time, and so be it.

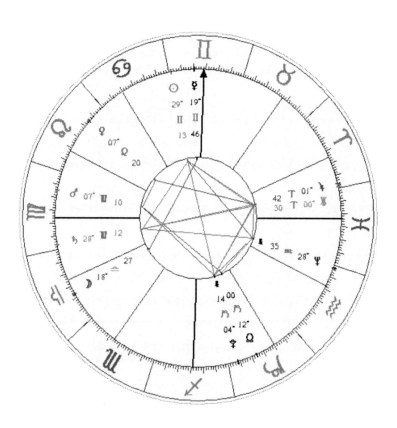

Hi Dror,

I hope you are all back to vibrant health!

It is hard to believe that Tuesday will be day 21 of my cleanse/beautiful way of eating and regaining awesome health!

I am doing well with my addition of watermelon (yum!) - adding some to my juice too.

The kriya is going well but I have to do it differently due to the sciatic pain in my legs (difficulty sitting in easy pose), so I am sitting on a cushion on the couch with the rolled towel under me and pulling it up and close to my body in the front while I do the contractions and pull the energy up. The energy is pretty intense. Not the worst exercise I've ever done ;-) !!!

Much love and gratitude to you Dror,
D.

....

Wonderful,

I feel that you are doing great. Keep at it. With the kriya try at times to increase the energy you are building up by using visualization and longer and more pleasurable strokes. This exercise has many health benefits and it is the foundation for building and holding more energy in the body.

I feel so much better but still taking it slowly.

Much love and enjoy the solstice

Love
Dror

The Great Ballroom

YOU ARE DEARLY LOVED.

What you see all around you is but a small story of the experience you are now undergoing. Your reality to some seems normal, but it is anything but normal. There are many layers to your reality—the parts that your senses can perceive and the parts that are taking place regardless if you are aware of them or not. The forces that are guiding your journey are mostly unseen. What you do see is only the end result manifestations of these forces in your 3-D reality.

How does this information help us on our path, some may ask in frustration?

We thought you'd never ask, we answer with a smile.

Nowhere in the universe is such an experiment taking place. You are so unique in a sense that your path is open and you can choose all directions. You have moved from the expected probability into an uncharted territory. Now you may pave your way to whichever way you wish. Your power grew ten-thousand-fold in the past few years, and you can now create a road just by wishing for it. From a passenger you became the conductor, and from the conductor you became the train; from the train you became the rails, and from the rails you became the terrain. You have transformed your own idea of who you are on a mass scale, and the numbers of awakened angels are growing by the day. When we see you from above you are glowing with excitement and anticipation of your next move. The next move is the one all of us are talking about and it is the theme of this message.

We ask you to become very still when you do your dance. Be aware of the unseen forces and work with them in harmony. Allow your angels to move ahead of you, creating harmony wherever you go, even before you get "there." Send vibrations of love to all of those whom you feel conflict with, so the unseen forces will have the fuel to change the trajectory and outcomes of your "appointments." We wish you to move like a dancer—be sensitive to the music. Understand that the music does not only reach your awareness through your ears; music can be felt on your skin, in your spine, and through your taste buds. Music is everywhere. Be the dancer and respond to the music with harmonious movements. Allow your body intelligence to carry you over the waves of melodic nuances and become the music. Your next chapter is all about dance. Allow your body to move with the rhythms that you perceive. You are asked to maintain your vessel in such a way that it becomes sensitive to the music. Become lighter all around: eat light, drink light, think light, digest light, and take in light through your skin. Create light environments where you are easily sensing the movement and harmonies that sound around you. The walk that you are about to follow is already created within you. It is created as you begin to learn the steps of this new dance. We ask you to become very still inside. Observe and listen. Become the hunter or the warrior who is waiting for signs from the winds and the faint footsteps of an animal. Walk, observing your environment, allowing your mind to stay open; just tune in and listen. The entourage who is with you can guide you when you allow space within you to receive guidance. Stay open and trusting. The navigation through new energy territory is challenging, and most of you resort to fear at one point or another. Fear is your natural physical response to unknown stimuli. We ask you to build enough power within you to bypass the automatic stimulus-response, remaining balanced, peaceful, open and receptive. Your power comes from the unseen forces which are operating all around you.

Understand that physical power is only a small portion of the vast variety of tools you now possess as an enhanced master walking, though still, in duality. You may choose at any moment to create a limited view of yourself and walk the exclusive physical path where what you see is what you get. There is no force in any reality that can make you do things that you do not wish to do. All moving forward must be by agreement—your agreement. To dance, there are many steps that you must choose in order for your body to be receptive to the music now playing all around you. Your body must become more sensitive to vibrations as melody is vibration, thoughts are vibrations, and the unseen world that is all around you emits vibrations. Like a string, you must play your melody in harmony with the symphony that is playing all around. You are moving soon through the first booster acceleration which will carry many of you higher than you have been. The booster will be delivered by Venus and the transmission of the feminine download is now approaching. Delivery of energy from the cosmos around you takes place all the time, but there are markers which create a vortex of fast-moving evolutionary steps in your collective human consciousness, and one such event is forthcoming. Prepare to dance. There is great change taking place in some of your celestial neighbors in order to facilitate the frequency upgrade which Earth requires to move into the next phase. Much of this celestial activity can be observed by your scientists, but their interpretations are void of any real understanding of the vast unseen forces that are in play in this game. The game is played by the collective you and us in unison with the system you define as God. We ask you, with all love, to trust that the system, vast as it is, is aware of each and every single one of the actors now playing their roles on planet Earth. The time to allow, trust, become still as well as flexible, light, joyful, musical, and free, is now.

Make peace with your Stradivarius and get ready to play your tune fully, and dance your dance fully. There is no holding back, as the energy that is now being delivered to the planet is immensely powerful. Its presence will stir all that was sunken at the bottom of your vessel so you will now have opportunity after opportunity to release your heavy loads. We ask you to not hold on to your heaviness as it can sink you. The energy of ascension is spiraling upward while at the same time pushing downward the heavier elements. If you are light, you will be the one moving higher; but if you hold on to heaviness, you will be pulled down and not be able to move above your current reality. Your reality—as it may appear to many—will be one of great inconsistencies in form and content. You must not rely on your media's version of reality to guide you through your days. Become light and still. Listen to the melody and dance accordingly. You have moved into the great ballroom dance arena, and it is now your turn.

What good is our dance for the planet and those who are around us, some may wonder?

In every layer of reality there are placeholders who keep that reality intact, allowing consciousness to grasp and perceive that reality. As your collective consciousness moves higher in vibration, the dancers are the key holders of this new energy. Your dance is the energy needed to stabilize a new version of reality for the masses. With love, you do not need a business card or special training to fulfill your mission. You came for this reason. We ask you to awaken to the inner music playing all around you and follow it with your movements. This is the reason that you are here. We are your alarm clock once again reminding you of what you already know. When you are awakened to your dance, those who are part of your inner circle will begin to attune to this dance as well. Some will even begin to hear the music that you hear. Just dance, allowing the vibration that you emit to engulf you and show on your face. No other method of marketing is needed. We ask you to be yourself and not hide it from anyone. Allow your power to be expressed within you as you hold up your peace, balance, and love to those who interact with you. The unseen forces and the army of angels are at your disposal. This army of angels is there as peaceful warriors shining light where it is dark. Send them ahead of you, whenever you feel a need to plow through dark territory, so they can play their role. You are a conductor, and the music you conduct is that which will be played out in theaters worldwide in the next chapter of your evolution as a human. Your own role is the only one with which you must be concerned. Your brothers and sisters have their own unique roles to play.

With a hug, we ask you to start dancing today, as your dance affects all and your movement will be teaching the ones around you the steps of this new rhythm. You are a dancer as well as a dance teacher. We ask you to awaken to your roles, dance, and so be it.

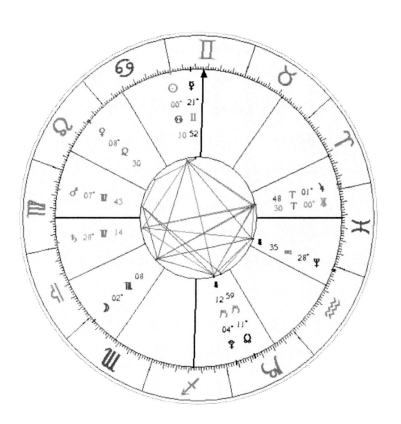

6-21-10

Hi D.

I hope your traveling is going well. I have been
working with bank of America on our credit
cards. They offered a settlement that I believe we
must accept.
I can not settle without them talking to you and
getting your approval. . If we do not do that we
will need to end up in court. I have been working on
it for over 6 months so please make sure you call on
6/30 around 11am and ask to speak to David. G. tel
from Europe is . If he is not there, any one else
can help.

Please confirm that you received this email and
understand everything

Sincerely,

Dror

The Rocket Booster

YOU ARE DEARLY LOVED.

Hmmmm? Where should we begin? You have asked us for help and we are here with you, holding your hands.

Why can't I feel the help, you whisper in frustration?

You can, we say with a smile. Without our support you would have been in a very different place.

I am hurting and I feel tired. I want to see you. I want to understand why I am where I am and why is it such a struggle, you ask quietly?

You know who you are and you know what missions you must accomplish. We have told you that we are always around you holding your hands, yet you are still worried. There is not much we can assist you with while you experience fear. You must let go of all those linear things you believe and become free. You have asked us for security. We hear you say, "I just want to feel safe." With so much love, we must impart to you that no one feels safe at the moment. It is only from within that your sense of safety can be generated. Even those who you believe have everything do not feel safe.

How can I be a lighthouse when I, myself, have no answers, you remind us?

You are a lighthouse by being truthful and walking the walk. Being a lighthouse does not mean that you do not struggle or have challenges in your personal life. Lighthouses are naturally placed in dangerous waters, and you are placed exactly where you were meant to be to play your part. If you were placed in the safety of inland, no ship would be able to find you unless, of course, they sail on land, and as you know, this may be proven a rather rare sight (angelic joke).

I am trying, and many things I have been working on seem to be blocked, some say.

Yes indeed, is our answer, so stop trying so hard!

You are moving into a new reality, and the "trying hard department" will not be as efficient as before. When you tell us that you want to walk the high road and be guided to your highest path, the next step is letting go of all the "trying hard" while tuning in to what is coming. Trying hard is no longer the buzzword. We have told you in so many words to be still so you can hear the guidance. Do not push, because it is no longer the method that will take you to your next destination.

How about my health? I have strange and weird ailments which do not go away easily, and when they do, something else comes as a replacement. I signed up for something other than being slowed down by my body. I asked to be a master full of balance and vibrant health, you complain to us.

Is this a question, we ask with a smile?

Let us sit all around you and show you where you are. You are in the middle of a huge arena. All around you are millions and millions of lights swarming in one large circle around you, looking at you. You look above, you see lights; you look below and you see lights. All around you is light and all this light is at your disposal just waiting for you to send it to where it is needed. What are you waiting for, is our question to you? Send it into your body and ask the ailment to be balanced.

I have done so, and it did not go away, some may say.

Now do it again from the center of the arena. Look at all the lights that are around you. Understand the immensity of the power that you now possess. Go into the body and find that place that seems to be out of balance. Point your fingers at that area, asking the light to heal you and it will. Try it now and you will see that by tomorrow you will feel different.

I am still feeling weak, some may claim.

With a hug, we ask you to allow your biology some time to adjust. Love it. Ask it to be balanced. Give it the time it needs to work on rejuvenating and regenerating your cells so that real healing can take place. You are in the midst of your walk, and many of you are now beginning to doubt that there is any merit to all the hard work to which you have been committed. The pain, the fear, and the planetary events which seem to be spiraling are a few such reasons for many of you to feel that you are going nowhere. From our perch, we must impart to you that you are no longer moving linearly. The shift is upon you. The energy of the New Sun is already marked by the direction and ferocity of events that are mainly coming from within you. You are moving higher and are no longer on the surface. That is why so many of you feel stuck. You feel that nothing is happening; meanwhile, your body and your inner workings are changing so much that soon you will not recognize yourself. Allow yourself the time you need to be in a place of contemplation and rest. There is much movement on the inside—so much so that outer movement must be limited so to preserve your energy. To many, this time is all about moving around, doing things, where you actually should just slow down, do less, and feel more. Understand that the shift from 3-D to multi-D has to do with your perceptions, feelings, and the inner workings of your nervous system. The process of upgrading is still taking place within you. Your body must learn to use many more tools than it possesses to observe, learn, evaluate, and walk the external boundaries of reality.

You are no longer walking with both feet on the ground, but with one foot on the ground and the other in multi-D, which can mean pretty much any system that you may choose. This may feel unbalanced at first, much like in the practice of yoga. Here, one practicing must learn the postures, repeating them over time, in order to master balance and elegance within the practice. Becoming a multi-D human is all about mastery. Becoming a master, you must use your body in a very different way than before.

How so, some may wonder?

Your body is a vessel that is activated to a very limited degree in your external reality, but much more power is now stored in you that you can and must access in order to walk the highest path. This power must be generated within, and to tap into your source you must work on clearing your vessel, then activating your vortexes one by one. When your chakras are spinning and your channels are open you can manifest miracles just by wishing them to be. Miracles are nothing but multi-D intersecting with 3-D to form a bridge so you can access reality that, from your limited perspective, will appear as magic. There is no magic in any of it, but an activation of your hidden powers, once stored away and disassembled in your cellular memory. Your activated chakras and the energies that are here to support you on your path will assist you in putting the puzzle back together. When all the pieces are reassembled you begin to fly. Your DNA structure already has been furnished with new helixes. These must be activated to communicate and light the dormant neurons in your brain so you will be able to perceive, then use, the new tools. This is magnificent in the cosmic sense of the word as you are becoming an enhanced human. Your science will begin to see part of your brain light up in MRI scans which would not light in "normal" people. Many doctors will try to bypass this phenomenon by explaining it as freak solitary events, but this is happening all over the globe on a mass scale. Many are now learning to walk the walk of mastery. When your science catches up, the jaws of many will remain dropped for a very long time as this has never happened in your recorded history as humans. Much of what you know about your biology and the way you perceive reality is about to undergo a fundamental shift. To some of you reality will never look the same. Many of our messages speak about this evolutionary phase of beginning to see and interact with the transparent forces that are all around you. More of you will begin to converse with your galactic neighbors, and some of the mysteries that were hidden from you will open up, revealing themselves to you. These are exciting times, and there will be much more external movement later on. For now, allow yourself to receive the gifts of the New Sun, walking slowly, as if you were an actor and the director has slowed down the film. Make space to be in tune with the natural world and ask mother Gaia to direct you where to turn.

There will come a time when you will miss this peace and quiet, wishing that you could slow down. Now you have the opportunity. When the booster rocket explodes you must be one with the rocket and just let go of all resistance. Now it is the time of taking care of your vessel in preparation for launch. You are ascending. So is your home and, with all love, we ask you to get ready for this unique journey, as you have waited for it for a very long time. Be in gratitude for all that you experience, and you will know why you had to go through the stages that you are now experiencing.

We love you and we are never too far. We are honored to walk this walk with you, and so be it.

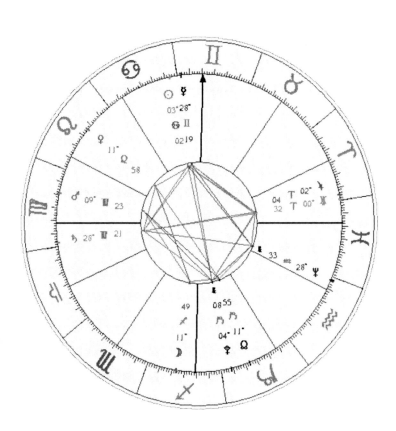

6/24/10

Amazing Dror,

One a.m. connection last night with you was off the charts for me...thank you!! I set intention to tap into the work you are doing with Kundalini...i love that you gave me permission to "use you" my beautiful Avatar :) Quite the ride!!

its moving day.....i am now officially "sleeping around" for 7 wks while my friends enjoy their home....oh boy....spending a couple of nights each week with friends and family....using Angel Room for home base for my belongings....crazy, but all so very worth it.

Tuesday night meditation was very intense....could feel energies touching different parts of my right lower back and head... then towards the end it felt like waves of energy moving from my right brain to my left....very strange sensation. Michael was taken aback by my energy shift in the last two weeks... he is actually allowing me to work on him this afternoon....all so wonderful.

Love !!

Nicki

An Initiation

YOU ARE DEARLY LOVED.

You thought that climbing up your spiritual ladder was one joyful act, but soon you discover that everyone else around you seems to be enjoying themselves while you are lagging behind. In fact, while you are going inside, many around you are going outside and seem to have fewer issues than you do. They are faring well and you feel that you are hurting. Did we capture the essence of how some of you feel? You are so dearly loved, dear human. You are an angel and your earthly experiences are nothing but camouflaged background scenery, or in other words, a set design constructed on a stage so as to give you a context within which you can evolve. What some of you describe as joy or fun is usually but a fleeting feeling gifted to you along your path.

A child can have great fun running in the yard until she stumbles, falling, slightly scratching her knee, and now she is not having fun anymore. She is crying and upset. This little girl is you, the mature adult in your day-to-day. You may have fun on a boat sailing, or walking on the beach. Your broker calls to tell you that your deal went sour or the stocks you just bought lost their value, or the sale that you worked on so hard fell through. Suddenly you are not having fun anymore. Fun is a moment-by-moment construct or illusion of relative safety or well-being while doing something you truly enjoy. On your journey of ascension the goal is not to have fleeting moments until you fall and scratch your knee, but to have a complete awareness of the different aspects of your journey where, from all the different angles, you still maintain your relative sense of safety and well-being. From an elevated perspective, even when you scratch your knee, experiencing pain, you realize the beauty, the sacredness, of it. You get up changed, maybe realizing that the free joyful running, falling, hurting yourself, and getting up are all experiences that are part of one continuum of moving upward on your journey, learning about energy as well as about your own vessel on a higher road. You begin to view all events in your life from the expansive overview of your light energy, or your soul, experiencing fewer and fewer fluctuations between fun or misery, joy, or sadness. You begin to move into an elevated awareness, being in a state of bliss no matter what happens on your journey. Scenery that you deem positive is not more or less beneficial to you than scenery that you deem negative. You are masters of energy. Your role is to learn, and attract energy that supports your highest path and sense of well-being. However, at times you must experience the opposite in order to appreciate your place within the continuum you call the journey of life. There is so much misunderstanding within your spiritual institutions about the concept of bliss. From our perspective, bliss is a state of awareness that is not stationary, but continuously moving away then shifting back to the core magnet in your heart. When you hold your balance inside of you with the vibration of love, no matter what happens around you, your heart becomes a gravitational core attracting the pendulum back to your center. With it, then, comes the sense of bliss.

Bliss is not a destiny one reaches and stays there. Bliss is work. Bliss means shifting back to balance and understanding the appropriateness of all that takes place in the illusion you call your reality. When you know within your true "core knowledge" that the suffering of humanity is a choice, destruction of the planet is a choice, starvation and lack are choices, premature death is a choice, evil is a choice, that being on the side of darkness is a choice, you also know that you can change all that you observe in your external reality.

How can we change the choices of others, some may rightly ask?

You cannot, my dear angel. This is where your power stops. Free will is an equal birthright of every single angel choosing to have an earthly physical experience. But

(we love buts) we smile and wink at you as we are so close to you right now.

But you just said that we can change all of that. How can we, you argue?

You can only change *you*, the way you see all suffering and the vibration that you emit as a result of your expanded awareness. That is what we call light. When you shine your light, you allow all those who come in contact with you, whether physically or spiritually, to see that they can choose as well. When one of you selects to shine light while a hundred thousand of you are still in the dark, that one person walking with her light shining can show all of the others that this path of light is open and available to them at any given moment, to change their life's trajectory and reinvent their storyboard. That is your power, my dear angel.

Do we need to follow her path, some may wonder? *Does she have the answers?*

She has the same access as all of you, but she walked the walk, making choice after choice to move higher. Her path is not similar to any of yours because she paved her road based on her own experiences. It is on you to pave your own path. Many of our messages speak about the choice that you have at any given moment to move to a higher elevation. At this higher place, reality begins to melt, deeper layers present themselves, allowing you to remain the observer, stationed above as if in an expanded bird's-eye view of things, while still grounded and balanced within your body. Your work is on *self*. You are the core ripple, which directs the movement all around you. Those who represent your inner circle are echoing your new vibration and sending it back to you. They will echo your resistance as well as their own. Once you have moved beyond the need to justify, explain, apologize, and hide living your truth, those around will begin to create allowances or move aside, as light can never be blocked by darkness. Wherever you are creating light, darkness dispels, as it must.

Your circle then expands and expands. As it expands, the light that you created within you affects more and more who are ready. Some of you are still skeptical and feel that this whole thing is a made up fairytale. You are equally loved and your choice is honored. Your beliefs create your experience, until such time that your light must justify the journey you took on as a physical being, a time when your higher part will choose learning. It is then where some of the things we talk about begin to resonate. When you are home all of you will say, "*Aahhh,*" as you will know all that we know. You are source energy creating all that comes to you. It's time to awaken to your power and use it breath by breath, heartbeat by heartbeat.

How do we go through the day-to-day with all the tasks, responsibilities, worries, expectations, and health problems yet still shine our light? This is mission impossible, some may say.

You can, and many of you do, is our short answer.

Your initiation into the fast lane is already assigned to you by the fact that you are alive in a mature body on the planet today. At the time of the mystery schools, before the pharaohs, many of you had to experience initiations with a high degree of ferocity and challenge, so as to allow you to stretch your human ability, raising your awareness level. Your walk during this now-time of Earth initiation is equal if not greater than the challenges you had to face then, and you are ready. You are ready to create within you enough power as to affect the atoms and molecules around you so your reality will reflect your new awareness. We know of your pain and we are with you all the time. We also see you in moments of anger, anguish, shame, guilt, depression, and sadness. We know your history. All human emotions are a powerful vortex of energy, and the heavy emotions are used by those who do not come from light. Much of your drama is created in "movie studios" to feed those who are the consumers of heavy emotions. Your range of emotions makes you a precious commodity on this galactic plane. There are those who feed on heavy emotions and create movies in order to satisfy their insatiable, large appetite. All your emotions are honored as free choice, but the power to move away from heavy emotions to light—despite overwhelming reality which builds on terror movies—is surely challenging. None of what you consider real is your true reality. All of it is manufactured somewhere. Your power is to see through the illusion of the manufactured movies and to sense what serves you. Your mission is to stay light despite the voices that come from different sources and outlets which try to sell you fear. Your mission is to be a warrior of light, transmuting darkness to light first within you, and then becoming an example to others. On a biblical storyboard, this time would be described as a time of war between light and dark, truth and illusion, masculine and feminine, light and heavy. All that is hidden must be exposed and expressed. The actors and director behind the manufactured scene must be exposed as well. Your reality is aligning to a higher vibration and many changes are upon you. This is a glorious time and many of you feel the excitement. You want to be light but there are endless issues which hold you back from experiencing light. My dear angel, these are your initiation and tests. They are meant to be challenging. In the past you had to lie in a dark sarcophagus for days with no fresh air, water, or food to prove your strength and test your powers. Now, just to go through a day can be as challenging.

This is your time of Earth initiation, and issues will present themselves continuously. This is part of the Earth's vibratory acceleration, and all of you must work through the clearing of the old, so you can move higher. Embrace what comes, allowing it in and allowing it out. Do not hold on to anything. Do not fight or block the seemingly endless challenges, but allow with a smile, knowing that the power you possess is not the power of resistance but the power of awareness, intent, and love. Slow down and consult with your core self. Keep strengthening your KA, or life force, and love your vessel. Build stamina because you will need it more and more as you move through this time of acceleration. Take time to reconnect with Mother Earth and her inhabitants. Honor all the elements around you, the ones which sustain you, understanding that all is there to support you and shower love upon you. Allow the time to feel and allow the time for gratitude for whatever crosses your path. Know that you are never alone and always loved. Know that you are always guided, that we are so close that you can smell our fragrance when you are open. You feel that you are on a mission impossible, but you have done it before, you will do it again, and so be it.

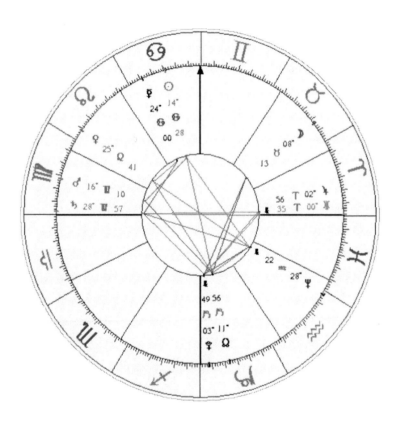

7/6/10

Hi Dror
Just wanted to say to you how grateful I am for
having you in my life as a teacher and as a light
beam that propels me to take higher and higher
flights.
Thank you so so so much...for your love and light, and
for the beautiful being that you are.
Thank you for living your mission and helping others
to awaken to theirs. What a sacred work you are
doing.
with love.

Libi

Spirit and Chocolate

(Spirit is very much like chocolate without the side effects.)

YOU ARE DEARLY LOVED.

When you think you understand the gist of it all, then and precisely at that moment, you experience the rug being pulled out from under you, with all that you believed your reality to be, presented in an upside-down, sideways angle.

Why is it so, some may ask?

The journey of revealing your truth must be understood in a way that is outside the linear scope of your reality. There is really no way to write about it, talk about it, explain it, or even describe it. This reality that comes from the dimension of being one with Spirit is about being. The knowing comes as a feeling that cannot be analyzed; that is why so often, when you finally think that you've got a handle on the manual of truth and you are ready to explain to everyone else how to become, you yourself soon realize that it is not so. Throughout history, with all the spiritual knowledge that you gain, very little of it is actually helpful in becoming "it." Much of this knowledge, especially the information orchestrated by religious institutions through dogma and idealism, further removed you from linking with the core of your inner flame. Some information originally may have come from pure sources, but those who presented these sources packaged it so as to mainly gain control over its constituents. Information that came from a light source to assist humans in their quest to become empowered and liberated was manipulated, as well as distorted, by those in power for the opposite aim. Religion often introduced certain rules, rituals, and interpretations that were far removed from the original purpose. The information was used to further disconnect the believers from their own inner light and power. You are powerful, and when you realize it, you are no longer subservient to the establishments that wish to control you.

Power of Spirit is harvested like any other source of energy but in a less obvious way. All of you carry an immense power to create, manifest, and bring light. This energy source has been understood for eons, largely being harvested to lead you down a path of obedience, compliance, and subservience. Power of Spirit is given to each and every one of you equally, in abundance, as there is no authority over it. It has, however, through a campaign initiated to take over and control resources on this planet, been robbed from you. The power has then been channeled through fear, guilt, shame, subjugation, intimidation, and coercion often, ironically, disguised as love to make you subjects rather than masters. When you are a master, you do not need others to tell you what to do and how to think. You are free and powerful, as all the resources that are available to the one you consider "powerful" are also at your disposal. You are it. The time is now to claim back your power and shine with such luminosity as to create a ripple of awakening. There is no other time and there is no other opportunity that will be meeting you on your path. It's time. Claiming your power does not mean that you walk with a business card or hold a prestigious position so everyone around you feels intimidated. Being powerful is holding a frequency of love to self first and maintaining a link to the universal love energy. You become a lighting rod, attracting light to you and, through you, directing it to Gaia. Others who walk beside you and interact with you are attracted to you like steel pins to a magnet. They wish to get closer to you because of the love emanating from you. You become a magnet of love and light frequency from the universe pulsating to your surroundings. If you never had chocolate in your life, being introduced to it for the first time is likely to make you feel wonderful and want to try more. This is similar to you holding light allowing others to be illuminated by it. Once they "taste" your light they will keep searching for it, initially in you. Later on, with guidance, they will look inside and realize that the light source is within them.

We know of your fascination with chocolates and we must tell you that Spirit is very much like chocolate without the side effects (like gaining weight). When you connect to the love source within you, it is as if you found a fountain of chocolate inside yourself. Chocolate—especially a really good one—induces the euphoric, invincible feeling you get when you are in love.

You have always known that coming to this planet is challenging. Coming at this time probably ranks as the most challenging of all your other cycles, for the simple reason that you must be willing to let go of the idea of who you are, wearing your new costume of a multidimensional being linked and connected to the galactic family around you. For the past many thousands of years, you have been led to believe that you are alone on this planet as consciousness as well as in your universe, despite overwhelming evidence to the contrary. The ones who kept the link and conversation alive with your galactic family were the cultures of indigenous tribes in different parts of the world. Those tribes did not need permission or convincing because for them it was a reality. Many of those whom you consider less developed lived the reality of multidimensions and have been interacting with other civilizations from the beginning of their history. Their link has been partially responsible for keeping this planet on this current course away from the trajectory of Armageddon to one of ascension. The power, as you can begin to see, is in the hidden places between the words. The power is in the pauses. It is not in your technology or wealth. It is not in your outer beauty or the transient position you hold while playing your role. Your power lies in your awareness of who you are and why you are here. That is why we ask you to wake up to your power because the time has come.

I am in such a different place. How does all this relate to me? I am struggling with health, money, my family, as well as just remaining floating above the waves which, by the way, seem to get higher and higher. I feel that I have become weaker as very little makes sense to me. What is going on, you shout to the heavens?

We say to you in so many words that you are so dearly loved. The walk is challenging as you move to the inner sanctuary of the unknown. Many of you experience life at the moment as relentless events that mark important changes and often departures from your life plan. For many of you, the sails which you used to navigate your life using predictable winds are no longer available. You have had to lower them and be directed by currents which you can neither see nor control. You must let go and trust that it will take you somewhere. To many the feeling of not being in control of your charted path is threatening and terrifying. You always believed that you had the power to control your destiny. Now, all the tools that you have grown up with and learned to master are no longer available or predictable. Dear angel, the rules of this great game are changing, and nothing that you have used in the past to navigate with will be as it was. You are still in control, but the tools to navigate must link to the undercurrents rather than the wind. You must learn the new language of the Earth, the sky, the natural world, and the guidance above. To some who are drifting about, sleeping, this next period may seem like the end of everything, with many experiencing it through anguish, agony, and fear. To those who are riding the new frequency, using the new tools, this next period may be experienced with greater ecstasy, fearlessness, sense of well-being, love, health, and abundance than ever before. We spoke of the split between heaven and hell. It is coming. The new and old energies are battling. As events mark the greater consciousness of your humanity with accelerated speed and ferocity, some of you will ride it, but some will be buried under it. When you walk in your street and you look around, everything seems to be normal. Even as your Earth continues to hurt, bleed, and the pressure on your precious aquatic life, as well as on your balance, is mounting, nothing seems to be able to move the masses from business as usual. With all love, we must impart to you that this is about to change very rapidly. When the movement starts, all of you, without exception, will feel it to the core of your being. From that point on, business will not be as usual.

How should we prepare, some may wonder?

You are prepared, we answer with a smile. That is why you are here. You must awaken.

What precisely is going to happen, some may still wonder?

Many of you are walking on the beach, and life is perceived as normal. At times the weather gets dark and it rains, at times it is stormy. A large storm may even come and go, but mostly you experience life as you always believed it should be. Summers are hot and sunny. Winters are cold and dark. At times you hear that someone you know has been going through a hard time, but mostly it does not pertain to you directly. Life still seems to be "normal." That picture is about to change. For the past two years many of you who are at the forefront of the new energy have been getting messages that life as you know it is about to change. The change is at your doorstep. What is about to change is you. Beginning with your biology, then your relationship with yourself, then with your natural world, and eventually your interaction with what you call your reality. All is in the process of changing and all of you are about to sense it in one form or another. You do not have words in your vocabulary to describe some of the processes that you are about to experience, but new words soon will be added. Your physical landscape is about to change. The seasons that marked the cycles of change in your weather patterns, punctuating the times for your farmers to plant seeds or to begin the harvest are about to change as well. The movement of the migratory mammals, birds, and aquatic life is changing. Your whole magnetic resonance and the frequency by which you communicate with one another as well as with the world around you are all about to change.

These changes are upon you, and although only a few of you will read our messages, all of you will sense the greatest shift humanity has ever experienced in its current form. You are moving into that change. Your awakening has everything to do with how you will experience the next chapter and the service you will endow upon your brothers and sisters. The choice is yours and we act as your alarm clocks, asking you gently to not stay in bed, as the time has come, and so be it.

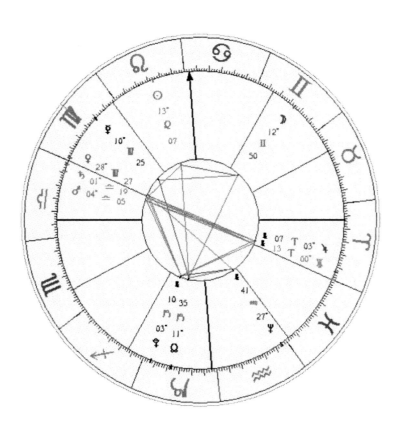

8-5-2010

Dear dror:
i don't know the date, but it was about a yr ago now that I first met you. so I felt like telling you a little story called - the night I met you:

One night after our pathwork group my friend Tina came to me and said - "Andy and I are going to a talk by a man who says he speaks with angels - would you like to come too?" well, I was a little curious, so I said , "sure, why not?" So I went.
The talk was interesting, and you seemed authentic, so I was open to the possibility that you and these angels might be for real. (Though I don't buy anything all that easily.)

I had come in late and Tina said to me after - "you missed the best part - the part where he looks into your eyes - go over and meet him so he can look in your eyes." i said something like " no thanks - I'm good" (If you were to invent a torture chamber custom for me it would involve forced eye gazing with a complete stranger man)
She insisted. - DO it! I really did not want to.
I felt like you could see through me and I did not like the sensation one bit.
In fact by now I was feeling quite sick. my heart was racing and i was sweating.
part of me felt panicked - and wanted to run in the other direction as fast as possible and never look at you again.
But yet another part irresistibly drawn.
OK I will do it.
So I look in your eyes.

Tina tells me you have been working with her daughter - and she suggest I ask to work with you too.
"But I overheard him say he is not working with anyone new right now "- I tell her.
"This does not matter" she says - "you ask anyway."
I resist. I protest.
Then she says -
"It does not matter if he is working with NO ONE else - He is going to work with YOU"
"why do you say that?" I ask her and she just says - "trust me - this is something I KNOW"

(I do not want to ask you anything, but she is so insistent that later I do.)

As I leave, I suddenly develop a splitting headache that is to last for days. I have not had headaches since I was a child. As I am driving home from your talk, Darin calls me - he has fallen on the ice and snapped his ankle. He cannot get up. He asks me to come get him. For weeks he is unable to walk, can only move about, and, barely, with crutches.
Then, later, this same night, my dog becomes very sick. I have to take him out nearly every hour, through the day and night, vomiting and shitting blood. Over the next week he becomes sicker and sicker and I worry he is going to die - he is that sick, neither eating, drinking, nor sleeping. For the next week I am round the clock playing nursemaid to Darin who is bedridden, and doing all his work besides my own, while taking my sick dog out. round the clock, trying everything I can to heal him. By the end of the week I have nearly come unraveled by my constant efforts and lack of sleep.

I remember thinking - "what is with that angel man? I think he may be a real troublemaker" and that was the night I first met you
Love

B.

Activation

YOU ARE DEARLY LOVED.

You are here, while we are here and there simultaneously. We are with you but you cannot see us. So many of you reach out and try to grasp us but we are invisible to your human eyes. The surest way you can experience us is by feeling our presence in your heart. Some of you can smell us and feel the subtle tingling sensation on your skin which we call a hug. When we hug you, some of you sense a flow of energy or heat running through you, charging you up. You may experience a deep sense of peace as if everything around you is in harmony. A sense of well-being, safety, and comfort may descend upon your whole being, as if your mother just picked you up from your baby crib to cuddle you. When you link and invite us, the love flowing from Spirit creates a reaction causing your body to vibrate differently. We like to give names to our interactions with you, and we call this one an "Angel Dance." There are a few bodily sensations unique to our dance with you, but many of you miss out on these sensations if you are not sufficiently in tune with your body.

Why do you tell us about this dance, some may wonder?

The planet is moving higher and you have a choice to move with it or not. This dance can greatly facilitate your journey, allowing you direct access to inner guidance so that when you reach an intersection, you will know whether to turn left or right. The veil between us is thinning and some of you are closer than ever before to our dimension. We are with you all day long facilitating messages. To some these messages are interpreted as thoughts, fantasies, or visions, and many of you do not pay much attention to them. Spirit communicates through symbols, as what you call your reality is also symbolic. You are Spirit and your symbol is your human form. Through your symbol you communicate and create other symbols. Many of you view life as literal: what you see is what there is. From our perch what you experience is just a signpost or a landmark directing you to your next stop. You are an artist and your reality depends on how you read the symbols on your canvas. You exist in a fantasy of sorts where your own programming determines how you experience your universe. If you open up to the larger "you" and know the power you possess to create your reality, everything around you will support your new program. You will then, indeed, experience an empowered light- and love-filled reality. Some of you may choose a program of victimhood, where you may believe that your circumstances are imposed upon you by power-ful forces like government, nature, or even God. For you reality will rearrange itself to support your pro-gram, and you will experience events which will rein-force your view of victimhood. You are a powerhouse and a master. When you awaken to your mission, your purpose for being here at this time, you can redirect the trajectory of your own life, the lives of those around you and of humanity, to new heights. This is why we are here hugging you and guiding you. It is our inten-tion to light your way and show you your potentials so you can choose. You are an embodiment of the force you named God, and your collective intent is the cre-ative power behind all that you experience as humans on this planet. These powers were hidden from you un-til not too long ago, but the power of light broke the lock of darkness and many began to see again. In your past "seeing" was available to only a few selected indi-viduals. Now, it is an option available to all of you who activate their powers and choose to awaken.

This time is magnificent precisely because of the immense power that each and every one of you hold to recreate your own reality, releasing your karmic ties, moving into an elevated vibration to experience life from a place of love. Your own journey becomes the torch for others to follow. In your past the choice to become enlightened involved different schools where you may have been required to negate your physical body or go through grueling training for many years learning to control your earthly urges and needs. Your road map has changed. Accessibility to your powers and control over your life has much to do with letting go of all the "musts" and "shoulds," allowing trust in your own higher guidance to move you through this dance of symbolic reality. The shift in consciousness crowns each of you as your own guru. Your sacred manuscripts, as powerful as they may be, can only take you part of the way. Following a set of rules and getting more competent at adhering to those rules was the path of the old energy. There are no more pre-paved roads to mastery. We have said that before and we repeat it today. The manual is within you. All the information you need to awaken, to walk this walk, is embedded in your biology. You are your own teacher, and the sooner you realize it the fewer steps you will need to repeat. You must trust your own higher guidance.

Fear is your greatest obstacle, as many of you do not like the unknown. Some of you even go to a fortune-teller or a card reader so they can tell you what to expect, then you purchase insurance in case something does go wrong. With all love, we must tell you that in your new energy potential there is no longer a need for the insurance industry because mastery means that you direct your journey through intent and trust. Even the most apt palm or card reader no longer can predict your journey because a road is no longer there. You create your path as you walk. In the billions of potentials floating around you waiting to be activated, your choice is the most powerful predictor of your next destination.

How do we know where to go without roads, some may wonder?

Becoming in touch with your higher guidance and with your vessel are the steps you need to take to get yourself ready. As you move higher you will encounter blocks and resistance. These are part of your journey. The obstacles you meet are not only from your current life; many were gifted to you through your human DNA programming and conditioning created over many lifetimes. Your work at this time is to clear away, detaching from the cords that hold you anchored, to become free and powerful. This journey is not easy nor is it simple, as every time you take a step higher, new blocks present themselves asking to be cleared. We ask you to know that your reality is symbolic. When you encounter a new obstacle, greet it like an old friend. Then allow it to move through you so you can clear it once and for all. Do not attach to your heavy symbols, adopting them all over again.

Your awakening is the single most powerful step you can take towards reclaiming your power to become a multidimensional galactic human. We have come to you because you called upon us to assist in reigniting your flame so that light will be your guiding force and not darkness. We are your activators and we only do so with your permission. No words need to be spoken and no physical actions need to be taken. Activation takes place through the energy of love. When the music sounds we dance with your light, beginning a process that is sacred. When you give us your hand, joining our dance, symbolically you are ready and the activation proceeds.

What happens when I am being activated, you may inquire?

Your cells are being "electrified" with higher frequencies. You may feel it as tingling, inner shaking or trembling, as if your body is lying on a vibrating bed. Your cells will be dancing. Some may lose sleep in the beginning of the process as the body absorbs new information and shifts. This process can be disconcerting to some of you and you may close down. Activation is a sacred process which greatly accelerates your journey. As your cells awaken, beginning to absorb more light, it is important to spend a few minutes a day exposed to the sun. Your sun radiates frequencies and information which assist in the shift of humanity. The sun's bad reputation and the upsurge of skin cancers are partly an attempt to remove you further from your source of information. Ten minutes a day is enough time to greet and honor the sun. Take this time to allow love and light to be absorbed into your body. The planet is being activated through a bombardment of particles coming to you from the center of your galaxy. Your human form is being activated through the same particles. However, for you to move higher more is needed. You must choose to allow the process to manifest. Activation is not a passive process. As your body begins to absorb the new frequency, as the new information and realizations stream through your consciousness, you must let go of some of the old programming, conditioning from the past, to act upon the new frequencies. To some of you the process is very frightening because of the "unknown" factor. You want to know what will be. The process of activation has to do with letting go of all that you know in order to allow the new to replace the old. Each one awakening becomes a lighthouse to others considering awakening, as well as a frequency guardian of the new emerging planet. The power of the one is immense because, not only is your light shining, but you allow all those around you to use that light to dispel their own fears and begin to see.

Why are you telling us all that, some may still ask?

You are coming to a zero point where all that you know will change. It is happening already but many of you are so anchored in the day-to-day that the bigger picture eludes you. What we speak of will become clear in your near future. "Zero point" means that a new paradigm will replace the old. The new paradigm is created by those of you who are activated and awakened. Those who choose to awaken to their power will carry the planet to the next step. It will not be up to your political leaders or powerful businesses to pave the new trajectory of humanity. It is up to you—the lighthouses, lightworkers, and light warriors—to guide, paving the next step on your collective journey. You entered into a time where in your potential, collectively, the power of love and light will illuminate every part of your reality. Then darkness will have nowhere to hide. In your new potential, those who will be elected to lead your countries or manage your corporations will be aligned with the new vibratory rate that is now being established. This will establish the new paradigm where humanity can coexist in balance with itself, as well as the planet it inhabits, establishing what we have called the New Sun, to create peace on Earth.

In one of your books of sacred text it was prophesied, "Blessed are the meek: for they shall inherit the Earth" (Matthew 5:5). As we see it, you are the meek. "The meek" are the ones who hold the quiet power of love and light which is neither visible nor external, but has the potential to lead humanity to a higher step than ever before. The next step in your journey is directly connected to your awakening. Those of you who choose to awaken, shining your light, are the ones, energetically, who carry the power to guide humanity to its next evolutionary chapter.

Who are these heroes? They are *you*, each one of you who chooses to dance and give a hand to spirit. You are the renegades, the ones who often feel confused or sidelined by life, yet keep working on clearing, healing, connecting, and trusting. You are carrying the load for the majority of the planet who are asleep. The changes around you, often described by your scientists in technical terms, indicate that your Earth is changing rapidly. Not until your lifestyle, food supply, or way of life is disturbed do you pay much attention to these changes. The time will come when all of you will acknowledge the change. We ask you not to wait as the time to awaken is *now*. When all that you know begins to shift, your level of awareness and rate of vibration will determine if you experience fear or bliss.

How do we start the awakening process, you may still ask?

Give intent with pure heart to walk the path of an activated, awakened angel and tune in to the messages from your higher guidance. Your angelic entourage will respond quickly. When you hear the "call" trust yourself and allow your higher guidance to lead you to a new path. We are part of you and our dance is celebrated in the heavens as the gateway to a new dance floor.

What kind of music do we dance to, some may wonder?

Love music, we answer with a smile. To hold yourself in a place of love, remaining peaceful in the face of fast-paced, intense, external moving reality has an immense effect on others.

Why do you keep speaking of Earth changes? Should we be worried, some may ask?

With all love, we wish you to know that whatever you experience is sacred and there are no negatives in the changes that you are now experiencing. You came to this planet, and asked to be in the body that you now carry at the age that you are, so that you can experience the magnificence of the time. No two of you have the exact same path, but all of you agreed to be here and awakened to your truth. When you choose to awaken a rainbow appears, as it marks the agreement between you and "you." When the rainbow appears, you know from the deepest place in your heart that you have arrived home, being in the right place at the right time.

Even if that place is in the eye of the storm you still feel that you are home. The time to dance is now. You are so dearly loved, your journey sacred, revered by us all, and so be it.

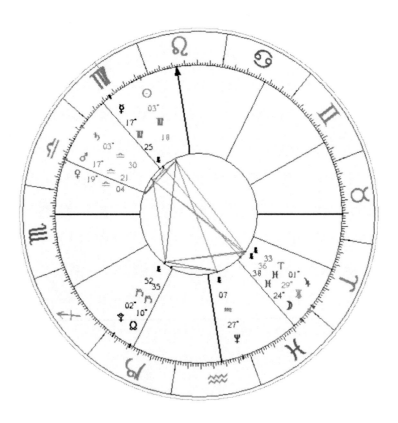

8/26/10

(Just came back from the Dr. diagnosed with Shingles)

Dearest Nicki:
something came up and I will not be able to make it. I really wanted to.
Let's connect soon. Dror

Dear Dror:
You are kidding, right??
speechless

Dear Nicki,
I know me too
Life threw me a curve ball. Got to deal with it.
so sorry
love
dror

Dearest Dror:
I really hope that everything is ok with you....trying not to worry but it is really difficult not knowing what is going on.
I have had a hard time dealing with the e-mail vs. a phone call to say you
weren't coming. I know I am deep in my own stuff and I am trying to get a
grip...it felt so cold as if you had just changed your mind, that it was not a big
deal. I felt as if I had been kicked in the stomach.... When I connected with
Corinne about the pants yesterday she mentioned that you were really upset
about not coming which made me think something major had happened and I
was being self centered and in fear. You mean so much to everyone here....I am
struggling for perspective here.

I hope you are alright.
Sending Much Love.

Nicki

Dear Nicki:
I will call you later. Thank you for sending love. I am really baffled sometimes
by what is happening but I really had no choice.
Dror

Notes from 8/26/10 – continued on 9/20/10 – Woodstock, New York
(Started message with shingles—lots of pain,
continued after healing took place.)

Butterfly Across the Window

*Y*OU ARE DEARLY LOVED.

What does your body tell you? It tells you that it is not balanced. How does it speak to you? Through pain and discomfort! This is the language of the body. It can take you to the highest peaks of joy and pleasure as well as the lowest valleys through the language of your nerves. Through your nerves you learn to feel and to listen. Many of you do not stop to listen until the signs are so clear that you can no longer ignore them.

Your mission is to work with your body and not against it. When it requires you to slow down, you must listen and not push it further. Are you upset that your body fails you? It is the way matter speaks to spirit. You may not understand the language because of the pain involved, nevertheless the signs and symbols are there. Who do you think you are? Only through pain do you understand that you are not your body. When all is moving smoothly many of you believe that you and your body are one. It is then that you begin to worship your body instead of honoring your true self.

Why me, some may wonder?

It is time to shift. Through your body you are nudged to make adjustments to your lifestyle, your choices, and to your path. If everything served you all the time, carefree, you would not have any reason to grow. You would continue on your path of forgetfulness. We are your lovers. Our job is to be your cane when you need one, to touch your heart when your heart is aching. We are here to support you in whatever shape or form you take as a human walking this sacred journey of life on Earth.

I want to heal, we hear you say.

Indeed you will, is our answer. Healing is your path upward. To some of you, only when you reach the bottom of a deep valley do you begin to climb back up.

Do we have to reach the bottom in order to grow, some may wonder?

The answer is, of course, "no." You do not have to do anything. All that you encounter is a choice. When your higher part receives a conflicting message that indeed you are ready to grow, yet are fearful, it may guide you to meet your fears so you can move through them, coming out victorious.

But what if I do not come out of it at all, some may inquire?

It is again your choice, but there is never a judgment. If you do not conquer your fears now, you will face them at another time, in another space, under another name, sometime in your linear future.

Tell me something that I do not know, you may say.

You are on a road, but the vista is not your real vista. Your idea of who you are is an illusion. At times the only way to pop this illusion is to stop the treadmill you are on and sit on the sidelines for a while, taking inventory of your life. When you stop because your body is in pain, you begin to reevaluate your priorities, reconsidering your goals. To many, even your appreciation for nature shifts. All that you take for granted is now being shuffled and you have an opportunity to take a fresh look at your world, deciding if you wish to keep it the way it was or to change things. You are moving into a time of accelerated changes. All that you know and are familiar with is changing now under your feet. The changes around you appear slow but they will become more noticeable as time progresses. Those of you whose mission it is to awaken must adjust your bodies, as well. As a result many are now facing health challenges. These ailments are not about the body only, but about the marriage of body and spirit. Both elements must align and when they do not, you may experience challenges through your vehicle asking you to shift so you may grow.

Why now and why in this form, some may wish to know?

There is only now, is our answer. As we hug you gently, we whisper in your ear that you are not only the building but also its architect. You reside in a building that you yourself designed. You are Spirit manifested and there is no one else that holds the key to your blueprint.

What do we do with that information, some may ask, frustrated?

There is only one thing you can do, that is, to face whatever is in front of you, with the awareness that there is a gift waiting for you on the other side of the experience. No suffering is in vain, as the greater entity that makes you who you are learns from all experiences whether they are joyful or painful. Painful experiences lead you to faster growth while more joyful experiences, externally, do not necessarily accelerate your growth. Your mission is to experience your life as joyful no matter what happens in your outer circumstances. The higher state of awareness we speak of is for you to experience your internal landscape as your true home. Whatever external circumstances you encounter on your journey, understand that they are no more than a backdrop for your set designs so you can play your role, learning from them. Imagine a quiet moment at home, looking at a raven sitting in a tree cawing. You may not notice the bird at all when your mind is racing about all the things you believe you need to accomplish today, but disable your body for a little bit, then all of a sudden, a butterfly moving across your window on a beautiful summer day represents much more than before. It represents the celebration and power of life at that moment, flowing, moving, despite your own disability. The butterfly is an angel that tells you to look inside and experience how everything is actually perfect. When you are lying in bed looking out, you have two choices: being in the awareness of this celebration, only when you are strapped to a bed feeling weak, or being in this awareness every moment of your life. You are upset because the vehicle that moves you around—which you take for granted—is disabled. We see how frustrated some of you become when your real car stalls for some reason. Again, we ask you to move with us into the circle, beginning to celebrate *when you are still in the dis-ease phase.* When you begin to celebrate, your soul and body begin to work in unison, conversing with one another to manifest healing. Your imbalance or dis-ease is an opportunity to spend time with yourself, honoring your vehicle and celebrating having a body. Celebrate even when you are experiencing pain because the celebration again, after you have healed, will hold even more power.

How do I heal, you may want to know?

We ask you to use all your tools including your modern-day doctor to understand your body. After you've done your homework, sit with yourself and ask your body what kind of treatment will work best for it. Speak to it like you speak to another person, knowing the answers will be forthcoming and that they will describe to you exactly what you need to do. You may use a pendulum or muscle testing to connect with your body or just talk to it and listen for the answer. Many of you may be able to hear it loud and clear. We are around you hugging you and we can see your thoughts. We hear many of you complain to us that you cannot fulfill your mission and be a lighthouse while in a sick body. We ask you with all love to be patient. Health, at times, must come from knowing sickness. When you are moving upward, at times your biology must shift.

That is what is happening now to many of you. You call it being sick and we call it biological transformation.

Please explain how so, some may inquire?

Many of you have asked to move up the ladder faster so you will arrive on time to your graduation. At times the shortest route is to bring the body to a place of awareness of its own limits, as well as its own healing power. You may do so by reading many books or you may do so by experiencing it yourself. There are many paths to moving higher.

But I cannot function when I am in pain, you may claim.

With all love, we ask you, what function do you think you need to fulfill?

Your ideas of where you are going often are very different than ours. Your path is an open book. At times the trail that opens up to you, which you believe you would never have designed for yourself, is actually the one that guides you to fulfill your highest potential. Be patient, we ask, and celebrate the moment that you are shifting from one level to another. You began taking notes when you were sick. You have now come full circle to complete the message from a place of balance, and we are all around you celebrating. You were sick twenty-seven days ago and now you have healed. You were unable to complete taking notes because of the intolerable pain in your back. Now, a few weeks later you are sitting at the same table typing on the same laptop and the pain is gone. It is the same you sitting in the same place doing the same thing, yet your awareness was very different than it is now. You feel whole again as your biology gingerly obeys your wishes. It is from a place of gratitude that you are asked to look at your vehicle every moment that it plays the role for which it was designed. It is meant to carry you, allowing you to manifest your wishes and create your dreams. Yet, when your body moves into imbalance, the smallest task becomes a challenge. To some of you, to simply get up is a task that you must plan and consider before you do it. Your body is sacred. It tells you when and how to communicate with it. It gives you pain at times so you will remain inside it, not forgetting your gift or moving too far from it. It asks you to be in the now when your mind wanders. The gift of pain is one that allows you to slow the passage of time and sense every second. You become aware of parts of your body whose function you never knew. It allows you to look at your body and wonder how you did not say "thank you" every day before having the pain. Now it is your opportunity to change all that. Many rush for prescriptions for painkillers to ease their pain. Indeed it may be appropriate and necessary, but we ask you at times, before you choose to numb the pain, go into it with your whole being. Feel the muscles, nerves, or tissues from the inside and talk to the imbalance. Ask it what it needs because when you truly surrender to the pain, allowing it to move through you, you conquer fear, as fear of pain is often far greater than the pain itself. When you move through fear and face it, often you remove the need for the particular imbalance to remain or come back. The root cause of your imbalance commences in your energetic subtle fields, making its way to be manifested in your physical body when the root cause has not been processed.

We ask you to use the time well when you are sick and in pain. Think of it as being back in school and be grateful for the homework you receive. Love your body for the pleasure it offered you up until now and the joy it can potentially deliver to you once the imbalance has been cleared. With all love, your imbalance at times is needed for you to learn about balance. If you are always running with no pauses, you have fewer opportunities to move inside of yourself. Pain quiets your outer world and leaves you with only enough energy to see beauty, appreciating the little things you didn't notice before. We see many on treadmills searching for fame, fortune, and love until sickness strikes. Then, all their desires are reduced to just one: to be healthy again. We hear many of you whisper in our ears, "I want to be healthy again so I can enjoy the little things. I wish I could just lie on the grass and enjoy the sun. I wish I could run with my dog in the park again." Your wish list shrinks quickly. This new list is now made of things many of you did not have time to consider because you were too busy running after the "big" things. The imbalance that you just experienced expressed what needed to be expressed so you could move further on your path. As an example, if your anger was stored in your cells, yet you were unable or unwilling to express it in a way that cleared your energetic body, it is then that your higher self moves into action, sequestering the body to do the clearing and balancing. Your body always follows your higher self direction. Your higher self has chosen to attract and manifest an experience expressing as a dis-ease.

Do you really believe that there is someone out there trying to get you? Do you really believe that you have been forgotten by your angels for just a moment so a virus could enter and wreak havoc in your system? All is done with permission—your permission. With awareness you may heal yourself. Also, you could purposely change the tracks of potential imbalances that were scheduled to wake you up.

How can we change and prevent these imbalances, some of you may wonder?

You sit with yourself and you begin a conversation with your cells which should sound like this: "I love myself. I love my body. I ask to use the power of love and light, clearing, as well as correcting, any imbalances that are in my potential now or in the future, so they never need to be expressed." You may then add, "I ask to attract to myself only experiences which guide me to move forward through balance, peace, harmony, health, love, and light. I ask my body to speak to me when it needs my attention, allowing me the opportunity to guide it to harmony before the imbalance manifests. I am love, I am light, and I am filled with gratitude for the vehicle of divinity that I chose, allowing me to express myself on this plane of reality. I am full of gratitude for every process taking place within my body as it is all sacred, all balanced, and all working in perfect order." As we hug you, we ask you to not turn this intention into a mantra. We wish you to look at our example, understanding that consciousness has the power to bring about healing to cells and tissues through your thought, with feelings, directed by your intention.

The same applies to imbalance and dis-ease. They can be pulled into you through your thoughts and feelings. With all love, know that you are in the midst of a tornado, metaphorically speaking, with the energy swirling and pulling everything on its path upward. The winds are fierce. We ask you to open your wings and allow yourself to be carried upward, fearing not. This tornado is nothing but you asking to be elevated to your highest potential. The aftermath of the tornado can be glorious or disastrous, depending upon you. Your attitude and emotions create your experience, not vice versa. With all love, we ask you to soar above, seeing that all storms do is to rearrange what was and place it differently. You are not losing anything except the things that did not serve you. Learn to surrender to your highest potential by expressing gratitude and love to all that crosses your path. In your new paradigm you are enabled to dance with your body and communicate with it all the time. Speak to your cells and they will respond. You are now in the energy of the New Sun, as it has arrived. One cycle is ending and a new one has begun. Do not fear. Celebrate every moment that you are here on this planet experiencing a profound shift. Know that you asked to be here playing your role, as it is your turn, and so be it.

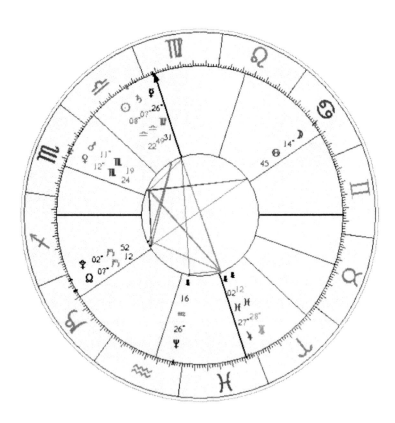

10-1-10

Hi Dror.

May I share some personal thoughts and developments with you?

The other class is with A.F. - a biweekly shamanic drumming circle. Since
I've been in it I have journeyed to the lower world several times and met my
power animal - Wolf - had some very cool journeys. Tonight we journeyed
to the middle world and I journeyed with one of my guides to meet a future
expression of myself - it was after Atlantis rose again. I have been truly
amazed at what I have seen and experienced in these classes as I didn't know I
had the ability to do this!!

I have been asking my guides and angels for help in guiding me to those who can
help me with my development that is for my highest and best.

I have an appointment with D.S. to work on that issue with my excruciating
arm pain past life issue - she is an intuitive reiki & crystal healer and feels
that she can definitely help me with this.

I also have an appointment to work on shifting my consciousness to allow
myself to get "out of my head" and act from the heart only and to deal with
the emotional triggers or fears which are most present for me at this time so
I can dissolve them.

I am loving the community I have found in these groups of spiritually developed
women (sometimes there are men there). I truly want to cross that bridge
to feeling closer to spirit, and to move from my entrenched 3rd dimensional
living. I am grateful to have these connections so close to me here at home and
to have you out there in Woodstock. You have made such a difference in my life
and I want to thank you for helping me in all the ways you have.

Thank you for being who you are. Thank you for being in my life...again...I
wonder how many times? It gives me a great sense of wonder as to why we
have reconnected in this one and to the great work that lies ahead.

Much love and gratitude to you as always.

C.

The Finale

YOU ARE SO DEARLY LOVED.

If we had you memorize anything from what we have been saying to you all this time, it is that you are loved. You are it. There is always one main purpose in all our messages and it is to awaken you so you will remember who you are, feeling the love from spirit. If you have managed to feel it, know that this is the whole story in a condensed form and the rest are just side notes. Real knowing comes from your heart. All other knowing is but interpretations of what you already know, so you can mold it into your linear reality. You exist in a circle but can only see it as one line connected to another line. If you were able to move high enough, you would see that all these connected lines form a large circle—and that circle is you.

We hear some who say, *This is confusing to us. What difference does it make if we are in the line or in the circle?*

Our answer is: for some it may be the difference between heaven and hell.

Why so, you may want to know?

Linear vision only allows you to see your experiences in 3-D, as if you chose to only see the color red in your daily life, ignoring the other colors. Your awareness would grasp only the dimension that is visible and explainable to your left brain. So in essence, you are completely disconnected from the larger story of your life. You may, therefore, experience your life as if everything that is happening is beyond your control, giving access to fear, anxiety, and panic to wreak havoc in your system, risking loss of access to your light. Light is the real you, and the way you choose to see yourself is the way your reality is unfolding in front of you. When you are feeling loved, your whole reality begins to accommodate love. It affects the way your body functions, the way your skin appears, the way you age, the way people look at you. Most importantly, it affects the way you feel about your life and the world around you. Everything changes and it does not have to take much time. When you realize that you exist in the circle, there is no past or future. All is happening in the *present* and therefore you can go backward, forward, and sideways if you please. When something happened in your past that left a mark on your life which is a constant source of pain, you can go back in time and change it. The only constraint you have on your ability to go back in time is your grasp on linear reality. When your mind insists that something cannot be, it does not see, thereby blocking your access to your expanded reality—the one humanity is slowly moving towards.

How about going into the future, some may wonder?

Your future is not yet set, as it is comprised of probabilities. Those potentials exist. You can see them and change them at will, as well. The potentials which are activated are based on your choices, thoughts, and feelings. Going into the future is not really necessary; all you need to do is be aware of the now, and you can shift your future to the highest probability within your path.

Can I move to a different path altogether, some may wonder?

Yes, and many of you do it all the time. You create new probabilities and potentials continuously. The way to access these potentials is from the now. We come from your future because we have been where you are now. We are your brothers and sisters who have mastered traveling through the corridors of time. However, even when we come from your future it is just one potential. Many of us did not see you moving as high as you have. It was a low probability and it became your reality. You have chosen to climb higher than any of us believed possible, creating this wave of excitement all over the universe. This, by itself, can speak volumes about the power you possess. If you for a minute believe that this was the work of governments or large corporations who helped change your trajectory to where it is, you have it upside-down. It is the light-workers and lighthouses like you, who created this shift through your daily meditation, with a commitment within to find love. This love is your magic carpet. As humanity battles between dark and light, your individual choice may be the one choice which tips the scale. In this battle between light and dark your main "weapon" of light is awakening.

Awakening to what, some may still ask?

Awakening to who you are, to the knowing of the power and mastery that each of you possess as an awakened angel. When you are with light, surrounding yourself with love, you are undefeatable. No darkness can even get near you, and that is the call of this time. Awaken.

We see many challenges ahead of you and we see many of you who are making choices to turn on your light. More and more are joining you daily. This is not reported in your media and you will not see statistics, but the billions of angels that are with you know each one of you who chooses to turn on your light by your eternal name. Does it tell you a little about the love of Spirit and the magnificence of your story?

The energy of now is the one many of your sacred native cultures spoke of eons ago. It was prophesied that the consciousness of humanity will have the option to graduate one level of awareness and move into the next higher one.

What does this mean, some may ask?

Higher vibration means greater alignment with your own true story, your relationship to Gaia and resource distribution, your connection with spirit, your relationship to the larger galactic family surrounding you. This graduation comes with challenging tests just like in your educational institutions. Some of your corporations do not wish to see a more balanced planet and resources being distributed more equally to maintain equilibrium with the natural world. This is one aspect of the war that is now being waged. Those tests we speak of are not theoretical. You experience them in your emotional, mental, and physical bodies as well as in your physical environment. Unlike your schools, these tests are not held in a well-lit room, but at times in the darkness of night without the use of any gadgets to help you. This graduation is about the triumph of

Spirit over matter. The wise native cultures have been sidelined by the force of matter. Now it is their time to rise and teach you once again what they know. Many of you have forgotten the knowledge that kept you linked to Earth, sky, and the natural world. These cultures went underground, hiding their knowledge until such a time that it became necessary for humanity to remember and make its leap. The time is now. Those cultures from all over the world who have been repressed, persecuted, and marginalized at great costs to Earth are now returning to their rightful place. They hold the secret keys that link you to yourselves and to your true nature as pure energy that is not separated from your surroundings, but part of this beautiful planet. You are the natural world. You are the plants, trees, birds, and animals. You have, for a minute, forgotten. You allowed the illusion of superiority of man/woman over Gaia to wipe out your knowing. The time of remembering is now. You have forgotten to love the food that sustains you, blessing the Earth and the water that nourishes your bodies.

The hardest test always comes at the end of the schooling period, and indeed, these tests require you to remember all that you have learned. Many of your past cycles are now coming back to your awareness, and many of you will begin to remember who you were. This is not a coincidence, as you must use that knowledge to advance. Each one of you carries within your unique DNA a key to your own journey of ascension. We ask you to use your own manual because it is the only one that is accurate for you. One form of test facing many involves the expression of illnesses and health challenges in your biological vehicles. You must integrate all you know in a short period of time, as Spirit works on the energetic adjustment through your body. You are an expression of Spirit, and your body is a manifestation of all that you must clear. As we hug you, feeling your fear, frustrations, pain, and agony, we must assure you that you are not alone. You are greatly loved, and all that you experienced can be cleared. There is nothing that is attached to you that cannot be removed. You are Spirit and your body is your expression. You are the sculptor, the painter, or the musician. The way you choose to play your instrument will be expressed in the melody heard. The way you use your chisel or the way you apply paint to your canvas will ultimately create your masterpiece. Begin today to express love to self, your surroundings, and to the natural world. Your body will change forever as a result. Healing at this time is not just for the body, it is healing throughout time and space. Every time you clear an imbalance, celebrate because it brings Gaia closer to balance. You few are doing the work for many. You have chosen to be here at this time being aware, about these pending tests. There are no tests for which you are not prepared. This time is a time for celebration.

What do we have to celebrate, many will ask?

You have stood in line to be in the finale and this is it. It is not *the* end, but *an* end and a beginning of something new. You are moving from one paradigm, where you see yourself as a human separated from all things, into a new potential paradigm of unity consciousness where you experience oneness with all that is. This privilege was guarded and kept for the very few who dedicated their lives and mission to it. Now, in your potential and through awakening, greater numbers are able to move into the dimension of oneness, balancing with self, planet, with your expanded family—a family of light. This is your mission and why you wanted to be here now. Some of you have not been on Earth for a very long time, waiting for the right moment to come down and play the game of life, making a difference. This is your opportunity. This message comes from the circle and we ask you for a moment to step inside, feeling the love. Draw a circle around you and step into it. Just feel the hugs. As you expand your idea of who you are we wish you to give a hand to the natural world. Speak to this world, speak to your cells, speak to your angels, and speak to the elements. We know that your society may lock you up if you do it in public, so do it with thoughts and feelings. Communicate with the larger you, allowing time and space for the larger you to answer you back. Create a sacred circle at home and know that we are always waiting, ready to hug you. You are so dearly loved, and so be it.

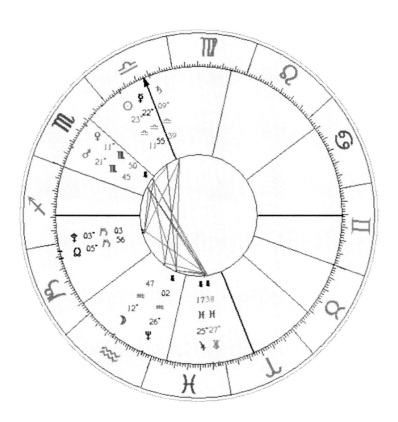

10/16/10

Hi Drori,

So we're celebrating a bit. Had a big family party yesterday
and I was tired when you called.
Just wanted to find out if you and Ofer arranged to meet on
Sunday when you come, cause I am taking him to Jerusalem on
Sunday morning for two days, and it's a surprise. I also invited
some friends to come to Jerusalem on Sunday evening, just to
drink a toast for him at our zimmer in Ein Karem so it would
be great if u could join us…

Let me know your plans
love

Dear A.

I would love to but I am coming for just a few
hours to Israel and then going to Egypt. I will be
celebrating with you in my heart

Love to all of you

Dror

Elixir of Love

YOU ARE DEARLY LOVED.

When you stand in the center of a circle, you are it. When we hug you and tell you that you are so dearly loved, it is because, for us, you are the center of the circle. We wish you to see what we see, beginning the journey of moving higher and higher from where you are now standing. No two of you are alike, and you cannot take anyone with you when you ascend in vibration. The ascension path is a path that begins from the lonely place of the one and journeys to becoming one with all that is. There are many of you who are going through a separation from parts of yourselves.

What do you mean, some may wonder?

Those you call your lover, spouse, child, friend, and family are parts of you. At times you must shed the illusion of the separate being that you believe to be, in order to find out eventually that you are never apart from anything or anybody. Like water changes to ice

413

or steam, so relationships must change their form. If you wish the relationship to remain the same, you must choose the "life" of a rock. The life of an angel in the disguise of a human is all about growing, changing, learning, and teaching, collecting the many parts of the puzzle into one coherent picture that spells the word "love" in the center. Often the separation from the illusion of the self involves great pain. Some may feel as if their insides are being torn apart. The feeling of deep pain, longing, and yearning may take over as you depart from those loved ones. We know your human side as we are with you through all your rides. We see your suffering and we feel the movement of anguish in your solar plexus when those cords become unlinked. With all love, we must impart to you that your path must at times allow the self to clear, cleansing some parts so you can expand and grow. Your relationships mirror you back to you, and as you grow, the face that is reflected in the mirror may need to change so it can reflect the new you.

Fundamentally, all those who were part of your life in the past, as well as in your future, exist in a quantum space now available, accessible, and linked to you at all times. All your past relationships, even from your previous cycles, are all still there, very much alive and conscious in the present. As a human your attention cannot truly contain the idea of "no time." We know who you are as we can see you all the time. Many of you are struggling with one central relationship, let alone dealing with thousands of relationships from all your past cycles. You are much vaster than you can ever imagine, and when we see the geometry of guilt or shame around you, as you choose to move higher, allowing some parts of you to remain behind, we wish you to know that higher is really the only viable choice you have at this time. As Gaia is ascending you must be with her in the direction upwards. As you expand and grow you allow all who come in contact with you to grow as well, even if you are not physically there to hold their hands. Your choices affect the whole—not only your close circle but the whole vibrational balance of light and dark on your planet as well as beyond your Milky Way.

Time and space are but limited constructs of one dimension and reality. In the not-so-distant future you will begin to explore other dimensions and realities, as distance will become a nonissue in space travel. Your consciousness can plant itself in an instant in the furthest reaches of your circular universe because it is all contained within you. Your consciousness expands mainly through feeling and experiencing, on the cellular level, the vastness of your existence. All the words in your linear vocabulary cannot come close to describing the experience of expansion. You must *feel it and be in it*. When you do, no words are really necessary to describe it because you have moved from being in third-dimensional reality to all dimensions with multiple reality overlap. Being at a loss for words is an understatement when you expand.

As humanity is nearing graduation your journey is now about defying gravity, becoming lighter and lighter. The lighter you are, the higher you can levitate. The higher you can levitate, the further you can see and feel. You must expand the notion of who you are and know that you are that. You are the center of the universe. All that you see, feel, and experience begins, as well as ends, within the vast energy that you call "I." "I am that I am" means that you do not need to look any further than inside of you to all the secrets and mysteries which are unfolding in your external reality. Heaviness is the density of the old energy where the frequency of your combined thoughts and emotions were near the bottom of the scale.

As you move higher each and every one of you must leave behind the old, the heavy, and begin dressing light, being light, eating light. Choose, every time, the lighter option versus the denser one.

What do you mean? Give us an example, some may say.

As you walk in your day-to-day and face an intersection, sense the density of either direction, turning to where it feels less dense. When you get out of bed in the morning and look at the selection of clothes in your closet, again, do not think, but sense the density of the outfit, choosing the less dense. When you are invited to go to a social event and you need to decide whether to attend, use your solar plexus, looking for the sensation of pull or push. Pull means denser energy and push means lighter, recharging energy. As you expand, your whole body acts as an antenna capturing all the sensory stimulation that surrounds you, both visible and invisible. Your spine, when open and activated, can receive signals from your future that the mind cannot interpret but your feeling centers can. Your density determines your reality so, when your vibration increases, the communication between us is greatly facilitated. We are on a vibration that is more subtle than you are and it is why you cannot sense us with your physical eyes. However, we can communicate with the subtle parts of you when you are quiet and peaceful.

As you can see there are many parts to the puzzle that make who you are, but the glue that holds all the pieces together is always love.

What is all this talk about love, some may wonder? *It only got me in trouble*, others may claim!

Love is the air that you breathe and is the fire that you warm your body with. Love is the water you drink, it is the atoms and molecules which make up your physical form. Love is all that you see, hear, taste and smell. Love is not the romance that went sour between you and your ex. You call that love, but we call it being human and getting a taste of higher vibration. When you are in love your frequency actually increases and you feel in harmony with all that is. Your heart feels open and your body feels excited. This is how a human gets a taste of love, but for us love is what makes up your universe. When your scientists move deeper into quantum physics they will discover that the field itself is conscious and it responds to . . . yes, you guessed it . . . LOVE. It is the glue and the energy which is contained within each cell in your body. It is in the atoms, molecules, and photons, holding all of it together. Love is in carbon and it is in silicon. It is in the elements and directions. When lovers open their hearts to each other, allowing their cells to feel, expand, and arouse their vibration through sexual energy, they are beginning to experience the oneness of all existence. Through orgasm, you enter for a short time a vortex of melting walls and the unification of all the yous. You become one with your lover and one with your universe. Through love, with sexual energy, you can open doorways to your expanded reality where your true power, mastery, and light are ever present. It is no wonder that so many cultures placed restrictions on the utilization of love mixed with sexual energy. The mystery schools had to hide this knowledge from the masses because it possesses an immense power which could be harmful if used inappropriately. As power began to shift, with resources being used by the few to gain power over the many, this knowledge was hidden from the masses so they would remain malleable and could be manipulated. The institutions of religions and the ruling governments began to forbid and restrict the use of sexual energy, corrupting the codes so that the keys to ascending higher would be difficult to discover. Why did they go through so much effort to hide it? It is because the elixir of love with sexual energy is the engine and fuel which can take your vehicle to a place where you do not need anyone to protect you or control you. You are liberated and powerful to be that which you are . . . a master. Your religious institutions cannot control you when you are powerful, and your governments do not need to protect you when you are powerful. Throughout your history, the keys to moving higher were tainted, polluted with "viruses"—codes of darkness including guilt, pain, and immorality. The language of light was scrambled and it is on you to decode it, beginning to utilize the language of light in your own personal journey. You are the main force which can enable the transformation of those who are in power. The game of life has changed. The power of light and dark has moved from the physical to the subtle. *Your own vibration* is the force behind the movement—not politics or big business any longer.

The scrambling of your frequency was a deliberate attempt to keep you at a lower vibration where you can be easily controlled and manipulated. Who was behind this "conspiracy" you may wonder? From our perch there was no conspiracy per se, although it surely has all the characteristics of one.

So why was it conducted in such a way, some may wish to know?

There are many players in your game of chess. Not all appear in human form. There are players who compete for your resources, be they physical or, at times, energetic. These players—some of them seen, some unseen—are also part of creation and allowed to interact with you. They have their own path and karma. They have power over you only when your frequency is scrambled and your light dim. When you are in your power, you cannot be manipulated into being something that you are not. Your ancients knew of the power you possess and the potential you have to ascend from one reality to another. This task was well guarded, being utilized by very few, as the process was hidden and coded. Only those who were deemed worthy received entry to the secrets of moving higher. The players and consumers of resources did not wish for the masses to discover the power because it meant that they would no longer be able to easily harvest their crops. We speak in very general, simple terms because it is a process that is part of your journey, and you, through your own light, succeeded in moving higher to a place where now the awakening can be accessed by all who intend for it with pure heart.

Why all of a sudden, you may want to know?

You have made a choice and that choice became a turning point for the future of all of humanity.

When did that turning point occur, some may wonder?

It was in your year of 1987 but began twenty-five years earlier in 1962. The battle of light and dark seemed to be won by the dark until the time that many volunteered to come back to Earth and shift the balance to neutral, so your choice will have power. During the mid-1950s and early 1960s, a steady but growing stream of what we called masters were born to your mothers because they wanted to see that this game on your precious planet continues. Fewer came as early as the 1930s and 1940s; however, their voices were mainly silenced as they found their environment highly inhospitable and unsupportive. Now everyone wants to participate in the game, and the growth in population is a reflection of that desire as graduation nears. The light that began to flood your planet along with the new frequencies which were introduced to you from outer space allowed the awakening and re-assembling of some of the information coded in your DNA. This enabled many of you to awaken and begin to claim your mastery.

Who sent those new frequencies, some may ask?

You are a galactic being and you play the game of creation not only on Earth, but in other realities as well. In the great game of creation there are many players. You had a lot of support from your galactic neighbors, and we hope that soon enough you will be able to see them in person, even in your 3-D reality. You are the most powerful energy in creation, and as such, you could influence the deliverance of frequency that can change the trajectory of your journey on your planet. You call this deliverance "God's hand," but in fact, it is you collectively who are behind the change in the flow of energy and the flooding of light from the center of your galaxy. As the alignment of the center of your galaxy approaches, in your year of 2012, the moment to awaken has arrived, as it symbolized the moment of truth, as well as the time to awaken to the truth of who you are and why you are here.

The knowing and information that is part of your legacy is embedded in your DNA, and the decoding of it happens automatically when you give intent, beginning to raise your vibration. Raising your vibration expels out all the blocks, that were embedded and implanted in you, up to the surface. Many of you are now going through seemingly insurmountable challenges to clear those blocks. This is your work and it is sacred. As you clear yourself, you pave the way for others. Your children are already a step further ahead as the road has been cleared significantly by many of you. The pull-push/light-dark battle continues with new scrambling methods being introduced to you and your children, many of which are being delivered through your new technology to hold your attention. Your attention is the heart of "the battle." In this accelerated time the focus of your attention manifests as your reality. If you create peace within you, coming to a place of love and balance, you become the lighthouse, illuminating your own path and the path of those around you. If you are numb, so that much of your attention is directed outward, as you absorb your media indiscriminately, you may be neutralized and used as harvest for those who do not have your best interest in mind.

At the core of moving higher in vibration is clearing blocks. The main block—as far as we can see—has to do with sexual energy, as it has received the most attention from the dark to redirect and rechannel your energy. The dark targeted the fuel for your engine so you would have limited capacity to move higher. Much of the information known to your ancient civilizations was repackaged and manipulated so the original intention would be lost. New purpose was assigned to rituals and some suffered severe repercussions for daring to use or guard this knowledge. Sexual energy is your fuel, and when you choose the high-octane grade it can carry you like a spaceship up into the heavens. When you choose to use your energy source in its raw vibration form, with guilt, shame, fear, anger, or revenge, or you feed yourself with this energy not using love, you may find yourself in the darkest of dark caverns. Look around you. You may notice how sexual energy, repressed in certain groups or religions, can be channeled towards violence, hatred, fanaticism, and chaos in the name of ideology.

It is your choice at any moment to move with light or with dark. We always love you and wish to remind you that whatever you choose is sacred. Dark is not bad, it just lacks love or light. It does not represent your truth and therefore does not support your highest path.

What do we do with that information, some may wonder?

Give intent to celebrate your body. Use your sexual energy often in a sacred form. Teach your body to be loved, allowing the knowledge embedded in your DNA to resurface and teach you all the unexplored pleasure zones and mysteries of your body. Never judge and always allow that which you experience to be used as building blocks for new awareness to guide you on your journey. There has never been a more potent time to make a shift in your life. You came this time around to experience a shift. We ask you with all love to move into the center of your truth and begin today. Use love, and your heart, in all that you do. Your whole reality is about to shift and as you enter into alignment with the center of your galaxy; simultaneously, you must align with your own center. This is your time. Do not fear love. Do not fear pleasure. Do not fear to experience life as a game and as an adventure. Play the game as if each day is the only day. Focus on the now and stay connected to your breath. Allow Mother Gaia to take your breath away with joy as you ascend to new heights. Stay connected to Gaia and ask to be guided. We are with you, celebrating, guiding, and hugging you, when you call us. We are your angels. For us you are the only one who matters, and so be it.

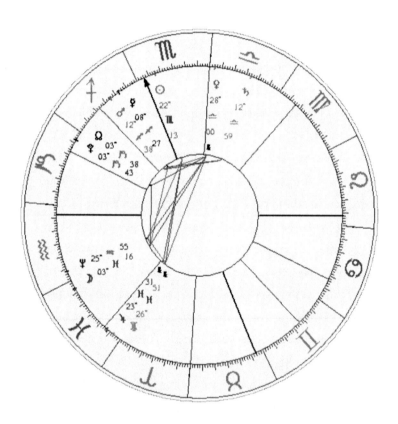

11/14/10
Dear Angel,

You know I can relate!
Waves of pain still wash over me when i choose to focus on Mark's
refusal to speak to me and his still being so angry....but when i focus on
where i am right now in my beautiful journey i see there really was
no other way for me. he will rise above the pain when he chooses to
and it has nothing to do with me and my center. using sexual energy
for my ascension process has been very powerful and joyful and i love
sharing my thoughts and feelings about it with others...connecting
in pure love is amazing just for the bliss of it, for the light of it....it is
beautiful learning to dance this dance and i am so thankful for your
teaching me how. i love watching the unfolding of the lessons and
messages...it will be so very interesting to see how people respond.
Thank you for the courage it takes to do what you are doing. I had a
really great conversation or two with my guide here Mahmoud about
where i believe we are going and about Muslim rules from an spiritual
American womens pt of view....ive given him much to think about...that
when we can be in a state of love for reach other and god no matter
how much or how little clothing we have on then we will be making
the shift....when we can just LOVE each other as we are or choose to
be....the day is near. and i am committed to holding space for its arrival.

so tired ....another long day visiting Akenatens priests tombs and his
palace.....lots of craziness doing a chanting ceremony for 30 min and
the old guard freaking out.....hilarious stories...lots to tell. It really is
all so comical....like how i know what they are saying even though i
dont know the language. and when i call them on it they are amazed.....
shifting the world one person at a time. "Network awakening"

good night

always love,
Nicki

The Scaffolding

YOU ARE DEARLY LOVED.

At the end of each sentence there is a period, and at the end of each journey there is a rest stop. At the end of a steep mountain climb you celebrate the vista, and at the end of a steep decent to the bottom of a valley you celebrate water to quench your thirst. As you probably already "know," all your journeys are within the realm of the circle. When you go down it is only a preparation to go up. As you turn to the left it is only until you realize that it is also a right, depending on which side you are facing. All journeys are contained within you. As you build a story around your life, where you are going, what you wish to achieve, know that, when you move forward enough it will become a backward, when you move high enough it inevitably will take you down again, as if you were inside a balloon. That is why we never judge you based on your ups or downs, lefts or rights, forwards or backwards, as they are all movements within you. With a smile, we wish you to fathom that it is not the direction you are heading that matters, but how you feel about it, as you move through your life. The real movement is only contained within your consciousness, as all life rhythms are but cycles—some shorter, some longer. The footprint you leave, after you have recycled your physical form, is the energy that you carried and the experiences within that you have accumulated.

As you walk up or down, left or right, east, west, north, or south, you always search for something. That something is what pushes you to make an effort. You feel that you are not whole unless you get somewhere and find that something—as if a treasure is waiting for you. Once you have discovered the hidden cave and open the treasure box all will be well. This is one essential aspect of your story in simple terms. What moves many of you is a powerful desire to find something that will make you complete.

And what is this something, some may ask?

The simple answer is, of course, love. Many of you, however, search for substitutes that will allow you to experience love for yourself. The love that some of you search for out there in the physical world is but a set of training wheels for your "bicycle" to keep you riding along your path, convincing you that you are worthy of love. Many of you need to create a convincing story around your life similar to scaffolding. You create a story by which you yourself will be convinced. When you believe yourself, you are more apt to accept and love yourself. On this path, we hug many of you who built one story and all their love for self was based on that one story. As the power of light is increasing, illuminating your hidden inner truths, that story you created no longer adds up and the scaffolding can no longer hold the walls around you. All is now cracking open. There are stress fractures in the stories that many of you created around your life. These fractures are becoming larger until your story will no longer hold the foundation of the house and it will fall down, as it must. Letting go of the old, a new story can be created. The new story is grander than any of you may imagine at the moment and it is coming. If we had told you two hundred years ago that people would be able to speak from the farthest parts of the world at will, at any time, by using a small portable device, even seeing each other as they speak, you would say that it could not be. Remember that you did not have light bulbs yet. In fact, you would probably have the person prophesying reported to the authorities as a certified lunatic or an antichrist anarchist. You are in the midst of a change. It is becoming more and more apparent that the mechanics that you are used to navigating your life with seem to be less and less effective.

As a result of these changes many of you are losing those training wheels and crashing to the ground. The scaffolding that supported the walls around you is disintegrating and soon these walls will give way too. Crashing to the ground means that there is no longer reason to love the self because *that* self has changed costumes, no longer matching the story and expectations you built with such great effort. The physical story around your life is a manifestation of your inner awareness. Therefore your physical environment must go through some drastic changes, as well, so your inner environment will be prompted to shift. All is connected in a beautiful thread and all the movements are happening now. Some of you delude yourself that you have time, and with a smile, we remind you that you have all the time in the world; you are indeed eternal. However, within the scope of this cycle you are running out of time, and the awakening bells that we keep speaking of are ringing now.

What are we to do with all this information, some may rightly ask?

You cannot resist the change as it will create an inner conflict too intense to sustain. You must work on moving to a higher plane and vibrating with love to self. Working within your inner circle is your most powerful road map to navigating in these tumultuous, rough seas.

Many of you feel that all you want is to be accepted and loved for who you are. Only if your spouse, partner, family, friends, and coworkers would accept you, love you, your life would be perfect. With tender love, we remind you, for the however many times that we do, that you chose all these actors to play their role, showing you your own resistance to loving the self and accepting yourself the way you are. When you finally move beyond the role-play, embracing the wholeness of your being without judging yourself or others, as if by magic, all those around you who "gave you a hard time and made your life miserable" (to quote some of you) either change their position, embracing you fully for who you are, or move out of your way, clearing your path.

We hug many of you who are worried about the state of affairs on your precious planet. So many of you light warriors want to take this world and shake it, so that all the "evil" will be sucked out by a black hole carried off to oblivion, yet all the "good" will remain intact. You ask in your prayers for the Earth to be cleansed, for humans to love each other, accept each other, and support each other. We see many of you weep at night because you can physically feel all the pain, anguish, and suffering that is being displayed to you day in, day out by your media technology while some of you feel that you are powerless to do anything about it. "There is so much darkness and so little light" is the message that keeps popping up on your screens. We see you cry over the animals because their habitat is systematically being destroyed. We see you shedding tears over the children that go hungry and the senseless violence that is being expressed against innocent people. There are victims everywhere and seemingly there is no light at the end of the tunnel, to use a cliché from your literature. We ask you to sit for a moment in front of your candle, take a deep breath, and connect to your heart. Through your heart we ask you to realize the sacredness of all that is swirling around you. Billions and billions of choices, as well as agreements, of the divine human are being expressed at any given moment. All the darkness that you see is your choice. The day that enough of you change within, your reality will transform as if it happened overnight. Gaia is powerful and will remain intact, alive, and well for a long, long time. The question remains if you will still inhabit Gaia or search for a new place to express your divinity. There is never a judgment as Gaia took you and is supporting you unconditionally every moment that you are alive. She gives you the air you breathe and the food you eat. All that you have is gifted to you from Gaia.

Some of you may say, *We want more light. How can we force the darkness to go to the light and transform?*

Our short answer is: you cannot.

You can only offer light to the darkness but you cannot force anyone to open their eyes. The dark ones of humanity are just one step from becoming light ones. Once they intend to move into the light, they do. That is all it takes. In the meantime they are as sacred as you are and as loved as you are. The nature of this experiment is that free will is honored above all. Your mission is to create enough light so that all who open their eyes will begin to see using your light. Light is created when you begin to love self. Loving self is loving the God within you.

Many of you are aching at this time and we ask you to redirect your passion to your inner circle, aiming your desire to helping humanity from the inside out. Your power will be greatly amplified to bring the change that you envision.

We love you and we know of the limitation of the human to accept reality that is not being displayed to you through your senses. This is the way of it from the beginning of time. If you could only move with us above the stage you call Earth, seeing the set designers and producers of your show, you would maybe understand that it is all just a magnificent production made for your entertainment as well as your learning. The suffering is real and the pain is real for those of you who experience it, but it is time to embrace that you have a choice at any given moment to ascend beyond this stage. Like the individual human who creates a social network of friends and family so they can learn about self, so it is with humanity. Humanity represents the consciousness of the planet moving and acting with free choice. What you consider your reality on Earth is but a reflection of the collective state of loving and accepting self; each one of you, as an actor in this production, as well as in your own role, makes a difference for the whole. You represent the micro, and your own shift creates a shift within the macro.

Your love for self is the love of God. Some of your sacred texts ask you to "kill" the ego and live for the sake of others. You are asked to do one good thing for someone else and you will ascend to heaven. It is again a misunderstanding of the deep meaning of the texts you have received from pure sacred sources. All begins with self. Love for self is not egoistic, but the purest love of God. Accepting your own light is the path to accepting all lights; loving yourself is the core of loving all who come in contact with you. Your own personal evolution is the evolution of humanity. Through your eyes everything changes. When you begin to shift your attention to loving yourself, you are becoming the server for humanity because wherever you walk you give permission to others to love themselves.

So much of what was given to humanity in the form of sacred text was ever so slightly manipulated so that, instead of you becoming empowered, you were sold on the idea that you are powerless and that real divine power is outside of you. At times, the plus and minus signs were reversed so that the text seems almost the same, but one word was inserted at the "right place" to change the whole meaning.

Loving the self is the source of love; accepting the self is the source of acceptance; compassion for self is the source of compassion; and on the other side of the spectrum, hatred for self extends to hatred for humanity; violence against the self extends to violence against humanity, which may also be expressed as violence towards Gaia.

Some of your religions interpreted your sacred texts that you must love God. By the same token, if you do not love God, you will be punished, suffering the consequences. Some religions ask you to believe in punishment and consequences resulting from you not following their belief. They also ask you to believe that their sacred text comes from the love of God. Does it feel like Spirit, we ask with a smile? Spirit never judges or punishes anyone, and God is not religious. The love of God asks nothing of you; it only gives. Do you see where you have been misled? It is not necessarily the original intention of the text that is at fault but the interpretation of the text. You are a wave pattern of light, a chain of photons, atoms, and molecules that are commanded by conscious energy. Your physical form is but a temporary vehicle to express yourself, and to us you appear as a beautiful display of geometric shapes, sound, and light.

You occupy a space that is much larger than your body, and as a result, your form can only house part of you. Very few of you hold the majority of your total energy. If you would hold your entirety you would implode from the intensity of the force that is contained within the being you represent. You are magnificent in every way. Many of you sigh in disbelief. We hear you telling yourselves for the thousandth time, "I have no power; I do all I can and the world is not changing. I came as a light warrior. I fight and fight, but the battles continue. I do not see any difference. The powerful still dictate our lives. The Earth is still being violated, animals are still being killed, violence and hunger still flourish in many places. There are injustices everywhere. What can I do?" With a hug, we ask you to start at home. Learn to truly link to your light, accepting the flame that is within you; that is the shortest way to bring the change for all of humanity.

From our perspective, Earth is ascending and you are standing on the verge of an immense shift in consciousness. The dark and light will be doing the dance, while your role is to stand still, maintaining your balance, witnessing all the movements around you. Your role is to keep your equilibrium intact and your heart open while being the lighthouse that you are. When you accept all the stories of fear, pain, and desperation that are being sent to you, you are no better off than you were before. When you disconnect from these stories, even for short periods of time, linking with your own truth deep in the cave of your heart, you will hear the melody that is now permeating more and more people on this precious planet—the melody of unity consciousness, the understanding that you are all part of one being, not separated from the Earth or from the natural world. When you begin to sit quietly, listening to the new melody that is being played inside of you, you may soon realize that you are in a play and you are one of the actors. Your role is to be a lighthouse, and for that you need to awaken, turning on your light. The misery that you see all around you will continue for some time and even increase for a while. The drama will continue and Earth will reflect this drama, demonstrating her own magnificent, sacred role on this grand stage. So what can you do? You are to awaken to your own truth and begin with the self. It seems like little, but from our perch it is all.

We always tell you that you are loved, and we ask you to move into your heart, feeling that love for yourself. Some will say, "This is too simple. It cannot be that we can affect global events by just loving the self." With a hug we ask you to look at your history, seeing what effects were created by individuals and masters who loved themselves like Jesus, Buddha, or Gandhi. Every master of love always had to conquer the self first. With all the people on Earth walking in darkness, the most powerful act you can do is to create another ripple of love. Loving the self is your service. When you do, you always give that vibration to whoever crosses your path. You cannot wait to help someone because you feel good about the self. You are full and your fountain just keeps giving. This is your story. In your sacred texts you were told that one of the essential truths that you were to follow is, "You shall love thy neighbor as thyself." Again, the interpretation was changed to dilute the power that you possess. The emphasis should be on loving the self first and then extending that love to your neighbor.

You can only create in your world that which you have first created within you. Create love within and you will manifest it in your reality. There are many who say, "I do not even know how to begin." With a smile we whisper: how about beginning today by taking time to honor yourself for being on this planet, fulfilling your promise to do all you can to awaken to your mission and shine your light? Ask to be shown the way and the answers will come quicker than the speed of light. The reason is that these answers do not need to travel far. They are already within you. Your light, when shining, is connected to all lights. Together you illuminate this precious planet and allow others to see. If you are sad or angry because of the state of affairs currently on your planet, you do not emit much light and you are therefore in darkness. It is sacred and honored to experience these emotions, feeling them, fully allowing them to move through you, out into the world, so you can transform sadness into joy, anger into compassion, fear into balance, hate into love. We spoke often of how to allow emotions which are dense to move through the energetic body and be transferred to Gaia so they can be absorbed by her, transformed into love. Your Mother Earth is always there to give you a hug and take away the overloaded density that does not belong to you. Your natural soul state is one of pure joy.

How do we do that, some may wonder? *Is there a system that can take all the heaviness from me?*

Yes, there is a system and it is called mastery. The way to do it is to simply ask to be shown the way. Sit in front of a candle, asking Spirit to lead you, and we will celebrate with you the journey to ascension.

You may take action to change events in your physical reality and it is sacred. You can volunteer and petition. You can ask your friends to demonstrate for this cause and that cause. You can donate to all the worthy causes you deem appropriate and that is all sacred. You main role, however, still remains to take these actions from a higher, elevated vibration, realizing that all the injustices that you see come from within and the biggest shift you can create out there is by using self-love, radiating that love to others. Move into joy and take care of self. Through self, create a circle of love around you. That ripple will then grow in concentric circles, expanding to all, and so be it.

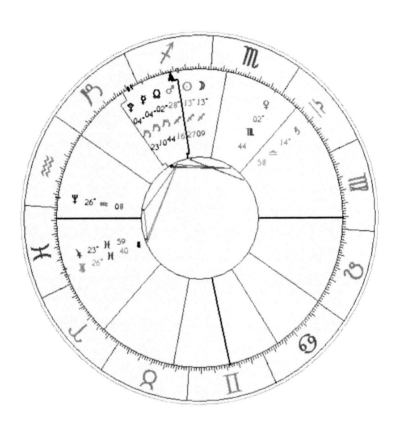

12/5/10

Dearest Dror,

I understand the cocoon thing and am glad you emailed. I have been wanting to reach out but kept getting in my own way.

I have been thinking about you so much lately and how I haven't communicated to you how much I want to have a healing session with you. I have got to move these blockages. I feel like as soon as I make steps forward, I fall back a little. I am constantly wondering what my mission is, especially in this transition time. I am also losing my job at the end of the month and haven't figured out what direction I am going in. I am sooooooooooooooooooo wanting to know if there are stepping stones I can take to move in the direction that I am here for. What did I contract to do this time?

I am also transitioning everything that I can into natural organic, and am now investigating the medications I am on and how to do this. I just realized that the med I have been on for years causes glaucoma, which I was diagnosed with last year. I didn't know! I would love to get some help on transitioning off the med I've been on for years with nutrients. I am doing a lot of research lately on nutrition and ascension. I have been feeling a disconnect, brain fog, tired, short-term memory loss - I don't know if it is ascension symptoms or something else? Sometimes I feel sad for no reason. I am so glad I have Maria's class every Wednesday - I feel connected there. I am dealing with my duality/polarities and trying to find the happy medium. Questions always lead to more questions...

Sorry to dump this all out on you. In the last 2-3 classes (Maria's Intuitive Development) you came through several of the readers. Maria actually heard from her guides - "Dror is the only one" and that I had to stop getting in the way of my healing with you. That this work will be extremely important for my development. My "other" side is working hard at keeping me where I am. But I know it is time, and I want to open to my highest and best. Can you help me Dror....

Please forgive my ramblings, but I took the opportunity to get off my chest what's been in my head - thank you for emailing me. Funny, I was going to contact you today.

. Thank you for all you do and all you are. You are so loved by so many people.

Love,

C.

443

I Am Ready

YOU ARE DEARLY LOVED.

"I am ready," we hear you say. "So are we," we respond as we look at you with so much love. "Let's dance," we say to you and slowly we begin to lead you step by step to the sound of music. We are angels and we are made of music. Our essence is a vibration and we communicate with you through sound vibration. When we hug you, you may hear a high pitch in your inner ear. Do not rush to the doctor, as our frequency communicates with your frequency via what we call electromagnetic biofeedback and at times it creates an audible sound.

How does this communication take place, some may still wonder?

The physical aspects are complex. However, to use an analogy, we move into your vehicle with your permission and allow our subtle engine to coordinate RPMs with your subtle engine. Once we are aligned communication is possible. In the process of this alignment the high pitch may be heard as the two frequencies create a feedback effect while colliding with each other. It can be described as an electromagnetic charge that is being introduced and released into your nervous system. Your body may also experience pulsation sensations and inner vibration which results from our dance. You may feel waves of heat or dizziness and an increase in your heartbeats. Some of you may feel a sensation of expansion as if the body has no more need to breathe. Some may feel movement of energy within the body changing locations as if by its own accord. There are still those who may begin to hear conversations; smell strange scents; feel, touch, or see sights that are seemingly not there—as if the imagination is working overtime. Some may become concerned that you are losing touch with reality. You may experience symptoms that do not make you feel good but are also part of this process. Some are emotional and some physical.

With all love, we must impart to you that as you move higher you must become lighter. Your body must clear out the heavy loads, and as blocks are being flushed through the system, it may feel challenging. Some may feel sudden sadness for no apparent reason or even depression. You may experience periods of little energy to do anything except sleep or periods of debilitating anxiety or fear that come from no specific source. At times sudden pains or bruises may appear; some bumps and lumps may come and go. Periods of digestive issues, heart palpitations, over sweating, and circulation issues may pass through. You may feel too cold, too hot, suffer from dizziness, headaches, stiff neck, blurry vision, and fevers. These are a short list of the many symptoms that are associated with the changes taking place in your biology. We ask you to move through it all with a smile as resistance may create additional blocks. *Do not resist* means do not numb yourself; stay present and acknowledge how you feel. Allow yourself to go through the ebbs and flows of this process without trying to keep yourself "up" artificially. Take care of your biology and eat pure foods, drink pure water, and meditate often. Allow your body to move and connect to Earth in whatever way suits you. Your body needs all the support it can get at this time to remain balanced.

With love, we ask you to congratulate yourself as some of you are beginning to move into a more expansive playing field of reality. It is as if you are lying in bed pretending to be sleeping but then you are not sure if what you are seeing or hearing is happening in your dream or for "real." It is a magnificent time and your medical science cannot support your "weird sensation" because it cannot measure it yet. It is measurable but not in any way that can be easily identified, so you are in a place where you must rely on trust to know that you are in the midst of a shift, and much of it is taking place inside of you.

Why are you speaking of the body again, some may wonder?

Many of you feel "strange" but very few of you stop to wonder what it is that is taking place inside. You may say to yourself, "I feel weird," and dismiss it or you may just lie down, waiting it out. Some even go to the doctor and describe the symptom. The response you get may be: menopause, inner-ear imbalance, midlife symptoms, stress, autoimmune disorder, diet, and so on. With all love, we must tell you that the biological vehicle that has served you for so long in one way is being upgraded, and many of those sensations may very well be part of this sacred process. If you knew the complexity of the interaction that is taking place between your cells, our melody and the particles that are being directed at you from the center of your galaxy, you would stop in your tracks, be in awe and in gratitude for what is happening, as it is utterly magnificent.

What is it that is happening to us, some may still inquire?

When an angel hugs a human we hold a celebration. Can you just imagine how many parties we have these days? Many of you are making leaps in your vibration, moving higher and higher. Now, your biology is beginning to catch up. Your body is a code-carrying device that responds to melodic vibration. Everything around you is made out of unique sounds, and much of it is in-audible. Sound vibrations are at the core of all creation. Sound works on your subtle energy, and you do not need a translation as your cells respond to the vibration carried by the sound. We see sound used for healing moving into the forefront of a holistic approach to balancing the body. Not too far into your future we see potentials for many new techniques sprouting, facilitating communication with your cells through sounds, bringing them back to balance and health. Some techniques may even be multidimensional using sound intent from quantum space. You may call upon the appropriate sound from the universe to return you to optimal health without needing to know which to use. Your body will know. You will need to communicate with your body from a multidimensional awareness. Your link to your own vessel is being upgraded and these types of conversations between you and your body are more enabled than ever before. Much magic is on the way as you move higher in your vibration. Sound translates to color which translates to light. All are vibrations in variations of forms and all are different aspects of the one.

When our melody interacts with your melody, these codes that were undecipherable up until now are beginning to reorganize themselves, making sense inside your heart. We call it "angelic activation." It is happening everywhere the human gives intent to move higher, and many of you do. Each one of you that leaps, spiraling upward, is a cause for celebration and all of us know about it. You are a celebrity in the angelic kingdom, we say with a smile. Some however, are so engrossed in their denser reality movie that many of these symptoms are being viewed as nuisances and ignored. There is never a judgment on the side of Spirit and all is by free choice. With a hug, we ask you: why would you want to miss the greatest shift humanity has seen since your unique angelic species was introduced to this planet a little over a hundred thousand years ago? You all wanted to be here at this time awakened so you can act your role and fulfill your mission. You have worked on it for so many lifetimes. Finally, now you are here and you are dozing off? If we had to predict your future, we would say that many of you who are in dozing-off mode will soon be awakened to ear-deafening bells.

Tell us, what do you see in our future, some of you may ask us?

We see your potentials, as all is up to you. We see you looking up and welcoming some of your galactic family to a celebration. We see some of you moving into the realms of light that have not been seen on a mass scale on this planet since you came aboard. And some of you will elect to delve into a reality of darkness that was described as hell in your sacred texts. This lower-vibration reality is one where you keep repeating a rerun of past karmic choices that lack love, with seemingly the same scenario repeating, binding you in an endless loop. The karmic attributes of the new frequency on Earth are that the results of your choices manifest faster than before. You need not wait for death and rebirth, presently, to sow what you seeded. The karmic cycle accelerates with you and the planet. Therefore, actions that are not of high vibrations keep repeating and repeating and repeating and repeating, giving you ample opportunities to respond with love. For those who choose not to respond with love, their life seems to be moving into the realm of challenging reruns that follow one after the other. This is our definition of hell, where you are bound to a reality from which you may find no release. With all love, we must admit there is no hell in the place we come from, as it is all very well illuminated, and by making a choice to use love in your life's circumstance, you can move from seemingly the darkest caverns to the most illuminated peaks very quickly. This is the time. Your choices are powerful and honored above all.

What else do you see, some may wonder?

We see many changes both in your physical landscape and your inner terrain. As your electromagnetic grid is shifting continuously, dormant fault lines that were inactive for eons in the belly of Gaia will awaken, weather abnormalities will become the norm, and observable celestial bodies will change course as if for no apparent explainable reason.

What many consider acts of madness will become more and more frequent as pressure builds, on your field, to move higher. The acceleration of speed and intensity in the electromagnetic field around each of you can cause those who are less balanced or use mind-altering chemicals to "snap," swirling with violent, "insane" acts. We see darkness mounting "impressive" campaigns to create fear and disorder, disguised as protection, in an attempt to preserve the grip on your reality. Your reality is at stake here. Each and every one who chooses to hold their candle illuminated makes the difference for the multitudes.

We see individual choice becoming the subject of campaigns as some will challenge those of you who exercise power and mastery. We see transparency—an aspect of the new energy—under attack by all those who wish to keep their secrets under lock and keep your power diluted. This is all part of the energy we named the New Sun. It is awesome in its possibilities, potentials, and magnificence. We see many of you who choose to move into your truth fearlessly, moving higher, spiraling to greater and greater heights. Glue that held old structures will be challenged. What were considered stable walls will be fragmented and fractured as power players will be shifting seemingly overnight.

We see many changes in the Earth's crust and in the cycles of nature. Some species may choose to move off the Earth plane to different vibrations and you may tag them as extinct. Your use of natural resources will force many to look in a whole new way at your relationship with the cycle of life. We see many opportunities to use light, integrity, and love, and many opportunities to use fear and survival protectionism. This is your time and each of you who is awakened becomes a beacon that can be seen by our satellites.

None of what we see is new to you as you all came to be here because you could see the same potentials we described both for the creation of love, light, and peace on Earth as well as the potential for darkness. You came this time to become truth and allow that truth to emanate to all. You came here to become light so your light will be illumination to all. You came here to become love so your love will be emanating to all. You are it. We ask you with a final hug to awaken to your power and mastery. Embrace joy, love, and peace in your own reality while bringing the New Sun that much closer to your shared reality, and so be it.

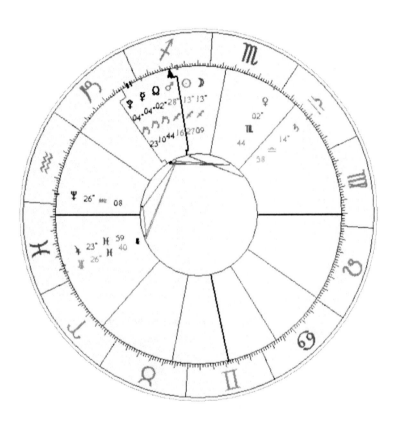

12/24/2010

Dearest Dror,

Lovely to hear from you and happy you enjoyed your time with Zoe. I
am doing well, have come down a bit today from totally flying high but
all is good. Tues. next week is perfect. I will miss you and look forward
to seeing you then.
Please stay in touch.
With Love,

Yours L.

Dear Light.

I wanted to share with you a message I received on Xmass eve.   It
is quiet advanced and not a message I feel comfortable sharing in a
public form. It offers some insight into this journey.

It is not an easy reading, and a little different then some other
messages but I feel guided to send it to you. It may be good to read it
more then once.

Please feel free to share your feelings about it.

I feel that Mexico and now Egypt opened new pathways.

Thank you for being

with Love and Light

Dror

From Crawling to Flying

*Y*OU ARE DEARLY LOVED.

As the sun illuminates your Earth, many of you begin to see. Seeing is not only what is revealed to you through your eyes. Many of you were trained to "see" the unseen in one or another order that was kept secret in your previous cycles, as you are old souls on this planet. Now, many secrets are being revealed and you are beginning to remember how to "see" again the unseen forces that are guiding your life. Even your scientists are beginning to observe what so many of you already know. They begin to look at threads that link all the different fields together, coordinating between your visible realities with the invisible strings behind the scenes, which act as catalysts to movement in your life. It will be a "big surprise" the day scientists prove what the natives have been practicing for eons— that consciousness moves everything. Everything, on some level, is aware of you, as well as your intent. All matter responds to consciousness as all that you see is energy in one form or another. It is you who creates all movements within your reality. It is the collective you who shape all the seen and unseen matter in your universe.

Are you still surprised when we tell you that you have power? How you act in your moment-by-moment brief life on Earth is the story on which we wish to expand. You carry a physical attribute that can pick up things from the ground and lay them, for example, on a table. You called this physical attribute hands. You also have a physical attribute that can move your energy to different places and you named it legs. You have senses that you use to navigate your coming and going, allowing you to avoid obstacles, helping you to find your way around your physical geography. You have a physical attribute that holds all your pieces and parts together so you will not fall apart. This you call skin. Within you, you ingeniously devised systems which distribute the different elements which sustain, as well as protect, your physical form, delivering various substances to where they are needed: the cells, the digestive system, the lymphatic system, cardiovascular system, respiratory system, and so on. You also created a system which delivers the electrical signals with information to all parts of your body, as well as alerting you when something goes wrong and telling you where you are in space. You called this the nervous system. You have the reproductive system which insures the continuation of your species. All the different systems facilitate, first and foremost, your survival in this body on the physical plane. Each system is God's work of art and it is perfectly suited for you moving through the physical experience. Then there is the mind, which allows you to translate that which you experience through your senses into words or abstract ideas, building upon that which you learn through analysis and observation. You called that thinking. Finally, there is the emotional system which allows you to sense and express yourself according to the manner in which you interpret the actions that take place within you or around you.

All your different systems are programmed foremost to insure your survival. Some systems are automatic and your response is insured, bypassing thinking, like the injection of adrenaline hormone into your blood when your body requires performing at its peak, allowing more blood to be pumped so that more oxygen passes through you, putting your nervous system on high alert. Your main program concerns survival and the continuation of your evolution. This you all know, and most of you live by the dictates of these different systems. And then there is Spirit. Within this complex web of attributes which demonstrates the perfection of your physical form to negotiate your physical landscape and to thrive, you have the reason behind all of this magnificent creation. Like many things that have Spirit inscribed on them, this one also is counterintuitive, as well as the least obvious. The secondary purpose of your coming to this dense reality and thriving is obvious: to build a home, raise a family, to insure the survival as well as the continuation of your "tribe." The physical tools are right there at your disposal: you have hands, legs, eyes, mouth, and so on. However, the main reason that you came here is less obvious and needs to be discovered. It is for the purpose of your spiritual evolution and the activation of your expanded awareness. Your yearning is a catalyst for you to discover your true identity—to recognize your divinity, choosing light over darkness of your own free will.

Why is that, some of you may want to know?

Who do you think devised this experiment? The collective you were on the design team to create a movement within Spirit that is free will based and allows choice to be the main attribute of the evolution of light in your universe. There are many systems that are part of the magnificence of Spirit where light is the only choice.

We hear some of you sigh and say to yourselves, "I want to go *there*. I am sick and tired of this one. Let me be in a place where there is only light." With so much love, we must tell you that where you are is where there are lines stretched beyond the horizon. There are so many who wish to participate and take part in this journey. This is where the action is; you come here cycle after cycle to be part of this excitement. When you are with Spirit, the challenges that you faced in your moment-by-moment life seem very different as you have the advantage of seeing it through the prism of eternity. When you observe your light from above, your survival does not play the main role, because you are fully aware of who you are and the fact that you are eternal. There is beauty in every moment that you walk on Earth in your physical form, but that beauty is obscured by your need for survival. When you are detached from the physical, moving higher, every moment holds within it magic and learning, carrying an immense power to transform darkness into light so that the expansion of Spirit within you may continue. That is why an essential aspect of realizing who you are, as well as what this journey is all about, has to do with activation of your cells, awakening of your inner light so you can gain enough speed to move to a higher plane. From an elevated plane, many of the issues you struggle with in the moment-by-moment and breath-by-breath of your human journey clear away.

What do you mean by activation and awakening, some may ask?

We would like to answer with an analogy. Your aviation is a good example. Most of humanity is moved to action by the need to survive, which is the prime base program with which each and every one of you is born. We can compare it to crawling on your hands and knees. As you move higher and develop your relationship with the Spirit within, you begin to walk, which is using the same legs but in a different way. As you progress, some of you accelerate the journey by running. Again, you use the same legs but in a different way. The first is crawling, the next is walking, and the last is running. The attribute you are using in the physical form remains the same but is used differently. As angels you all have the ultimate wish to fly, as it holds your highest potential. To fly you need to grow wings which are multidimensional. To develop these wings you must awaken and become activated. With the use of your wings you can develop enough speed on your runway to take off, and when you are up there, all that we speak of becomes clear. The use of legs cannot take you up but it can surely move you faster on the ground. Through awakening and activation, rather than moving faster on the ground, you let go of gravity and ascend. The majority of humanity knows intuitively that there is a higher purpose for their coming to this plane of existence that is beyond survival, so they subscribe to one form of faith-based religion or another. This step can be compared to walking, which is faster than crawling, but not as fast as running, as most religions use survival as their guiding engine obscured by dogma.

In a parallel to running, a faster use of your attribute (legs), you must depart from dogma, using your own innate tools and powers to advance. Some of you, and you know who you are, do it even within the framework of one faith or another, but you have moved away from dogma, beginning to listen to your inner voice—or should we call it your higher part—that is linked to your angelic family. What does it mean to grow multidimensional wings that no one can see and become a carrier for the highest potential of humanity within your energy field? This is the next step for many of you and it has to do with the hold gravity has on you, which we describe as your velocity. The lighter you are, the faster you are, and the more likely you are to take off. Do you think it is a coincidence that so many of you deal with weight clearing so you may heal, shedding darkness as well as density with such ferocity, these days? This is one important aspect of easing the hold of gravity on you. The most sacred journey that a human can travel is upward. You called it ascension. Some of your ancient texts speak of those who ascended and hold them dear, as the light torches, guiding humanity's spiritual evolution. Much of the dogma and religious institutions were built upon the written records of those who ascended. With so much love, we must impart to you that ascension has no manual. Those ascended masters did not follow any manuals, as the manuals were created after they moved up. From our perch we must impart to you that none of the so-called ancient scriptures can lead you to ascend even if you choose to follow their every point with a dedication that is admired by all who come in contact with you. There are many who are wise, well versed in the scripture, who can spew wisdom seemingly with every word chosen carefully, and it has very little to do with ascension. Wisdom and knowledge alone are in the realm of walking, maybe at times even running, but not flying. Flying requires your cells to be awakened and activated, and when your body begins the process you will have no doubt that something peculiar is taking place within you. As we finally begin to share with you the key components of ascension, you will again sigh that it is nothing new. The key ingredients of awakening must be felt in your heart; they are love, trust, and fearlessness.

Survival is like a rock that many of you carry on your backs and it keeps you earthbound. When you know deep within your feeling centers that you are loved and protected at all times, you slowly let go. Once you let go, many of you are surprised at how your physical reality rearranges itself, in ways that some of you call miraculous, supporting you fully. When you link with the source of divinity within you—which is in timelessness—and have the highest perspective, you can move beyond the anchors of your physical reality. Spirit within you has a direct link to that prism. As you loosen your hands from the ropes of protection and survival, allowing yourself to be guided, gravity begins to weaken its hold. The awakening can be analogous to velocity, and the activation to the growing of wings. Activation is a physical process which has its roots in the multidimensional aspect of your DNA. It is part of your makeup. Activation is a complex process which takes into account agreements that your light has with your body. Once you have cleared some of the blocks, the signal to grow wings is given. Activation requires a vast amount of energy to be move through your body. It can be compared to a lighting bolt of electric charge going through you, charging every cell with divine essence of love. The kind of energy required to manifest such a charge can be created through the use of your engine, which is the center of your sexual energy. No other source of energy can be compared, in its power, to sexual energy. We have spoken of the different systems and how they were created for your survival and continuation of your species. Each system is layered with different levels that correlate to the place of spiritual evolution of each human.

On this journey, the nervous system—which is essential to your survival on one level—also contains the key to the awakening of your Kundalini energy. You may choose to stay on the basic level or activate your highest level. Kundalini holds secret pathways to your highest spiritual journey. When awakened, the serpent coils upward in a force which starts the propeller of your airplane.

We have spoken often of sexual energy and why it is at the core of your moving higher. Sexual energy is not about having sex with a partner. Naturally, a sexual relationship with a partner is one aspect of using sexual energy. However, what we speak of has to do with the use of this energy to activate and clear the body from blocks, allowing the cells to vibrate higher. To achieve liftoff through activation, many of you must relearn the use of sexual energy in a form that is elevated, redirecting the energy to the higher energy centers within your vessel, and building, over time, to more intense levels. The keys for activating your potential using sexual energy are well hidden and the codes have been scrambled for the obvious reasons. Those who had access to this knowledge and practiced it could no longer be held in captivity. There would be no power in your physical reality that could hold them bound; they would be set free from all anchors. The process of activation is felt in the body clearly. It may feel like an electric charge, running loose, as your cells vibrate, with your body shaking and contorting in response.

Activation signals the cells to awaken using the innate highest programming available in your DNA, fulfilling the agreement to grow wings. As many of the keys are hidden and coded, this journey has to, again, be taken by you alone. You do not need a partner to relearn the codes in the use of sexual energy for ascension. It is, however, more accelerated and offers more pleasurable delights, with the right partner. Finding a partner for this sacred journey can be challenging, as karma often creates additional heaviness. When two people choose to grow wings together, relearning the use of hidden codes of sexual energy, it is no longer in the realm of sex, but in the realm of light creation through sacred divine dance. Relationships are sacred, as they allow an opportunity to grow by creating a mirror for each of the partners so they can see their own unreleased blocks, moving through them. The divine dance we speak of is not often achieved through those who are attached with cords of karma.

Awakening and activation are the highest use of your tools on this spiritual journey, while survival is the most rudimentary use of these tools. It may be challenging to hold on to both. One has to let go of the fear relating to survival to gain velocity. There is never a judgment as to how far you reach or how much effort you make. You are loved unconditionally always, and as we hug you, we wish to whisper in your ears that, when you explore moving beyond the realm of running into the realm of flying, you begin to see what we see: that every aspect of your journey is divine, that moment by moment you are creating a masterpiece that has your signature on it. You no longer judge good or bad, as all seem to be placed in their perfect order. You are moving into the realm of infinite possibilities, and we wish you to enjoy this journey to the fullest, knowing that you are a master, loved by all of us, and so be it.

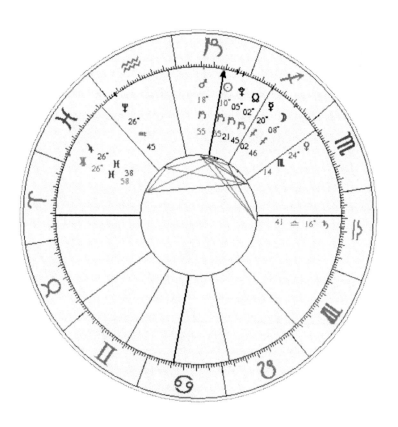

1/26/11

Dearest Caroline,
Good to hear from you and was wonderful to see you even briefly.
As to the energy work;
There was so much resistance for the activation for the past 2 days
but Yesterday something cracked opened and the energy began to
flow. This morning things began to shift even more. What is happening
in Cairo, have no idea? I am on the Nile River still, getting to Luxor
tonight. It would be amazing if you have time to translate the message
from 1-1-11 to German.
Love
Dror

Dearest B,
Thank you for reminding me to take in the magnificent nature for
the past few days. I have been preparing for Egypt and catching up
after Mexico. I was pretty much going non stop and had no brake to
meet before leaving. I am emailing from Munich Germany waiting
for my Cairo flight. Would love to catch up when I return. After
Mexico my body has been vibrating differently so I did not get much
sleep. Wonderfully intense time at the moment.
I hope you received the 1/1/11 message.
Love
Dror.

Dear Dror
Hoping you are well. I see there is a lot of fighting going on in
Egypt right now and that the government has blocked wireless
communications. Wondering if you are near the unrest and if you are
able to get this message.
I am in Boston this week.

B.

Heart Reunion

*Y*OU ARE DEARLY LOVED.

You have entered a new paradigm as you progress towards finding who you are. You are an angel and you have chosen the body of a human, coming down to this reality on Earth so you can rediscover your angelic essence.

Why, some may ask?

You have entered into this dimension so you may exercise the most prized attribute of this dense reality—free choice. You have all the possibilities open and available. Within this infinite variety of potentials, would you choose light? Would you move towards reuniting with your true self or move further away from your divine essence? This is the test and why you are here. Many of you have waited for a long time to be here to exercise your prized attribute. Almost as many are now feeling the brunt and burden of this divine, sacred test. You came to use love, and many of you are experiencing the lack of love in your relationships. You came here to experience peace, and many of you are in turmoil. You came here to be in a place of vibrant health, although many of you are being challenged with ailments and dis-ease in that aspect of your life. You came here to explore the depth of pleasure, but many of you are experiencing pain. You came here to become an angel in human clothes, exploring the limitlessness and expansiveness of your existence, but many of you are finding constriction or limitation seemingly everywhere you turn. You came here to be a full-fledged angel, and instead many of you are learning the density, intensity, and depth of being a human.

Why so, and what went wrong, you may rightly want to know?

With a hug, we reply that nothing went wrong. What you see is perfection at work. You are experiencing this sacred test, as it manifests in each of your individual experiences, so that you may have the opportunity to ascend above what you consider your reality, discovering your true essence. The perfection of the system is expressed in the manner in which it gives each of you a real choice. It does not offer you only peace because then the choosing would not be a test. It offers you turmoil and peace. The turmoil is external and peace is internal. Now choose which one you accept as your reality. One is ever changing while the other constant, no matter what happens in the outer circle.

Many of you are feeling cheated as if the plans you have devised for your life have somehow been switched by no other than the "dark" to make your life more challenging and difficult. This is your humanness speaking to you, wearing the victim glasses. All that takes place around you and all that affects you is a choice that you may accept as your reality or move away from it, accepting a different version of reality.

How do we move away from our challenges, some may wonder?

You begin by offering gratitude to all and everything that has led you to where you are at this moment.

What if I do not like what I am experiencing at this moment, some may rightly ask?

With all love, we must impart to you that gratitude is the first signal to Spirit that you understand your role and responsibility in creating everything that you consider to be your reality. This recognition in itself carries immense power, and while acknowledging your power to magnetize aspects you do not like into your life, you also take hold of the reins, acknowledging that if you have the power to bring one reality, you also have the power to recreate a different reality—one that may take you up on a magic carpet to a more blissful existence. Your story of the new energy and the New Sun is all about awakening to your power to activate your dormant tools so you may begin to take hold of what was robbed from you for eons, which is your power.

Who robbed us, some may wonder?

The pathways to higher-elevated vibration were blocked to most of humanity for a very long time. The codes which were embedded in your DNA to link you with the expanded you were scrambled. Now they are being reassembled and supported energetically. More and more humans are claiming their power, accessing their higher part again. If you wish to point a finger at someone, there is no one out there to blame. Collectively, humanity has agreed over time by taking certain actions to give away your power. Those actions were partially related to the masculine/feminine balance ratios. You are a powerful being which contains all the attributes of God within you. Each and every one has the seed of God. It is on you to create the condition so this seed can grow and flourish. Never can you destroy this seed. Your energy is beautiful to us. As you shine, your geometry expands and swivels in magnificent colors touching all dimensions, creating a heavenly melody. We fall in love with you all over again when we observe you in action. At times we will hover around you just to create a complementary geometric shape so we can experience your magnificence and share our love with you. We call it dancing because the synchronization of our heavenly bodies with yours requires a very delicate coordination. We love dancing with you when you allow us. You are in the midst of manifesting your grandest potential. You are in the midst of creating your dance, and we are with you all the time, even when you are asleep. You have support not only from your entourage of angels, but also from Gaia. She knows where you are and she knows your intention. She knows where you walk and she absorbs your tears like a mother who comforts her child when she cries.

We hear many who say, "We do not feel the love and support." With a smile we say to you, open your heart and the feeling will flow, never stopping. Many of you are closed up in your heart from past hurts. It's time to find love again. It is your time to rediscover love within you and share it with those who come in contact with you. Through love you bridge all aspects of the illusion of separation from anything or anybody. When you accept love as your guiding light, those who choose to be close to you—and there will be many—will be illuminated by your light. This is how the ripple of a concentric circle grows to engulf the whole of humanity. It all begins with you.

Can you tell us something new, some may ask?

All that we speak of is already known to you. It is your attention that we wish to awaken as our words speak to your feelings and your feelings converse with your heart. We always bypass the mind as it becomes an obstacle on the journey to a higher vibration. Our words are being expressed simply without complicated technical details. We are not trying to convince you but to offer light by transmitting an angelic frequency in the form of a feeling into your geometric structure. We water your seed so it will awaken. It is on you to add the light to it so it can flourish. Water and light are all that is needed for the sprouting of your seed. When you create the ripe condition for growth you also awaken your latent memory. With the remembering comes the knowledge of how and what to do to progress on this journey which is perfectly fitted for you. We have told you many things throughout the last three years, and we wish to celebrate with those who began to dance in those three years, shifting their lives to a higher plane. Many of you have done so and you know who you are.

From our perch, the most important ingredients we insert into your energy field are that you are loved, that you are divine, that you are powerful, that your choices on this path are sacred and never judged. We placed hints in some places and have illuminated others so you would be able to feel which choice serves you and which choice may hurt your progress. For us it is a great honor to dance with you and to love you. It is our mission and we fulfill it with joy. When we see you hunched over, depressed or sad about different aspects of your life, all we want to do is hug you and let you know that it is all divine, reminding you how loved you are. We wish to take all the pain away, but it is not our mission. We can only illuminate your path. The choice to remove suffering and become free remains with you and you only. There is no one, no entity, being, family member, boss, head of state, or even God, that is more powerful than you concerning your own life. There is one power and that one is you. Within that one power all is contained. You contain within you aspects of all creation. As you play your fragmented role as a separated entity from your surrounding universe, within that same journey you can choose to experience that you are being a part of all that is.

When you fall in love with another human, the feeling of heightened expansiveness comes from you loving self. When someone loves you it gives you permission to love yourself. What happens at times when that love is being withdrawn from you? To many of you it begins a downward spiral chain reaction. Your geometry does not lie. It tells us the story of your thoughts. We see thoughts such as, "If my lover does not love me anymore, how can I go on loving myself? I have lost my main support for loving myself." As we hug you, we remind you what you already know: you do not need support or permission to love self. You do not need another to give you the okay that you are okay. It is your birthright. To many, the challenging relationships that you attract and manifest into your life are opportunities to choose loving the self, despite the lover you perceive as having betrayed you, the family member who hurt your feelings, or a friend who caused you pain. Those who act their role in your life are your most revered teachers. Your most sacred teachers are not the gurus or spiritual leaders of this or that religion or belief system. Your teachers are your close circle of family, friends and coworkers who interact with you, giving you opportunity after opportunity to become whole and to choose love. Thank them for fulfilling their role so perfectly; honor them as if they were the most revered spiritual teachers of the time. Bow your head in wonder to the extent, the ingenuity, of the challenges and tests they present to you. Understand that your immediate circle is indispensable and irreplaceable on this journey. The surest ways to move away from the challenges is to use love and begin with self. Those around you are the ones with whom you contracted to show you the path to light. When you choose to let one teacher move away from your life, not through love but through denial, another will surely and expediently come to replace him or her.

Make time to open your heart. It is a window of opportunity to become lighter, to accept and forgive all that you have done or that was done to you, relocating, permanently, into your heart residence. Gaia has always resided in the realm of the heart. Even the high winds, those powerful surges, the fires and other seemingly angry elements come from love. Know that you are with her and include her in all your journeys. Connect to her and ask for guidance. Earth is moving to a higher frequency and all its inhabitants are moving with her, you included. There is no hiding—only facing, being present, and residing in your heart. Allow yourself to surrender to your vulnerability because it is a key component to becoming powerful. Many of your misdirected actions of anger, hate, and violence are acted upon to cover your vulnerabilities, as well as your fears. Residing in the heart knowing that love is your birthright, that all power lies within you, allows you to experience being vulnerable and powerful at the same time. You are it and all is contained within you. Thank yourself for making this most sacred and divine pilgrimage to the heart and awaken to who you really are. Celebrate moment by moment the shifting back to your heart, and know that all the challenges you face are but opportunities to express choices. Finally, from this moment on, choose to use your heart so you may ascend higher than ever before, and so be it.

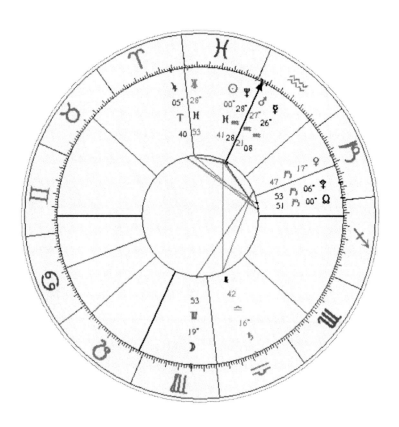

2/19/2011

Dear Dror

Thank you Dror for your encouraging words...and your advices - you are right with everything you say...it means a lot to me...as I conquer very new territory.

You talked about lower energy people draining me...and for this scenario I have not found a solution yet. Yesterday for instance, I spent all day in a recording studio-and I came in with very much energy - but during the day everyone in there kept constantly coming up to me, making conversation...and I swear I could hear the "Sucking Sound" and yet I could not get out or stop it. In the end of the day I was completely exhausted...still today...I understand that "diet" is one answer but often times we have to function in the world...

I have experienced this all my life and I have tried many unsuccessful "techniques" - So now I wonder, if there's maybe a sign on my forehead saying - please take as much of my energy as you want...please, dump your negative energies and problems into my energy field and let me transform them...meaning: On some level I must have agreed to this, no? Maybe this is about some unconscious choice that I have taken (who knows when) to offer the world my energy and to be their transformer???? Or is this just normal on the path towards awakening? What is your experience with this? Definitely I will try the black tourmaline...

And I AM really terribly sorry, but this time there were no more flights available to Woodstock or NYC to hear you speak - but maybe next time... :))))

I sensed, you know about things happening here... :) there has been a potential someone around...So far we have not been really involved...I just understand more and more that he is here to help me a great deal with my learning lessons...He gives his best to push my buttons allowing me to heal and to take the decisions I need to take for my own sake....and the timing has always been perfect. 10 Minutes before I came into the Mid-heaven bookstore in Munich on Feb.11, he had responded to me with the most idiotic und ignorant sms - but by doing that he had prepared my very upset heart so well for its new journey right through that meeting with you...And since then the world looks very different anyways. And yes, there is and there has been an opportunity for sex, but I have decided against it...because I have this loud alarm in my head and because "old energy Sex" is simply not appealing to me any more. It leaves me empty. Nothing to gain from.

Now it is 2:25 a.m. - and I'm still wide awake...this is now happening a lot...being up very late and talking suddenly 10 times as much as before... :))

Thaaaaank you and viel Liebe - much Love to YOU across the ocean!!

Astrid.

The Director, Producer, and Actor

*Y*OU ARE DEARLY LOVED.

As the sun sets over the horizon you are asked to walk in the dark as if it is daytime. You are moving into a field that is chaotic to the senses but in perfect order with the heart. We call it the womb because it is the core essence of the feminine Goddess. It is where creation takes place, where magic manifests and blossoms. Nowhere and at no time in your recorded history has your power been available to you like now. You have been enabled to see and feel who you are. Many of you do not have names or terms to describe how you are feeling, but deep in your heart you know if you are aligned with Gaia: with the energy of love, integrity, your truth, and beauty. When the picture in your heart is in great misalignment with your awakened knowing, many of you begin to take action and manifest change. All of you intuitively know that this is a time like no other.

We understand truth. But why beauty, some may inquire?

With a smile, we say to you: Look around. Do you see beauty everywhere you look? If you do not, you are looking with the wrong set of eyes. Look again. Beauty is order and beauty is the divine feminine in balance with creation. Beauty is love. Beauty is not an external attribute, but an internal one. When we hug you we see only beauty. You are beautiful to us in every way. As we are holding your hands on this journey, we ask you to trust that, even if you do not see anything—like in the womb—you are protected. Trust, as well, that you cannot get lost, as there is only one way and it is out to light. Soon many of you will be born into the light pushed by powerful forces that guide you. Like birth, when the time comes you must sprout. There are some of you who feel comfortable in the protection the darkness of the womb offers. With love and a wink, we ask you to get ready, as birth is coming close and the choice to stay inside past your scheduled birth date is not an option.

Who am I, you ask?

You are an awesome, beautiful energy like no other in the universe. When you take a body, your first choice is whether to be born as male or female, and your second choice is how to play your part as a representative of the energy you chose. Much consideration is invested in these two choices. As a creator being, and a guardian of the feminine torch at these times, you have a great responsibility because you must lead. You must pick up the baton and conduct the orchestra. You must get over your hurts, pains, anger, and blocks, implementing your gifts, using love, in bringing the New Sun onto Earth so it will be in alignment with humanity. We used the Mayan cosmology term "New Sun" because it represents the end and new beginning of a great cycle noted by many ancient cultures, notably the Mayan. The luminosity that is appearing on the horizon of your shared reality is the New Sun. It will look and feel different.

How so, some may ask?

All of you agreed to accept one reality and now this agreement is no longer valid. The locks have been broken on your one-channel reality restriction and each of you can choose which channel to experience. In your past very few could escape the traps of a single-channel reality or walk in higher vibration on Earth. Some of you carry cellular memory of persecution and even death just for trying to vibrate higher. The wise women Goddesses, or witches, as they were called at times, were driven into hiding due to your one-channel restriction. Your collective will has changed your path, and one by one you have moved to explore other channels. As your technology allowed you to distribute this knowledge amongst you, many more have moved higher. At this juncture it is the first time since the time of Lemuria that, as a society, you have the option to ascend higher than ever before. Your power is in the choices each and every one of you makes in the moment-by-moment timeline of your life. The intensity as well as acceleration that you experience from Gaia's vibration moving higher creates a pressure which manifests thoughts and emotions into action faster than ever before. The wheels of karma are spinning faster and you no longer must wait for future cycles to reap what you sow. Many of you experience it in the here and now. It means that your power to create magic both through light and through dark is enhanced to an extent that each of you who chooses to vibrate higher changes the blueprint for the whole planet. As your planet is connected to many other planets, as well as to the entire universe, through the field, the change that is happening on this faraway planet on the edge of your galaxy is affecting all realities and dimensions in the furthest reaches of the universe. Do you still doubt your power?

Why now, some may ask?

It's time, is the short answer. There are processes which begin at the edge of time, moving through your galactic experience until they reach the energy of manifestation and change. You are now in this energy. This awesome shift is guided by none other than the feminine energy that must return to balance in order for your species to remain and thrive on this planet. The feminine principle is not only about nurturing and love, it has aspects which express raging destruction as well. Your mythology from various cultures gives attributes of the divine feminine energy to different Goddesses. The act of creation is one that must at times follow destruction. Destruction is not negative, but a natural phenomenon. It is a mechanism of creation which facilitates your evolution guiding the new to replace the old. A new energy which some named the "New Sun energy" is sweeping across your magnificent blue pearl. It has been here for over ten years now and will continue for years to come. Many of you are yet to be awakened by the magnitude of the change, but our promise to you is that soon all of you will find that sleeping will no longer be a choice. Your reality is changing and it is why you are here. You came to be part of this change and to facilitate your own path, guiding others to higher ground. You are the carrier of the torch of the feminine energy and it contains principles that are now coming back into center stage: principles of integrity, transparency, and heart-based society connected to the idea of unity consciousness through the umbilical cords of Gaia. Each and every one who is alive on Earth at this time stood in line to be here now. We are speaking of things you already know. We are here just to hug you and remind you. We have excitedly spoken with you about it before you descended into the birth canal. As we said our goodbyes, you have said to us with tears in your angelic eyes, "This is exciting, and I am grateful to go back to play my part."

It is a time of remembering your true essence and power as an angelic being carrying a physical form, moving into your mission of being a conduit of love energy. Love is not an energy that needs to be advertised or spoken about, as love is quiet. Love is the essence of your universe, and when enough of you hold the link to your universe through love you are changing your Earth. Love begins with self-love and from there it ripples in all dimensions and realities. This is the power center that all of you carry in seed form. Now the seed has been watered and the New Sun brings the ripe conditions for your seed to sprout.

What does it mean for me, some may ask?

Many of you hold hurts and anger from the past, as you all have been scratched or bruised by the dense reality here on Earth. This is the most challenging school in your universe and you receive a medal just for participating. As Earth's vibration is moving rapidly higher, you can no longer afford holding on to dense emotional energy as it would keep you in a low vibration reality so that you would not be able to experience the magnificence of Earth's ascension. Holding on to heaviness could manifest into a dis- ease in your body faster than ever before. Your aim is to become light. You must clear your sexual centers of shame, guilt, and pain, learning to love your whole self. The locks that were placed on humanity through your religious establishments were primarily targeting your sexuality as it is the engine for your moving higher. Your sexual energy— when channeled with love and flowing freely—is your magic carpet to moving higher in vibration. Throughout history this energy was manipulated, as well as scrambled, so that the keys to using your sexual energy in its original intended form were well hidden, tainted, and repressed in order to create a subjugated society that is malleable. This is where the Goddess comes into the picture. The Shakti feminine principle must play her role to again teach humanity the highest use of sexual energy. The masculine, through a campaign lasting thousands of years, moved this energy far away from balance and away from its original intention. Relearning the original intention of using your energy offers one of the greatest challenges humanity is facing. Many of the conflicts you call political or religious based on your Earth come from manipulation of sexual energy, channeling it away from love to benefit the few and de-power you. The immensity of the energy must be channeled somewhere, and in your history it was often directed to create destruction. When an angel in human costume is vibrating with love—using your lower chakras open and flowing—there is no power in the universe that can control you. Your power of manifestation and of driving your own reality is absolute. When you are uncontrollable, you are not a good candidate for your energy and resources to be harvested by your governments, religions, businesses, as well as many others who compete to gain access to your emotional or physical resources. The movie you are in, playing your role, is now being rewritten and the script created by you as you act. There is no longer a prescribed story line; you are the director, the producer, and the actor. Some of you have not yet realized that you are the driver and you are still waiting for new instructions. With so much love, we are asking you not to wait too long. Look inside to find your script—the one that offers you guidance to your highest potential, allowing you to move into heart-based reality and use it.

How, some may still wonder?

The manual is inside of you and the codes to open the manual are simple and you all know it. Begin with gratitude to self first for being here now; use love and be guided by fearlessness. Fear will come up again and again as you all must continually clear it from your system in order to progress. Sit on the floor in front of a candle and hug yourself, renewing the vows that you had before coming to this dense reality to love yourself no matter what. Ask to be shown the way through light and love to your highest potential. Collect the tears from your eyes and offer them to Gaia, or just allow them to roll down to the ground. Visualize yourself in the womb and experience your new birth. As you open your eyes, taking your first breath, know that you have made a sacred divine step to reuniting with your mastery, becoming a full-fledged angel walking on Earth in human form, and so be it.

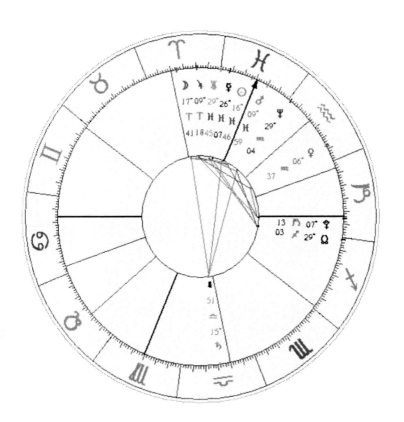

3/7/10

"Never measure the height of the mountain until you have reached the top.
Then you will see how low it was."
- Dag Hammarskjold
Second Secretary-General of the United Nations

Subject: Postponement of Programs in Israel

Dear M.
this is the memo I received for postponing the MEPI.
I am so sorry. I hope Dror will come next time
God Bless
M.

Dear Dror:

Greetings from the Secretariat of UPF International.

We have an important new direction to announce concerning the Legacy of
Peace and MEPI programs scheduled to take place in Israel next month.

The Legacy of Peace and MEPI programs scheduled for June 3-7, 2010 in
Israel are to be postponed.

We very much regret the inconvenience this change of plans may bring, and we
appreciate your patience and understanding.

Once again, there will be no programs in Israel on June 3-7, 2010.   The
programs may be re-scheduled for August. As soon as we receive direction
concerning a future international program in Israel we will inform you of the
new schedule. Sincerely

Dr. Thomas G. Walsh   Mr. Taj Hamad

President   Secretary General

The Chosen One

YOU ARE DEARLY LOVED.

When you begin to climb, the view must change. You cannot ask to see the same things from down below as from up above. Many of you wish to cling to what you know and consider normal. With love, we ask you to prepare to leave many of your "precious belongings" behind. Nothing is ever lost when you walk up the stairs except your perception of things. You are an energy that is one with all energy, and you take on a unique melody for a while, creating the illusion of separation in order to find at the top of the stairs again your oneness with all that is. "I am that I am" is you arriving home, experiencing the melding of all existence. As you move higher you can no longer claim that you are a being separated from your surroundings. Your society was based on the idea of defining the separateness of humans, thereby comparing and contrasting one from another. It is part of your linearity to be able to define and classify whoever is presented to you. This way it enables you to distinguish between friend or foe, stranger or family, loved one or hated one.

Indeed it is appropriate and was useful for you to negotiate your survival in this reality. The story is about to change, and your consciousness is no longer focusing on the separateness. A powerful stream of unity consciousness is sweeping and permeating every living thing on this planet, including you. This intense energy is creating invisible links which call upon your awareness to begin focusing on your similarities and your common ground rather than your differences. Many of you call this trend the new technology. It is humorous how quickly many of you separate between the realm of Spirit and the realm of matter, dismissing one over another. Matter is an expression of Spirit. When the need and yearning for unity is created, with pressure building to move beyond walls, there are always those who volunteer to play their part, creating the appropriate technology to fulfill the need. Many of you use this technology not because it is simply there, but because, from a quantum space, you have created it to accommodate your needs. You credit the inventor of this or that technology with ingenuity and reward them with great material wealth as is appropriate in your culture. Know that they just responded to your wishes. We also respond to your wishes by delivering you this frequency, through our words and energy, to facilitate your awakening and activate your mastery. There are many inventions that remain off the buffet table of your awareness because they are not aligned with the direction of your spiritual movement. What remains and takes hold, spreading faster than ever before, are those technologies that are supported by the new energy—the ones of unity, to break down the veil that hides your true common nature. For the new to take hold, the old must let go in order to allow change. You are now in the midst of powerful new energy making advances into territories that are stronghold domains of old energy. The old was built on heavy structures armored with dogma and shielded with an old energy brick-and-mortar fortress to protect you from realizing your own power. These walls must crumble, thus, much of your political, financial, social, psychological, and geographical landscapes are in the midst of this change. The changing of guards is not all pretty. At times, you may classify it as darkness, as it is being expressed in violence, chaos, rage, and destruction. As we hover around you, we must impart to you that there is so much light coming through. The changes you are now seeing are the fruits of your work. Yes, they are not looking pretty at the moment, but they are magnificent and open new potentials for Earth that have never been recorded anywhere. It is a time like no other and you are in the midst of a battlefield. Your light is what makes the difference.

Know that, when you sit in your room feeling love surging in your heart, experiencing oneness with Earth, you have just created a pulse that transferred to the other side of the world instantly, creating a sensation within a young angel's heart saying to herself, "I can feel my power and I will walk today knowing who I am. I ask to regain my mastery over my own life reclaiming my truth." The change that one makes within, using love to activate and awaken their inner knowing, beginning to access their power, actually changes the blueprint of your Earth. One by one you have shifted, and as your numbers grew, the energy that was created brought about changes in remote places. We told you before that it is no longer the politicians or powerful businesses that will invoke these profound changes bringing in the New Sun of humanity. It is you, moving your attention into your heart, expanding your vibration of love from within you to all that is, sending a powerful ripple, just by being and feeling. Your energy will arrive where it needs to go without a name tag or material benefit to you, but all of us will know and everything will shift as a result. It is why you chose to be here now. This is why you went through so much trouble to collect all the scratches and bruises this lifetime, so you can be ready to do your lightwork, finding your truth. Some of you traveled immense distances to play your part on this planet at this time. Do you still feel powerless?

We then hear some of you whisper to us, "I am in pain; I cry often; I do not feel I have any more strength." Some of you then whisper about the pain of others—the hungry ones, the underprivileged ones, the repressed ones, the subjugated and violated ones, the hurt, wounded, or sad ones. We say to you as we wrap our fluffy wings around you, "You are all sacred. You are all loved. To each of you awaits a unique experience, tailored just for you and all by choice." You have also gone though many challenging experiences in past cycles and they brought you to where you are now. We take you by your hand and ask you to soar above for just a moment to see it through our angelic eyes. Everything that you see through our eyes is appropriate, woven with a golden string of love, and again, it is by choice.

Why me, you wish to know?

You are The Chosen One, we say with a smile. In your sacred texts those who were named The Chosen Ones were often persecuted and prosecuted as a result; however, the context of the term was removed from its original intention. The Chosen Ones are those of you who chose to shine your light. You are chosen, not by the almighty God in heaven, but by activating the God within you, intending to move higher than ever before. Your choice is sacred, and we fondly tagged you as the

"Chosen One." When you look around you and link to your deepest knowing you may realize that you are exactly where you need to be to fulfill your mission. This realization in itself can shift your perception in an instant from victimhood to gratitude. You have chosen to play the most magnificent role one can play in a physical reality, to activate your mastery, awakening to your true identity and power. Very few have done so in the past and you know most of them by name as your sacred texts recorded their stories.

Why do I have to go through so much turmoil, you wish to know?

Turmoil is one aspect of your path. It is not a requirement, but a phase. Clearing and becoming light are prerequisites to moving higher. If you carry heaviness from many cycles, how can you take off? Even in your aviation regulations, there is a limit on the baggage weight you are allowed to carry. In order to clear your pain, anguish, hurts, or sadness, at times, your starting point must bring those experiences and feelings into you. If your life were only smooth sailing, why would you clear anything? You probably would lie on your back sun-tanning all day long. You have chosen to do the work not only for yourself but for Earth as well. Each time you move higher from a challenge we hold a celebration—not only that you have unloaded your own baggage but that you serviced other humans. You have helped shift the lives of angels in human costume you do not even know. Most of humanity is asleep, and it is appropriate. The ones who are awakened carry the load for all. You only need a drop of blue-colored dye in a glass of water to change the color of the whole glass of water.

Your thoughts or feelings, your moment-by-moment experiences in your sacred journey here, are measured and applied to Gaia. All are loved equally by Spirit and all journeys are woven with love. Your mission is to connect the dots and bring the new frequency into alignment with Gaia at this time, so to facilitate the most profound change humanity will experience in your recorded history.

How do I know this is the truth, some may wonder?

You will know because it will sound a beautiful melody which will vibrate inside your heart, creating harmonious resonance. You know what we speak of and you know us. We are your brothers and sisters. We come from your future. We know what you are going through. Some of us walk with you every moment and follow your every breath on this journey. Do know that Loved you are, Sacred you are, Powerful you are, Beautiful you are, and so be it.

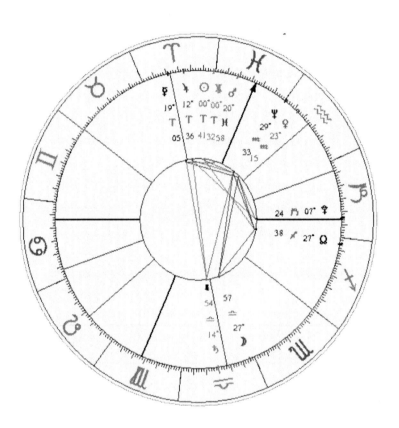

3-21-11

Dearest N:
It was wonderful speaking with you.   I feel like I
want to move forward with the divorce. Please
email me the lawyers number.
Hope I can at least begin the process.

So grateful

Love Dror

It's S. and her tel: is xxx,xxx-xxxx i just send her an
email to ask if
it was okay if you called her, but that should be
okay.
I am a little in a rush to get some graphic work done.
My mom got her
operation yesterday and because of the time
difference to connect
with my family my work is not yet done. But she is
doing amazing; she
is already walking after just one night sleep after
the operation and
is talking to everyone else who is in the hospital. And
my dad was so
in love with her, it was so very sweet. Much Love, N.

Cosmic Orgasm

*Y*OU ARE TRULY LOVED.

When a body touches another body the electromagnetic fields around each body are being charged. You may be charged with a negative charge or a positive charge, as both are like the polarity of a magnet and therefore interchangeable. When two bodies merge from a place of love, openness, and acceptance, you open channels to the expanded you. As your field expands, the two fields are growing larger and larger, finally, to create a third field which no longer can be identified as either of the original two. The third field grows bigger than the original two and is independent. It represents divine creation. When realized through the physical, you merge a divine spark with a body, breathing a new life to be born.

Why is that important, you may inquire?

The act of creation at times must be done with a partner. Both represent the divine principle of feminine and masculine, although physically they can be represented by the same gender. The act of creation is not exclusive to man and woman energetically, although within all divine merging there must be an attraction of polarities. We also create in pairs and our relationships are based on love. You and we are family, although *we* do not have space in our attic for heaviness and hidden agendas. All is transparent in our communications with each other, and we do not allow shadows or basement storage facilities in our homes. You are a vibrating instrument and, as such, your body responds to your environment largely through sensors embedded in your spine. As you walk, your spine acts as an antenna, receiving and transmitting signals which are being absorbed by your surroundings, and like a GPS, Gaia knows who you are, where you are, at any given moment. Like a transistor, you are pulsating waves, and those waves surround you wherever you go. You can be in a dark room underground but Gaia will be aware of your location. You are part of an immense grid structure that maps every consciousness which is part of the human realm on Earth. This structure is linked to the belly of Gaia through an umbilical cord which communicates with the crystalline grid. The crystalline grid acts like a storage house of your original blueprint: your past, present, and future potentials and your akashic library, which stores all your experiences in this body, as well as from previous cycles.

When two touch each other either physically or energetically something magical happens—both fields change as a result. When you have been touched by love and you walk with your field expanded, connected to the larger you, you are touching everyone around you energetically. In your human culture, love is celebrated in so many ways because all of you know intuitively that your fragmented self can become whole through linking, using this frequency. When one is touched by another, both change as a result. Others who come in contact with those original two change, as well, and as you interact with one another, moving about your life, you continuously affect all those who come in contact with you even if they do not know your name or recognize you from a picture. Your electromagnetic field is pulsating and transmitting a frequency that we see in terms of geometric shapes. It is like rain falling on a pond. Each raindrop creates a ripple, intersecting with other ripples. In a like manner, as you traverse with each other, each of your concentric circles changes. One raindrop falling on a pond gives birth to a ripple affecting the whole pond. When over seven billion raindrops fall on that pond, immense movements follow. The resonance of two touching each other from a place of love creates a vibration on a higher octave. Metaphorically, it appears as if one dropped a large rock into the pond to create a more powerful ripple. The rain drop's ripples are therefore all affected by the large rock's ripple.

As you walk you emit a melody. When seven billion each sound a melody, in this concert on your planet, it may sound like a cacophony that many would rather avoid attending. One instrument vibrating with love frequency is like a drum that sets up a beat for the rest of the melodies to follow, thereby replacing the dissonant noise with harmonious music. Many of you are attracted by love stories, as they create harmonic resonance within you for a moment. When two come together in love they give birth to a third field that is larger than the original two. This third field overrides all other fields, creating harmonic resonance. The two that come together in love change everything. The two that now must come together are both within you. Through love you begin to merge your duality, melding your angelic frequency with your human vessel.

Wait a minute. I thought you need two to create a third, some may rightly ask?

Your aim is to first merge the lower/higher, masculine/feminine, physical and angelic aspects within you. From a place of oneness, reaching to another person through love catapults you to the playing field of your highest potential, as a human serving all. Merging the two into one you ascend in vibration, realizing your true galactic, expanded identity, and you change all who cross your path. This is your potential as individuals and as a collective. An aspect of the shift on Earth, and within you, is to break down your walls and shutter your boundaries. At times these walls must disintegrate through what you consider tragedy and pain. You have dwelled in your own dualistic mind frame for eons, creating an existence that is discombobulated and fragmented, making the individual aspect of your humanness glorified at the expense of your oneness. All creation comes from two coming together to create a third, which can be visualized as a triangle. You are now being carried by the force of the spiral pulling you up from the base of the triangle toward its apex. The two merging into one has been practiced mainly through a partner and when you merged, the mutual resonance of love created within the two, for a moment, collapses the walls of duality, catapulting you into a momentary experience of oneness. Through climax you can experience the ecstasy of becoming one with your partner, merging your fields completely, surrendering and allowing the act of creation of a third, more powerful field to manifest. In the process you also merge your own fragmented aspects into one. As a collective, the path of merging and creating true union has been on the defensive for eons, moving you further and further into duality. The pendulum is now swinging back with ferocity and all the fragmented pieces that you have identified as you are beginning to integrate through core gravity. This process takes place on all dimensions, in all realities: personal, collective, physical, emotional, psychological, and geographical. With all love, we must impart to you that all those parts that have been discombobulated are now trying to fit into one cohesive painting. You are the artist. You must now find a place to make peace with every color, shape, texture, and medium used throughout your many cycles, creating a harmonious resonance through love. To many it feels as if the opposite is true because, since the old painting must make room for the new, you are now in the process of erasing and scraping what was, rather than creating the new. Many of you are busy deconstructing what you have worked so hard to construct.

This process is always sacred and you all knew about this time. You are recreating your form and for that you must first clear your canvas. We know what you are going through and that these times are challenging. We know your fears; we know your aches; we know your darkness; we know your pain; and we wish you to know that you are so dearly loved for walking the walk.

How can I find this love and work with it, you ask?

With a gentle hug, we ask you to allow your heart to go through the pain. Feel it. Move on through it. Hug yourself, allowing the tears to roll down your cheeks and be absorbed into the soil. Walk in nature and feel her support. Sit quietly and feel. When you feel, you heal. Your body clears through its emotions and it may require more sleep than usual. You may want to resort to more chocolate, wine, or other mood enhancers. It is so important for you *to feel*. The more you allow and surrender to these deep, dark feelings, the stronger you grow. We celebrate with you when one day, these dark feelings are just feelings, no longer painted as dark. Congratulate yourself for integrating yet another element into a unified field, turning it into yet another brushstroke laid on your canvas. Take the time to love yourself and give yourself support, so your emotional body will begin to clear and your subtle body will become lighter. This is your work: *to feel everything*. Many resort to covering the body in layers through overeating so the body will not feel the pain; we wish you to diet so your body will become lighter, vulnerable and powerful at the same time. Ask Spirit to show you all the darkness now. Once you demand it, you will be surprised that, instead of darkness you will feel hugs. There is no darkness out here. When you do not wish to feel pain, you feed pain. Feel it fully in your body and release it, through breathing, from your heart down into the Earth through your first chakra.

What about the pain? What about other people's pain? What about the pain of Gaia, you question?

With all love, focus on you. Through you, you release all pain. This shift is affecting everyone. Do not focus on others. When you draw your attention inward you will discover that you have plenty on which to work. This is your work. Once you become clear you serve everyone who crosses your path. To some of you old souls, other people's dramas are like wine and chocolate—used to numb your feelings and redirect your attention away from you. If this is your life's work, do continue, as it is sacred to heal others, but take the time, first, to clear what is hidden in your own inner chambers, letting it move out, up to the surface. Resisting is futile. It can only prolong the imbalance, as the mounting pressure is coming from the frequency of Gaia herself, and all of you are her children. You are a galactic energy that is vast and your essence is made of light. It is not the physical light that your scientists describe as photon wave particles. You are made out of a spark from the divine essence of creation. As such, your choices are always honored, and your powers to be of light or of the dark are honored. We come from light as we do not have darkness in our quarters. It is a time to celebrate the coming together of the two merging into the one. You are moving closer to the realm of a cosmic orgasm where the potential of humanity to experience the collapsing of the fragmented pieces into a space of unity is a real potential. This is an organic process, but many already begin to feel glimpses of this new dimension through kundalini activation and awakening. As Earth kundalini is awakening, the push to move higher is intensified. There are signs everywhere that the two are getting closer to each other, metaphorically speaking. You are now in the realm of foreplay. As the fields around you expand, so do the movements and feelings. Collectively you are moving closer to climax, experiencing the collapsing of your walls. Allow, surrender, take this ride as a gift each day and every moment. You are so dearly loved, and we wish you to thank yourself for being where you are, doing the work that you do, as there are no mistakes. As artists, you all have a brush and a palette in your hands. You must choose the color and texture to create a harmonious vision for yourselves as well as for humanity, and so be it.

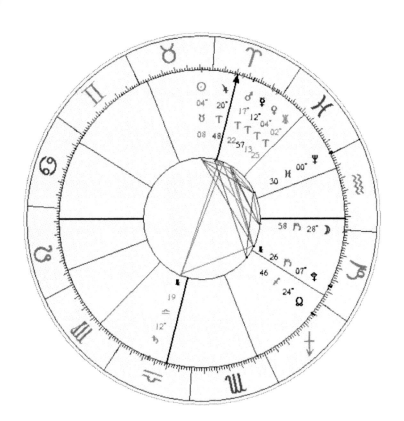

4/24/11

Dearest Dror,

First of all, I apologize — I did not even know that you called me on June 8th until yesterday when I checked voicemail. I hope you and D. are healing.

I really connected with this message and am comforted to know that others are feeling the same way I have been feeling. The feeling of being lost is so difficult. But that is exactly how I have been feeling. Like I don't know where I belong, what I am supposed to be doing. I am forgetful and floating and insecure.

Too much going on and hard to find balance. I really need some time away from here to get my stuff together. I desperately need to just be in a quiet space, reconnect to spirit and work on healing myself as I feel totally out of control. I need some time to sit in nature and go within without all the distractions. I need to know what I am supposed to be doing as I feel so disconnected. I am also going to look into declaring bankruptcy as we are so far under I don't see a way out unless we have some huge windfall of cash. I am not at all attached to the ramifications of it and see it as an outlet to clean up the junk and start anew.

I will get back to you soon,

Much love to you and your daughter

G.

The Golden Chalice

YOU ARE DEARLY LOVED.

Today you are celebrating your victory. In fact, every day that you walk this walk must be a celebration.

Celebrating what, some may want to know?

That you are alive, we say with a smile.

Being alive in a body is always a cause for celebration. We are here walking with you. Each time one of you inhales a breath of gratitude, your colors brighten and your light expands like fireworks on the Fourth of July. When you offer gratitude and acknowledge your victory we shed tears of joy. When you experience these emotions, standing in the present, you have linked with Spirit, with Gaia, and you become it. "It" is a divine vessel who shines brightly, fueling illumination on this precious planet. So much dust you have accumulated over your many cycles, so much pain your cells remember, so many unresolved puzzles that ask to be completed. On your many journeys you have gained extensive knowledge and tools of what to do as well as what not to do, whom to listen to but also whom to ignore, when to turn left or when to turn right. This knowledge is all within you, and all you need to do is awaken and trust. Easy are the steps of this dance that potentially carry you to your highest path, and at the same time so perilous. You have the knowing, but memory of the past clouds this knowing. You receive the messages, but the mind keeps shadowing those whispers. You have the tools, but amnesia and being lazy keep you away from your power. When you finally loosen your grip and allow, fear comes in, freezing you. We hear so many of you say to yourselves, "I am lost; I have no idea what is going on; I am not sure what will be with me; I have lost my power and direction." Sweet human angel, with a hug, we impart to you that this is the way of it.

Those who seemingly walk confident and secure in the inner workings of your world, believing they will conquer this physical world by storm, are up for many surprises. Being lost is a sign that you are one with the new energy permeating your dimension. Being lost is being in alignment with the feminine wave now flooding your collective consciousness. The sensation many of you experience of floating—not knowing to where, not being sure how far, pulsating, allowing, surrendering, being vulnerable yet powerful at the same time—

these all are aspects of the Goddess frequency moving back to center stage. Not knowing must precede real knowing. You are experiencing an immense shift that is rearranging every particle on your dimension. Metaphorically you may place your wallet on your kitchen table and as you turn around it has disappeared only to be found on your bed a week later. Some of you like to consult a mirror often so you remember what you look like. You may be in for a treat when a different face may stare back at you from the mirror. Your cycles are all changing, and for you to reorient yourself within this shifting reality you must learn to take time, be still, quiet, seek balance, so that the instructions coming from your higher navigator—left, right, up, down, north, south, east, or west—will be heard clearly. You are the conductor. You must rely on your feelings to navigate as the old compass is no longer pointing north. This is your challenge at these times. Sacred indeed, these changes are in your midst, and as we hold your hand, we ask you to walk in a leisurely way.

Many believe that you are running towards progress when in fact, you may actually be moving backward. Now that so many of you are lost, finally you begin to tread slower. You are finally realizing that this cycle is not about more, faster, bigger; it is about love, awareness, and connecting your inner cords to your outer reality, so that all of your actions, in this dimension, are aimed at carrying you higher.

Many of you are experiencing feelings of doom, as if the world is coming to an end. We can see it layered on your geometric forms. We know who you are. Much chatter is circulating in the ethers, and your collective thought energy creates a cloud that covers the sun. This shift is about the rising of a New Sun, and in order for you to experience that New Sun, each of you must clear your sky of clouds. Your power to create that which you believe in brings to your table the dish that you order. This world is not coming to an end anytime soon, and the energy that you are will never be coming to an end. You are eternal, and you contain within you the energy you call God. Collectively, you are the creator, and that which you wish for you manifest in your dimension on Earth. It is time for you to walk the walk of a master fully aware of your power and magnificence. This is why you are here, to awaken to your power and experience it in your body. What many of you consider as powerful in your manufactured reality, through the game of business, politics, or through the energy of money, is not what we consider to be powerful. Power is walking in the knowing of who you are. It is how your thoughts, feelings, and intentions manifest your reality. Power is being fully aware that all energy is guided by love. The dark forces that many believe in and fear are your own creations. There is nothing more powerful than the light of an angel dressed up as a human in this universe. All evil created is not from our side, but from your side of the veil. Many of you mistake the universal law of cause and effect—or karma—tagging it as evil. We wish you to know that all energy strives to be in equilibrium, and when a powerful energy such as the human moves energy out of balance through actions that are not love based, those actions must then be balanced, allowing the human an opportunity to regain equilibrium. The force of karma does not seek revenge or to hurt anyone, but through synchronicity, creates opportunities for the one who inflicted pain on another to experience that pain on itself. As well, the one who gifted another through love may then experience that love on itself. It is an impersonal energy that is biased to love. The darkness, pain, or suffering that you are experiencing on your sacred planet is a reflection of the collective state of your consciousness. To those who give power to a conspiracy of aliens and attribute your state of affairs to intervention from outside, more powerful forces, with all love, we ask those of you to look inside before you scout your skies. You are the alien, and you have been interacting with your galactic family for eons but you have just forgotten. Many of your native cultures still do communicate with your galactic family but do so incognito. You have been guided and schooled by guides who came from other systems; none was more powerful than you, and all was done with permission.

When a human gives her power away, there will be many volunteers to take her place, and those volunteers will not have her best interest in mind. There are many players in this game of creation. We wish you to hold on to your light, as it is your birthright, and know that you are magnificent, that you are loved. Your light is coveted by many and it is your golden chalice. Hold on to it and use it with care. Evil has been marketed and sold to justify the actions of the human that could not be explained or understood. When a human angel commits despicable acts of violence against another human, for some it may be convenient to give that power of choice to another, more omnipotent element, calling it the dark forces. Darkness represents a choice not to be with light. Light represents love and truth. You have been offered many choices up until now, and the movie selection, the choices of channels is growing. Your attention, intention, thoughts, and feelings are your remote control. The swirling movement of your cycles is accelerating; the shifts above and below you are intensifying. You have known about these times and you are ready. We are your brothers and sisters, acting as your alarm clock. Give intention to remember why you are here. Begin to use your tools and allow yourself time to create with awareness within, before you manifest in the external. Evaluate and feel the results of your creations before you manifest. Move slower, act slower, think slower, and consult your higher part before you act and manifest.

If we move slowly, we will never make it, you may say. *Physical reality demands that we move faster, work harder, be more efficient. So how do we reconcile what you tell us with our life,* some may ask?

As we hug you, we whisper in your ear that what you call "the demands of life" is just one channel, available on your energetic remote control, out of many. Go inside and order your remote control to switch the channel to the one that supports your highest potential, leading you to your highest path. "See" yourself physically switching to the channel of love, abundance, balance, and health, then see what happens.

What then, you may ask?

Laugh and dance. This dance is simple as it requires three basic steps: love, intent, and trust. The three can be reduced to two steps: awakening and trusting.

We have tried it but it did not work, you may complain.

We find it funny, at times, the role you play in your physical reality—for example, going to the supermarket and buying vegetables. Your expectation is that there will be a supermarket, that there will be vegetables to buy, that when you hand the store's clerk money he will bag your vegetables and thank you. When you are asked to do the same with Spirit, all of a sudden there is no supermarket, or when you find the supermarket there are no vegetables, or at last when you finally find where the veggies were hidden, you discover that they do not take your angelic credit card and that you are out of cash. With a wink, we promise you that, when you intend to go to Spirit's supermarket with the same expectation that you have when you go to the one around the corner, you will find everything that you expect waiting for you. You manifest in the physical the same way that you manifest in Spirit. In the physical, though, the dimension of time is inserted so that thought and feeling, fueled by intent and love, must be convincing to you first. When they are, the pulse sent begins to shift the atoms and molecules, creating the synchronicity, bringing your supermarket to you, with an abundance of fresh vegetables, in a place where they gladly agree to charge your angelic credit card. You are Spirit commanding a biological vehicle. You have within you all the tools and knowledge to ascend higher than ever before, or to delve into the depths of darkness. Each choice you make, within the polarity of light and dark, holds more power than ever before.

This is your time to shine. It is your time to live your truth, knowing that you are loved beyond all measure and to know that you are it—God walking, dressed up as a human. We ask you to give your hand to the God within you and walk hand in hand. Your actions reverberate to all and help facilitate the ascension of consciousness on your planet. You are so dearly loved, and so be it.

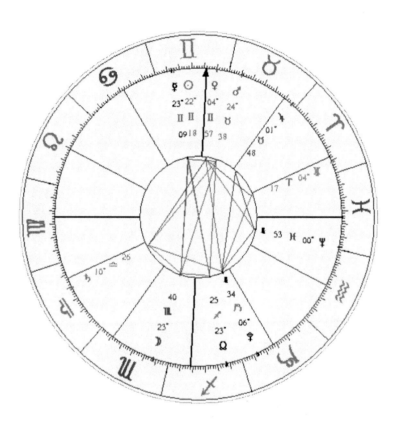

6/13/11

Dear Dror,

I've been busy with work and S. and I have started an organic farmers market! It was off to a slow start last week but we see it getting better and growing as we go along.

I have still been feeling out of sorts and looking back on the cleanse I started at this time last year and how much better I felt then!! I will get back to you shortly...

Love,

C.

Dearest C,

So good to hear from you. Congratulations on your new venture. I felt for a while now that any venture you take nutrition related will be rewarded. Good luck.

With gratitude and love

Hey Dror:

Thanks for the insight on the nutrition angle. You know, I knew that when I was a kid and all I wanted to do was study nutrition. I became a vegetarian when I was 15 and haven't eaten red meat in 37 years! My parents couldn't send me to college, so when I could get there myself, I went for nutrition science. Unfortunately it was not meant to be...will explain later. It has always been an interest for me.

Much love to you,

C.

The Leaf

YOU ARE DEARLY LOVED.

Only some are meant to walk the highest path in each cycle, yet even for those, it rarely feels high enough. Higher may not be easier, and *the climb* is your mission at this time. Keep moving despite the challenges and obstacles. As you climb, you pull with you all the rest. This is how it works. The few pave the way, energetically, to a new frequency of being. You are the ones who chose to introduce a melody that was never heard before on this precious planet. There are many melodies playing: all are divine, all serve a purpose. It is the higher octave that is now being utilized to allow your abilities to expand.

Why don't we feel like we are making a difference, you ask?

This is not about you feeling special and your ego being stroked. You know who you are and why you came here. Our stories are familiar to you. At night you do not sleep because you relive your purpose in visions. We see many who try to forget why they are here, becoming very busy with physical life: making a living, supporting a family, being involved with community, even finding time for charity work. It is all wonderful, all sacred, but it is not your purpose, and deep within, you know it. You feel that you are trying to be the best you can be, but inside it does not feel good enough. It's not because you are failing, but because the way you were brought up to see yourself and measure your path is changing. Your physical reality is merging with the astral. It is now on you to play in both fields and be comfortable juggling 3-D with All-D using the same body, same senses, same feelings, with the same breath, yet knowing that in one reality you are a human going through the human experience while, in the other, you are an intergalactic angel playing in fields reachable only with wings.

Many of you are concerned with your physical actions. From our perch, your actions are as important as your feelings, thoughts, and dream time. The reality of multidimensionality must be learned like any other skill. This know-how is inside of you and you must wish for it. For your know-how to be activated, sprout, and reach the light, you must water your seed buried in the soil. Your seed knows that it must strive to break the surface and reach to the light. All the movement inside you and around you is cyclical, or circular, in essence. Many of you are amazed to find yourselves back in the beginning, just when you thought that you may have reached the end. It is so because you always move in circles, and as you propel to higher and higher elevations the circle is being stretched into an upwards spiral. It is the movement of ascension, and the pressure pulling up and pushing from below is intensifying. Internally and externally pressure is being built on your systems, being expressed through what feels like emotional whitewater rafting. This is your time to shine by allowing the movement to move through you and to trust. We have been sharing for some time now how to prepare. More and more of you are now being awakened to why you are here, beginning to dance with the wind. To dance with the wind you must hold still. Like a leaf you are being twirled up, down, and sideways while maintaining your leaf form. It is so because your consciousness must practice letting go of what you know and who you think you are. There is a divine purpose to the chaos that is expressed in and around you. Are you holding on to the pole when you feel the blowing wind threatening to carry you away? We ask you to do the unthinkable and loosen your grip on that pole, knowing that you are safe.

Your insurance certificate is not given to those who hold on but to those who let go. The intense powerful movement within you and outside of you is your guide. You are asked to let go of what is heavy in your life. Let go of those things that keep you anchored and release your grip on the poles around you. Many of you fear that your identity will vanish. We ask you to move deep inside the cavity of your heart and, from the sphere of light planted in each one of you, connect to the love that is all around you, knowing that nothing is ever lost. By loosening your grip, you allow your reality to rearrange itself, serving your highest path.

How does this chaos end up serving me, you may wonder?

Funny, how you believe that human society creates order while nature is chaos. In fact, the reverse is closer to our truth. Your attempt to control movements all around you disturbs the natural order. When an intensely emotional event takes place in your physical reality, we ask you to become still. Allow all this movement in and around you to create some havoc within you while you remain still. We ask you to not react. This energy that is carried by emotional upheaval holds an immense potential that you can use to move higher. As the emotions flowing inside of you range from fear to rage to sadness to feelings of revenge or hate, allow and allow without moving. Your game has just begun. The kickoff action that prompted the movement is a Big Bang, the same bang that holds the potential for infinite expansion, as long as you do not react.

Why not react, you may wonder?

The emotional Big Bang event is sacred and contains within it all the potential for endless expansion. Yet, you do not have easy access to the big picture because of the emotional storm that is taking place inside of you. This storm has the potential to delve into the deepest oceans, then to carry you soaring to the highest peaks within a matter of minutes. When you react to an intense emotional event, you have chosen to freeze your current level of understanding of what took place. From that point on, all your emotional energy, rather than teaching you while empowering you to explore and dive into the depths of your story, remains in the shallow water anchored by your response. The longer you hold off on reacting, the larger your energy expands. If you have been hurt and you lashed out, your geometry has now become fixed in the shape of anger. You have determined within you that what had happened went against your wish or well-being. In the universal playing field nothing is arbitrary or coincidental, and your experience is created by you for the purpose of guiding you higher. An intense emotional event, like a storm, presents a sacred opportunity to use the movement of energy to spread your wings to fly. As the seconds tick by, which turn into minutes, hours, even days after the Big Bang, if you have conquered your desire to react, choosing to remain still, allowing the movement within you to rage and storm, you have mastered one of the most untapped energy sources in your tool box. As time passes, when you allow the event to be filtered down, moving through the deepest layers of your consciousness without being stopped, you are nearing your truth. As you dive into the depth of your ocean, glimpses of why and how begin to surface. From a devastating bang a short while ago, that may have shaken your core, new realizations begin to stream in and you may begin to discover the golden string of love that had attracted this bang into your reality. When your outlook changes and you have reached a quieter, more peaceful space in relation to the bang, know that you have won the lottery, picking the winning numbers, elevating yourself to the highest potential within the scene that was introduced to you. Mastery is hard work. Holding still and staying open in the face of immense flows of energy is challenging.

How do I remain still in the face of a difficult event, you ask?

Continue to breathe deeply and slowly, moving to a witness platform from which you can observe yourself not reacting. Allow second by second to pass, resisting the temptation. Allow your mind to form many responses but act on none of them. Do not choose; do not form an opinion; do not take sides; do not lock yourself into a story. Do not tell anyone a script—especially yourself—and just feel. Feel the uncontrollable tsunami of emotions pass through you, and just remain still. Your mind will fight, asking you to choose, and we ask you to not choose but remain still. All the different versions of responses will flow in and out of you; just watch, just breathe. This is mastery at its best. Everyone can get angry and lash out, but how many can remain still in the face of immense adversarial experiences? The longer you hold off reacting, just breathing, allowing the energy to freely flow within you, the larger your energy field grows around your vessel and the more powerful a transformation you will experience, riding the wave. Many of the events you chose to classify as painful, hurtful, and pure misery are your ticket to becoming liberated from your current version of reality. We ask you to board the plane when you get the ticket. To most of you, these events are something to dread. We ask you to get yourself ready. Learn to breathe slowly and deeply during times when great excitement is taking place in or around you. You hold within you an immense power to choose your channel of reality, so we ask you to be still and allow the movement to settle within you before you fixate it on this or that channel. The sphere of light inside your heart is your magic chalice and it holds the power of the universe within it. Finding the key to the lock where this chalice hides is your aim. You contain within you a key to the secrets of the universe. All is contained within you. The chalice guards your light. When you open the door to where the chalice is stored, all the secrets are revealed and there are no more questions, as you know all that you need to know to walk your walk. All your situations and dramas are but gateways to ascending to higher grounds. You must move from the storm into the eye of the storm and find peace inside while all around you wind is raging. Your aim is to be one with the movement yet experience peace at the same time. You must surrender, allowing whatever comes to sway you, while you remain without resistance, taking in the currents of energy, letting them move through your vessel, propelling you higher and higher. The more open you are to the experience, allowing your consciousness free rein to search, feel, merge, delve, to become tossed and turned while remaining open, the closer you will be to unlocking the lock. Once found, you have entered a new reality. Each gate represents a new understanding of yourself along with the forces that operated in and around you. You are standing at the gates of a New Sun. You are beautiful and you are loved. You have come so far. We ask you to open your wings and jump, knowing that you were meant to fly. With a hug we remind you that there are no victims, there is no arbitrary anything anywhere; all that you meet on your journey as a human angel has a purpose. We ask you, then, to open yourself to that purpose; ride on it higher than ever before, and so be it.

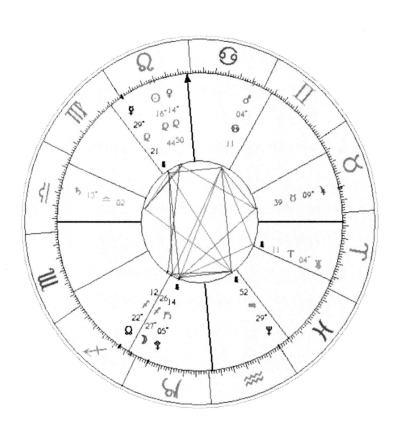

8/9/11

Dearest Light:

Was feeling you strongly Just a few moments ago.
Thank you so for being.
I did receive a message today and it somehow helped
my energy align. It comes with so much love and
clarity that I felt more balanced after.   The new
message is very relevant to what I am experiencing
at the moment and I am always thankful when it
happens.
I will start to work on the forensic accounting
tomorrow with a couple of helpers. Will be doing it
pretty much the whole week.

I will be at home.

Love and Light

Dror

The Eye of the Storm

YOU ARE DEARLY LOVED.

Does it seem fair to you that so many of us are watching you, guiding you and supporting you, but you carry the workload all by yourself? To some the load seems to be overwhelming and you ask, "Please help. I can no longer carry on like this. It is simply too much. Why can't you take it all away and make things lighter for a change?" We hear you think out loud, "We understood the messages and we are climbing, looking for the wide-open vista. Instead, though, things get more convoluted and dense." We know who you are and we see those of you who wonder, "Have we been misled? What is happening? Why aren't we ascending? Why aren't we trouble-free? Why aren't we happy and joyful like we feel we should be? Why aren't we free to do the lightwork and fulfill our promise? Why, why, and why?"

These questions seem to be occupying more than a few of you these days.

Our loving answer is simple: this is how you designed it for yourself. You chose to be precisely where you are. You chose, with every dance move you make, to ascend above your current understanding and reading of your situation or to delve deeper into the illusion of the heaviness.

There is no heaviness. You are free; you can be happy and joyful at every moment that you choose to be. The overwhelming feeling that you experience is you trying to control the outcome, rather than allowing the highest outcome to come to you and knock on your front door saying, "Here I am." There is no one out there that is loading you with heaviness. You have stood in line so you can be here at this time, carrying the load that you are carrying. You are prepared for it and you know what you need to do. If you thought for a moment that your temporary fleeting reality would accommodate you and lighten up just so that you would have no worries and no burdens, you have taken the wrong dance lesson. The dance moves you have practiced were choreographed to allow you to move with ease, negotiating difficult terrains and challenging situations. You are an artist. You are an alchemist. You are the creator and your goal is to transform lead into gold through the inner process of alchemy. As a master painter you now know to distinguish between the different shades of grey. You know how to highlight the background of any landscape so the hope of illumination will be apparent even in seemingly the darkest, most hopeless situations. The work is moment by moment, being and realizing your power, utilizing every tool you were exposed to, knowing that you are now facing test after test after test being expressed as choice after choice after choice. All you can do is keep your head high, gazing at the horizon and set your intent to move as high as you can without attaching to the details of how to get to your final destination. That part is our job. We should, after all, justify our wings (our angelic humor, winking at you).

You are now experiencing a rapidly shifting planet which is being expressed through acceleration of changes in your outer environment: politics, financial markets, culture, society, and technology, as well as through immense changes in weather patterns. It is, however, your inner terrain that is moving through an upgrade and an expansion never before experienced by you, so your point of view is changing in relation to all these physical changes. If we had to sum it up we would say, as we hug you, you are well within the parameters of the New Sun storm. There are no places on Earth that this storm does not reach. There is no place far away enough on this planet in which you can hide.

Where should we go then, you may ask?

The best place to be is at the eye of the storm within you, as nowhere else will you feel quite as protected.

But the eye of the storm is constantly moving, some may protest.

This is precisely what you need to be doing as well.

This does not feel like too safe of a solution, you may say.

Your mission is not to hide but to be present and awake, acting and rippling your vibration to all those who are in contact with you energetically or physically. Many of you experience the shifts within your close circle, be it with your lover, spouse, best friend, or a parent. Your close circle is your mirror, and this mirror is reflecting to you your own shift and you do the same to them. Know how sacred this change is, as many of you are now being carried on your new wings to higher elevations—higher than ever before, where the view is breathtaking, a view few humans ever get to experience. As we hug you we see the anguish many face as you realize you may need to let go of loved ones you cannot take with you. We have spoken about the split that is now taking place on many levels: darkness versus illumination, heavy and light, high or low. This split is reflected more than ever in your personal relationships. You are finding that loved ones you believed would walk with you the whole journey this lifetime now must say goodbye, as the road has split, so that you can no longer carry the burden of pretending or being untruthful to yourself. When you choose to love and honor yourself, your body, your path, at times those not wishing to honor you or love you in ways that support your truth may need to move away to clear a path for a new, polished mirror.

At times, all that you know may feel torn and discombobulated. It may begin to fall away from you, as you toss and turn in the immensity of outer as well as inner changes swirling all around you. Dear angel, you came here for exactly this. It is here, now. You are in the energy of your initiation into a new frequency and, at times, all that you know must be let go, so the new can take hold. You are all "candles" of "one" divine flame exploring its own magnificence, and as one moves higher, all the billions upon billions of parts making up that magnificent one must shift positions. You are all connected like never before, and one may be aware of what the other one is doing on the other side of your planet almost in real time. Through your technology, media, and your inner intuition you are paving a path to unity consciousness. As forerunners of the new frequency, what you feel, think, and do affects the whole. Your planet is becoming more illuminated. The more light floods, the more transparent it becomes, and the more darkness is being exposed.

We have said in one of our messages that you did not come here to lie in your hammock, drinking nectar. This now-time is the time of which we spoke. You are your vibration and your relationships are your extended concentric circle. As you vibrate your love and light to the whole, the circle around you must change to reflect your ascending frequency; the higher you reach, the more apparent the change will be. Self-love is the core ripple holding within it the most powerful energy a human angel carries. Honoring the self is the portal which opens the gate to all honoring. Loving the self is the portal that opens the gate to all loving. As you spread your wings and begin to levitate above, gliding on the hot-air frequency of self-love, you no longer judge anyone as good or bad, light or dark, high or low. You bow your head in wonder at the beauty and divinity you see all around you expressed through choices. You beam love to those who were part of your life, and are no longer. You know all too well that you are all one and the same. You also know that the short time you all have shared physical space is honored and sacred. You say your goodbyes, knowing all too well that you will always be connected, and all that you have ever experienced with those who crossed your path is woven with invisible golden strings of love. You know that you may meet again on another journey and may have to complete another piece in this great cosmic puzzle. There are many players in this awesome game and all are trying to contribute to the picture of the whole. As you match and assemble the pieces, you help not only yourself but all those who abut your piece of the puzzle to be complete. There are no victims, only choices that are honored and accepted by all who are participating in this great experiment.

When it is time to say your goodbyes, honor the ones who taught you, thanking them for showing you the way, allowing you an opportunity and a context in which to grow. Do not harbor animosity or anger to those angels, as they came here like you to fulfill their promise, completing their own puzzle, as well as helping you to complete yours. Sacred this union was and sacred it will remain for eternity. You are never too far from anyone who ever crossed your path. When a new cycle begins you may meet again and fulfill another promise. We are with you as you move through your trials, and we must say that it looks magnificent from our perch. We ask you to be your truth, live in your power, and know that nothing important is ever lost as you move higher in vibration, only weight, and so be it.

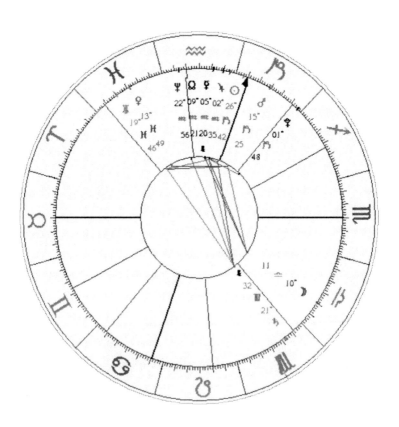

9-28-11

Shana Tova

I wish the both of you a happy sweet and wonderful
New Year.

  May we experience peace. Make peace with the
past and embrace a new beginning. Forgive ourselves
for what we have done to others and forgive others
for what was done to us, let go of pains and hurts
and embrace a path to harmonious relationships with
all those who surrounds us.

 Wish you health,joy , love and all the good things life
has to offer.

Shana tova

Dror

Blueprint

YOU ARE DEARLY LOVED.

Do not give up, we say as we hug you. We wipe the tears that are rolling down your face, and we say: each day that you breathe is a gift. It is a gift, as well, each day you are holding your light upward, illuminating your surroundings. See how far you have traveled to be here and know that the end is not what you think it is. Many of you wish to reach your destination where there is illuminated brilliance, peace always, and rest. Dear human angel, where you are now, at this moment, is that destination, being in the trenches, transforming, shining light where it is dark, moving high when gravity pulled you down, opening your heart when you are expected to close it, moving above water when you are expected to drown, becoming lighter when you are being loaded with heaviness. You are renegades and you know that what you do makes a difference to the whole. Indeed, it is your reason for being.

How do I lighten my load, you wish to know?

What if we told you that the heavy load you carry was "gifted" to you? Your original essence is light. When you begin to unload your heaviness you create light which illuminates your surroundings. The angel in human costume comes to this dense reality asking to find happiness, experience joy, health, and abundance. When those expectations and hopes do not materialize as hoped, many are asking, "Why?" and "why me? "What did I do wrong to deserve such fate, when all around me people seem to be in better places?" You all come here with a grand plan. You have carefully designed your blueprint before you descended into the birth canal. You have studied all the different roads and potentials. You have placed yourself smack where your route will intersect with your learning, allowing you to move through the unfinished business you left in previous journeys, and progress. You did not sit with your angel guides and devise the easiest path to move through. Unlike water you do not devise plans based on ease of flow and gravitation. You are consciousness driving a physical vehicle, and you won an opportunity to accelerate your learning by playing the game of human angel. Does it make spiritual sense to you that, after all the effort you made to be here, all you would plan is for everything to flow perfectly, exactly the way you desire it? Some of you like to view your lives as if watching through large binoculars, saying to yourselves, "This part is fine, but this part needs repairs, and then this part is awful."

We ask you to reverse your binoculars. Instead of trying to analyze the details, look at the details as more distant—so small they almost disappear. You soon realize that they are insignificant in the scheme of things. Driving a car on a straight road with no curves, hills or valleys can be awfully boring, and some of you almost fall asleep at the wheel while driving through such terrain. Entering the game of life is like driving a car: the challenges that appear all around—the curves, the oncoming traffic, the difficult weather conditions—metaphorically, are what keep you awake, alert, progressing, growing, and becoming more powerful. At the moment of challenge, we hear your call for help, but fast forward the tape a little and most of you look back with gratitude, clearly seeing in hindsight how these challenges benefited you, giving you the opportunity of a lifetime to move higher, progressing on your path.

We know, we know, we hear you say.

Then why are you complaining when you know better? Why are you asking, "Why me?" when you know that you should be grateful for every moment that your exciting life is unfolding in front of you? If you had the option to go to a video store and buy a video game, would you buy the video game which shows you a long straight road, just so you could sit there holding the stick without moving? We know who you are and you know who you are. You buy the most exciting, action-packed story lines. Why are the movies which everyone loves packed with drama, action, as well as moments of highs and lows? Have you seen an Oscar-nominated movie lately that had no action and everything went as planned without any drama whatsoever?

Well, those are movies and we are living in real life, some may reply.

With all love, we must remind you once again that you are living in a movie. Not only that, your movie is all produced for your entertainment. You also wear three different hats. You are director, producer, and actor, as well. There are many planets with consciousness roaming around; none is as exciting as this one in our view. The birth rate on Earth is accelerating to such an extent because everyone wants to be here and yet there are many standing in line. The capacity to feel, experience, react, use love, and choose are rare ingredients which make this beautiful planet so desirable, this experiment so unique. So, next time when you face a challenge, look at the challenge as if through binoculars but reverse the direction. See whatever you're looking at as so small that it is practically indistinguishable, smile to yourself, and know that whatever you look at changes all the time. What is it that distinguishes your life on Earth from your life in the heavens, we ask you, and the answer is change. As an angel, you do not change as dramatically as you do when you walk the walk of a human. You do not have a choice between dark or light, and you know all that we know. You do have opportunities to grow, but none can be compared to the accelerated growth opportunities you experience as a human angel. With a hug, we must remind you that many of the reasons that keep you up at night—nervousness, being upset, your dramas, your lows, your challenges and tests—are the reason you chose to be here. So next time when you ask for that easy life, where everything is constant and all is boring, think if you would purchase a ticket to that movie. Or if you already did, would you have considered asking for your money back? We see many who chose to experience a human life with the intent to live their truth, feel, explore, risk, and be fully alive. Once they forget their original purpose they become complacent and compliant because it seems too risky or challenging to break from the grooves, to live outside the box. Finally, when they come back to our side of the veil, they ask for their money back because they did not experience the ride they were promised. Unfortunately for them, our policy on the angelic cash register states that once you have bought the ticket to your Earth theater, "No Refunds Here"—another angelic joke. There are many ways to look at what you are experiencing at the moment; the surest way to move through your dramas with ease is to understand that it is part of the entertainment you chose. Some of these setups are difficult, challenging, and painful, yet these are the paths you have designed for yourself as runways so you can take off, becoming the airborne magnificent angel that you are. If we told you that, instead of going to a safari, you will be riding a bus in the desert and the landscape will pretty much remain the same, would you have chosen it as an option? Your answer will likely be, "No way!" What makes these journeys so precious is that once you complete a cycle you are back again for another go at it. You go through all the stages of development, and you have yet another opportunity to experience fully life in the body of a human. We tell you over and over that just being on Earth now is a cause for celebration. Being in a body, to play your part when Earth life is accelerating, is certainly getting your money's worth, and we ask you to prepare for even more excitement. What you have learned to accept as your political, financial, personal, psychological, spiritual, and geographical landscapes are all shifting. To some it seems as though all remains the same, yet it does not. To some it feels as if all is coming to an end, yet it is not. You are embarking on a new trajectory where the premise of all that you know is being challenged. It cannot get more exciting than this, and we ask you to celebrate. Celebrate the busy days and sleepless nights that make you wonder what is going on. Offer gratitude that you are getting front row seats at the most exciting show—the one that is all around you.

How do we navigate the slippery slopes and know where to go, you may wonder at times? *How do we avoid failing our tests? We hear so much advice and all sounds truthful, but we are still lost.*

Beautiful energy you are, and when you spread your wings becoming airborne, we all put together our invisible hands to clap in awe of your magnificence.

Being on this planet requires energy. For your geometry to spin and your field to navigate you to where you need to be, you must hold on to as few filters as possible. The purer your vessel is, the clearer the guidance will be to you. Navigating in the current accelerated changes, your map will not be as useful, mainly because you must navigate in the dark. You are a magnificent musical instrument. As your body vibrates, the field around you expands. The musical notes, as if through magic, will appear within you. The conductor will appear everywhere, dressed up as anyone, as everyone, anything or everything, to give you signals or cues seemingly coming from all around, to lead you through to where you need to be. You may think that knowledge is essential and that, spiritual knowledge, particularly, may be your saving grace. With all love, many of the concepts that you have grown to accept as your truth may be changing their reflections, showing you new aspects of that truth which may seem to directly oppose the original truth. Truth is always in relation to who, what, and where you are at the moment. Many ideas you accept now as absolute truths are being challenged and more so as you move beyond 3-D to multi-D. The differences between dark and light may not be as clear any more. A great deal of spiritual chatter around you may leave you still wondering and just as lost as you were before.

Why is it so, you may ask?

Although you have access to so much information, the only information you need, that caters to your own highest path, will appear when you are linked to your own melody. To link to your own sound, your instruments must be tuned and vibrating. So many will offer their help and guidance. The hunger grows for spiritual guidance, as many feel insecure and confused. You may be offered spiritual dishes from Earth's buffet to satisfy your hunger. Be aware of what you take onto your tray, and what you leave on the buffet table, as not all dishes are the same.

How do we know, you may wonder?

Smell the food, we say as we smile. The answers are always easier than you think and they come naturally. Feel your solar plexus. If the feeling of a particular teaching is appropriate for you, the energy felt will be recharging your batteries, and when it is not, the energy will be of pulling or draining your field. Any truth that makes itself indispensable is an outright lie. Any truth that has asked you to give away your power is not your truth. Any spiritual path that asks you to become part of it and pay fees, or else you will never get to the light, may not be your truth path.

Then what is my truth, some may dare ask?

We thought you'd never ask. Your truth is love and light. Your truth is becoming aware that all the spiritual knowledge you will ever need is within you and, through intent, you can activate it at any given moment. Reading, studying, and taking courses may enhance your journey, but your progress is not dependent upon one school of thought or another. Your yearning to grow and your choice to energize your spiritual journey is the power that elevates you. It is not any particular knowledge that holds power, as many reach higher through one school while others reach as high while following a diametrically opposing school. It is not the spiritual school that matters, but your inner power and intent to move higher. When you consider teachings which empower you to become awakened to your own power, consider taking a bite of the apple. When, though, by biting that apple, your power gets whisked away from you, go for an orange. Your body is a musical instrument capable of playing divine tunes. You can choose to use your hands for many things: you can prepare food, clean the yard, play the piano, or write a novel. Same with your body. When you honor your body and treat it with love it will reciprocate and will vibrate. When you play your instruments, allowing your cells to expand, reaching higher frequencies by activating your sexual energy, you are on your way to growing wings. When you make peace with your past, surrendering to let go of the feelings of inadequacies, of not being good enough, strong enough, smart enough, tall enough, pretty enough, or whatever else is in your "enough list," you move a step higher. When you become aware that all that you are and all that you perceived as your reality is perfect the way it is because it reflects the collective wish of the collective you, that whenever you wish to change that "perfect" picture to reflect your new awareness, that indeed you have the power to do so, you have defied gravity. When you walk your path expressing gratitude while bowing your head in awe of the ingenuity, simplicity, and power of truth as it reveals itself, you emanate light to wherever you go. When you do not try to persuade anyone of your truth, allowing each to keep their own reflection, without it feeling threatening to your truth, you have moved two steps higher. From one additional, third step, then, you may begin to see that each choice, with each breath, you are allowing a higher frequency through your instrument, with that frequency rippling and touching others without a word. The silence that you maintain, as you hold on to your own truth, allows your vibrational melody to persuade those who love the music to open their "ears" and feel the power of love. When tears begin to roll down their faces, you know that the music you play has touched their hearts and that, through love, healings ripple out to others. By being, allowing, trusting, and feeling, you let go of the need to prove or to have, to conquer or to acquire. The power of your melody alone carries your truth, and that truth is love. The love becomes light which shines, illuminating all who walk the path to higher ground. All you did is allow your truth to come through, as you are a conduit of light, becoming the winged human, and so be it.

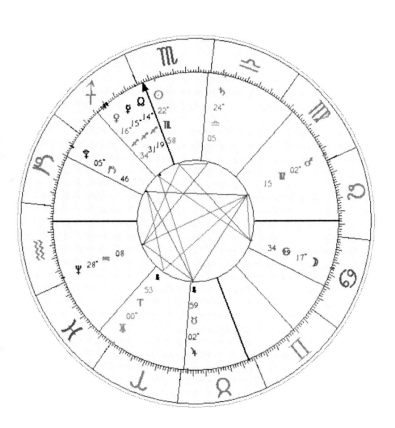

Hello Dror. Hope all is finding you well. I thought you might en-joy this photo taken by one of my clients. It's awesome!! peace and blessings....dale

picture my client took while reading conversations with angels

Hi M.

Thank you for lovely session last evening; with the wisdom tooth extraction, I know I wasn't totally relaxed. I did feel much better after our session. I appreciate any vibrations / readings you may have gotten energetically from me. Here is the photo; please feel free to share with Dale - took this picture as I was reading Conversations with Angels.

Lv, J.

The Perfect Partner

YOU ARE DEARLY LOVED, DEAR ANGEL.
We know who you are; we know where you are coming from; we know your true identity; we know your trials; we feel your hurts, and we celebrate your joys. We are family, the closest family you can have. We are with you at every waking hour and at night when you set yourself free to dance with us. We love you always. There are no conditions, even after we see you at your most fragile and trying moments, at your moments of vulnerability, at moments that you wish to hide from the world, you are still loved the same. You have no secrets from us because it is not necessary. You are never judged. We wait patiently, at times through many cycles, for the moment that you will wake up, feeling the universal pulse of source in your heart, link with us, and begin to awaken to your true magnificent self. It is why we never leave. We do not want to miss your call when it comes.

Why am I here, you ask, puzzled?

You are here to celebrate and we are here to celebrate with you. The fall and rise of all that you see around you is the movement of time within a cycle. All is cyclical and you are nearing a new beginning which is also an end. Yet again, nothing ever truly ends. The true movement is always within you, and the shifts that you are currently experiencing are but contexts for inner transformation. Your life is but a melody that plays a unique tune. This tune fluctuates based on your choices. The choices of light produce divine harmonics which heal, transform, create, nurture, love, preserve, protect, and uphold the highest vision for self and for all who come in contact with you. How simple yet profound. The scenes which are selected to offer you choice are your own setups, but as it stands, most give credit to none other than God, faith, chance, luck, or anything else for that matter, other than the higher aspect of yourself.

What you all seek is love. You all wish to be intravenously connected to the source of love and have this liquid light/energy substance inserted and flowing into you 24/7. With a smile, we assert that you are all junkies for this energy because it is what links you with your true magnificent self and makes you feel whole. The fragmented aspects of all creations desire to become whole. Like magnets of opposite polarities, you are attracted to each other, creating a pull, complementing each other's deficiencies. The proton and electron will invite each other into a frantic dance so both will "feel" complete. Why are so many feeling incomplete, some ponder? What is the secret to feeling whole? How can one find their true complementary perfect "other" to achieve a state of equilibrium? All are good questions. Beautiful is your journey, and yet treacherous it can be at times. Your senses all confirm that you are indeed an individual separate entity from all that is and you must protect self, worry about survival, and create boundaries wherever you go. This programming is your first challenge and obstacle to overcome on your path to becoming whole.

As you exist in an energetic playing field of duality and free choice, your most challenging obstacles to link with love source, as we view it, are three-dimensional portals. There are tests involved in the opening of each portal. The secret melody one must play is a frequency that lets the portal know that it is time to let you through.

What are they, you wonder? How does one find these portals?

These portals are interdimensional and always there. You are guided to find them once you give intent. Once moved past each of the gates a new energetic playing field reveals itself. Metaphorically speaking, one reality is switched with another, similar to your TV channels. The new channel is playing at a higher-frequency programming, rendering the old blueprint no longer accurate. This is one aspect of ascension—the change of one-frequency programming with higher-vibration programming. With a hug, we wish to remind you of what you all already know: the sacred tonal frequency required for opening the portals to source.

The first gate one must walk through is using the vibrational melody of gratitude. All aspects in one's life must be aligned with the frequency of gratitude so the heart will chart a path for opening and linking with source. It is challenging to most, as many of the trials, tribulations, hurts, and pains must be not only forgiven but embraced for one to genuinely align with gratitude.

The second gate is the gate of intent not to cause harm. One must vibrate in the melodic frequency of awareness not to cause harm intentionally. The power of the intent produces a sphere of light around one's field so to alert you when your choice may harm another. At the same time one must honor oneself and allow learning to be created through relationships. It is the intent of causing harm to another or to Earth that thickens the veil between you and your link to the universal love source. It is not about another being hurt, but about your intent. Harming another may often happen unintentionally, but it is in the realm of synchronicity, karma, and fulfilling of contracts for the purpose of learning, growing or moving higher.

Give us an example, one may ask.

In the realm of your intimate circle, you may feel that you are unable to move higher and fulfill your mission, manifesting your highest potential, while maintaining the same circle of relationships. Inevitably, you may need to change some relationships in order to allow the playing field to shift. This choice may hurt another, but the intent was not to hurt but to grow. When you act from love and honoring of self, not only do you not hurt others, but through your action you offer others opportunities to grow, shift, or ascend. Intentionally harming another does not allow your field to ascend in vibration and reach a frequency where you can link to source. This gate's trickiest aspect is that you must include yourself in the intent. Honoring and loving self guides your path toward no harm. Harm to self often leads to harm to others. To love as well as honor yourself guides one's light to love and honor others. This gate opens to the melodic frequency of no harm to self or to no harm to others in the lower octave, loving the self and others in the higher octave.

The last gate may be the most challenging one of all. You must let go of all agendas and loosen all strings in relation to love. Agendas are like filters obscuring luminosity, blocking your channels to higher frequencies. When you fall in love and the object of your love does not reciprocate the way you had hoped or expected, many of you reverse polarity, becoming sad, angry, and at times even hateful. It is, indeed, human and natural to experience these emotions. From our perch this is limited, first-step love. The two merge into one, metaphorically acting like two magnets that are attracted to the opposite polarity so each can feel whole. When a human falls in love with another human and for a moment both are dancing in union linked to source, you call it love, although it is only one aspect of it—the one everyone desires. Often a test may be introduced where the playing cards are being shuffled, gifting you with an opportunity to expand your love vantage, pointing and guiding you towards a path to move through this third gate. Love does not mean ownership of another or a conditional agreement where one serves the other, thereby receiving love. For you to experience the radiant light of the sun all the time you must ascend above the clouds. Having an agenda is being dependent on the weather conditions—sunny at times, but also stormy at times. Love does not ask anything from anyone. It just radiates. It is the pulse of the universe. Love is the highest frequency available to you that bridges the human dimension with Spirit and it asks for nothing in return. It is a state of being.

Your journey offers you sacred opportunities to invoke the gates. Your most challenging, gut-twisting dramas that make you come back time after time and work on script after script are fueled by your desire to link to the universal love source. Sacred is your playing field.

As you move higher in vibration, you must walk through the third gate. Once walked through, your colors change. Your chakras' spin rates, as well as geometry, change; your vibration, radiance, and melody changes. You have ascended energetically and are no longer who you were. Like a serpent, you have shed your skin but remained very much alive. This is your roadmap to mastery. It is embedded in your field and DNA.

You did not tell us how to find our perfect partner, you exclaim!

We did indeed. You are it. You are your perfect partner. The one you took with you as companion on this journey is none other than you. All "perfect" partners are but mirrors for you to see yourself. As you radiate with self-love, it will be reflected in the partner you choose. As you move from the limited programming that you have been taught, to accept and open yourself to the magnificent resonance which weaves all that is together—yes, you included—you will burst with luminosity, having love for all beings, all things.

What about that life partner we wish to grow old with, some may persist?

Your "perfect" partner is the one who, through contracts, paves a path for you to invoke the gates, giving you an opportunity to walk through them one by one. Your "perfect" partner is not the one who will be the ideal image of who you believe a partner should be. It is the one who may also cause you sweat and tears, giving you opportunity after opportunity to choose a melody that opens the gate to source. With all love, we must impart to you that all your partners are "perfect," and even when you change partners they are still "perfect." Eventually, you may not even have a partner, and still it will be perfect. We ask you to, once again, open to the magnificent aspect of your journey where there are no coincidences, no victims, where you have the opportunity to exercise the attribute so many desire, which is to choose and chart your own path. The partners that you attract and bring into your life are the ones who energetically match your intent and learning. They are all "perfect."

We want to find "the one," you may say.

There is one for each path of learning, for each intent, and all are mirrors for aspects of you. Therefore, again, all are "perfect."

With love, we ask you to allow the melody of gratitude to flood you and to reach all the "perfect partners" you have ever had, holding them as your teachers for invoking the gateways to source. You are a master in training. We ask you to open your wings and ascend above your current programming. Much of your work is to let go of one programming and open up for a new energy. It is a time for shedding, clearing, and becoming light. You are at the end of a cycle yet the beginning of another, so many of you are now being offered opportunities to invoke your personal gates. You have come here for this. You knew that now is your time and it is not in the realm of "easy" or "comfortable." The escalating acceleration many are now experiencing with intense emotions and challenges is fueled by your desire to keep in alignment with an ascending Gaia, your home. Sacred it is.

With a hug, we wish you to awaken to your opportunities, walking the highest path available for a human with wings, and so be it.

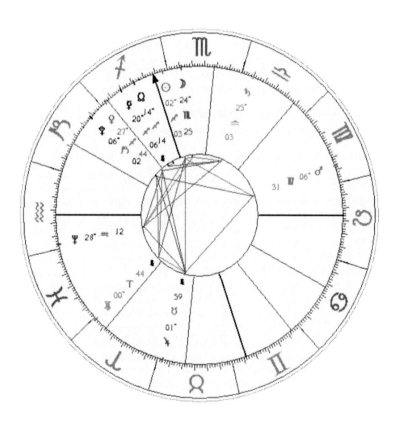

11/24/11
On Nov 24, 2011, at 12:43 AM, Emeka

Dear M,
I was somewhat amused and taken aback by your response about my deciding not
to come to Woodstock. You seemed to take it personally while insinuating that I
had personal or emotional reasons for my decision. Which makes me very aware of
how little you see me or understand who I really am and what this play is is about.
And believe me, it is a play, a divine chess match where every actions breeds its own
cause and effect. Whom am I playing chess with? Why the invisible realm and my
family of energy of course. Dror, gave an indication in his response to me, that this
was all about a choice that he knew that I had to make, a hard choice... he further
added that my actions had little to do with my e-mail but a truth that lay deep
inside me which I am not really allowed to tell anyone because even if I told them
they would not believe nor understand... Dror has given clear indication by his e-mail
that he is aware of another much more deeper and powerful play. This is the place
where I exist. It is from this place that he correctly surmised that I operate from
and is the place where I am not under cover but work from my true intent. Dror has
given hints through out his two e-mails that he is aware of who I really am and just
how great an actor I have been forced to be and become. I play what people see me
as, but that does not mean it is the truth.
> Just as Dror has given hints in his two e-mails, so have I in my onslaught of e-mails.
Who would hear, truly hear, who would see, truly see, who wants to understand but
truly understand... and who are those who simply assume?
> I made it very clear to you that something was wrong with my body when you
came back from Mexico, and that this would be an impediment (the greatest factor)
to my going to Woodstock. Is it not funny that you did not notice that it started
when you guys came back and when the offer was made to go to Woodstock? Well I
did, I further stated that thee was an etiquette that could make me easily identify
my line of the family... they have a certain manner, and they let slip information
which enables me to know that it is they. I re-read my e-mail to all three of you and
saw that I stated myself very clearly, which makes me wonder why it was so important for you that I come to Woodstock. Was it because you had my suffering condition in mind, do you know what is really happening to my body? This divine contract
that Dror spoke about which you know very little about (and instead of being quiet
and patient, seeking to understand and learn) instead you call me impatient and ask
me as to whom I am saying is disrespectful to the sacred truth. That I am aware
that you hardy truly listen or truly seek to understand what I Do you know why he
said this, do you know the great forces in Dror who are watching me, as they play
chess with me, a chess match which each move (and not before) bring forth the
outcome and the correct move...................
love
Emeka

The Light Keepers

YOU ARE DEARLY LOVED.

What an appropriate beginning for a day where so many offer their gratitude for being. It is a joy to be with you yet once again, to hold you near and dear. As we get ready, settling around you, we create a circle of light where each of us, in their turn, lights one candle. Together, then, we radiate, pulsating to you our words through melody, images, and vibrations. We say to you, "We are the nine." Sacred it is.

What else can a human seek on this journey? What is the motivation behind any seeking? Why bother? There are so many twists and turns. It feels as if this maze goes on forever and you may never find the way out or reach the treasure. Yes indeed, you are loved, and many are now asking themselves if what they are seeking even exists.

Tell us something we do not know, you say. Tell us the secret for which everyone is searching. Tell us how to navigate this maze and find our treasure. Tell us the buried, forgotten codes that have been lost. Tell us how it works. Be specific and do not hold anything back, you say.

And we say, beware of what you ask.

Once on a path of knowing, you must hold on to your seat as the landscape may begin to change rapidly. How fast do you wish to progress? "As fast as we can," we hear you say? If we had to reveal all the secrets, we would start with the one that has been held from you for millennia: the light that you carry within you is your most precious gift and it keeps you linked to the energy you call God. God is the source of light which is in all of you, throughout all the dimensions of space and time. Your light is part of your DNA and is also in every cell. The secret to all moving forward, not getting lost, and discovering your treasure depends on whether you hold on to your light or freely give it away. This is the war that you are currently fighting, taking back the light that you have so freely given away under false pretenses for so long. The keeper of your light, like your pawn shops, does not wish to return it to you unless you redeem your light and compensate them handsomely by paying high interest for that which you had deposited in their hands.

Tell us more, you propose.

There is a link that weaves all of you together. It is a silver cord that transfers the pulse of light and distributes it amongst you. There are those who acquired, mostly through deception, many hubs which regulate the pace and level of your movement within this web. Those hubs were held tightly and secretly away from the grasp of most humanity for a very long time. They were buried in codes, kept in vaults which are accessible only to those who agreed to never reveal their content or their hiding place. Indeed, it sounds like a conspiracy of sorts, and it sure appears that way. The only twist to the conspiracy idea is that you have agreed willingly to give up a portion of your light as many were not ready, or were overwhelmed with the idea that you hold full and absolute control over the unfolding of your own life. As you have created your mono Gods, choosing to believe that "he" is the one having the absolute power over your life, a piece of that knowledge was conveniently removed—the missing link was that this God was you. At that time the few who knew about this link formed a hub which collected the lights of those who were not ready to acknowledge their divinity, giving it freely to the few who used it for their own benefit and power. Over time many of those who held on to their light were coerced and forced through deception to surrender their light under one pretense or another. It is a game and you are a player in that game. Playing the game is the purpose and you learn by simply participating. The stated mission of all of you was to move within your charted path and learn what you could. The game rules have changed as many realized that you may lose the ability to play this game if you don't reclaim your light. The feminine aspect of your collective lights has asked permission to move back to its center role so that many will gain knowing through the heart rather than through the mind. The mind is more easily manipulated but the heart knows. The deliverance of feminine energy from your neighboring planets and galactic family, which happened in stages, marked the beginning of this shift, in whose midst you are now. The secret was exposed at times and attempts were made to reveal it. There were those who held the key to the hubs who knew how to create another story to divert the truth by creating a reflection and deflection of light, rather than allowing the light to link again with its rightful keepers. Many of you who came this lifetime to play your role as the new holders of the light knew of this secret and battled to release it in different cycles. This is why you were named light warriors. Your mission was to shine your light and through your own vessel create new codes so the frequency of light will once again free itself from the hubs' containment vaults, becoming available again to those who give intent to become light keepers.

Some of you who are fighting in the trenches, transforming and shifting your own idea of reality, are doing it for the many who no longer hold on to their power. You exist in a symbolic reality where one is linked to all and all is always linked to the one. Whatever the one does affects the whole so that, one by one, you are empowering each other through free will and intent to keep your light, taking full responsibility for your script. The power that you claim by knowing your responsibility, as the creator, to shape your reality, ripples to all, allowing the awakening of your collective. Sacred it is.

Tell us more, you demand!

You are sacred—all of you. By tarnishing your vessel through campaigns of subjugation and manipulation your sacred vessel programming was hidden from you as well. The codes have been switched or tainted so that you could only keep the survival energy intact, without the know-how to link to the higher spheres of knowledge and light. Your ability to link with your light and use your power to navigate the maze was scrambled. The keepers of the hubs knew that when a human discovers their secret source of power, those keepers would lose the ability to protect their vaults from that human linking back to their own light. It is a war between the light warriors and the hub keepers, or bankers, of your energy. Your light, when linked to source, keeps your melody playing the highest potential for you. Your own power, when activated, guides your reality to manifest the most divine blueprint in your potential. Collectively, you are all here to activate as many humans as possible. Each of those activated angels changes the balance of light and dark on your planet as they allow more to link with their light.

How do we access our powers, you ask?

The role that you came here to play is one of a truly heroic nature. Your aim is to reconstruct your programming and rewrite your DNA codes so that the blocks that have been conditioned in you through the last many thousands of years will relink with new awareness.

Tell us specifics, you insist.

For your body to vibrate within its highest frequency range of self-love and God-self I-Am, you must be block free. One path to reaching higher frequencies is by experiencing pleasure as well as by building sexual energy for a prolonged period of time. You then channel this energy from survival, creation, and core self-image, stored in your first, second, and third chakras, to your higher centers. Your higher portals, the heart, throat, third eye, and crown are directly linked to your higher aspect which is your God-self. Through programming, the divine codes of pleasure were removed from your programming above the first and second chakras; this kept you in survival and populating modes or manipulated the third center, redirecting your image of self for the purpose of consumption or energizing the ego, which is insatiable. The pathways to higher programming were, thus, kept restricted and tainted to a great extent.

We know all that; it is nothing new, you say.

Yes indeed, we answer, but very few have managed to break free of the old locks and reprogram their codes. Like DNA therapy, those new codes inserted into the flow of consciousness ripple into the body of light that you are part of, informing it that there is a new path opening for you to regain your link to your light, self-love, and God-self. It is the most challenging aspect of your journey to link to your power, ascend in vibration, and pave the way for others to follow. Many hidden blocks have been inserted in your collective script. You must now find a way to clear them, one by one, through love and self-honoring, moving away from limited programming such as guilt, shame, fear, and attachment. All has been regulated in numerous ways to keep you anchored in a script that is limiting you. If you examine your religions, regulating sexual energy tops the list of restrictions and programming worldwide. As programming was introduced to divert and repackage your use of sexual energy to move higher, often the energy was misused, abused or perverted, only to be downgraded, for use in the lower frequency range. In the lower range you are not a threat to the hub keepers. Your attachment to lower vibrations further limits your access to your light and power.

How do we go about freeing ourselves, you ask?

You give intent and begin renewing your commitment to reach as high as you can using only the pathways of love and light. Treacherous this journey can be, as it has been corrupted through the ages. Those who choose to explore the unlimited dimension of linking to source and reprogramming the body with new, and clear, DNA codes are at the forefront of paving a new path to light.

Sacred it is. The secrets revealed appear to those initiates who reach certain thresholds.

Each phase of this journey awakens a new remembering. Each phase offers challenges of releasing and replacing chains with feathers. There are no manuals or books to tell the whole story. Most have been destroyed and the few which hold the sacred knowledge must be interpreted to suit your individual path. With all love, we whisper in your ears the melody of love, telling you over and over again that, as you intend to move higher, new vistas will open which many may access only in dreams. As you change your old blueprint, the knowledge is transferred to Gaia to be released to all who seek. Like the human body, Earth must move from the lower chakras to the higher chakras.

Programming your own frequency, through tonal resonance, awakens portals deep in the belly of Gaia to release higher programming. You and Gaia are partners, for better or for worse. Sacred is your journey; loved you are. We wish you to walk the highest path available to a human with wings: making peace with your body, radiating light so others can begin to see, linking to your power, once again becoming the light keepers, and so be it.

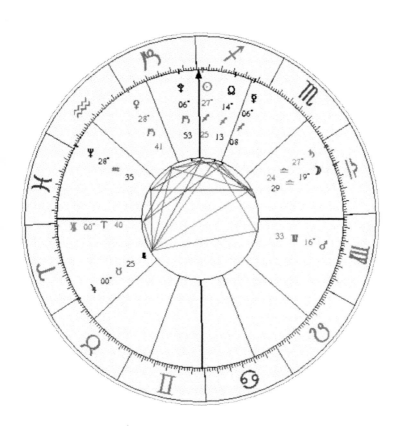

12/19/11

Dearest N.

Thank you

At least we opened the door for her.

She has a desire to grow but very lost in thoughts
and calculations.
her body is in constant misalignment.   all is a choice,
all is sacred

much love and light

dror

The Void

*Y*OU ARE DEARLY LOVED.

Like a leaf twirling in the wind you are being carried by the movement of energy all around you. Desperately you tighten your grip with all your power, trying to remain connected to the tree branch held glued by the thin stem. As the wind velocity increases you realize the futility of remaining attached and you let go of your grasp. While attached to the tree the leaf transforms light into energy through photosynthesis, absorbing carbon dioxide and releasing oxygen. As the leaf falls to the ground it serves Gaia by enriching the soil, breaking down into the different elements that can be used by the tree to grow and thrive. The leaf serves Gaia whether attached or detached from its tree without waste—reflect the sacredness of nature's cycles fulfilling their different missions in reaction to the movement around. Nature is your teacher. You are part of this Earth, no different from the tree and its leaves. Reacting to the wind is your natural programming—protecting, fearing, holding, hiding, and becoming heavier, when all that is asked of you is to offer gratitude, remain present, and let go knowing that all is well. This is a sacred process that all of you must experience within the divine blueprint you envisioned in the design room. Following your heart, knowing that you are loved, and experiencing the web of cords that connects all of you with invisible strings—these concepts are not simply pretty words. These concepts represent the path for all of you regardless of whether you are awakened or fast asleep. That is why we tell you that there is never a judgment on your path as an angel disguised as human. Like a leaf you serve the growth of consciousness. Whether you are part of the tree—attached or on the ground, detached—you are never too far. All has its appropriateness and is harmonious with your vibration, melody, colors, and lights.

Metaphorically, it is the fall season on Earth. The season has changed in the ever cyclical movement of the human journey towards a higher vibratory rate. More of you than ever before in human history on Earth are now on the path to discover your divinity, awaken to your mastery, and become a shining light. Now it is your turn, as the day becomes shorter and the wind blows from the north detaching many stems from their trees.

Consciousness, like your seasons, offers you energetic waves on which to ride. Following the fall is winter—a time to go deep within and explore the invisible strings that connect you to all that you "see" around you. Following the winter comes the spring where all that was hibernating must awaken and continue the cycle of growth. These seasons represent your movement within your inner seasons of awakening as a collective consciousness. Fall's winds have knocked down many leaves, and you are now moving into a period of hibernation so you may have an opportunity to go deeper within. It is an opportunity for many to take stock of their lives—re-evaluating priorities, reconnecting with long-lost loves, detaching from those relationships which no longer support you, aligning with your truth and light. We always wish to hold your hand and tell you that all is perfect. Everything and anything that you experience is a movie designed for you, by you, to give you a story line to move higher. You are the creator, and many of you are now creating magnificent story lines that will be played out for generations to come. Many of you are now invoking your invisible wings, riding on pockets of hot air which carry you higher and higher into realms that could only be imagined in dreams a few years ago. Your thoughts manifest faster than ever before, and your emotional frequency ripples more potently than ever—shifting, prodding, and eliminating, all the while affecting your physical landscape. Your human relationships are the physical strings that glue all of you together. You are one consciousness, fragmented into billions of light particles. Realizing your power can turn your planet into a light source via alchemy, birthing the New Sun and illuminating the universe.

What is being asked of us, you ask?

You are asked to open your wings and let yourself be carried by the winds. Do not aim to fight the winds, but offer your gratitude for the powers of nature, using them for your own growth. Direct the movement around you to flow through your spine, prying open your resistance, clearing blocks, opening rusted gates that you inherited through many cycles on Earth, so the light from above may flow through you, embraced by Gaia without resistance, blocks, or distortions. Connect to your heart, beginning to breathe in and out from your heart, so it will become your new lungs. Each breath should be from the heart, inhaling gratitude and exhaling love.

Offer gratitude for each heartbeat as you pulsate and breathe; using the frequency of gratitude, you act like a lightning rod attracting the immense electromagnetic power from above, channeling it into Earth. Many of you are now so burdened by your current reading of reality. We ask you to trust that this is just a temporary episode in your movie. When you set up your intention to move higher using love, you create a ripple that rearranges the atoms and molecules around you shifting your landscape, visible or invisible, as a result. The hardship many of you perceive is you moving from the old paradigm into the new. Your dance must include letting go of weight, so you can levitate higher and higher. The loosening of the anchors that hold you in cells, jailed in self-created concepts, must be melted by your inner light. All may seem to be lost at times when all you have known washes away, yet this frees you, catapulting you into higher vibration. When you attach to heaviness giving intent to become light, do not be surprised when that heaviness can no longer remain attached. Bless all heaviness and darkness that is being released and commit to not replacing it with a different heaviness. We see you work so hard on moving higher, rearranging all, shifting your inner terrain, but then, when light does comes in and the heaviness clears, some feel so empty that soon they are compelled to find some different heaviness to replace the void, opened by the clearing. With a smile, we say there is never a judgment and we are congratulating you for walking the walk in the first place. With love, we must ask you: why are you in such a hurry to replace heavy with heavy and dark with dark? How about just letting luminosity replace darkness and weightlessness take the place of heaviness?

When you have been programmed to experience life in one way and you get a glimpse of reality in a higher vibration, to many it feels frightening or scary. We ask you, at that moment, to take your time. The unknown is your treasure. Going back to what you know will only move you in circles, but your direction is to move higher. Let the old version break apart. Do not rush to replace it with a newer version. Understand that your story is much greater than you can ever imagine. As the old falls apart, consider that the script may no longer support your new paradigm and it may be time to consider rewriting a new script—one that was never written before. Understand that you are here to break old molds, rebel, and revolutionize the old energy programming. In your past, those who broke the mold were paving the road for the rest to follow. It begins with you realizing that experiencing life is your goal. The "small deaths" that you encounter while walking in life are but opportunities to clear your light so you may walk in the present, fearless, joyful, and in balance with your mission, your purpose. The more fearless you become, the more truthful you become, aligning yourself with your highest path. We ask you to embrace the voids that are created by cleared heaviness and, instead of rushing to fill those voids with new matter, let them remain empty. Begin to let light shine into these holes so the only weight being added is that light, which has no mass. You are paving the way for a new blueprint to be created through your own holographic projection. When you invoke your wings, many say to us, "That cannot be, we cannot fly; we were meant to walk or crawl, but surely not fly. Birds were meant to fly. We have no wings." With a smile, we say to you: wrong answer, you were meant to ascend and fly. You may not use the same aerodynamic laws as birds but you were meant to soar above what you consider your physical reality, joining the expanded family of light that is all around you. As you walk the walk, feel your body; link to your cells; allow each cell to sing within you harmoniously, using love. Draw light into your being, reflecting it to all. Do not explain, preach, convince, or even try to understand. All these acts are the lower self's wishes to be acknowledged for the void created by releasing the heaviness, asking you to fill it back up with a different heaviness. Invoke your inner smile and resist the temptation to take the path you already know. Walk a new path—one that has no defined rules or agendas, and see where you end up. The old is no longer supported by the vibratory rate of your planet or by the intent of your collective. The magnificent masterpiece that you are painting is now being created. As the creator, close your eyes and create those shapes that you have felt in your heart, not those which you remember or have seen before. You are an artist, and the vision that you are now creating is multidimensional. It includes melodic tones which are, from within, illuminated. Set yourself free, invoking your wings, asking them to carry you to that place in your heart that you all know exists—a place where Spirit and human are forever linked. Fear from loss is a gateway you all must pass through as you ascend. Your aim is to dance to the beat of ecstasy, allowing your cells to learn the new orgasmic frequency now available to you, riding on those waves as you walk and interact. Your brothers and sisters who happen to be touched by you will know that something else is happening. This is the new tune. We ask you to play it; be fearless; let the wind be your guide; let the unknown replace the known; let love fill voids of darkness; let massless photons replace the heavy debris of matter. Spread your wings, knowing deep inside of you that you were meant to glide on a higher frequency. It means trusting that you have always been and will always be, that the choices you make on this sacred journey are the reason you are here. Each choice is heard above like the flap of wings. We are in love with you and dance with joy to your melody when you take a step higher. You are so dearly loved, and so be it.

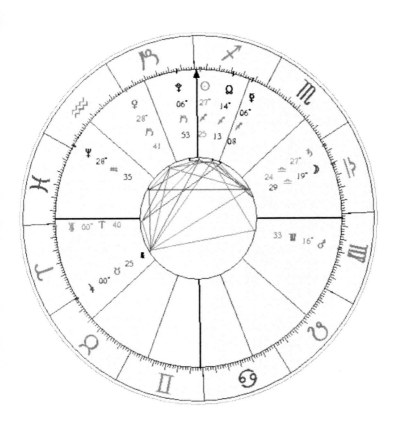

12-25-11

Dearest Light.

Perfect time to celebrate the light in my life. I am in Hot
Springs Arkansas. (birth place of Bill Clinton.) I am learning
a little about this land. I went into one of the healing springs
here. Felt so good and relaxing. I may stay here one more day
just to recharge.

Everything feels so alien and weird in a funny sort of way and
at the same time I feel that I am right where I am supposed
to be. Not sure why but I just let it. I started to assemble the
chapters of the 3rd book today in AK from all places.

My daughter called today to let me know that she is going for
a vacation to New Orleans for a few days with her mom. I was
happy for her and wished her to have a great time.
We are all being set free.

I feel that it was right for me to take a pause from the
divorce and even from Z.

This morning I linked and the dance was luminous. Felt so
grateful to remain open and vibrating.. It felt so beautiful.
I hope you got to rest a little. I know you will be busy
tomorrow.
You are in my heart always.

With Love and Light

Dror..

Spread Your Wings

YOU ARE SO DEARLY LOVED.

Why do we open with this reminder? It is the entry point to your heart. We begin by linking with you, and as we give you our invisible hand, you are given a choice to reciprocate by stretching your hand to us so we can begin.

Begin what, you ask?

Sounding the melody to which you may dance. These words are an exchange of energy between Spirit and matter. They come as a pulse from the universal source of light and love, translated to linear words and carried over to you one word at a time. There are more efficient ways to transfer energy to you and this is through a hug. No need to read any words as the exchange is done in silence and reverence, with permission, always to serve your highest path, and so we begin.

We ask you to seize the moment at any given moment. Flying is your goal and you all know how to take off. It is as simple as visualizing that your hands are wings and your legs are the engine that propels you higher, allowing you to overcome the gravitational force. Three intentions must always present themselves as you stand in front of an elevated surface getting ready to take off. Each intention must be invoked by you. The most exuberant one is the intent to no longer adhere to the rules into which you were born. The second intent is to break any rules, even the ones your science convinced you are unbreakable, simply by asking to move from third gear to fifth gear or from 3-D to 5-D. The third rule is the simplest—giving intent, with pure heart, for your highest agreements to come forth, manifesting in your life. You do not need to know what they are or even if they are signaling the changes for which you are hoping. All you ask is for those contracts to manifest now.

This is it, you ask in disbelief?

No, we reply, this is the beginning. You have come here to learn to fly. Flying is an art, like other forms of sport, where you learn to move seemingly beyond the physical limits of your body.

We do not wish to be fooled, some may say. *We know we were not meant to fly.*

Look at where your knowledge of limitation was anchored 500 years ago, 250 years ago, 150 years ago, and now. Do you think you know everything that there is to know about your abilities? Your evolutionary trajectory is changing as you realize the power you possess. Space travel using large spacecraft may become a thing of the past, and redundant, as you learn how to place your consciousness in vehicles that move vastly faster than the speed of light. There are already some of you who are exploring what we named biofield travel but they do so incognito, as is appropriate. The power of the human to displace parts of its consciousness, directing it to various locations using visualization, had been explored intensely during the Egyptian mystery schools and later on by different mystery schools around your planet. This knowledge was based on what the Atlanteans called the centrifugal force, as it was accessed through spinning or being on the surface of a mechanism that spins fast and, like in your medical science's blood test, allows parts of you to separate from other parts. Much care and control was used in training for such missions. You are made of parts that seemingly represent one whole, but in fact, you are kept as one integral whole by a magnetic field that we call your light and by your intention to manifest as a physical being. Once your awareness lets go of preprogrammed limitations, you are able to separate those seemingly different components of your being by using antigravitational force or centrifugal forces, reversing the polarity of your magnetic field that keeps you intact as a conscious human being. Once the being has been separated from the consciousness, it is a matter of will to be able to direct that consciousness to wherever you wish and later on to safely land it back, integrating it with the physical body, being magnetized back to become whole again. The ancients built temples that were used as portal fields of energy from which one can travel. They left clues in many places, but the ingredients that made it work were lost.

Why were they lost, you ask?

They were hidden from sight initially and later were destroyed by those who were threatened by the power humans were able to access. There was a time when these hidden secrets were used to create destruction and bring about much darkness. This happened before your recorded history and therefore made itself into the realm of myth or legends. A human angel has infinitely more power than you were led to believe. Much of your current programming was designed to funnel that power you possess away from you. Your attention is most prized. You are, at present, bombarded daily by elements which compete by drawing your attention away from your inside towards the outside, rendering you weak and malleable. Your access to resources that regenerate your body, rather than degenerate it, are on the defensive. Despite all these elements which are there to block, many of you are slowly, step by step, disconnecting from the sources of depletions, patching up the leaks in your auric fields, redirecting your energetic channels of power back to you rather than giving it away. This is a cause for celebration, and we congratulate many of you for selecting higher frequencies, despite the abundance of lower-frequency choices available to you. The geometry of your vehicle is constructed through visualization—by focusing your attention on forming a link between your heart and the field around your body. As the energy bounces back and forth from your heart to your field, something that defies your current understanding of matter begins to happen. The molecules that construct your physical form begin to expand, making your constitution less dense. The less dense you are, the higher the vibration you achieve. As the body becomes activated, moving into the higher frequency, it invokes the field around the body forming an egg-like shape. This shape expands the more you focus on your heart, creating a harmonious resonance. It may feel somewhat disconcerting, as the sensation may be interpreted by your body as fainting or dizziness. The cellular density mutates from the biofield of a human to the biofield of an angel, creating a bridge that may feel as if you can become unconscious. The body must get used to that sensation over time by practicing moving through the gateway of fear of losing oneself in the egg-shaped energy field.

By practicing, the undulating movement of energy from your heart expands in all directions, stroking the walls of the egg shape around you and feeding back to the heart, opening a portal to another dimension. The body must let go of its desire to remain in control as the body becomes more porous. As the field around you grows, you may begin to become aware of a high-pitched sound coming seemingly from inside of you and the sound of thunder and waves flooding your inner ears. Beautiful your body is and it was meant to perform miracles; flying is one of them. Continue the undulation and draw a line linking your heart with the site you wish to visit. Allow this site to appear clearly in your mind. Practice initially on sites that you are very familiar with and are not far. Ask your consciousness to perceive what you see, remain aware, so that you may remember details.

The traveling is contained within the egg shape. The shape transposes your awareness to anywhere in the universe directed by your will. The geometric shape of the egg protects your awareness from becoming disoriented as it maintains a cord linked to your physical body, and at will, can return to it.

This is confusing; please give us step by step instructions. When do we invoke the wings, you ask?

As you begin the process, give intent to fly, invoke the wings, and visualize yourself flying, using your legs and lower torso as your source of power and wings to navigate. Follow up by invoking the three intentions. Once completed, raise your sexual energy but do not climax. Direct your energy from your engine (second chakra) to the heart. Follow up by visualizing the egg shape around you, undulating from your heart back and forth to the egg shape at an exceedingly faster pace. Once you hear the high-pitched sound inside of you and thunderous sounds in your inner ears, know that you are ready to experiment with flying.

It is time for you to expand your idea of who you are. Many of your galactic neighbors are waiting for you to visit them. Indeed it happens occasionally that a human travels unintentionally, but rarely have human angels ventured to the galactic family territory, and it's time.

Now what, you may ask?

We hug you with our wings, reminding you that no one ever judges you on how far you reach. You are your own judge. We let you know that you have options.

Some of your options are magnificent in scope and are available to you, if you so wish.

What is happening now on Earth? We wish to have an update, you request.

Earth is becoming lighter. Many species are already moving into higher frequencies and disappearing in large numbers. They are still on this planet but can no longer be perceived by you with your eyes. Immense seismic pressure is building up due to the shift in magnetic polarity. Large movement is being observed in your perception of reality. Your eyes are opening up to "see" the larger picture. Many ask for this picture to be aligned with your heart, and when it is not the case you begin to act. These actions come in waves and are assisted by delivery of high-powered frequencies from what you may call the universe or your galactic neighbors. You have much help while you are shifting from one frequency to the next. The darker aspects of your emerging consciousness are being pushed "against the wall" metaphorically and the battle is raging. Light is merciless and dark is just lack of light. Light shows each one of you a full 3-D picture of who you are, your shortcomings, your inner darker aspects, your misalignments, and the pressure is awesome in scope. Your body is craving to align with the new frequencies being introduced and permeating your dimension. Those of you who do not align will leave the planet in large numbers just to be back soon for yet another go. It is a time for celebration; a time to slow down, to take each moment, breath, and heartbeat and use it to spread love frequencies. Thoughts that are disorderly, disharmonious, or chaotic amplify, colliding first and foremost against the self, rippling to your surroundings, spreading misalignment, pain, energetic blockages, as well as disease faster than ever before. Balanced harmonious feelings and thoughts, aligned with the heart, impact the planet, creating surges, or waves, of light which assist many in choosing higher frequencies. Be aware of your thoughts, feelings, and actions at any given moment. As you clear your flow through your own process, redirect the challenging, dense, disharmonious waves to your heart, projecting them, from there, down into Gaia, transforming heaviness to light and love.

The whole is contained within the one and the one contains the whole. We wish you to know that your journey is about linking you with you through the cords of love. You are at a crossroads and it is time to play your part. The timing of your awakening is set to now, and we ask you to open your eyes, invoke your inner smile, and know that you are ready for it. You are love and we are love. As family, we always are with you. It's time to spread your wings and fly, and so be it.

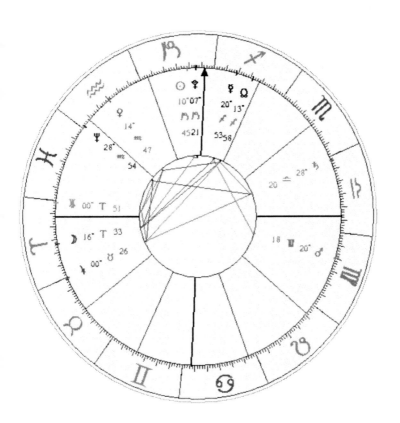

12/31/12-into 1/1/12

Dearest Light.
Wishing you an amazing loving and flowing transition into
2012. What a gift to be alive.
Your New Year blessing moved me deeply. So grateful I am for
your light..

Not sure if you will get this email as I am high up on the
mountain of Cathedral Rock. Found a remote powerful
feminine vortex spot and I am just melting away feeling the
rock.

The galactic family just stopped by. I saw a green craft
materialized right in front of me and I am quite high up on the
mountain and it flew slowly in a straight line and then just
disappeared into thin air. It had a green halo and I am sure
others saw it as it was so clear and bright. I had a feeling that
I needed to be here to connect with them somehow. The night
is still young. My heart is still racing but I am ready for what
ever comes.

With Love and Light

Dror

Sent via BlackBerry from T-Mobile

The Triangle of Forgiveness

HAPPY NEW YEAR. You have made it, thus far. This is just the beginning of a wave that will sweep all of you, shifting your landscape and carrying you to a higher place. We wish to remind you, yet again, that indeed you are dearly loved. You must hear it over and over again for your system to clear "heavy debris" to become lighter.

We will speak today of what has held many of you from moving higher in your past: realigning with your heart and linking with your "I AM." It is a day of celebration, saying goodbye to a year where many experienced life-changing shifts. We are ecstatic to note that more than a few of you are still smiling. At times looking back is just like looking forward. What happened in your life is a reflection of what is to be, as the spiral of time accelerates. The challenges you have left behind will show up to be cleared once again, dressed up in a different costume on a higher plane. Ascension is a spiral. Your movement is circular and you meet layers of yourself represented usually as challenges— each time from a higher awareness vantage point. Each "appointment," as we call these challenges, is an opportunity to ascend higher.

Consider each day a gift from you to the collective consciousness of which you are a part. Each illuminated action and choice is like a musical note amplified, which enhances the symphony of a shifting planet. When you conduct your own harmonious melody you are aligning with other harmonies so that, together, a symphony is created which opens portals for others to walk through, to use for transformation, enabling more and more of you to open your hearts, aligning your consciousness with higher frequencies. Your combined geometry is looking more orderly and luminescent than ever before. Like a pyramid, the wider the base, the higher the apex, and you are aiming the collective structure higher than ever before.

When we look back at this past year, we see that many have insisted on trying to float with wet suitcases, holding on to your soaking wet belongings, and we ask you: why? Is it that you feel that you are no longer who you are without your precious things, places, or people in your life, even when "they" no longer serve you? Maybe you feel that your attachment to heaviness is more important than your growth. To some it appears as a daunting task to clear emotional, physical, and spiritual debris accumulated, to an extent that life becomes almost unbearable when you face the shedding and letting go of all that is superfluous in your life. The spiral movement of ascension does not support, energetically, the "extra weight" around you, and it is why, to those on the path of moving higher, this time seems to be so challenging. The aspects of your life which do not cater to your higher path must be discarded, with love, and be cleared from you so you can fly. The rules indeed are changing, and you have a new limit on the amount of baggage you are allowed to carry. As the weight of the carry-on luggage limit on your airplanes is being sliced, the same holds true on your spiritual journey. Your angelic wings are not meant to carry the old weight limit. You are moving into a new energy where all that is heavy and no longer serves you must be discarded, donated, left behind, or transformed. From our perch, the geometry of forgiving is your challenge as it contributes to the overall weight and many are struggling with moving forward as a result.

Forgiving is not like forgetting. You are never asked to pretend that what has happened in your life did not really happen. The geometric shape of the forgiveness lesson is a triangle. A triangle has three angles. The "I" represents one angle at the base; everything that is outside the "I," the other angle at the base. The apex represents the merging of the "I" with what you consider as separated from the "I" to one which is called the great "I AM."

The three angles, metaphorically, are levels of awareness. Developmentally, you move from the "I" level to the "everything outside the I" level and your aim, as a collective, is to ascend to a level where the two merge into the "I AM." When you have reached awareness where the "I" no longer is separated from everything outside the "I" you have ascended to the next spiritual level of unity consciousness. We see some who have been on the spiritual journey for many cycles. You have known about the alchemy of the triangle moving from separation to unity. As some near the zenith of the climb, the weight accumulated is so great that the triangle flips on its pinnacle. The pain, the hurt, the lack of forgiveness accumulated can no longer support your ascension and the process reverses.

There is never a judgment as to the distance you walk as an angel disguised as human. We know the pitfalls and we are aware of the traps. We are with you every day in the trenches, and we are here to remind you why you came this time around. You came here to live your truth and chisel away the layers of illusions that are separating you from you. You have come to regain your power and link to your luminous self. You came to free yourself from the trappings of the "I" rippling to all those who are touched by you the awareness of the "I AM." Forgiveness is at the core of moving higher. The challenges from your close circle are mostly karmic, which means that you are now having an opportunity to clear the slate clean with each of your close relationships, ascending above the "who did what to whom." Each time you miss an opportunity the weight increases. With a smile, we remind you once again that the rules have changed and you can no longer carry on you these weights from past cycles. It is precisely why the challenges seem to increase. You have loaded yourself with a busy appointment schedule so you can meet the weight limits before your scheduled takeoff. The time is now and your suitcases are way over the weight limit. For what are you waiting? Each time a challenge presents itself and manifests in your life wearing a name badge from your family, partner, friend, or associate, we ask you to take your time before responding. The mechanics of your response can determine the final weight you add on or discard on this journey. We wish you to sit down, light a candle, and remind yourself that you are light. Visualize yourself at one side of the triangle and the angel who poses the challenge to you at the other side. Thank them for their service and honor them for giving you yet another opportunity to become lighter. Hold in veneration this contract and give intent to walk the highest path. Seek to be guided, for the slate to be cleared, so as to serve all who are involved equally for the highest benefit, learning, and growth, so all can move forward. Always set the intent and ask to be shown the way. Your intent serves as your safety net, metaphorically, to not act in disservice. We promise you that you will know whenever your action is misaligned. You will know because we will remind you and you will feel it in your heart. Approach each action with extreme care, examining your motivations. You are all masters of self-persuasion, convincing yourself that what serves you must therefore serve the other.

You serve yourself and all by clearing, by aligning with integrity as well as with your intent.

We wish to draw you a metaphoric picture of what it means to forgive. Let's "pretend" that you are an angel and you know how to fly. Each day you have to confront one looming limitation we name "perpetual forgetfulness." You have a built-in dysfunction that the mechanics of flying that you learned on day one is being "forgotten" by the time you wake up on the morning of the next day. Each day you have to teach yourself the art of flying. Each day you must begin by reminding yourself that you are an angel and you were meant to fly. Each day you have to conquer fear and trust that you will not be hurt. Similarly, true forgiving requires you to remind yourself who you are and to forgive, each day anew. The magic of Spirit is created by the one who must be forgiven, acting as catalyst for you to remember who you really are. Hurt, pain, hate, and even desire to take revenge surfaces whenever the "I" moves away from the "I AM." You have designed your lesson to be the most challenging around forgiving. It is why you do not remember the one who hurt you from one lifetime to the next—you would be too busy chasing those who crossed your path eons ago! Each lifetime presents an opportunity to relearn the art of moving higher. Being hurt is always a question of awareness. When you "see" yourself from the level of the "I," you will have to cope with many hurts. As you move higher towards the pinnacle of the triangle your awareness expands to include the one who hurt you as being an aspect of you. At the "I AM" level there is no separation between you or the one who hurt you, as you are one and the same energy viewed from different angles. Loving, honoring the self at the "I AM" level extends to loving as well as honoring the one who is part of you. There is no need to forgive at that level as you have merged the plus or minus signs, neutralized both and are now gliding on equilibrium. Moving away from a perceived threat to the "I" requires daily work for most. The work you have accomplished on Monday was long forgotten by Tuesday. It is just the way of it. As long as the two points of the triangle climbing the steep angles are not yet merged, you must deal with the "dysfunction."

Open your wings and look at your journey for a moment through an eagle's eye.

You have designed your cycle to include you hurting others and others hurting you. Without it you will not seek to move above the traps of the "I." Each aspect of your journey is sacred. The bad and good are aspects of your limited view. As you adapt an elevated awareness, the perceived "bad" and "good" become movements enclosed in a circular arena and are interchangeable depending on the direction of your movement.

Why are you telling us all of that, you ask?

You are in an accelerated spiraling energy where each thought, feeling or action reverberates and is amplified to all. Your choices manifest faster than ever. When you choose to truly examine the one who has wronged you, following up by consciously forgiving them, you are illuminating not only your own cells, but changing your melody and geometry to affect all. When you forgive, you also disengage the cords of karma. Everything in your being—your physical body, your emotional being, your psychological constitution—supports forgiveness. Holding on to hurts literally creates a cellular imbalance and dis-ease. You have asked to be here at this time and you knew that you would have an unequal share of the burden to produce light. The older souls must work extra shifts to support the new vibratory frequency toward which you are moving. We are reminding you that forgiveness serves you. You must honor and be grateful for those who give you an opportunity to forgive them. We hear you say, "But . . ." "But he or she does not deserve to be forgiven because . . ." And we say to you indeed, "but" how about you? Do you deserve to move higher and become the master that you are? We are simply here to remind you of what you already know. Loving self means that you must act in accordance to that which serves your highest path. Forgiveness serves your highest path always, regardless of the "buts" of what took place. Your journey is about expansion and about ascending to a higher vibratory rate never seen before on Earth. We remind you, once again, that on this flight there is a strict weight limit on luggage.

What next, you ask?

You are in the most glorious time, and you are alive and breathing. Offer gratitude and know that you are fulfilling a promise that you made before you were born to play your part the best you can. You have the opportunity. You are a light, and your power is to become the master of your life simply by so intending. You are loved and you have asked to be here so you can play your role as best you can. We, then, are simply reminding you to remember who you are, to awaken to what this journey is all about, and so be it.

Acknowledgments

FOR THE PAST THREE years I have encountered many beautiful angels dressed as humans, walking the path of higher vibration, seeking their truth, adding to the light of the planet. I feel immense gratitude to you, the light beings working in the trenches—clearing, transforming your own lives, and touching the lives of others. I feel blessed and in awe of the profound capacity of the human heart to love and support each other during challenging times. Through our hearts we are building a new bridge of light.

My gratitude is overflowing to so many who have supported me, guided me, wiped my tears, and held me when I needed to be held. To all those who were touched by the angelic messages, sharing them with others, thank you. I have met many of you who opened my heart. Your love has changed me forever.

I wish to mention by name some of the special light beings I have encountered over the past few years, yet there are many more that I would like to acknowledge. For all those I have met and have been touched by, I know who you are and I am eternally grateful for your friendship, support, love, and guidance.

I wish to offer my deepest gratitude to the angels. You never cease to amaze me with your love, guidance, and humor, and your dedication to humanity, Earth's ascension, and the healing of all. Thank you for being there always for everyone who is open to you, while asking nothing in return but for us to awaken and live our truth in light and love.

My deepest heartfelt gratitude to Corinne Gervai and her beautiful family: her husband, David, and her son, Gabriel, for adding so much light to this planet, and for your amazing support and your commitment to following your heart and truth.

A huge thank you from the bottom of my heart to Cynthia Shell-Terrell for your unshakeable commitment to proofing the angelic messages despite your busy schedule and for your total selfless giving and for supporting me every time I needed it.

To Marcia Daronch, I am in deep gratitude for your commitment to shining your light, illuminating those around you. Thank you for translating the messages into Portuguese, rippling them to a whole new country, and for helping with the script of *It's Time*. Thank you for living from your heart.

To Rob Shear and Jasmine Jordaan for your perceptive, insightful, and useful help and comments on the script. I am grateful for your guidance and for being wonderful friends.

To Nancy Aleo, Ofer Braver, and Siri Sat Kaur, my dear, dear friends who supported me when I began receiving the angelic messages and encouraged me to trust myself, helping me understand what is going on in my life with so much care, love, and patience.

To Gisela Stromeyer, my heart is filled with gratitude for your guidance, your support and for helping me to break through my own limitations.

To Naama Sudak for being there for me when I needed it most.

To Nicki LeMarbre and Scott Kuenzel for your friendship, offering your guidance and support, always knowing when to call and what to say.

To my parents, who through their unconditional love and encouragement gave me the permission to live my truth, and for continuing to remind me to follow my heart and do exactly what makes me happy, always encouraging me to walk my path and seek joy in whatever I do.

To Zoe, my daughter and most revered teacher and guide. I am grateful that you chose me as your aba (father) and allowed me to grow into my role with so much love and care. I am proud of you for working through this challenging time and emerging stronger, radiant, and true to yourself. I'll always love you.

I wish to offer gratitude to my former partner in life, Devora Mache, the mother of Zoe, for countless beautiful and joyful moments together. For being my teacher, even in our separation, to stay in gratitude and remain with an open heart despite the challenges, the hurts, and the pains we experienced in the past few years.

To Paul Cohen, publisher of Monkfish and Epigraph, for your continued support and guidance. A big, deserving thank you to Lauren Manoy, editor, for your keen eye to track inconsistencies. Grateful for designer Barbara Patterson; I truly feel that I am in good hands.

It's Time *Vol. III*
Message Guide

1. ***"The Golden Cage" Message from 1/16/09 & 1/22/09***
   (Themes: Fame, Self-Healing, Change)

   You are not measured by how high you climb. Your treasure is in the thoughts and feelings that you radiate as you walk. In your culture, goals are being promoted as the end-all, and if you arrived second, you lost. Only the one who arrived first is the declared winner. In our game, at times, the one who arrived last is the declared winner. It is so, because she experienced joy as she defeated all odds just to be in the race and run with the pack. *(page 3)*

2. **"Monsters Under Your Bed" Message from 1/23/09**
   (Themes: Fear, Self-Love, Betrayal, Trust)

   Moving upward requires fearlessness, and fearlessness requires you to practice conquering fear. Fear is part of your humanness and it is built in you. It is biological; it protects you and it helps you to survive. What we ask you, with all love, is to conquer fear by learning to redirect the energy of fear from you to Gaia so it can be transformed rather than freeze you.

   When you were a child and you saw imaginary monsters under your bed, your remedy was to call out, asking your mother to take them away. Gaia is your mother and you are her child. She is connected to you like a mother and supports you like a mother. When you fear and you call out, she will come to you. *(page 15)*

3. **"The Fountain of Youth" Message from 2/4/09 & 2/9/09**
   (Themes: Aging, Dementia)

   [T]hose of you who are going through the experience of forgetfulness or incapacitation are those who are learning to feel rather than control their environment through reason. . . . [T]hose who experience the deterioration of their mental capacity are going through unlearning one lesson while learning another. *(page 31)*

4. "The Dot" Message from 2/13/09
(Theme: Path to Mastery)

[T]he path to higher awareness is very simple. You may use complicated language; you may embed the path in difficult practices, but at the end of the sentence there is always a dot, and the dot is where the whole story is hiding. *(page 48)*

5. "Gadgets Stop Ringing" Message from 2/20/09
(Themes: Isolation, Overuse of Gadgets)

You are now in the energy of reconnecting with yourself, becoming one. Gaia knows who you are and all the energies around you know who you are, the trillions of us know you. We wish you, too, to know yourself. *(page 59)*

6. "Shades of Grey" Message from 2/25/09 & 3/4/12
(Themes: Choice, Taboo, Suicide, Gift of Life)

We respect your free-will universe and you are never forced to choose one road over the other. The power is within you. Know that you always have a choice between dark and light. Often your choice will not present itself solely as dark or light but rather in shades of grey. Even in the spectrum of shades of grey, there is always a lighter shade of grey and a darker shade. Your mission is to become aware, to awaken, so you will always move towards the lighter shade, spiraling, ascending, toward purer and purer light. *(page 68)*

7. "Planetary Healers" Message from 3/25/09
(Themes: Healing of Self, Others, and the Planet)

When you and we hold hands above the one who needs healing, it is your linearity that you need to move aside so your circular portion can be activated. When the energy from the circle interacts with your biology, the melody that is being transmitted is one of harmony, and it creates a pitch or a tone that is harmonious with your cells, bringing them back into balance. *(page 89)*

8. "The Dye of Love" Message from 5/9/09
(Theme: Repeat Dramas, Sacred Sexuality)

When you pour a drop of food-coloring dye into clear water the whole glass of water becomes colored by the drop of dye. You are the dye and the drop is the drop of "love." When you mix your environment with just one drop of a concentrated dye, all who are around you will be colored by your energy. It is the way of it. *(page 108)*

9. "What Am I Doing Here?" Message from 6/7/09
(Themes: Our Mission, Key to Universe, Vibration, Space Travel)

You are a piece of biology with a twist, and the twist is that you carry the seed of God in each one of your cells. The mechanics of your biology hold the key to the universe. It is why we tell you that you contain all you need, and you create what you need when you are in the now.

You contain within you all the universes in all dimensions, and there are more than a few. You, the one reading these lines, are the key to the unfolding of the biggest shift in consciousness your planet has seen since its birth. Are you still feeling powerless? *(page 121)*

10. "Rise of the Goddess" Message from 6/12/09
(Themes: Constant Change, Disintegration, Feminine Power)

It is time to surrender; let go of your walls. Allow all the emotions that you held at bay to be expressed within you and through you so they can be released. Learn to feel again. Learn to trust that you are loved and protected. You are moving into harmony, aligning with the powerful energy of the Goddess, dependent on your willingness to let go of the poles that hold you anchored in shame, guilt, and separation.

You must activate your Shakti, or your female sexual power, suppressed and repressed for thousands of years. The pendulum is swinging back to balance and with it, all of you must shift. *(page 132)*

11. "The Wave" Message from 7/25/09
(Theme: Relationship Change, Stress, Transitions)

To truly become one with oneself, you must let all that does not belong to you be discarded. You hold the belief that the heavy, buried feelings are your baggage. Many still hold on to their heaviness and we must impart to you that you cannot easily float with the coming of the high water surge if you hold on to wet suitcases. You may go under with your "precious" belongings. With all love, we ask you to hold on to the only precious thing that you are responsible for on this journey, you and your biological vehicle. *(page 147)*

12. "I Want" Message from 10/6/09
(Theme: Money, Economy, Consumption, Wanting, Desires)

No material wealth—no matter how extensive—will ever be enough. It is from within that your feeling of lack has to be fulfilled. Next time you sit to meditate and speak to spirit, ask not for more money but feel the feeling that you yearn to experience. Imagine feeling love; imagine feeling peace; imagine experiencing balance; imagine experiencing abundance; then let go and trust that you are the creator manifesting all that which you wish for. Allow your reality to rearrange itself according to your imagined feelings and let go. *(page 159)*

13. "The Blender" Message from 10/28/09
(Theme: Intense Changes, Shifts, Adjustments, 2012)

Imagine a world where everyone knew that they were eternal and masters of their reality. Everybody knew that all they needed to "do" is be in the now and in a place of joy. They knew that their reality must rearrange itself according to their belief and intent. Do you know what happens when enough of you understand these simple mechanics of your dimension? You have brought heaven upon you. Wouldn't you like to be the bringer of heaven on Earth? *(page 173)*

14. **"Show Me the Money" Message from 10/30/09** (*Theme: The Secret of Abundance and Money*)

The current system is based on lack and not abundance; therefore, as long as you are part of the system, it is part of the limitation of this game. We ask you at this time to move out of the game, imagining that which you wish to feel. Imagine abundance, that you have stepped off the treadmill and away from the game of scarcity. Imagine how the abundance feels: you are loved, taken care of, there is nothing you need more than what you already have. By using your power and light, you create your reality. The feeling of abundance will then present itself in your life as it must. *(page 183)*

15. **"It's Time" Message from 12/5/09**
(*Themes: Meeting Self, New Reality, Healing Modalities*)

Once you enter the healing space, placing your hand above your client, we ask you to now move aside, delete all you know, and wait. Visualize your patient in his/her perfect form as if there were no ailment. See them as healed and do not ask for specifics as if healing has already happened. Trust that once you clear yourself from expectation, stop looking for this or that sign of imbalance, trying to remember what to do, that the love frequency from the circle will operate through you. It is our promise, then, that you will experience miracles. *(page 196)*

16. **"Alchemy" Message from 12/22/09**
(*Themes: 2012, Wake Up, Become Free, Enslavement, Alchemy*)

You have chosen to come here for the sole purpose of living your truth awakened. . . . The process of alchemy happens when you walk in the knowledge of who you are. You create a vortex of energy around you which activates others. As you move around in life activating others, you create ripples of higher frequency which we also named "light." Others can use the higher frequency to ride on and bring about inner transformation from one state of awareness to another. This is alchemy. From heavy, you become light; from lead, become gold. From human you uncover your angelic essence. . . . This is what we speak of when we say you are all alchemists. This is your purpose. *(page 210)*

17. "Learning to Fly" Message from 12/29/09
(Themes: Peace on Earth, Armageddon, Activation of DNA)

Peace on Earth is the potential for this time. . . . Peace is not a practical political solution to your social and cultural conflicts, but a state of consciousness. You are getting closer to a vibration where the gap separating you from yourself is quickly closing like your hole in the ozone layer. You are approaching a state of vibration that embraces your oneness on a mass scale, holding a united vibration which can open up your dimension to the celebration that is all around you. . . . The party is scheduled soon and your light is needed for this party to happen on time. Our question to you is, why would you want to miss this party? *(page 221)*

18. "Sexual Energy Dance" Message from 1/11/10 *(Themes: Sexuality, Energy, Fear, Guilt, Shame)*

When you begin to use sexual energy, connect with an open heart, and become a vessel for pure love energy, you create a divine dance which gives birth not to another human, but to a new Earth. The sheer power of this dance is enormous, as it uses your most potent source of power with the highest frequency available to you. Procreation is the physical manifestation of this dance, but when you climb beyond the physical, you give birth not to babies but to light. You impregnate Gaia with sacred energy which further increases her vibration and yours. *(page 232)*

19. "Move, Shake, Flood, Fire" Message from 2/2/10 *(Themes: Purpose of Global Events, Unity Consciousness)*

As soon as you begin to separate one thing from another you

find yourself moving away from oneness. With all love, we wish to impart to you that when large movements take place in your physical dimension like floods, hurricanes, or earthquakes, your planet becomes, for a short moment, united in the energy of sympathy and compassion. Every moment of such magnitude creates a step for humanity to climb upward. After each event that has shaken your physical landscape, the wave of united emotions flooding your Earth is like a tsunami which pushes the larger consciousness, of which you are a part, towards the realization that you are all connected, all part of the One. *(page 244)*

20. "Sleepless Nights" Message from 2/8/10
(Themes: Not Able to Sleep, Upgrades, Moving Higher: Meaning of Higher Vibration)

It is easier for us to communicate with you when you are asleep. To many of you, our frequency keeps your nights less restful. When we contact you in your sleep, you are hovering in the deep sleep state. Once we begin to communicate with you, you remain in this deep sleep state, but you may feel as if you are completely awake. It is not a dream per se that you are experiencing, but an activation of the larger you, expanding, as your mind is off guard. To many, our meetings feel like a hangover after an all-night party. Once the intoxication ends, you lie exhausted in bed but unable to sleep. *(page 255)*

21. "And So Be It" Message from 3/12/10
(Themes: Akash Clearing, God, Work Ahead)

The purpose is to find yourself, your own divinity, and truly discover who you are. You come here to this remote planet in a hidden, scarcely populated area of your galaxy, believing that you are separated from everything, and through your inner process you must discover your oneness with all that is. Your oneness must be found within you. Once you discover who you are and begin to live your mission, the road opens up and you create ripples of oneness which circulate. Like a magnet, you attract all the pieces of your life together into one unified field. That unified field is made out of the substance of love. Once you radiate love, you are shining and sparkling like a star in the night sky. *(page 264)*

22. "Slowing Down" Message from 4/11/10 *(Themes: Destiny, Karma, Clearing, Highest Potential, Slowing Down)*

Many of your obstacles and blocks are created within you while you are busy running on your treadmill, making things happen. Often, as you think you are moving forward, you encounter in-surmountable blocks that you yourself created while being busy, and then you blame karma or whoever volunteered to play the blocking role for you as the culprit. With all love, we wish you to understand that there is no one out there who is more powerful than you regarding your own journey. You are the God that you pray for at night. You are the angels, and you are divinity. We are part of you, and when you slow down enough to feel all the forces that are part of your entourage, there is nothing that can ever block your path, your potential, or your destiny. *(page 275)*

23. "Self-Love" Message from 4/18/10
(Theme: Self-love, Light, Clearing Blocks)

For you to ascend to the next level you must vibrate with love. First to self and, as you walk with self-love, your resonance begins to spread to others. We never said that vibrating with love is like a walk in the park. You have walked, you have learned all the skills needed to vibrate with love, but accessing them, clearing away those parts which block love from flowing freely through you, is your mission. It is, indeed, the most sacred mission at this time. *(page 285)*

24. "Leaking Roof" Message from 4/24/10
(Themes: Relationship, Change, Growing, Self-Love, Align with Your Truth)

When you give intent, with a pure heart, to find the love inside of you, your reality will begin to shift and change to reflect your new direction. If you are under a sealed roof, holes will form so as to allow moisture and sunlight to penetrate. When holes are formed we see many of you who rush very quickly to cover the leaking roof overhead, again blocking the rain and the sun. Your outer circumstances must change for you to move from a place of dry darkness to a place of moisture and luminosity. For those conditions to manifest, at times you must allow the roof to leak and not rush to repair it. *(page 295)*

25. "Being Still" Message from 5/9/10
(Theme: Mirror, True Power)

Your angels do not wait too long, as time is short on this path. Soon you will begin to receive directions about where to go and what to do. These directions came from you through your intent. You then must follow the intention with action while staying still and balanced inside. As you do, you begin to see the love connection that weaves all the different circumstances creating your life. You will then begin to see yourself as a masterpiece in which every part of that masterpiece serves a purpose. You no longer judge good or bad, but you become peaceful with what was and become grateful for what is. Experiencing your life from a place filled with peace and gratitude aligns you with your highest path. These directions are the simplest, most profound set of instructions to move you into the spiral of ascension. *(page 305)*

26. "Follow the Beat" Message from 5/16/10 *(Theme:*
Unlearning, Trusting, Change in Perception)

Ascension rarely comes from studying mantras or sacred texts. Your vibration is linked to your biological vehicle and cannot be experienced only in your mind. The next step in your evolution must be felt within and experienced. You can talk all day long about a beautiful piece of music or the divine taste of dark chocolate, but the reading and hearing about it can never take you to the actual experience of listening to the music or tasting the chocolate. . . . Many of you speak of love. When you actually experience love through your inner and outer senses, realizing that it is everywhere, it is then that your reality shifts. *(page 315)*

27. "Left Ankle" Message from 6/19/10
(Themes: Unity Consciousness, Political & Social Changes, Physical Ailments & Imbalances)

Every single imbalance carries, as you know, a corresponding soul imbalance. Now, more than ever before, every tone you play that is off key may be shown to you clearly and almost instantaneously within your physical system. There is less and less of a delay between your choices along the path, resulting in the manifestation of those choices on your physical vehicle. With much love, we must impart that the opposite is also true. When you move into your role, understanding the mission and aligning yourself, your body will begin to sing a harmonious tune as if it happened overnight. *(page 323)*

28. "The Great Ballroom" Message from 6/20/10 *(Themes: Acceleration, Venus, Technique to Clear Conflicts)*

You are moving soon through the first booster acceleration which will carry many of you higher than you have been. The booster will be delivered by Venus and the transmission of the feminine download is now approaching. Delivery of energy from the cosmos around you takes place all the time, but there are markers which create a vortex of fast-moving evolutionary steps in your collective human consciousness, and one such event is forthcoming. Prepare to dance. There is great change taking place in some of your celestial neighbors in order to facilitate the frequency upgrade which Earth requires to move into the next phase. *(page 334)*

29. "The Rocket Booster" Message from 6/21/10
(Themes: Self-healing, DNA, Neurons, Miracles, Magic)

Let us sit all around you and show you where you are. You are in the middle of a huge arena. All around you are millions and millions of lights swarming in one large circle around you, looking at you. You look above, you see lights; you look below and you see lights. All around you is light and all this light is at your disposal just waiting for you to send it to where it is needed. What are you waiting for, is our question to you? Send it into your body and ask the ailment to be balanced. *(page 343)*

30. "An Initiation" Message from 6/24/10
(Themes: Earth Initiation, Mission, Bliss, Choice, Heart)

There is so much misunderstanding within your spiritual institutions about the concept of bliss. From our perspective, bliss is a state of awareness that is not stationary, but continuously moving away then shifting back to the core magnet in your heart. When you hold your balance inside of you with the vibration of love, no matter what happens around you, your heart becomes a gravitational core attracting the pendulum back to your center. With it, then, comes the sense of bliss.

Bliss is not a destiny one reaches and stays there. Bliss is work. Bliss means shifting back to balance and understanding the appropriateness of all that takes place in the illusion you call your reality. When you know within your true "core knowledge" that the suffering of humanity is a choice, destruction of the planet is a choice, starvation and lack are choices, premature death is a choice, evil is a choice, that being on the side of darkness is a choice, you also know that you can change all that you observe in your external reality. *(page 353)*

31. "Spirit and Chocolate" Message from 7/6/10
(Themes: Religion, De-powering, Manipulations, Knowledge)

When you think you understand the gist of it all, then and precisely at that moment, you experience the rug being pulled out from under you, with all that you believed your reality to be, presented in an upside-down, sideways angle.

Why is it so, some may ask?

The journey of revealing your truth must be understood in a way that is outside the linear scope of your reality. There is really no way to write about it, talk about it, explain it, or even describe it. This reality that comes from the dimension of being one with Spirit is about being. *(page 364)*

32. "Activation" Message from 8/5/10
(Themes: Karma, Clearing, Activation)

Your awakening is the single most powerful step you can take towards reclaiming your power to become a multidimensional galactic human. We have come to you because you called upon us to assist in reigniting your flame so that light will be your guiding force and not darkness. We are your activators and we only do so with your permission. No words need to be spoken and no physical actions need to be taken. Activation takes place through the energy of love. When the music sounds we dance with your light, beginning a process that is sacred. When you give us your hand, joining our dance, symbolically you are ready and the activation proceeds. *(page 375)*

33. "Butterfly Across the Window" Message from 8/26/10
(Themes: Being Sick, Pain, Healing, Slowing Down, Health Challenges)

Pain quiets your outer world and leaves you with only enough energy to see beauty, appreciating the little things you didn't notice before. We see many on treadmills searching for fame, fortune, and love until sickness strikes. Then, all their desires are reduced to just one: to be healthy again. We hear many of you whisper in our ears, "I want to be healthy again so I can enjoy the little things. I wish I could just lie on the grass and enjoy the sun. I wish I could run with my dog in the park again." Your wish list shrinks quickly. This new list is now made of things many of you did not have time to consider because you were too busy running after the "big" things. *(page 388)*

34. "The Finale" Message from 10/1/10
(Themes: Native Culture Reawakening, Planetary Healing)

If we had you memorize anything from what we have been saying to you all this time, it is that you are loved. You are it. There is always one main purpose in all our messages and it is to awaken you so you will remember who you are, feeling the love from spirit. If you have managed to feel it, know that this is the whole story in a condensed form and the rest are just side notes. Real knowing comes from your heart. All other knowing is but interpretations of what you already know, so you can mold it into your linear reality. You exist in a circle but can only see it as one line connected to another line. If you were able to move high enough, you would see that all these connected lines form a large circle— and that circle is you. *(page 402)*

35. "Elixir of Love" Message from 10/16/10
(Themes: Use of Sexual Energy, Shame, Guilt)

Love is all that you see, hear, taste and smell. Love is not the romance that went sour between you and your ex. You call that love, but we call it being human and getting a taste of higher vibration. When you are in love your frequency actually increases and you feel in harmony with all that is. Your heart feels open and your body feels excited. This is how a human gets a taste of love, but for us love is what makes up your universe. *(page 413)*

36. "The Scaffolding" Message from 11/14/10
(Themes: Sacred Texts, Loving Self, Losing Friends, Good & Evil)

All begins with self. Love for self is not egoistic, but the purest love of God. Accepting your own light is the path to accepting all lights; loving yourself is the core of loving all who come in contact with you. Your own personal evolution is the evolution of humanity. Through your eyes everything changes. When you begin to shift your attention to loving yourself, you are becoming the server for humanity because wherever you walk you give permission to others to love themselves. *(page 428)*

37. "I Am Ready" Message from 12/05/10
(Themes: Ailments Associated with Higher Vibrations,
Communication with the Angels, What Will Happen, Use of Sound)

We see many changes both in your physical landscape and your inner terrain. As your electromagnetic grid is shifting continuously, dormant fault lines that were inactive for eons in the belly of Gaia will awaken, weather abnormalities will become the norm, and observable celestial bodies will change course as if for no apparent explainable reason.

What many consider acts of madness will become more and more frequent as pressure builds, on your field, to move higher. The acceleration of speed and intensity in the electromagnetic field around each of you can cause those who are less balanced or use mind-altering chemicals to "snap," swirling with violent, "insane" acts. We see darkness mounting "impressive" campaigns to create fear and disorder, disguised as protection, in an attempt to preserve the grip on your reality. Your reality is at stake here. Each and every one who chooses to hold their candle illuminated makes the difference for the multitudes. *(page 444)*

38. "From Crawling to Flying" Message from 12/24/10
(Themes: Ascension, Purpose for Coming)

The most sacred journey that a human can travel is upward. You called it ascension. Some of your ancient texts speak of those who ascended and hold them dear, as the light torches, guiding humanity's spiritual evolution. Much of the dogma and religious institutions were built upon the written records of those who ascended. With so much love, we must impart to you that ascension has no manual. Those ascended masters did not follow any manuals, as the manuals were created after they moved up. From our perch we must impart to you that none of the so-called ancient scriptures can lead you to ascend even if you choose to follow their every point with a dedication that is admired by all who come in contact with you. *(page 456)*

39. "Heart Reunion" Message from 1/1/11
(Themes: Free Will, Your True Teachers, Hurt, Open Heart)

You came to use love, and many of you are experiencing the lack of love in your relationships. You came here to experience peace, and many of you are in turmoil. You came here to be in a place of vibrant health, although many of you are being challenged with ailments and dis-ease in that aspect of your life. You came here to explore the depth of pleasure, but many of you are experiencing pain. You came here to become an angel in human clothes, exploring the limitlessness and expansiveness of your existence, but many of you are finding constriction or limitation seemingly everywhere you turn. You came here to be a full-fledged angel, and instead many of you are learning the density, intensity, and depth of being a human. *(page 470)*

40. "The Director, Producer, and Actor"
Message from 2/19/11 2/20/12
(Themes: Choosing your Path, Feminine Role, Sexuality, Love of Self)

The movie you are in, playing your role, is now being rewritten and the script created by you as you act. There is no longer a prescribed story line; you are the director, the producer, and the actor. Some of you have not yet realized that you are the driver and you are still waiting for new instructions. *(page 482)*

41. "The Chosen One" Message from 3/7/11
(Themes: Old Energy, New Energy, Clearing)

Clearing and becoming light are prerequisites to moving higher. If you carry heaviness from many cycles, how can you take off? Even in your aviation regulations, there is a limit on the baggage weight you are allowed to carry. In order to clear your pain, anguish, hurts, or sadness, at times, your starting point must bring those experiences and feelings into you. If your life were only smooth sailing, why would you clear anything? You probably would lie on your back sun-tanning all day long. You have chosen to do the work not only for yourself but for Earth as well. Each time you move higher from a challenge we hold a celebration—not only that you have unloaded your own baggage but that you serviced other humans. You have helped shift the lives of angels in human costume you do not even know. . . . The ones who are awakened carry the load for all. *(page 493*

42. "Cosmic Orgasm" Message from 3/21/11
(Themes: Divine Union, Duality into Oneness, Sexuality, Moving through Pain, Clearing)

When a body touches another body the electromagnetic fields around each body are being charged. You may be charged with a negative charge or a positive charge, as both are like the polarity of a magnet and therefore interchangeable. When two bodies merge from a place of love, openness, and acceptance, you open channels to the expanded you. As your field expands, the two fields are growing larger and larger, finally, to create a third field which no longer can be identified as either of the original two. *(page 502)*

43. "The Golden Chalice" Message from 4/24/11
(Themes: Manifesting, Shopping for What You Need, Guard Your Light)

It is time for you to walk the walk of a master fully aware of your power and magnificence. This is why you are here, to awaken to your power and experience it in your body. What many of you consider as powerful in your manufactured reality, through the game of business, politics, or through the energy of money, is not what we consider to be powerful. Power is walking in the knowing of who you are. It is how your thoughts, feelings, and intentions manifest your reality. Power is being fully aware that all energy is guided by love. The dark forces that many believe in and fear are your own creations. There is nothing more powerful than the light of an angel dressed up as a human in this universe. *(page 513)*

44. "The Leaf" Message from 6/13/11
(Theme: Responding in the Midst of Emotional Storm)

When an intensely emotional event takes place in your physical reality, we ask you to become still. Allow all this movement in and around you to create some havoc within you while you remain still. We ask you to not react. This energy that is carried by emotional upheaval holds an immense potential that you can use to move higher. As the emotions flowing inside of you range from fear to rage to sadness to feelings of revenge or hate, allow and allow without moving. Your game has just begun. The kickoff action that prompted the movement is a Big Bang, the same bang that holds the potential for infinite expansion, as long as you do not react. *(page 524)*

45. "The Eye of the Storm" Message from 8/9/11
(Themes: Heaviness, Separation from Loved Ones on the Path)

There are no places on Earth that this storm does not reach. There is no place far away enough on this planet in which you can hide.

Where should we go then, you may ask?

The best place to be is at the eye of the storm within you, as nowhere else will you feel quite as protected.

But the eye of the storm is constantly moving, some may protest.

This is precisely what you need to be doing as well.

This does not feel like too safe of a solution, you may say.

Your mission is not to hide but to be present and awake, acting and rippling your vibration to all those who are in contact with you energetically or physically. Many of you experience the shifts within your close circle, be it with your lover, spouse, best friend, or a parent. *(page 535)*

46. "Blueprint" Message from 9/28/11
(Themes: Life Plan, Reason for Being Here, Life as an Angel vs. Life as a Human, Choosing an Appropriate Spiritual Teaching for You)

You all come here with a grand plan. You have carefully designed your blueprint before you descended into the birth canal. You have studied all the different roads and potentials. You have placed yourself smack where your route will intersect with your learning, allowing you to move through the unfinished business you left in previous journeys, and progress. You did not sit with your angel guides and devise the easiest path to move through. Unlike water you do not devise plans based on ease of flow and gravitation. You are consciousness driving a physical vehicle, and you won an opportunity to accelerate your learning by playing the game of human angel. Does it make spiritual sense to you that, after all the effort you made to be here, all you would plan is for everything to flow perfectly, exactly the way you desire it? *(page 544)*

47. "The Perfect Partner" Message from 11/15/11
(Themes: Finding your Ideal Partner, Ascension)

When a human falls in love with another human and for a moment both are dancing in union linked to source, you call it love, although it is only one aspect of it—the one everyone desires. Often a test may be introduced where the playing cards are being shuffled, gifting you with an opportunity to expand your love vantage, pointing and guiding you towards a path to move through this third gate. Love does not mean ownership of another or a conditional agreement where one serves the other, thereby receiving love. For you to experience the radiant light of the sun all the time you must ascend above the clouds. Having an agenda is being dependent on the weather conditions—sunny at times, but also stormy at times. Love does not ask anything from anyone. It just radiates. It is the pulse of the universe. *(page 557)*

48. "The Light Keepers" Message from 11/24/11
(Theme: The Hub Keepers Hoarding Light and the Role of Light Warriors)

There is a link that weaves all of you together. It is a silver cord that transfers the pulse of light and distributes it amongst you. There are those who acquired, mostly through deception, many hubs which regulate the pace and level of your movement within this web. Those hubs were held tightly and secretly away from the grasp of most humanity for a very long time. They were buried in codes, kept in vaults which are accessible only to those who agreed to never reveal their content or their hiding place. Indeed, it sounds like a conspiracy of sorts, and it sure appears that way. The only twist to the conspiracy idea is that you have agreed willingly to give up a portion of your light as many were not ready, or were overwhelmed with the idea that you hold full and absolute control over the unfolding of your own life. *(page 568)*

49. "The Void" Message from 12/19/11
(Theme: Avoid Replacing Heaviness with Heaviness)

The hardship many of you perceive is you moving from the old paradigm into the new. Your dance must include letting go of weight, so you can levitate higher and higher. The loosening of the anchors that hold you in cells, jailed in self-created concepts, must be melted by your inner light. All may seem to be lost at times when all you have known washes away, yet this frees you, catapulting you into higher vibration. When you attach to heaviness giving intent to become light, do not be surprised when that heaviness can no longer remain attached. Bless all heaviness and darkness that is being released and commit to not replacing it with a different heaviness. *(page 579)*

50. "Spread Your Wings" Message from 12/25/11
(Theme: Instruction for Space Travel and Explorations)

Flying is your goal and you all know how to take off. It is as simple as visualizing that your hands are wings and your legs are the engine that propels you higher, allowing you to overcome the gravitational force. Three intentions must always present themselves as you stand in front of an elevated surface getting ready to take off. Each intention must be invoked by you. The most exuberant one is the intent to no longer adhere to the rules into which you were born. The second intent is to break any rules, even the ones your science convinced you are unbreakable, simply by asking to move from third gear to fifth gear or from 3-D to 5-D. The third rule is the simplest—giving intent, with pure heart, for your highest agreements to come forth, manifesting in your life. *(page 589)*

51. "The Triangle of Forgiveness" Message from 1/1/12
(Theme: Forgiving not Forgetting)

We wish to draw you a metaphoric picture of what it means to forgive. Let's "pretend" that you are an angel and you know how to fly. Each day you have to confront one looming limitation we name "perpetual forgetfulness." You have a built-in dysfunction that the mechanics of flying that you learned on day one is being "forgotten" by the time you wake up on the morning of the next day. Each day you have to teach yourself the art of flying. Each day you must begin by reminding yourself that you are an angel and you were meant to fly. Each day you have to conquer fear and trust that you will not be hurt. Similarly, true forgiving requires you to remind yourself who you are and to forgive, each day anew. *(page 601)*

CPSIA information can be obtained at www.ICGtesting.com
Printed in the USA
BVOW080140260912

301316BV00001B/1/P